'TIS TREASON, MY GOOD MAN!

Four Revolutionary Presidents and a Piccadilly Bookshop

'May God protect and guide you all, and may he still give peace and mutual friendship to the divided family of Britain, and promote the happiness, equally of the ancient root and the transplanted branches.'

Henry Laurens, writing from South Carolina, to his son John, studying at the Middle Temple in London, August 14, 1776

*

'The ancient Roman and Greek orators could only speak to the number of citizens capable of being assembled within the reach of their voice. Their writings had little effect, because the bulk of the people could not read. Now by the press we can speak to nations; and good books and well-written pamphlets have great and general influence.'

Benjamin Franklin to Richard Price, June 13, 1782

'TIS TREASON, MY GOOD MAN!

Four Revolutionary Presidents and a Piccadilly Bookshop

by

ERIC STOCKDALE

OAK KNOLL PRESS

THE BRITISH LIBRARY

2005

First Published by **Oak Knoll Press** in 2005
310 Delaware Street, New Castle, Delaware, USA
Web:http://www.oakknoll.com   and
The British Library
96 Euston Road, London, NW1 2DB, UK

ISBN: 1-58456-158-0 (Oak Knoll Press)
ISBN: 0-7123-0699-4 (The British Library)

Title: 'Tis Treason, My Good Man!
Four Revolutionary Presidents and a Piccadilly Bookshop
Author: Eric Stockdale
Indexer: Marc Vaulbert de Chantilly
Typographer: Ella Whitehead
Photography & document scanning: Adam Koster
Dust Jacket design: Adam Koster & Angela Werner
Publishing Director: J. Lewis von Hoelle

The British CIP Record for this book is available from
The British Library, London, UK

Library of Congress Cataloging-in-Publication Data:

Stockdale, Eric.
  'Tis treason, my good man! : four revolutionary presidents and a Piccadilly bookshop /
Eric Stockdale.
    p. cm.
  Includes bibliographical references.
  ISBN 1-58456-158-0
  1. Booksellers and bookselling--England--London--History--18th century. 2. Booksellers
and bookselling--Political aspects--England--London. 3. Stockdale, John, 1750-1814. 4.
United States--Politics and government--1775-1783. 5. United States--Politics and
government--1783-1809. 6. Almon, John, 1737-1805. I. Title.

Z330.6.L6S76 2005
381'.45002'09421--dc22

                                                              2004063644

Contents

List of Illustrations

Photo Credits

The Illustrations are by courtesy of the following:

1, 2, 11, 12, 13, 15 and 18: National Portrait Gallery, London
3: Historical Society of Pennsylvania
4: National Portrait Gallery, Washington D.C.
5: Honourable Society of the Middle Temple
6 and 14: South Carolina Historical Society and as to 6, the owner,
Mr. John Laurens of Charleston
7: British Museum; 8: Harvard University
9: Frick Art Reference Library, New York City
10: Bowdoin College, Brunswick, Maine
16: Museum of Fine Arts, Boston; 17: Yale University

Foreword

Eric Stockdale's historical work, *'Tis Treason, My Good Man!*, illuminates one of the least known but most interesting corners of history: that concerning American propaganda before and during the War of Independence, much of it written by English authors. With unique insight and the trained eye of a lawyer, the author takes the reader back to the turbulent years in London just before, during and after the American Revolution. We are introduced to a few, stout-hearted publisher/booksellers who dared print the colonists' side of *The Great Dispute*, in dire risk to their life and liberty. We learn about the byzantine tangle of British politics and the men who pushed England's famed Freedom of the Press to Lord North's and the King's great distress.

We are introduced to a cast of historic characters, both heroes and villains: Prime Ministers, Attorneys-General, Members of Parliament and 'bloody revolutionaries of the worst sort!' Benjamin Franklin, Thomas Jefferson, John Adams, Henry Laurens, Tom Paine and other radicals, all step forth and take their place in these times 'that try men's souls'. We come to understand the quiet courage and audacity of men like John Almon, John Stockdale and other pro-American booksellers, and the deadly edge of treason they had to tread. With excellent scholarship and research the author, a retired English Circuit judge, presents to the reader a comprehensive picture of John Stockdale, a remarkable English publisher/bookseller of Americana and his trans-Atlantic book trade.

This work will be enjoyed by enthusiasts of the Age of Enlightenment, American Revolutionary history, of British printing history and all those interested in Freedom of Speech and of the Press.

John Lewis von Hoelle

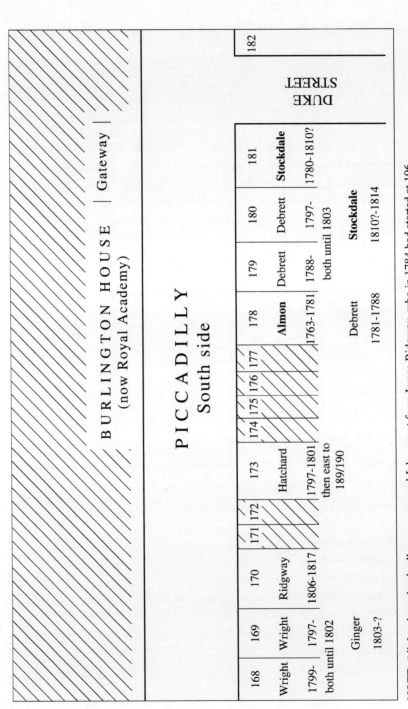

BURLINGTON HOUSE | Gateway |
(now Royal Academy)

PICCADILLY
South side

NOTE: All the above booksellers were named John, apart from James Ridgway, who in 1784 had started at 196. John Owen had been at 168 before Wright. Based on *Survey of London*, London: Athlone Press, 1960, 29: 253.

Preface

As I am not related to John Stockdale, the subject of this book, I owe it to his descendants and to the reader to explain how I came to undertake his biography. At the age of seventeen I joined my Inn of Court, the Middle Temple in London, to read for the Bar. One of the first subjects that all law students studied was Constitutional Law and one of the first cases, or rather series of cases I found of interest was that of *John Joseph Stockdale v. Hansard,* 1837-1840, which is discussed in the Appendix. After I had been practising at the Bar for some years, when on a routine trawl of the second-hand book shelves in Wildy's law bookshop in Lincoln's Inn Archway, I found and bought a copy of the book of the trial of John Stockdale in 1789, published by him in the following year to recoup some of his outlay on the fee paid to his counsel, the great Thomas Erskine. Both Stockdales were bookseller/publishers and both of them had done battle with the House of Commons and its advocate, the Attorney-General of the day. Each case involved important questions of law and had been followed by an Act of Parliament designed to deal with the problems it had underlined. As some fifty years separated the cases I assumed that John Stockdale might well be the grandfather of John Joseph; the *Dictionary of National Biography* disclosed that he was his father.

Some years passed before I had the time to follow the two booksellers up, but then the British Library catalogue revealed that the elder Stockdale had published John Adams. In the London Library I found the brief published note by Adams about his, and his son John Quincy's two-month stay with the Stockdale family over their bookshop in Piccadilly in 1783. Adams stated that it was 'where Mr. Laurens had lately lodged before me,' but that name meant nothing to me. Fortunately, the London Library had a copy of *The Papers of Henry Laurens*, as well as an excellent biography. A few more minutes in the library stacks made it apparent that Thomas Jefferson had in turn been introduced to the shop by Adams.

The obvious next question was: What and who had brought Laurens, a former President of the Continental Congress and a United States Peace Commissioner with Adams, to Stockdale's shop? The answer was to be found in the place where my studies had started: the Middle Temple, my legal home, or *Domus*, where Laurens had placed his son John to obtain a legal education, shortly before the War of Independence. After that discovery the pursuit of the Stockdales became irresistible even though I had no direct link with them.

It was extremely fortunate for me that the Laurens Papers were being published by the University of South Carolina Press; that Harvard University Press had for years been publishing various volumes of the Adams Family Papers; and that Jefferson's extensive correspondence with John Stockdale had been published by Princeton University Press. I am grateful to the three Presses; also to the South Carolina Historical Society and the Adams Family Papers (together with the Massachusetts Historical Society) for permission to use some unpublished correspondence. I am also indebted to C. James Taylor, formerly editor of the Laurens Papers and now of the Adams Family Papers; and to Peggy Taylor, Eric Emerson and Thomas Ashe Lockhart, a direct descendant of Henry Laurens and of John Rutledge. All that help related to Stockdale's connections with the four Presidents. The American Philosophical Society allowed me to quote from unpublished Franklin letters.

As there are very few collections of publishers' letters from the eighteenth century, I was also extremely lucky to find a significant number of letters that Stockdale had exchanged with five of his authors: three British and two American. Thomas Day, who wrote *History of Sandford and Merton* for Stockdale, has been the subject of several biographies and some of his letters are quoted in those, as well as elsewhere. Stockdale's correspondence with Mark Noble, a little known author, is in the Bodleian Library in Oxford, and relevant letters of Hester Piozzi (Dr Johnson's friend, Mrs Thrale) are owned by the John Rylands University of Manchester Library.

Stockdale published two of the first important post-Revolution American authors, David Ramsay the historian and Jedidiah Morse the geographer. Ramsay's letters were tracked down in various collections by Robert Brunhouse and published by the American Philosophical Society in its *Transactions* in 1965. Morse's letters are similarly scattered around the United States. Fortunately for me, Yale University library had copies of many of them and kindly lent me a set. Some of the Morse-Stockdale correspondence is at the New-York Historical Society, where I was also able to make notes from the John Almon correspondence in that society's possession. I owe a great debt to all those libraries and societies and their staff.

London is a wonderful city, packed with sources that can be tapped by researchers; I am indebted to the staff of at least twelve of the many libraries and archive centres in the capital. The London Library proved invaluable, particularly because of the open access to the collections and the borrowing facilities. The members of the British Library staff were always helpful, but I owe a special debt to Michael Crump, who, apart from anything else, encouraged me by inviting me to lodge an earlier draft of the book in the Library's Department of Manuscripts – as Add. MSS 71220. I also received help at the Public Record Office (National Archives), British Museum (Natural History), Guildhall Library, St. Bride Printing Library, Westminster City Archives Centre, London Metropolitan Archives, and the libraries of the London School of Economics, University College, the Middle Temple and the Athenaeum.

There are many others to whom I am indebted for help, friends and strangers: I have named only some of them in foot- notes. Some contacted me in pursuit of their own special subject and in doing so made me aware of another lead to follow. Others suggested possible lines of inquiry or chased up obscure references or publications for me in America, including James P. White, Russell G. Miller, Lincoln Faller, Gerald P. Tyson and Arnold S. Trebach. I am indebted to the three experts who kindly read the manuscript and made helpful suggestions: Robin Myers, Colin Bonwick and especially James Raven, whose many published works on the eighteenth-century book trade contain a vast amount of useful information. Morton Pollock and Gordon Turner repeatedly saved both my computer and its user from blowing up or breaking down.

Finally, this book is for my wife Joan, who has not only helped me with research, but has always been there to encourage me ever since I was a teen-age law student.

E. S.

Introduction

Before Independence, and for at least forty years afterwards, the principal source of books and pamphlets for North America was London and its booksellers, so that one can readily understand why Thomas Jefferson, in a letter written on August 25, 1775, referred to England as 'the land of literature and of books'.[1] Most of those booksellers were also publishers in the modern sense, in that they selected, financed and distributed the books whose printing they oversaw. In the second half of the eighteenth century two houses in particular specialised in American subjects. The first was that of the brothers, Edward and Charles Dilly, whose shop was in the City of London from about 1755 to 1800. The second was a shop in Piccadilly, but in two different hands and in two different premises, three doors away from one another. From 1763 to 1780, John Almon was active at 178 Piccadilly, and as L. H. Butterfield pointed out, he 'published a good many more titles by Americans and about the American controversy than any other London bookseller'.[2]

During his last six years as a Piccadilly bookseller, from about 1774, Almon employed a young man called John Stockdale as his porter, or shopman. When Almon retired in 1780, he handed his business over to John Debrett, who had never worked for him, but Debrett dropped the American baton. It was speedily picked up by Stockdale, who opened up his own shop in that year at 181 Piccadilly, and made the most of what he had learned

---

[1] See, chap.3.

[2] Butterfield, L. H., 'The American Interests of the Firm of E. and C. Dilly', *Papers Bib. Soc. of America*, 1951, 45: 293, hereafter referred to as Butterfield, Dilly.

from his master about bookselling in general, and about the American market and contacts in particular. As Butterfield put it, 'John Stockdale came forward as a vigorous backer of books by Americans and on American subjects, and he remained so until at least the close of the century.' In fact, he remained in business until 1814, so that he was active for thirty-four years, exactly double the time that his former employer operated his Piccadilly shop. After Independence, despite the continued dependence of America on London for a few more years, American authors were increasingly successful in the United States and, to a lesser extent, in England, with the help of specialist booksellers such as Stockdale.

We can only understand Stockdale's remarkable success as a self-made man, for he had never been apprenticed in the trade, if we consider his six years with Almon, that is, 1774 to 1780, the major part of the war between Britain and its American colonies, and also the eleven years before that, when Almon first displayed his considerable skills as a political writer. Almon was the principal pamphleteer and bookseller of the Whig opposition. It will be remembered that the opposition was not only opposed to Lord North's government, but especially to its foolhardy policies concerning the colonies. Almon's ability to write penetrating pamphlets, based on up-to-date inside information from both sides of the Atlantic, was truly astounding. This was underlined when a Minister of the Crown was asked in the House of Lords, shortly before the war, about American troop numbers, and replied that he did not know them, but indicated that Almon probably did have that information. A glance at Almon's connections with John Wilkes, the radical politician who published the *North Briton* – and notably, issue Number Forty-Five – helps one to understand the opposition pamphlet barrage and Almon's role in it. Wilkes was much admired in America for his stand against the government, receiving financial support from South Carolina, and a letter of encouragement when in prison from John Adams and some of his colleagues in Massachusetts.

Playing an important part in London before the war as a writer, often under the cover of a pen-name, was Benjamin Franklin, whose links with Almon will be considered only briefly, as Franklin relied mostly on his long-standing London friend, the printer and bookseller, William Strahan. It is easy to see why: Strahan had sent his favourite employee, David Hall, out to Philadelphia back in 1745 and Franklin had made him a partner. 'This three-way friendship was the basis of the first sustained book-importing enterprise in the middle colonies,' so much so that in the period 1748-1772, Hall imported over £30,000 worth of books and stationery from Strahan in London.[3]

Young Stockdale was fortunate in being able to take over Almon's American connections, but he would not have done nearly so well, had not one of his first authors been Thomas Day, a barrister, who preferred writing to practising law. Day, shortly before the war, had befriended a young law student from South Carolina at their mutual Inn of Court in London, the Middle Temple. He was John Laurens, who interrupted his legal studies to go home and become one of General Washington's closest aides in 1777, shortly before his father, Henry Laurens, became the President of Congress in Philadelphia. Henry Laurens was captured by the British in 1780, when on the way to the Netherlands to raise help for the United States, and was imprisoned in the Tower of London, charged with treason. He was detained there for fifteen months and only released after the British surrender at Yorktown, which had been negotiated by his son, as Washington's representative. While in the Tower, Henry

---

[3] Green, James, N., 'English Books and Printing in the Age of Franklin', in Amory, Hugh and Hall, David D. (eds.), *The Colonial Book in the Atlantic World*, Cambridge U.P., 2000, 277, 278. See also, Raven, James, 'The Importation of Books in the Eighteenth Century', *ibid.*, 183.

Laurens had little difficulty in getting minor contributions for the newspapers smuggled out, mainly to the *Courant*, which after February 1781, was published by Stockdale in succession to Almon. On his release from the Tower, Henry Laurens was befriended by his son's Middle Temple companion, Thomas Day, who acted as his unpaid secretary. More important, at some stage Day recommended his new publisher – already known to Laurens because of his *Courant* snippets – as someone who could provide lodgings for him above his shop in Piccadilly. As a result Laurens stayed with Stockdale on at least four occasions.

Henry Laurens was appointed one of the four American Peace Commissioners, together with Benjamin Franklin, John Adams and John Jay, who had succeeded Laurens as President of Congress. John Adams, as an author and bibliophile, had known of Almon's shop and had been published by Stockdale, but it was undoubtedly Laurens who recommended Stockdale's house as a place where there were satisfactory lodgings. For the book-loving Adams, the thought of staying above a bookshop must have been as tempting as the invitation to a child to live in a candy store. After signing the Peace Treaty in Paris in September 1783, Adams decided to bring his sixteen-year-old son, John Quincy, to London for a vacation. He also wanted to visit the waters at Bath for the sake of his health. After three days in a hotel in London that he considered too expensive, Adams and his son moved in with the Stockdale family in Piccadilly for a period of some two months.

The importance of that stay cannot be exaggerated. Stockdale in due course published further works by John Adams and by John Quincy Adams. On the recommendation of Adams, Thomas Jefferson became a customer and was then persuaded by Stockdale to let him publish his only book, his important *Notes on the State of Virginia*. The books by both Adamses and by Jefferson obviously helped to establish Stockdale as a specialist in books relating to America, but the link with Jefferson had another benefit. Thomas Day's main work was his great didactic book for children, *History of Sandford and Merton*, which became one of Stockdale's best sellers. Jefferson helped the bookshop to become an important source of children's books by buying such books by the French author, Arnaud Berquin, in Paris for Stockdale, who then published editions in English.

Laurens also played another part in furthering Stockdale's career. He recommended him to his son-in-law, Dr. David Ramsay, who was America's first important historian, and Ramsay in turn introduced Dr. Jedidiah Morse, 'The Father of American Geography', as he was known. Once Stockdale was selling their works in London, there could be no doubt about the importance of his shop as a first port of call for books relating to America. Laurens and Ramsay both recommended Stockdale to the Charleston Library Society and he was appointed as its London supplier. The relationship came to a speedy conclusion when Stockdale was sacked (like many another), but his letter of protest at his dismissal throws some important light on the nature of the problems of the trans-Atlantic book supplier.[4]

There is a dearth of correspondence relating to the London book trade in the years we are considering, but Stockdale's relationship with the Americans mentioned has had one great beneficial effect. The papers of Jefferson and of Henry Laurens for the relevant years have now been published in full, and the letters of John and John Quincy Adams are available in different forms. Fortunately, Stockdale figures in the correspondence of all four Presidents, notably that of Jefferson. Much of Ramsay's correspondence has appeared in print and although the letters of Morse are scattered in various American libraries, they are copied and available to the researcher. Both men's correspondence with the London seller of their books is revealing and gives a good picture of the problems faced by early American authors. The many biographies of Thomas Day between them

---

[4] Raven, James, *London Booksellers and American Customers*, Columbia: U. of South Carolina P., 2002, 288.

refer to enough letters to indicate the closeness of his relationship with his publisher. Finally, Stockdale's correspondence with two more of his English authors, Mark Noble and Hester Piozzi (Dr. Johnson's Mrs. Thrale) is fortunately kept in the Bodleian and the John Rylands Library, respectively.

When one puts together those letters with the books and pamphlets they discuss, a fairly comprehensive picture of one late eighteenth-century bookseller emerges. The correspondence also gives significant clues about the interplay of ideas and print, politics and publishing, and the contribution of the bookseller to the intellectual life on both sides of the Atlantic. The last quarter of the eighteenth century is one of the most interesting in the history of the western world. The shots fired in 1775, at Lexington, and later at Saratoga and Yorktown, had their echoes not just in America and Britain, but in France. Not all Americans agreed that the French Revolution mirrored their own. Some came to realise that France had become more of a menace than Britain, so for a time it was not clear whether the infant United States would side with one country or the other, or remain strictly neutral. Adams and Jefferson, for example, bitterly disagreed about France, as did Edmund Burke and Tom Paine. The booksellers, including Stockdale, encouraged discussion of the issues at the time, and they provided a record for us of our ancestors' views and disputes.

Although this book is mainly about Almon and Stockdale's American links – and particularly those with the past President of Congress and the three future Presidents of the United States – it is also about Stockdale's other lines. In Britain, the wars with America and France affected everyone, but there were other matters of interest in that fascinating quarter-century. India, the East India Company and Warren Hastings, were kept before the public. The voyages of discovery, the founding of Australia and the resultant books, with new maps in them, also lifted men's eyes above the horizon. Some of those publications increased the impatience of Englishmen wanting to see the world or to emigrate to the United States. Rousseau's works were beginning to have an effect on the broader education of the young. The campaign for free speech and a free press took a turn for the better. Thomas Erskine, the great advocate, was in the thick of that battle, repeatedly appearing for defendants prosecuted for writing or publishing books or pamphlets. Among those defendants were John Almon and John Stockdale, and we shall see how the latter's trial led to the Libel Act of 1792, which increased the powers of juries in criminal libel cases in England and influenced the thinking of President John Adams in America. All the topics mentioned impinged to a greater or lesser extent on the bookshop we are considering. Apart from his books on American subjects and those for children, Stockdale made a point of producing up-to-date publications on India and Australia.

What may surprise American readers is how closely many of the early stalwarts of their nation were involved with London during their lifetime, and how many of them had connections with a bookshop in Piccadilly. Most of those readers will recall that Benjamin Franklin spent so long in London that there was a 'danger' that he might stay there indefinitely. They will also recollect that John Adams was the first resident minister in that city. However, they will probably be unaware of the depths of the links between the two countries, for example, of the length of time spent in England by men such as Henry Laurens, or of the number of young men, like his son John, who came to London for a legal education.

There are now a number of books about the book trade, but few of them are able to show the eighteenth-century bookseller at work, defending himself against the authorities, bemoaning the consequences of war, complaining about the cost of advertising, nagging his authors, or defending himself against their charge of delay or failure to advertise their work sufficiently. Few, if any, of the earlier histories of bookshops are concerned with the political and military events giving rise to their books and pamphlets, but it is hoped that the reader of the present work will accept that the study of John Stockdale, and of the man from whom he learned his trade, would have been the poorer if those important factors had not been considered in conjunction with the correspondence and publications quoted.

Illus. 1. Richard Grenville, 2nd Earl Temple by William Hoare

1

John Almon and John Wilkes

The bookshop in Piccadilly with which this book is principally concerned is that of John Stockdale, who owned it for some thirty-four years, from 1780 to 1814, when he died. However, he had worked for a number of years before setting up on his own for John Almon, who ran his own bookshop, three doors further along Piccadilly, for a period half as long: the important seventeen years from 1763 to 1780, when he retired early. Almon had been apprenticed as a printer and bookseller in Liverpool, whereas Stockdale had never had a formal training but learned his skills as a bookseller and publisher from Almon, during the years he worked for him. Almon did not work as a printer either, but was a highly successful bookseller, who deserves special consideration as a trenchant and extremely shrewd pamphlet writer and journalist. He seems to have preferred political writing to the running of a business. In the late 1770s he increasingly left Stockdale in charge while he was away from the shop, hobnobbing with opposition politicians and others, preparing yet another devastating attack on the government.

This book is mainly about Stockdale and his American and British authors and customers. However, we need to consider Almon as the man who not only gave Stockdale the opportunity to learn the bookseller's trade, but made the valuable initial connections with Benjamin Franklin, Arthur Lee and other Americans in London, from which Stockdale was able to benefit. Almon was principally a writer and publisher of pamphlets, whereas Stockdale was not an author at all, and worked as a bookseller and publisher only. It is also instructive to compare the two men because of their differing allegiances. Almon consistently supported the Whig opposition and paid the price for his stance: he was arrested and prosecuted several times. Stockdale, though probably in favour of the American cause from the outset of his independent career in 1780, published materials at the request of the government and so was, with one famous exception in 1789, free from prosecution by the State.[1] In order to see how Almon became the principal publisher in London of the spate of publications in favour of the American colonies, it is necessary first to consider his links with John Wilkes and with the opposition to the ministry.

On October 23, 1760, King George II died and was succeeded by his grandson, George III, who then embarked on an eventful sixty-year reign. Two days later, a young political writer, recently arrived from Liverpool, where he had been born in 1737, was married at St. John the Evangelist, Westminster, to Elizabeth Jackson, by a new curate whose mind may well have been elsewhere at the time. The bridegroom was John Almon, who was already writing articles for Charles Say of the *Daily Gazetteer* and the curate, Charles Churchill, whose poem, *The*

---

[1] The only book on Almon, apart from his autobiography, is Rogers, Deborah D., *Bookseller as Rogue: John Almon and the Politics of Eighteenth-Century Publishing*, New York: Peter Lang, 1986. On Almon, see also, Rea, Robert Right, *The English Press in Politics, 1760-1774*, Lincoln: U. of Nebraska P., 1963, his two articles in the *Indiana Quarterly for Bookmen*: 'John Almon: Bookseller to John Wilkes', 1948, 4: 20; 'Bookseller as Historian', 1949, 5: 75, and his 'Mason, Walpole, and That Rogue Almon', *Huntingdon Library Quarterly* , 1960, 23: 187. See also, Werkmeister, Lucyle, *The London Daily Press, 1772-1792*, Lincoln: U. of Nebraska P., 1963, chapter 3.

Rosciad, was to be published in the following March, making him 'the latest literary sensation in England'.[2]

The young King was not prepared to accept the advice of the two principal ministers of the Crown, William Pitt the Elder and his brother-in-law, Richard Grenville, Earl Temple, about the future conduct of the war against France. The war had started in 1756, and was to be called the Seven Years' War in Britain, and the French and Indian War in America, after its conclusion in 1763. The two proud politicians resigned and were replaced by Lords Egremont and Bute. Bute was a Scot who was reputedly the lover of the young King's widowed mother; more important was the fact that he had great influence over his young monarch, having been his tutor.

One of the Members of Parliament who was extremely disturbed by the departure of Pitt and the arrival of Bute was John Wilkes, who since 1757, had been the fairly somnolent Member for Aylesbury in Buckinghamshire, or 'silent Senator' as the writer Junius was to call him. After this time, 'silent' was the least appropriate adjective to couple with the name of Wilkes. His constituency was near Temple's seat at Stowe and he owed a great deal to the Earl's patronage. Until Pitt's departure Wilkes was a political nonentity, but that event had a remarkable effect on him. 'It galvanized Wilkes into sudden life, so that within a few months this gay idler, who was known only as a profane wit and frequenter of Medmenham, became the moving spirit of public opinion, and was openly described by the Duke of Devonshire as the heart and soul of the opposition.'[3] Medmenham

---

[2] Green, James N., 'English Books and Printing in the Age of Franklin', in Amory, Hugh, and Hall, David D. (eds.), *The Colonial Book in the Atlantic World*, Cambridge U.P., 2000, 283. Green added that when James Rivington, the English bookseller who also published in America, put out an edition of Churchill's poems in 1768, 'American and British literary culture came closer together than they had ever been before.'

[3] Sherrard, O. A., *A Life of John Wilkes*, London: Allen and Unwin, 1930, 70.

Illus. 2. John Wilkes by William Dickson

JOHN ALMON AND JOHN WILKES

(also in Buckinghamshire) was where the notorious Hellfire Club celebrated its orgies, involving prostitutes dressed as nuns on some occasions – or so it was said at the time.

In March 1762, Wilkes produced his first pamphlet, anonymously: *Observations on the Papers Relative to the Rupture with France*, which put the Pitt-Temple case. In November, George Kearsley, a bookseller in Ludgate Street, published another anonymous pamphlet approving of Pitt's conduct. This was Almon's *A Review of Mr. Pitt's Administration*, which heaped praised on the former minister. 'Like a true Englishman, he was open, bold, free and honest. In a word, he was the spirit of the war, the genius of England, and the comet of his age.' The pamphlet was dedicated to Temple; it need scarcely be added that it went down well with both Pitt and Temple.

Fortunately, Almon was one of the few eighteenth-century booksellers to write his autobiography, *The Memoirs of a Late Eminent Bookseller*, which was printed for him in 1790. In this book, which bears the alternative title *Memoirs of John Almon, Bookseller of Piccadilly*, Almon told his own story in the third person. He referred to his dedication of the 1762 pamphlet to Temple and recounted: 'His Lordship requested to see the author. Mr. Almon waited upon him, and from that moment was honoured with his Lordship's favour and countenance, publicly and privately. Lord Temple afterwards made him known to the Duke of Devonshire, the Marquess of Rockingham &c. Mr. Pitt he saw at Lord Temple's in Pall Mall, where he did not fail to pay his devoirs once a week at least, and was always admitted. Through the same interest he became known to Mr. Wilkes, and many other gentlemen who were at that time in opposition to the court.'[4] Some time before this, Wilkes had become friendly with Charles Churchill, the poetical curate, who had married Almon to the wife who was to bear him ten children.

---

[4] Almon, *Memoirs*, 15.

In May 1762, Bute and his ministry began to publish the
Briton as a propaganda vehicle, with Tobias Smollett as editor;
one of its tasks was to counter the pro-Pitt arguments, such as
those contained in Wilkes's March pamphlet. Wilkes responded
by publishing, with the help of Churchill and the encouragement
of Temple, a weekly counter-blast, the *North Briton*. Both Almon
and William James Smith, a one-time librarian at Stowe and the
editor of the *Grenville Papers*, stated that Temple's contribution
went further than mere encouragement. Almon later wrote of
Temple, 'He frequently assisted his friends in the production of
these papers, not indeed with his pen, but with his information
and line of reasoning.' Smith asserted, 'There can be very little
doubt but that Lord Temple wrote several of the papers in the
North Briton; there are evident traces of his style, particularly in
the celebrated Number Forty-Five.'⁵

Despite some shortcomings, the *North Briton* was a great
achievement for Wilkes, whose membership of the House of
Commons enabled him to refer fairly accurately to debates
there. Parliamentary reporting was still prohibited by both
Houses at that stage; a few years were to pass before Wilkes and
Almon could jockey Parliament into such a ridiculous position
that it had to give way on this point and allow the reporting of
proceedings. The popularity of the paper was in part attributable
to the wit of both Wilkes and Churchill.

When Bute's ministry brought an end to the war by the
Treaty of Paris in February 1763, Wilkes considered the terms to
be much too favourable to France. He felt that many of the advantages gained by Pitt's earlier vigorous leadership were being
thrown away. It was his disgust with the treaty that led Wilkes to
make his classic comment that it was clearly the Peace of God,
since it 'passeth all understanding'. In 1786, John Stockdale was

---

⁵ Almon, John, *Biographical, Literary and Political Anecdotes*, London: T. N.
Longman and L. B. Seeley, 1797, 2: 11; *Grenville Papers*, London: John
Murray, 1853, 3: xlvi.

to publish a comment by one of his regular Civil Service authors, George Chalmers, making the fair point, 'To establish a peace after a glorious war, is one of the hardest tasks which can be assigned to British ministers, because their opponents never fail to turn the current of popular dissatisfaction on their measures, whatever they may be.'[6] It should be added that this hard task was neither confined to a peace after a war, nor to the British. Surrender terms granted by the victor after a battle were equally vulnerable to hostile comments by critics, whether American or British, safely miles away from the battlefield, as we shall see later in connection with the Conventions of Saratoga and Cintra.

Bute discontinued the *Briton* in February 1763, and resigned from office on April 8. Wilkes considered closing the *North Briton* in response, but as luck would have it, on April 23, he produced issue Number Forty-Five. Never before or since has one issue of a paper had such repercussions on both sides of the Atlantic. As early as July 9, Wilkes wrote to Temple, immodestly but accurately, '*North Briton* and Wilkes will be talked of together by posterity.'[7]

According to Almon's biography of Wilkes, both Pitt and Temple had played their part in the history of that famous issue. Bute was replaced as the head of government by Temple's younger brother, George Grenville. Grenville sent his brother, as a matter of courtesy, a copy of the King's Speech which was to be delivered next day, containing the new government's proposals in the usual way. Pitt was present when Temple received the copy of the speech, and both ex-ministers were indignant about its contents. 'At this instant,' Almon wrote, 'Mr. Wilkes happened to call upon his Lordship, having just returned from Paris. Mr. Wilkes agreed in sentiment concerning the speech;

---

[6] In his preface to Defoe, Daniel, *The History of the Union between England and Scotland*, London: John Stockdale, 1786, xv.

[7] *Grenville Papers*, 2: 75.

and when he returned home, he wrote a sketch of the conversation which passed on the subject while he was present. From this sketch, and some additions of his own, he wrote this celebrated paper, the forty-fifth number, which was published on Saturday, 23 April 1763.'[8]

The historian of the *North Briton* has stated, 'The story *might* be true, but Almon is too dubious a witness to believe without independent substantiation. Until such corroboration is forthcoming, Almon's account must be regarded as apocryphal.'[9] The warning – one of several urging caution before accepting Almon's version of events – may well be justified, for we shall presently see that Almon's account of the arrest of Wilkes is suspect.

Number Forty-Five contained a strongly worded attack on the Peace, disputing the suggestion that it was 'honourable to my crown and beneficial to my people'. It was only bribery, Wilkes claimed, that had seen this obnoxious treaty through Parliament: despite Bute's retirement, the ministers were still 'tools of despotism and corruption'. The reaction of the ministers is well-known. Lord Halifax, the Secretary of State, issued a general warrant for the arrest of anyone connected with the publication of the issue and for the seizure of their papers. No suspect was named in the warrant, so his messengers felt free to arrest forty-eight men, most of whom had nothing to do with the offending newspaper. Had three fewer suspects been arrested, it might have seemed as if there were some bizarre method in the minister's madness.

Almon claimed that he arrived at Wilkes's home shortly after his arrest there, and was asked by him to inform Temple. Almon added that he had gone at once to the Earl, who requested him

---

[8] Almon, John, *The Correspondence of the late John Wilkes with his Friends*, London: Richard Phillips, 1805, 1: 95.
[9] Nobbe, George, *The North Briton*, Morningside Heights, N.Y.: Columbia U.P., 1939, 207.

to hurry to the lawyer, Arthur Beardmore, so that he could apply for a writ of *habeas corpus*. Almon continued: 'It was to evade the writ of *habeas corpus* that Mr. Wilkes was committed close prisoner to the Tower; and Lord Halifax afterwards blamed the messengers for suffering Mr. Almon to go out of Mr. Wilkes's house.'[10]

After a few days, Wilkes's live *corpus* was produced in court before Sir Charles Pratt, later Lord Camden, the Chief Justice of the Common Pleas and a well-known Whig: he had been Pitt's Attorney-General and was to become his Lord Chancellor once he returned to power. He ordered the release of the prisoner because he was a Member of Parliament and protected from arrest as such. (It was only later, in the civil proceedings of *Entick v. Carrington*, that he declared general warrants to be illegal.) When Wilkes walked out of Westminster Hall, where the Common Law courts sat, he was greeted by a crowd, shouting 'Wilkes and Liberty!' The words were to reverberate on two continents. After his decision, Camden's name was often linked with that of Wilkes, especially once he had also spoken against the Stamp Act of 1765 in the strongest terms. Camden asserted in the House of Lords that Parliament had no right to tax America, adding, 'Whoever attempts to do it, attempts an injury; whoever does it, commits a robbery.' Leonard Levy made the fair comment, 'In the treatment and prosecution of Wilkes himself, the government found that it had mounted a tiger.'[11]

Heady with success after his release from the Tower of London, Wilkes foolishly decided to reprint all the issues of his newspaper, despite Temple's advice against such a dangerous course. In November 1763, the government attacked him in the Commons in respect of his newspaper, and in the Lords in connection with a pornographic poem that had been printed for

---

[10] Almon, *Memoirs*, 15.
[11] Almon, *Anecdotes*, 377; Levy, Leonard W., *Emergence of a Free Press*, Oxford U.P., 1985, 145.

him. The attack in the Upper House was led by the Earl of Sandwich, one of Wilkes's former whoring companions at Medmenham. The effrontery of the notorious Earl took people's breath away, even though they could not have known that as recently as March 8, he had written to Wilkes for his help in securing a directorship of the East India Company for a friend. 'Your activity and abilities would be of immense service to Mr. Sullivan, in whose cause both I and many other of your friends and wellwishers are most warmly embarked,' Sandwich wrote in the letter, which was seized with others in the possession of Wilkes, by virtue of the illegal general warrant.[12]

John Gay's *Beggar's Opera* was on in London at the time of the Earl's attack on Wilkes. MacHeath's line in the play about Jemmy Twitcher peaching, or informing on him, amused the politically-conscious members of the audience, who noted the parallel. After that, Sandwich was known as Jemmy Twitcher and early rhyming slang produced a new word for informer: a snitcher, or snitch. In his biography of Sandwich, George Martelli claimed that the Earl had been much maligned and that he was merely doing his duty, but the Wilkes documents in the Guildhall Library show how relentless he was in his zeal to pursue his 'friend' Wilkes: it was above and beyond the call of duty.[13]

Wilkes managed to score a palpable hit when he replied to Sandwich's sneering prediction that he would die on the scaffold or of the pox. 'That depends, my Lord,' was the famous reply, 'on whether I embrace your principles or your mistress.' For the sake of historical accuracy, it should be added that the unfortunate mistress, the actress Martha Ray, was murdered before Wilkes was tempted to embrace her – and that he never mounted the scaffold either.[14]

---

[12] London Guildhall Library, Wilkes MSS. 214/3.

[13] Martelli, George, *Jemmy Twitcher*, London: Jonathan Cape, 1962.

[14] For some unfathomable reason, both Miss Ray and her murderer

At the end of 1763, Wilkes decided that discretion was the better part of valour and fled to France, remaining abroad, but for short secret visits to England, until February 1768. During his exile Almon was one of his principal contacts and kept him well informed. In 1764, Wilkes was expelled by the House of Commons, convicted in his absence before the Chief Justice, Lord Mansfield, in respect of the two publications mentioned earlier, and outlawed when he failed to appear for sentence.

Almon was as indignant as Wilkes about the attempt of the administration to stifle criticism of the King's Speech, and wrote *A Letter to the Right Hon. George Grenville*, which J. Williams published for him in 1763. Freedom of speech and freedom of the press were two matters about which Almon felt strongly. He used the pseudonym under which he was to write some of his most powerful criticisms and to make some of his best points in favour of the colonies: An Independent Whig. 'Can any thing be more odious to Englishmen,' he asked in his letter, 'than an attempt to *exclude* them from giving any opinion or judgment on ministerial transactions? Englishmen will not silently and patiently suffer a yoke to be put round their necks; they value themselves on being free, and the right of communicating their opinions.'

These were dangerous sentiments to express but like Wilkes, Almon did not, at that stage, lack courage. We shall see later that, with increasing years and number of children, he became more cautious, but as a young man Almon was certainly bold. He had seen the dangers that surrounded the writer, printer and publisher of political works; despite that he set up on his own in 1763. If war was bad for booksellers, then the first year of peace might be a propitious time for a new one with drive. The London printing and bookselling trade had grown up centred on St. Paul's Churchyard and Paternoster Row, but it had spread

---

achieved immortality by being accorded their own entries in the *Dictionary of National Biography*.

westward both along Holborn, and along Fleet Street and the
Strand. Almon decided to open a shop in the new and
fashionable West End, near Temple's house, which was in Pall
Mall.

In his autobiography Almon recounted: 'Having been bred a
bookseller, he conceived that the exercise of that profession in
the vicinity of St. James's might probably prove successful. He
mentioned his design to Lord Temple, who gave him the
warmest assurances of support. Accordingly at Michaelmas 1763
he took a private house in Piccadilly [no. 178], opposite to
Burlington House, the lower part of which he converted into a
shop for books and stationery. But he preserved a connection
with Mr. Say, which was of mutual service. Lord Temple was
better than his promise, for he not only quitted his bookseller
and stationer, but engaged many of his friends to do the same in
favour of Mr. Almon.' When the opposition club, called The
Coterie, was established in nearby Albemarle Street, Temple had
Almon appointed as the bookseller and stationer to the club.
'This circumstance brought him a great flow of business.'[15] It is
interesting to see that the house in Piccadilly had until that time
been a dwelling-house only, which had to be converted for
business purposes. Almon and Stockdale, together with some
others, were to make the south side of Piccadilly, opposite
Burlington House, an island of booksellers in the rapidly
developing West End of London – as the plan at the front of
this book shows.

On August 14, 1764, Almon wrote to Temple about the difficulties of his trade. The *North Briton* conviction, he pointed out,
'has struck such a panic into the printers &c, that I am afraid I
now stand alone in the resolution to publish with spirit; however, I am determined to persevere, and whatever may be my
fate, I hope that in case of persecution (which I fear is threatened me, with the heaviest vengeance of the Administration), I

---

[15] Almon, *Memoirs*, 16.

shall have the assistance and support of all those who call themselves friends of the liberties of their country.' He did not need to add, 'especially you'.[16]

Almon published a number of pamphlets or letters written by Candor, Son of Candor and Father of Candor, which Smith, the editor of the *Grenville Papers*, was certain Temple had written. Today, there can no longer be such certainty about the identity of the Candor family.[17] One of the Father letters, *An Enquiry into the Doctrine, lately Propagated, concerning Libels, Warrants, and the Seizure of Papers*, was published by Almon at the end of November 1764 – and later republished with a similar title on several occasions. The letter charged Mansfield with having acted 'officiously, arbitrarily and illegally' during the Wilkes prosecution, by allowing a minor amendment of the charge at his house, rather than in court. That led to Almon's first experience as an accused. He was dismayed to find that he would not be tried by a jury, but by the Chief Justice, who had initiated contempt proceedings. Fortunately for Almon, events took a turn for the better. First, Mansfield decided not to take the case himself, then a procedural error saved Almon: a clerk had incorrectly headed the information with the name of Wilkes instead of Almon. Finally, the administration changed and this first case against the young publisher was dropped.[18]

By 1766, Almon was already well enough established to figure in one of the most remarkable poems ever to appear. Henry Dell, himself a London bookseller, published a poem of 427 lines, in which he managed to comment on no fewer than a

---

[16] *Grenville Papers*, 2: 428. For a study of the press in the 1760s, see also, Brewer, John, *Party Ideology and Popular Politics at the Accession of George III*, Cambridge U.P., 1976, chap.8; and for the later period, Werkmeister, *op. cit.*, and Lutnick, Solomon, *The American Revolution and the British Press 1775-1783*, Columbia: U. of Missouri P., 1967.

[17] Levy, 147.

[18] Almon, *Memoirs*, 18; see also, Fox, John C., *History of Contempt of Court*, Oxford U.P., 1927.

hundred colleagues in the trade in London and Westminster. Of Almon he wrote:

> Almon of late has got himself a name,
> But 'tis to W[ilke]s and P[it]t he owes his fame.[19]

While Wilkes was in Paris he managed to while away his days by writing various pieces for Almon; how he spent his nights may be gauged from a letter written to him by Edmund Burke. 'Since you are in a foreign pasture, I am glad (to use your own expression) that you feed among the lilies. We would all choose the home field for you, though our English roses bear thorns not a few.'[20] Wilkes started work on an autobiography but made little progress.

Almon, on the other hand, succeeded in writing and publishing his *History of the Late Minority* in 1765. Among other matters, he discussed the legality of general warrants, and referred to the motion in the House of Commons by Sir William Meredith, which had been defeated by the King's in-built majority, 'That a General Warrant is not warranted by law, and is a high violation of the liberty of the subject.' Almon continued, 'The Ministry dwelt particularly upon the impropriety, as they called it, of one House of Parliament only coming to a resolution upon a point of law; that such resolution was no security of liberty, that it was ineffectual as to the purpose intended, and that it would be nugatory in Westminster Hall, the judges there being bound to follow the law as made by the three estates, and not the sentiments of the House of Commons alone.' These ministerial arguments were to be upheld – and turned against the ministry – some seventy years later by Lord Denman, the Chief Justice, when he presided at the libel trial brought by John Stockdale's

---

[19] Belanger, Terry, 'A Directory of the London Book Trade, 1766'; this was a splendid and appropriate first article in the newly launched journal, *Publishing History*, vol.1, 1977.

[20] British Library, Add. MSS 30,877, f.57.

son, John Joseph, against Hansard, the House of Commons printer.[21]

Wilkes was displeased by some of the things Almon wrote about him. Almon was conscious of the fact that he had offended his friend, writing on February 3, 1767, shortly after one of Wilkes's clandestine visits: 'I am sorry I had not the pleasure of seeing you when you were last in England, but as I could not tell how far my company might have been agreeable, I did not choose to intrude myself.' On March 13, Wilkes wrote a conciliatory reply, saying that while he had been upset by parts of Almon's work, 'All that is now entirely over, and you shall always find me your friend and humble servant.'[22] After this exchange the two men remained on good terms until Wilkes died in December 1797.

Wilkes wrote some very interesting comments on the blank pages inserted in his own copy of Almon's *History of the Late Minority*, now in the British Library, which have been quoted by George Nobbe in his book, *The North Briton*. Wilkes noted against Almon's account of his arrest, 'All the particulars in this and the following pages are inaccurately related,' but he did not specifically assert that Almon had not been present at the scene at all.

In May 1767, Almon published the first of seventy-one monthly issues of his *Political Register*, which ran until the end of 1772. He had earlier written to Temple about the idea that 'a weekly political paper ought to be set up,' but in the end settled for a monthly issue, probably because there were already so many newspapers. By 1760, London was served by at least eighty-six papers.[23] By October 3, Almon was able to write to Wilkes, 'You are always heartily welcome to all my publications. The *Political Register* succeeds beyond my most sanguine

---

[21] For *Stockdale v. Hansard*, see the Appendix.

[22] British Library, Add. MSS 30,869, f.95; Almon, *Wilkes Correspondence*, 3: 135.

[23] Rea, Robert R., *The English Press in Politics 1760-1774*, 7.

expectations. It is become the fashionable political publication of the times. All parties buy it, and the public approve it.'[24]

Somewhat surprisingly, the *Political Register* was closed down by Almon in response to pressure from the King himself. He had published an account of the King's own plan for the reinforcement of the army in Ireland. Almon later explained: 'The day after the publication, the King sent Mr. Barnard, jun., to Mr. Almon, to know how he obtained that paper. Mr. Almon declined, in the most respectful terms, giving an answer to the question. But he rightly foresaw that his refusal would inevitably draw on him -----, and therefore with the view of deprecating such consequences, he discontinued the publication.' Although he was brave enough to refuse to disclose his source, his courage failed him when he weighed up the considerable powers of the 'constitutional' monarch. One can usually fill in the blanks deliberately left in eighteenth-century publications without difficulty, but this one is not so easy; 'the King's wrath', 'prosecution', 'persecution'?[25]

Wilkes returned to England, although still outlawed, in February 1768, and was soon afterwards elected to Parliament as one of the Members for Middlesex, Temple having given him some land in that county to qualify him as a candidate. His supporters made sure that Wilkes's triumph would be marked, as Benjamin Franklin explained in a letter to his son: 'The scenes have been horrible. London was illuminated two nights running at the command of the mob for the success of Wilkes in the Middlesex election. The second night exceeded anything of the kind ever seen here on the greatest occasions of rejoicing, as even the small cross-streets, lanes, courts and other out-of-the-way places were all in a blaze of lights, and the principal streets all night long, as the mobs went around again after 2 o'clock and

---

[24] *Grenville Papers*, 2: 457; British Library, Add. MSS 30,868, f.157.
[25] Almon, *Memoirs*, 47.

obliged people who had extinguished their candles to light them again. Those who refused had their windows destroyed.'[26]

Wilkes's outlawry was revoked by Lord Mansfield and in April he entered the King's Bench prison in Southwark to serve a term of twenty-two months. While he was there, Almon visited him 'every Sunday morning during the whole time of the confinement.' He also joined with others to open a subscription for Wilkes and made his Piccadilly shop one of the collection places. Almon conceded later that the idea had not proved very fruitful, but pointed out that it laid the foundation for the more successful 'society of gentlemen who called themselves Supporters of the Bill of Rights'. That society was to raise considerable sums to deal with Wilkes's crippling debts, which affected his freedom of action quite as much as his imprisonment.[27]

By 1768, many American colonists, especially those who received news and pamphlets from England, were beginning to identify with Wilkes: he was suffering from the same oppressive ministry, which was proving to be deaf to their reasoned arguments. On October 5, John Adams, together with four of his associates in Boston, wrote a long letter of support to Wilkes, then in prison. It included the passage, 'We feel with fraternal concern, that Europe in a ferment, America on the point of bursting into flames, more pressingly require the patriot senator, the wise and honest counsellor, than the desolating conqueror.'[28]

In February 1769, Wilkes was expelled from the Commons, despite a surprisingly supportive contribution from George Grenville, Temple's brother, which included a reference to the problems of America and echoed Adams's remarks. 'The difficulties we have to struggle with, arising from the interior

---

[26] Labaree, Leonard W. and others (eds.), *Papers of Benjamin Franklin*, New Haven: Yale U.P., 1959-, 15: 98.

[27] Almon, *Wilkes Correspondence*, 3: 287, 289.

[28] British Library, Add. MSS. 30,870, f.75.

condition of this country, from the disobedience of our colonies, and from the state of our foreign affairs, are augmented to such a degree, as to form a very dangerous crisis. The respect and reverence due to the parliament, and the confidence reposed in this House, are visibly diminished.' He then fairly asked, 'Under these circumstances does it not behove us to be doubly cautious, not to exceed the strictest bounds of law and of the constitution? Is it not more advisable, if the case can admit of a doubt, to conciliate the heated minds of men by temper and discretion, than to inflame them by adding fuel to discontent?'[29]

Grenville only learned of Almon's delayed plan to publish his speech when William Knox informed him of it in a letter of October 10, which is of interest as it shows how Almon dealt with the speech, and because it indicates how political comment could reach America. 'Almon, who is a thorough judge of times and seasons for publication, does not intend to publish it till the return from Newmarket races, which will be the week after next, when many persons from different parts of the kingdom pass through London. In the meantime he sends it to all those who leave orders with him for every new thing. I send by this night's post a copy to Ireland, to be reprinted and circulated through that kingdom, and I shall supply every American ship that sails with one, so that in a small space of time every part of the King's dominions will be fully satisfied of the wisdom and uprightness of your conduct.'[30]

Wilkes was dissatisfied with Grenville's speech and wrote a 130-page reply, *Letter to the Rt. Hon. George Grenville.* Temple asked Wilkes not to publish that criticism of his brother, but Wilkes brushed his request aside and got Isaac Fell to produce it. 'The consequence was,' Almon recorded, 'a total annihilation of that friendship which had subsisted between them above twenty

---

[29] *The Speech of a Rt. Hon. Gentleman on the Motion for Expelling Mr. Wilkes,* London: John Almon, 1769, 40.
[30] *Grenville Papers,* 4: 468.

years.'[31] 'It was typical of Wilkes to be offended by a speech in his favour, which happened not to contain all he would have wished. It was also typical of him to fall out with a useful supporter like Temple. In fairness to Wilkes it must be added that four years' exile, followed by a sentence of two years' imprisonment and expulsion from the House of Commons, would reinforce many people's paranoid feelings.'[32] Temple did not communicate with Wilkes again or return to public life, but Almon remained in touch with his patron until Temple's death in September 1779.

After his expulsion from the House, Wilkes was twice re-elected, only to have the government majority in the Commons declare the election void. When he was elected a fourth time, his opponent, Col. Henry Luttrell was invited to take the seat. Almon published a pamphlet, probably also written by him, which pointed out the grave implications of the House of Commons acting on its own, *Reflections on the Case of Mr. Wilkes and on the Right of the People to Elect their own Representatives*. The Society of the Supporters of the Bill of Rights gained considerable support from the alarm caused by the unseating of the democratically elected Wilkes, and proposed a series of tests for parliamentary candidates. Each candidate who wanted the support of the Society had to subscribe to the principle of 'a full and equal representation of the people in Parliament', as well as to a number of other principles, including 'the restoration of the sole right of self-taxation to America'. We shall see presently how much the cause of Wilkes, parliamentary reform and the case for the American colonies had become intertwined, and the important part played by Almon in the debates of the day.[33]

---

[31] Almon, *Wilkes Correspondence*, 3: 300. Wilkes's *Letter to the Rt. Hon George Grenville* has sometimes been wrongly attributed to Almon; see, Stockdale, Eric, 'John Almon and the State Prisoner', *Factotum* (British Library ESTC Newsletter), 1980, 9: 22.

[32] Stockdale, 23.

[33] For the American reaction to Wilkes, see Maier, Pauline, *From Resistance*

Almon's support of Wilkes cost him a great deal in financial terms. Almon explained that he could afford it as he was 'a frugal man', and that he never received any subsidies 'during the whole time he lived in Piccadilly'. That may well be true, but we shall see later that once he had moved to Fleet Street, he was certainly prepared to be subsidised by the Whigs. Incidentally, Almon's use of the words 'lived in Piccadilly' confirms that he followed the common practice of living over the shop.[34]

The unsatisfactory Middlesex elections led to unrest generally, but particularly in Westminster, the area of the county which included not only the Houses of Parliament but also Almon's house in Piccadilly. On January 16, 1770, Almon spoke at a meeting of Westminster electors at the Standard Tavern. Although he usually used the pen and the printing press to get his views across, on this occasion he made a stirring contribution, which Ian Christie has called 'a fiery speech full of class feeling', and which proved dangerous, for his next prosecution soon followed.[35]

In 1769, another supporter of Wilkes arrived on the scene. Letters signed Junius began to appear in the *Public Advertiser* and to infuriate the King and the ministry. One of the Junius letters was re-published in *The London Museum* and contained advice for the King on the subject of Wilkes. 'Discard those little personal resentments which have too long directed your public conduct. Pardon this man the remainder of his punishment.' According to Almon, John Miller, the printer, not only delivered some copies to his shop without his authority and in his absence, but advertised his work : 'To be sold also by J. Almon in Piccadilly.' When Almon heard that the printers were to be prosecuted, he

to Revolution, London: Routledge & Kegan Paul, 1973. See also, Bonwick, Colin, *English Radicals and the American Revolution*, Chapel Hill: U. of North Carolina P., 1977.

[34] Almon, *Memoirs*, 50; and see chapter 12.

[35] Christie, Ian R., *Wilkes, Wyvill and Reform*, London: Macmillan, 1962, 37; Almon, *Memoirs*, 56.

sent the remaining copies back to Miller. 'However, the ministerial runners or informers had been so quick,' he wrote later,
'they had bought one or two copies; and the ministers, as it
should seem, being now rejoiced that they had caught their
enemy, the prosecution commenced against him.' Almon was
particularly aggrieved, as Miller's conduct was quite usual in the
trade: both Miller and Edward Dilly swore an affidavit for the
resultant court proceedings, confirming the existence of the
custom.[36]

On June 2, 1770, Almon found himself appearing in front of
Mansfield, who had initiated the earlier unsuccessful prosecution
against him. The ministry were clearly determined to get him, for
the Crown was represented by both the Attorney and the
Solicitor-General, while Almon was represented, as on the
previous occasion, by Serjeant Glynn. The jury clearly believed
the defence version of the facts, for they asked the Chief Justice,
'Whether selling in the shop by a servant, of a pamphlet, without
the knowledge of the master in the sale, or even without a
knowledge of the contents of the libel or pamphlet so sold, be
sufficient to convict the master?' Mansfield answered in the
affirmative, so the jury had little choice but to convict. Fortunately for Almon, the penalties were non-custodial, though they
included a bind over for two years as a deterrent. The bind over
required Almon to refrain from publishing any further offensive
material; a breach would have brought him back to court for the
forfeiture of the money put up by him by way of surety. We
shall see later what he felt about the gagging effect of a binding
over on a publisher.[37]

Lucyle Werkmeister did not accept Almon's version at all,
claiming, possibly correctly, that Almon was the real publisher of
the paper in question, and that John Miller was merely his dupe,

---

[36] Almon, *Memoirs*, 62; Public Record Office, TS 11/177, 765.
[37] See chap.11; *R. v. Almon*, *English Reports*, 98: 411.

who was prepared to go to prison in place of Almon, on this and other occasions.[38]

Wholly undeterred by his sentence, Almon celebrated by publishing an account of the trial, including the offending words, but as part of the charge laid against him. He also included in the July *Political Register* the fair comment: 'But let me whisper in the ear of my reader, the secret is out, Almon was busily concerned in the Westminster Remonstrance, he must therefore, at all events, be punished: and the measure of proceeding against him will subserve the end in view of taking away the liberty of the press.'

In 1768, Almon made the important decision to challenge Parliament's prohibition on the reporting of its proceedings. He collected up details of speeches from various sources and published the results of his researches three times a week in the *London Evening Post*. The House of Commons became increasingly irritated and ordered various printers to appear before the House. In 1771, John Miller, the printer of the paper, refused to attend when so ordered, pursuant to a plan devised by Almon and Wilkes in collusion with their friends in the City. When the messenger of the House arrived in the City of London to take Miller to Westminster, a constable was ready and arrested him for assault. The messenger was brought, as arranged, before the Lord Mayor, Brass Crosby and Alderman Richard Oliver, sitting as magistrates for the City of London. They found the assault proved but granted the messenger bail. Crosby and Oliver were also Members of Parliament, and were speedily committed to the Tower by the House of Commons for contempt of Parliament. The members of both Houses of Parliament realised that there was a danger of their becoming a laughing-stock and so they abandoned their prohibition of reporting. Almon and

---

[38] Werkmeister (at p.130) was very critical of Almon, relying in part on the scathing attacks on him by Rev. William Jackson in the *Morning Post* for October 13, 16 and 20, 1784.

Wilkes and their supporters had achieved a notable victory for the freedom of the press: farce had proved to be a potent weapon.[39]

Apart from the obvious advantage of the public having almost contemporaneous reports, the publishers were thereafter able to produce regular volumes of debates for the use of members of both Houses, civil servants, historians and others. Once again, Almon was in the lead. In 1766, he started to publish, from the limited sources, *Debates of the House of Commons*. His next move he described as follows: 'When the new parliament met which was elected in 1774, and the dispute with America was approaching to hostilities, Mr. Almon resolved to compile and publish himself in monthly numbers, a regular and faithful series of the whole proceedings and debates of both Houses under the name of *The Parliamentary Register*. This was the first work of the kind ever attempted. He carried on this work to the end of that parliament, since which time the work has been continued by other hands with the same fidelity.'[40]

The hands which continued the work included those of Almon's successor, John Debrett and, after his bankruptcy in 1803, John Stockdale until 1812. Eventually the name of the printer Hansard, who first printed and later took over William Cobbett's *Parliamentary Debates*, was retained to the present day. The freedom of the press to report the proceedings of the legislature, nowadays taken for granted, may be said to be a permanent memorial to the co-operation of John Wilkes and John Almon – a formidable duo.[41]

---

[39] Almon, *Memoirs*, 119, see also, Rudé, George, *Wilkes and Liberty*, Oxford U.P., 1962, chap.IX, and Thomas, Peter D. G., 'John Wilkes and the Freedom of the Press', *Bull. of Inst. of Hist. Research*, 1960, 33: 86 and his *John Wilkes, A Friend to Liberty*, Oxford U.P., 1996.

[40] Almon, *Memoirs*, 120.

[41] Peter D. G. Thomas called Almon 'the bold pioneer of newspaper reporting', in his 'Sources for Debates of the House of Commons 1768-1774', *Bull. of Inst. of Hist. Research*, 1959, Special Supp. Nr.4.

Illus. 3. Benjamin Franklin, by Charles Wilson Peale

2

Benjamin Franklin and Almon

In the present chapter we shall see how Benjamin Franklin and John Almon, each in his own way, with pen and pamphlet, attempted to persuade the British government to see sense on the issue of the rights of the colonies. It will also become clear that they combined their efforts on occasion and that, partly because of Franklin's approval, Almon became the undisputed principal bookseller for publications on all American issues.

Had the thirteen American colonies been able to discuss and agree the appointment of a press secretary or public relations consultant, to work on their behalf in London and later, in Paris, they could hardly have done better than to give the post to Franklin. He has been praised for his various interests, abilities and achievements in many books over the years and most of them are relevant to our story. Franklin was a trained printer, some of his experience having been gained as a young man in London, he then turned to being a publisher and writer in Philadelphia and was so successful that he could afford early retirement. Apart from his literary and business skills, he was a scientist with an international reputation. In addition to that, he acquired experience of government as the clerk to the Pennsylvania Assembly and as Postmaster.

When Franklin returned to London in 1757, it was as agent for the Assembly of which he had been the clerk. He brought his son, William, with him, and entered him at once at the Middle Temple. William had already undertaken some legal studies in Philadelphia, but at the Inn of Court he studied to be

a barrister with other American and English students. William
became Governor of New Jersey soon after his return home,
and remained loyal to the Crown – to the great distress of his
father. William had a son, William Temple Franklin, who later
preferred his grandfather's political views to those of his own
father, siding with the patriots. He was to act as secretary to the
four American Peace Commissioners at the end of the War of
Independence, or Revolutionary War. One of the worst consequences of any civil war – and that was, essentially, the nature of
that war – is that brother can fight brother, father can meet son
on the battlefield. The three Franklins were fortunate in that
none of them had to fight under arms, but the fact that the
middle one of the three was a Tory loyalist and the other two
American patriots, caused immense pain. It is impossible to say
how many colonists were loyalists, but possibly a quarter or even
a third were; the Franklin trio were certainly split one-third, two-
thirds.

After a further five years in London, Benjamin Franklin
returned home, but he was back again in 1764, to start his
longest stay and to petition the government about the
Pennsylvanian constitutional problems that had arisen. He
lodged, as on his previous assignment, in Craven Street, just off
the Strand, and only minutes away from Piccadilly and the new
bookshop that had been opened by Almon in the previous year.

'No events in England gave greater encouragement to the
militant party in the American colonies than the achievements of
John Wilkes', Horace Bleackley commented. 'From first to last
they regarded his cause with as deep an interest as if it had been
their own. It was natural that they should sympathise with the
English rebel. In trying to vindicate the rights of the electorate
against the encroachments of the executive he was fighting for a
principle which all American patriots hoped to see recognised in
their own land.' William Franklin, by then Governor of New
Jersey, while not impressed by Wilkes, confirmed his importance
in America by writing to his father in January 1769, 'All the

nonsense about No.45 is almost as much attended to in the Colonies as in England.'¹

At this stage Franklin and his son still found it possible to agree on some matters. Franklin himself was not all that keen on Wilkes either. He did not approve of demagoguery and disliked the intervention of mobs in disputes: we have seen how he had felt about the Wilkes election celebrations. 'Wilkes was an ally Franklin could do without.'² We shall see later that in South Carolina, Henry Laurens held very similar views, as did many English supporters of the basic rights of the colonies.

However, apart from not sharing Almon's enthusiasm for Wilkes, Franklin probably agreed with him on most other matters. Franklin was to use young Almon's shop as an outlet from time to time, but he mainly relied on his stream of letters to the newspapers and on William Strahan, a leading printer in London, as well as a close friend. Franklin and Strahan had become friends by letter, years earlier. Franklin, when in America, had once ordered books from him, pointing out to him, 'Your authors know but little of the fame they have on this side of the ocean.'³ For many years most of the books sold in America were imported from England. In 1745, Strahan recommended his friend and favourite employee, David Hall, to Franklin, who also took to the young man and made him his partner in his Philadelphia business. 'This three-way friendship was the basis of the first sustained book-importing enterprise in the middle colonies.' In the period 1748-1772, Hall imported over £30,000 worth of books and stationery from Strahan in London.⁴

---

¹ Bleackley, Horace, *Life of John Wilkes*, London: John Lane, Bodley Head, 1917, 243; Labaree, Leonard W. and others (eds.), *Papers of Benjamin Franklin*, New Haven: Yale U.P., 1959-, 16: 5; hereafter cited as *Franklin Papers*.
² Morgan, Edmund S., *Benjamin Franklin*, New Haven: Yale U.P., 2002, 170.
³ Van Doren, Carl, *Benjamin Franklin*, London: Putnam, 1939, 102.
⁴ Green, James N., 'English Books and Printing in the Age of Franklin', in

Fortunately for Almon, he was able to benefit to some extent from the existence of this bookselling troika.

The Stamp Act, passed in 1765, marked the effective beginning of the British government's crass mishandling of its compatriots in North America. That Act imposed duties on many items in every day use in the colonies, from legal documents to newspapers, and Franklin and Almon both worked hard for its repeal. On February 13, 1766, Franklin appeared before the House of Commons to express the views of the appalled colonists. On April 7, Strahan wrote to David Hall in Philadelphia, promising to send a copy of Franklin's examination as soon as he could obtain one from the Clerk of the House. Strahan sent the promised copy on May 10, 1766, pointing out that he had only obtained it, 'with great difficulty, and with some expense.' He added a request: 'If you do print it, however, in any shape, pray send a dozen copies of it, directed to Dr. F. to save postage.'[5]

Hall published the Doctor's evidence, with the title *An Examination before a Great Assembly*. It was presumably Franklin himself who gave a copy to Almon for re-publication, for he put it out early in the following year, with the title changed slightly. Almon altered *Great* to *Honourable*. The Act was repealed in March 1766, but unfortunately that repeal was accompanied by the Declaratory Act, in which Parliament asserted its right to legislate for the colonies, if it so wished, and then by the Townshend duties on tea and other commodities. Almon was delighted with the repealing statute, commenting later: 'Mr. Almon was in favour of that measure, writing and publishing a good deal of support of it. This conduct was soon distinguished

Amory, Hugh and Hall, David D. (eds.), *The Colonial Book in the Atlantic World*, Cambridge U.P., 2000, 277, 278. See also, Green's 'Benjamin Franklin as Publisher and Bookseller', in Lemay, J. A. Leo (ed.), *Reappraising Benjamin Franklin*, Newark: U. of Delaware P., 1993, 98.

[5] Adams, Thomas R., *American Independence – The Growth of an Idea*, Providence: Brown U.P., 1965, 21.

in America, and the American writers constantly sent him their pamphlets and papers to be re-printed in England.'[6]

After this, Almon not only published many individual pamphlets about the American dispute, but also sold bound compilations. In this last venture he was assisted by Thomas Hollis, whose love for America led him to become a benefactor of Harvard College, as well as an early English supporter of the rights of the colonists. 'The association of the radical printer John Almon and Hollis was close during the years 1765-1770,' Caroline Robbins pointed out. 'They prated politics and certainly had some views in common.' She added: 'He was closely in touch with Almon in the autumn of 1765 and was concerned in the collection of tracts on the Stamp Act. In the following February, Hollis asked Almon to collect tracts relating to North America, and in August the printer was still at it – searching the booksellers throughout the city.' The two men were probably jointly involved in the compilation of the two-volume collection that Almon published in 1766 and 1767 with the title *Tracts Relating to North America and the Stamp Act.*[7]

On November 21, 1765, the *London Chronicle*, at the suggestion of Hollis, reprinted an essay from the Boston *Gazette*, with the title 'A Dissertation on Canon and Feudal Law'. He had been greatly impressed by the anonymous author's arguments in favour of the colonists. When he learned that a young Massachusetts lawyer called John Adams was the author, Hollis responded, 'He cannot be too much encouraged.' Three years later Almon, again on the recommendation of Hollis, used it once more, this time in a collection of pamphlets with the shortened title, *The True Sentiments of America.* John Adams's latest biographer has written of his dissertation, 'It was his first extended political work and one of the most salient of his life,

---

[6] Almon, *Memoirs*, 32.
[7] Robbins, Caroline, 'The Strenuous Whig, Thomas Hollis of Lincoln's Inn', *William and Mary Quarterly*, 3rd. series, 1950, 407.

written at the age of thirty. It was a statement of his own fervent patriotism and the taproot conviction that American freedoms were not ideals still to be obtained, but rights long and firmly established by British law and by the courage and sacrifice of generations of Americans.'[8]

Hollis paid Almon for sixty copies of the compilation: he regularly bought pamphlets in bulk from Almon for distribution to Harvard College and other friends. Robbins concluded that the relationship between the two men 'undoubtedly furthered the constant publication of American authors in London.'[9] The publication by Almon in London of John Adams's Boston essay also marked the beginning of another important connection: that of Adams with the Piccadilly bookshops of Almon and John Stockdale.

We have seen that Adams wrote to Wilkes while he was in prison. In his answer, written after the government had decided to clamp down on Boston, Wilkes once more demonstrated his support: 'I have read with grief and indignation the proceedings of the Ministry with regard to the troops ordered to Boston, as if it were the capital of a province belonging to our enemies, or in the possession of rebels.'[10] On one of his weekly visits to Wilkes in prison, Almon was doubtless shown the exchange with Adams, which fitted in well with his and Hollis's views and combined efforts.

At the end of 1769, a committee of Boston merchants, clearly aware of the fact that they had supporters in the English legislature, sent Franklin copies of their expressed views on the effects of the Townshend Acts, with their tax burdens, 'that our friends in Parliament may be acquainted with the difficulties the

---

[8] *Memoirs of Thomas Hollis*, London printed, 1780, 400, 401; Bonwick, Colin C., 'An English Audience for American Revolutionary Pamphlets', *Historical Journal*, 1976, 19: 355; McCullough, David, *John Adams*, New York; Simon & Schuster, 2001, 59.

[9] Robbins, 438.

[10] British Library, Add. MSS. 30,870, f.135.

trade labor under by means of these Acts'.[11] Franklin presumably passed a copy on to Almon, for in 1770 he published *Observations on Several Acts ... by the Merchants of Boston.*

The occupation of Boston did little to pacify the merchants or the restless populace and on March 5, 1770, there occurred the incident immediately called the Boston Massacre. A mob in King Street taunted some British soldiers, who eventually opened fire, killing three civilians and mortally wounding two others. John Adams defended the British commander at his trial and secured an acquittal. Adams, who sometimes displayed paranoid symptoms, attributed his own later unpopularity with some of his compatriots to the fact that he had defended Captain Thomas Preston, in the best traditions of the Bar, and possibly at the request of the leaders of the local patriot movement.[12] Twelve days after the shooting, a town meeting at Faneiul Hall in Boston, acknowledging his importance in the mutual struggle, voted to send Wilkes a copy of the representations made as a result of the incident.[13]

A little later Franklin received a copy of the American leaflet about the Massacre, with a lurid engraving by Paul Revere to illustrate it, which was soon published by Almon and by the pro-American Dilly brothers. Almon also devoted the front page of his *London Evening Post* for April 21-24 to an account of the matter. The back page of the same issue gleefully reported the swearing-in of Wilkes, newly released from prison, as an Alderman for the City – an office to which he had been elected while in custody, and which was to lead to the ex-prisoner becoming Lord Mayor of London before long.

The Boston Massacre was regarded by many as a turning point. Adams may have had a point when, years later, he wrote to Jedidiah Morse: 'Not the battle of Lexington or Bunker's Hill,

[11] *Franklin Papers*, 16: 273.
[12] Ferling, John, *Setting the World Ablaze*, Oxford U.P., 2000, 77.
[13] British Library, Add. MSS. 30,871, f.18.

nor the surrender of Burgoyne or Cornwallis were more important events in American history than the battle of King Street on March 5, 1770.'[14]

Between that date and the end of 1773, there were no major crises in the relations of the mother country and her colonies. On June 10, 1771, Arthur Lee, a very influential member of the Virginia Lee family, who switched from being a medical practitioner to being a barrister practising in the Middle Temple, wrote to Sam Adams, John's cousin and a leading revolutionary in Boston: 'The session of parliament is now at an end and without one offensive measure to America. We owe this to the difference with Spain, which engaged all the attention of administration in the first part of the session; and a quarrel with the City of London, which employed the remainder.'[15]

That quarrel with the City was, of course, the famous one engineered by Almon and Wilkes, to secure the right to report parliamentary proceedings. By fighting for their rights as Englishmen, they had unwittingly bought time for their American friends. One of Arthur Lee's brothers, William, was an ally of Wilkes and was also to become a City Alderman, while their brother Richard Henry was to sign the Declaration of Independence. It was Arthur Lee who had shrewdly got the Society for the Supporters of the Bill of Rights to include in their manifesto the aim of 'the restoration of the sole right of self-taxation to America.' (Sadly, Arthur Lee was later to cause trouble for Franklin and other compatriots in Europe, and eventually became seriously mentally ill.)

While the co-operation of Hollis and Almon proved to be very fruitful, Hollis never brought himself to work with Franklin in a similar way. The two men met regularly at various worthy societies, but unfortunately Hollis regarded Franklin as a

---

[14] Adams, Charles Francis, *The Works of John Adams*, Boston: Little, Brown, 1856, 10: 203, hereafter cited as C. F. Adams. For Morse, see chapter 16.
[15] Lee, R. H., *Life of Arthur Lee*, Boston: Wells and Lilly, 1829, 1: 213.

trimmer. On the other hand, Franklin co-operated with Almon from time to time, though he was still mainly relying on Strahan to introduce him to editors and others who could publicise the American case. Some forty of Franklin's letters were published by Henry Sampson Woodfall of the *Public Advertiser*, who also published the letters of Junius, but others were happy to publish Franklin as well. He did not always use his own name, but wrote under a large number of pseudonyms. He was angry about the insulting remarks made about Americans in some of the papers and constantly wrote to correct misconceptions, pointing out that his compatriots wanted nothing more than their rights as Englishmen.[16]

Verner Crane has drawn attention to the fact that Franklin sponsored the printing of some famous pamphlets: 'In January 1766, Strahan printed to his order the first and second editions of Daniel Dulany's celebrated tract, *Considerations on the Propriety of Imposing Taxes in the British Colonies*; and in February the first English edition of John Dickinson's *The Late Regulations respecting the British Colonies*. Both were published by John Almon, who was becoming a specialist in American tracts. It was Almon who brought out in 1768 the first London edition of Dickinson's more famous work, *Letters from a Farmer in Pennsylvania*.' A literary expert on the period, called Dickinson's *Letters*, which had first appeared in the *Pennsylvania Chronicle*, 'the most brilliant event in the literary history of the Revolution'.[17]

Dickinson is still sometimes referred to as 'the Penman of the Revolution' His famous pamphlet was the first of three landmark works of the Revolution published in London by Almon, but the only one of the three to be written in America

---

[16] Crane, Verner W., *Benjamin Franklin's Letters to the Press 1758-1775*, Chapel Hill: U. of North Carolina P., 1950, xvi, xxii, xxix, xlix; Greene, Jack P., 'Pride, Prejudice, and Jealousy', in Lemay, 119.

[17] Tyler, Moses Coit, *Literary History of the Revolution*, New York, 1897, 1: 234.

by an American. The other two, by Arthur Lee and Thomas Paine, were written by an American in France, and an Englishman in America, respectively.

Strahan's account book shows that in June 1768, he printed five hundred copies of Dickinson's 'brilliant' pamphlet for Almon, who did not undertake his own printing, despite the fact he had learned that trade. Strahan charged £1.3s. for each of the eight sheets required, and 14 shillings for each of the eight reams of paper used. The total sum of £14.16s. is shown as having been paid on May 14, 1770. Another entry on the same date shows a debit for Dr. Franklin for a part of the bill: 'To Mr. Almon, balance of the Dr.'s bill £1.17.6d.'[18]

Although Dickinson also read for the Bar at the Middle Temple, he left London in 1757, on the completion of his studies, shortly before Almon's arrival, so they never met, but Lee seems to have introduced them to each other by letter. On February 4, 1775, two weeks after the Earl of Chatham (Pitt the Elder) had, in the House of Lords, demanded the withdrawal of the troops from Boston, Almon wrote to Dickinson, in terms which indicated how well informed he was, enclosing a proof copy of Chatham's Bill, which had not even been published at that stage.[19]

Michael Kammen, who made a study of the colonial agents in London, noted that soon after the arrival of the Connecticut agent, William Samuel Johnson, in 1766, Franklin took him to meet John Almon. He pointed out that some of the agents became dismayed when Almon also published British replies to some of the pro-colonist publications, adding, 'Thus Almon's printing of an English edition of the *Farmer's Letters* in 1768 (with Franklin's new preface) was offset by his publication of Knox's reply to John Dickinson, the Farmer.' William Knox,

---

[18] British Library Add. MSS. 48,801, ff.40, 34.

[19] Maier, Pauline, *From Resistance to Revolution*, London: Routledge & Kegan Paul, 1973, 222; Library Company of Philadelphia, Dickinson Papers.

George Grenville's 'puppet', had timed his response carefully. On July 23, he wrote to Grenville about that reply, *The Controversy between Great Britain and her Colonies Reviewed*: 'The Paper is now in Almon's hands, and part of it already composed, but I shall not suffer it to be published till near the meeting of Parliament.'[20]

Franklin, himself a printer and publisher, does not seem to have ruled Almon out as a useful bookseller, merely because he published both sides of the argument on this occasion. Almon had done so earlier as well. In 1766, he had published *A Collection of the Most Valuable Tracts which appeared during the years 1763, 1764 and 1765 upon the subjects of General Warrants, etc.* In his preface he wrote: 'As they contain every substantial argument and material fact which were brought by both sides, in support of their several points lately agitated; and as several of them were known to be the composition of some of the most able and principal persons in the Kingdom, it was thought by many, that such tracts were too valuable to be thrown aside like the common reading of a day.' It was possibly Temple who had encouraged Almon to print that collection, for he began it with a letter from Candor, containing an important plea for both sides' arguments to be aired.

Candor had written: 'As Mr. Almon has hitherto published nothing but what is in opposition to the present Ministry, Candor thinks it is high time for him to show some impartiality, by letting the world see what may be said in favour of some of the great men in office; and for this reason desires he will be the editor of the subsequent pages. Seeing all people agree that the Liberty of the Press should never be violated, and that it does no service, in the long run, to any man that attempts it, every printer should be totally free, and therefore impartial.' The press

---

[20] Kammen, Michael G., *A Rope of Sand*, Ithaca: Cornell U.P., 1968, 218; British Library, Add. MSS. 42,086, f.70.

is not free if it has to conform with the view of the party in power, or even that of the majority of the electorate.

In May 1773, Parliament abolished all the Townshend duties, but for those on tea, a step which led to the protest known as the Boston Tea Party on December 16. That led in turn to further repressive measures, known in America as the Intolerable Acts, which brought armed resistance closer, and also led to the meeting of the First Continental Congress in Philadelphia. 'A little "tea party" in Boston had mushroomed into a mighty storm uniting the continent.'[21]

Thomas Jefferson, a lawyer who had been elected to the Virginia House of Burgesses in 1769, became ill on the way to the Congress and so did not attend it, but he passed a note of his views on to his Virginia colleagues. Recognising its value, they encouraged him to revise it. He did so and in the summer of 1774 the enlarged note became his first important document to appear in print. It contained a set of proposed instructions for the colony's delegates to the Congress meeting in Philadelphia in the September, and bore the title *A Summary View of the Rights of British America*. It also clearly contained some of the ideas later incorporated by Jefferson into his draft of the Declaration of Independence.

Jefferson made the point, 'Our ancestors, before their emigration to America, were the free inhabitants of the British dominions in Europe, and possessed a right, which nature has given to all men, of departing from the country in which chance, not choice has placed them, of going in quest of new habitations, and of there establishing new societies, under such laws and regulations as to them shall seem most likely to promote public happiness.' He fairly asked, 'Can any one reason be assigned why 160,000 electors in the island of Great Britain should give law to four millions in the states of America, every

---

[21] Peterson, Merrill D., *Thomas Jefferson and the New Nation*, Oxford U.P., 1990, 71.

individual of whom is equal to every individual of them in virtue, in understanding, and in bodily strength?' He was perhaps on shakier ground when he boldly asserted, 'The whole art of government consists in the art of being honest', but it was a charming idea.[22]

On November 7, 1774, Franklin wrote from his lodgings at Craven Street: 'Dr. Franklin presents his compliments to Mr. Almon, and sends him a manuscript, which he has perused, and thinks well written, so as probably to be acceptable to the public at this time. If Mr. Almon should be of the same opinion, it is at his service.'[23] The pamphlet was Arthur Lee's *Appeal to the Justice and Interests of the People of Great Britain in the Present Disputes with America*, but it did not bear his name. It was ostensibly written by a former Member of Parliament, so as to disguise the fact that the author was an American. Lee's knowledge of his country enabled him to make a telling point, which turned out to be amply justified by later events. 'I acknowledge, I admit, even to enthusiasm, the bravery of our troops; what men can do, they will do; but in a country furnished with fastnesses and defiles without number, intimately known to the enemy you are to combat, where discipline is unavailing or embarrassing, and valour useless, it requires more than human power to succeed to any permanent purpose. God forbid that the bravery of such troops as the English, should be so vainly, so fatally employed. Let us suppose it true, as some vainglorious military men have vaunted, that with four regiments you might march from one end of the continent to the other – what would this exploit avail you? The moment you quit one province for another, the commotions your presence suppressed, will revive. When you have marched through, you will have to march back again.'

---

[22] Peterson, Merrill D., *The Portable Thomas Jefferson*, London: Penguin, 1977, 4, 10, 20.

[23] Almon, *Memoirs*, 92.

This pamphlet was to be the second of Almon's landmark publications of the Revolution, but he was cautious about it at first, writing to Franklin on December 6, 'There having been only a small number printed, because upon so beaten a subject one is doubtful of success, till the public opinion can be taken; but this pamphlet being much approved, it is probable that it will be reprinted. Should be glad therefore of notice of any errors (by penny post or otherwise).'[24]

Lee himself made no mention of any contribution whatsoever by Franklin. In his autobiographical notes, he wrote, 'In the Spring of 1774 I set out with Mr. and Mrs. [Ralph] Izard to make the tour of France and Italy. While at Paris I wrote the *Appeal*, which I transmitted to my brother in London, who had it printed and published by Almon. This pamphlet went through five editions.' There was no love lost between Lee and Franklin, so the omission of the Doctor's part was probably deliberate: it is unlikely that William Lee would have omitted to let his brother Arthur know that he had passed his manuscript over to Franklin. Almon later wrote, 'But Dr. Franklin had a considerable share in the composition; and it might now, with no impropriety, be called Dr. Franklin's farewell address.' Having had only a small number printed at first, he was able to add, 'Many thousands of it were circulated.'[25]

In December, Almon, who was undoubtedly one of the first to appreciate the significance of the meeting at Philadelphia, also had five hundred copies of the Minutes of the First Continental Congress printed. Either he or Franklin asked Strahan to produce the work speedily, for the printer charged half a guinea 'expedition money'.[26] On January 17, 1775, Almon advertised

---

[24] American Philosophical Society, Philadelphia, BF 85.

[25] Lee, R. H., *Life of Arthur Lee*, Boston: Wells and Lilly, 1829, 1: 262; Almon, *Anecdotes*, 2: 325; Verner Crane (at li) maintained that Almon was mistaken about Franklin's share, but it was certainly he who passed the manuscript on to the bookseller.

[26] British Library, Add. MSS. 48,801, f.61.

the publication that day of the *Journal of the Proceedings of Congress*, and claimed that the work was 'published by order of the Congress'. That was true, and the advertisement bore the signature of Franklin, Arthur Lee and William Bollan, the Massachusetts agent, several of whose pamphlets Almon had earlier published. On the previous day, Thomas Becket had managed to print a garbled version of the proceedings, so on January 17, the three Americans published another announcement to denounce it as being 'surreptitious as well as materially and grossly erroneous'.[27]

Two of Franklin's clerical friends produced two of the most powerful pamphlets of the period. Despite the fact that both were published by Thomas Cadell, rather than by Almon, they merit a brief consideration. Jonathan Shipley, the Bishop of St. Asaph's, wrote *A Speech Intended to have been Spoken on the Bills for Altering the Charters of Massachusetts Bay*, which included the oft-repeated sentence, 'My Lords, I look upon North America as the only great nursery of freemen now left upon the face of the earth.' He added the sage words, 'He acts the part of the truest patriot in this dangerous crisis, whether he lives at London or at Boston, who pursues sincerely the most lenient and conciliatory measures; and wishes to restore the public peace by some better method than the slaughter of our fellow-citizens.'

The other was the best-selling *Observations on the Nature of Civil Liberty*, by Richard Price, the well-known dissenting minister, who was a friend of America, of Franklin and later, of John Adams. 'I hope, therefore, our brethren in America forgive their enemies,' Price wrote, 'It is certain they know not what they are doing.' Price's pamphlet ran to some 60,000 copies and was only surpassed by Thomas Paine's *Common Sense*, which Almon republished in 1776, as his third landmark work on the debate. Price, like Thomas Day and other English supporters of the Americans, learned that pro-colonist sentiments could

---

[27] *Franklin Papers*, 21: 452.

sometimes prompt angry responses. 'I have drawn upon myself a torrent of opposition and abuse,' he wrote on June 15, 1777, to Arthur Lee in Paris, 'but the satisfaction I feel in the consciousness of having endeavoured to promote the cause of liberty and justice makes me abundant amends.'[28]

Franklin greatly appreciated the worth of Price's works – and of the power of the pen generally – sending him a memorable letter after the virtual end of hostilities, dated June 13, 1782: 'The ancient Roman and Greek orators could only speak to the number of citizens capable of being assembled within the reach of their voice. Their writings had little effect, because the bulk of the people could not read. Now by the press we can speak to nations; and good books and well-written pamphlets have great and general influence.'[29]

During the Winter of 1774-5, the colonists began to prepare for war by assembling arms and undertaking some military training. Almon recorded a startling question and answer exchange in Parliament about the military preparedness of the Americans. 'A few months previous to the commencement of hostilities, the Duke of Grafton was called upon in the House of Lords (the Secretary of State not being present) to inform the House what number of the King's troops were in America, which he answered. He next was asked what force the Americans had. To this question the Duke replied that he did not know, but that those who wanted such information might probably obtain it by applying to Mr. Almon. Whether his Grace meant this as a sneer, or an acknowledgement of Mr. Almon's intelligence, is not now material.'[30] Almon was quite right: either way, the reply was extraordinary. Grafton must have been basing

---

[28] *Massachusetts Hist. Soc. Procs.*, 2nd. series, 1903, 17: 310.
[29] Morgan, W., *Memoirs of the Life of the Rev. Richard Price*, London: R. Hunter and Rees, 1815, 96.
[30] Almon, *Memoirs*, 93.

himself on his knowledge of the extent of Almon's coverage of the dispute.

On February 6, 1775, Wilkes, who had finally taken his seat in the previous year, made a statesmanlike contribution to the House of Commons debate on a ministerial resolution 'to stand by his Majesty against all rebellious attempts'. 'It draws the sword unjustly against America; but before Administration are suffered to plunge the nation into the horrors of a civil war, before they are permitted to force English men to sheath their swords in the bowels of their fellow-subjects, I hope this House will seriously weigh the original ground and cause of this unhappy dispute, and in time reflect whether justice is on our side, and gives a sanction to the intended hostile proceedings. The assumed right of taxation without the consent of subjects is plainly the primary cause of the present quarrel.' He later warned that the Americans, 'will sooner declare themselves independent, and risk every consequence of such a contest, than submit to the galling yoke which Administration is preparing for them.'[31]

The ministry had received similar good advice from Chatham and Camden in the House of Lords debate on January 20, but remained pig-headedly determined to stamp out the opposition in the colonies. Franklin had attended the debate in the Lords, but correctly thought that 'all availed no more than the whistling of the winds'. He realised that a showdown was not far off, and handed over his agency for Massachusetts (for he had accumulated several colonies as his clients) to Arthur Lee. Shortly before sailing for America he spent a few hours with Edmund Burke on March 19.

That last meeting clearly influenced Burke's speech in the Commons on March 22, as did the contents of Lee's magnificent pamphlet. Among Burke's objections to the use of force was one which echoed Lee's earlier written warning. Burke told the Commons: 'Permit me to observe that the use of force is but

---

[31] *The Speeches of Mr. Wilkes in the House of Commons*, 1786, 7, 19.

temporary. It may subdue for a moment, but it does not remove the necessity of subduing again; and a nation is not governed which is perpetually to be conquered.' He went on to make one of the most telling points of the time, when he maintained that one of the reasons why 'this fierce spirit of liberty is stronger in the English colonies probably than in any other people of the earth,' was that 'the people of the colonies are descendants of Englishmen. They are therefore not only devoted to liberty, but to liberty according to English ideas and on English principles.'[32]

Burke summed up the situation perfectly, so one can readily accept a recent assessment of Franklin: 'He knew himself to be the most reluctant of revolutionaries, an ardent Briton driven from the arms of the mother country only by a deep, personal disillusionment.'[33] Joseph Priestley later gave an account of Franklin's last day in London. Typically, Franklin saw to it that it was pretty much like many another the two men had shared. 'A great part of the day he was looking over a number of American newspapers, directing me what to extract from them for the English ones.'[34]

On April 10, Wilkes, as Lord Mayor of London, presented the King with the City's petition, which declared 'our abhorrence of the measures which have been pursued, and are now pursuing, to the oppression of our fellow-subjects in America.'[35] The King was not impressed by the views of the principal merchants and citizens of his own capital, but even if he had been, it would have been too late for anyone in England to prevent the next fateful step. On April 19, when British

---

[32] Burke, Edmund, *Speeches and Letters on American Affairs*, London: Dent, 1961, 89, 91.

[33] Brands, H. W., *The First American*, New York: Doubleday, 2000, 622. We shall see in the next chapter that Henry Laurens felt the same – as did countless others.

[34] Crane, xlvi.

[35] *Gentleman's Magazine*, 1775, 199, 203.

troops were on a raid from Boston to seize arms, there was a clash with armed colonists at Lexington and Concord. Shots were exchanged, with casualties on both sides. The British troops fell back to Boston, where they were swiftly hemmed in by large numbers of Americans, armed with anything from hunting rifles to pitchforks. The unnecessary war had begun.

Illus. 4. Henry Laurens by John Singleton Copley

3

Henry Laurens and Independence

In this chapter we shall meet Henry Laurens and his son, John, and see how the crucial friendship between John Laurens and Thomas Day developed at the Middle Temple. We shall then note some of the unsuccessful efforts made by Henry Laurens, Benjamin Franklin and others in London to avert a war. Also, John Almon can be seen to extend his interest in the cause of America by publishing further pamphlets on the dispute in the period before the Declaration of Independence.

Henry Laurens was born in 1724, in Charleston, South Carolina (Charles Town until 1783) and spent his early twenties in London, learning to be a merchant. Back in America he managed to combine that occupation very successfully with being a plantation owner, regrettably with slave labour, and before long became involved in politics. In 1757, Laurens was elected to the colony's Commons House of Assembly for the first time. As David Duncan Wallace pointed out in his excellent biography of Laurens, published in 1915, this 'became one of the finest training schools in statecraft imaginable. It was in this school that the leaders of the Revolution and the framers of a new government were to be formed – Laurens, Gadsden, Lowndes, Pinckney, Lynch, Rutledge.'[1] Thomas Lynch, John Rutledge and his younger brother, Edward, were all educated as lawyers at the Middle Temple in London. Lynch and the younger Rutledge were to sign the Declaration of Independence, while the elder

---

[1] Wallace, David Duncan, *The Life of Henry Laurens*, New York: G. P. Putnam's Sons, 1915, 42.

Rutledge was to help frame the Constitution. Laurens's eldest son, John, was born in 1754, and when thinking about his education later, Henry was to recall where some of his more successful political colleagues had received their basic legal knowledge.

During the Seven Years' War, Laurens took part in the Cherokee campaign in the South Carolina Regiment, and after that was quite often addressed as Colonel, until he became the chairman of the Continental Congress in 1777, when he was given the more splendid title of President – there being no President of the infant United States at that time.

During the crisis created by the Stamp Act of 1765, Laurens was confronted by the age old question of how to respond to the repressive acts of a strong government. Does one try peaceful arguments in assemblies, pamphlets and newspapers, or does one have to resort to violence to get any sensible response? Laurens was firmly on the side of non-violent reasoning, regarding the alternative approach as futile and merely inviting sterner measures. His house was in fact raided by a mob of local people who, quite wrongly, suspected Laurens of storing official stamps. That experience strengthened his resolve against violent resistance to the Crown. In the late 1760's, he fell out with the British customs authorities and learned how to use his pen in earnest: he resorted, not for the last time, to writing a pamphlet to put his case to the public.

At the end of 1769, the South Carolina Commons ordered their treasurer to send £1500 sterling to England 'for the defence of British and American Liberty'. The recipient was the Society for the Support of the Bill of Rights, which had been formed to pay John Wilkes's debts. He was regarded by many in South Carolina as a man who shared with them the burden of a tyrannical government and who deserved their support. Laurens was rather lukewarm about the idea, but when the British attempted to punish the Commons for their unique demonstration of support for Wilkes, he stood shoulder to shoulder with his more militant colleagues on this issue. The Wilkes fund dispute rumbled on until the outbreak of the Revolution, as did the support for Wilkes and his ideas.[2]

Like so many women at that time, Laurens's wife died as a result of childbirth in 1770, leaving the distraught father with three sons and two daughters to bring up. Fortunately, money was not a problem: Laurens was by then one of the most prosperous men in America. Leaving the two girls with his brother and sister-in-law, he sailed for England in 1771, as he had decided that his sons would receive a better education there. Thomas Jefferson was to write to a friend in 1785, 'Let us view the disadvantages of sending a youth to Europe. To enumerate them all would require a volume. I will select a few. If he goes to England he learns drinking, horse-racing and boxing. These are the peculiarities of English education.'[3] As Jefferson had not even been to England when he expressed this opinion, the apparent views of Henry Laurens, who had lived in the country for several years, may perhaps be preferred on this subject. In practice, he sent his older two boys on to school in Geneva for the first two years, before switching their education to England, but he spent most of the three years in London with his youngest son. He was able to make a number of useful contacts while combining business with politics, not least at the Carolina Coffee House, which John Almon visited regularly to pick up useful information about America generally. Laurens appreciated the usefulness of carefully planted accurate information and following Benjamin Franklin's example, made use of Almon's willingness to print pro-colonist items.

One of Laurens's oldest and closest acquaintances in England, who was to visit him in the Tower of London and then to represent Britain in the peace negotiations, was the Scot,

---

[2] Wallace, chap.13.
[3] Boyd, Julian P. and others (eds.) *The Papers of Thomas Jefferson*, Princeton U.P., 1950-, 8: 636.

Richard Oswald, who had lived in Virginia and was sympathetic to the colonists' cause. In 1774, he made the shrewd comment to Laurens: 'If Great Britain forces a war upon America, she cannot spare troops enough to subdue Virginia alone, if the people there will be faithful to each other.'[4]

Oswald introduced Laurens to various Members of Parliament, as did the agent for South Carolina, Charles Garth, himself a member of the House of Commons and a barrister. Laurens and his fellow-Americans received a mixed response to their arguments, but generally speaking found that once violence increased on the part of the colonists, deaf ears were turned to their blandishments. One Member of Parliament, who was prepared to listen to the colonists' side of the argument, asked, 'What then would you have us do, Colonel?' Laurens replied: 'Repeal all those laws which are calculated for raising a revenue on the colonists without their own consent. They are galling to the Americans, yield no benefit to the mother country; you disagree among yourselves concerning the *right*, and every man sees and acknowledges the *inexpediency* of such taxation.'[5]

One of the matters which hampered Laurens and his colleagues back home was the continuing blight of the Wilkes fund dispute. The ministry's response had been an Additional Instruction of April 14, 1770, which prohibited the South Carolina Assembly from passing any money measure until it had pleaded guilty to helping Wilkes. Laurens tried hard to get the Instruction withdrawn, but with limited success, so in 1774, paid Arthur Lee to write a long pamphlet on the subject: *Answer to the Considerations on Certain Political Transactions of the Province of South Carolina*, which Almon published.[6] Laurens probably visited

---

[4] Wallace, 127n.

[5] Hamer, Philip M. and others (eds.), *The Papers of Henry Laurens*, Columbia: U. South Carolina P., 1968-2003, 16 vols., 9: 300, hereafter cited as *Laurens Papers*.

[6] *Laurens Papers*, 8: xiii; Potts, Louis W., *Arthur Lee – A Virtuous Revolutionary*, Baton Rouge: Louisiana U.P., 1981, 122.

Almon's shop from time to time, and may well have been served by John Stockdale, his new assistant, but had no occasion to mention him in writing until after the war.

Laurens was by no means the only American in London trying to influence events. As discussed earlier, some of the colonial agents, notably Benjamin Franklin, did their best to influence public and parliamentary opinion. Michael Kammen wrote of Franklin: 'He wrote most often in rebuttal to specious opinions about America. To keep his authorship secret, create the impression of a regiment of pro-American writers, and perhaps compensate for his colleagues' failure to write, he attached various signatures to his essays.' However, by 1770, even the wily old Doctor doubted whether 'the freedom I used in declaring and publishing these sentiments had much effect.' As related in the last chapter, Franklin was to remain in London until March 1775, but his oft-recounted bitter encounter before the Privy Council with the Solicitor-General, Alexander Wedderburn in 1773, reduced his effectiveness. Laurens wrote after Franklin's Privy Council appearance, 'His influence is lost, we have lost our principal advocate. I long to be at home to share the fate, whether good or bad, with my countrymen.'[7]

Before leaving for home, Laurens made one last approach to the British authorities. He drummed up support from some thirty Americans merchants working in London, half of them from South Carolina, and presented their petition to the Earl of Dartmouth, protesting against the coercive measures introduced as a reprisal for the Boston Tea Party. One of those merchants

---

[7] Kammen, Michael G., *A Rope of Sand – The Colonial Agents, British Politics, and the American Revolution*, Ithaca N.Y.: Cornell U.P., 1968, 208, 216, 284; Wallace,197. It is interesting to note that in referring to one of the earliest colonial agents, Jeremiah Dummer, Kammen made the comment (at p.10): 'His Old World education won him friends at the Middle Temple and among the military.' He also pointed out that a number of the agents, both English and American, were barristers of the Middle Temple or of another Inn of Court (p.25).

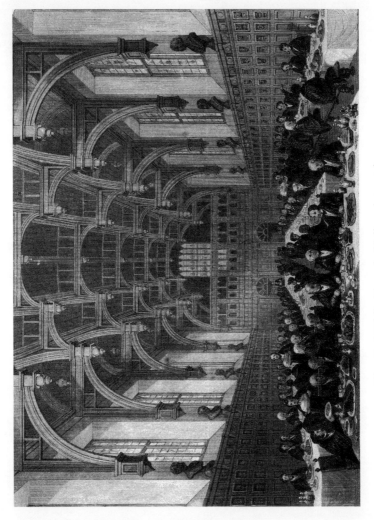

Illus. 5. Middle Temple Hall, artist not known

was Joshua Johnson, later to be the first United States consul in London and father-in-law of John Quincy Adams.[8] These last efforts of Laurens were of no avail, but the experiences he had in England, coupled with the contacts he made there, were to add to his political stature and to his acceptability, later, as a peace negotiator. He went home knowing a great deal more about politics, lobbying and the use of the pamphlet. Laurens left England in November 1774, and on his return to South Carolina plunged straight back into politics as an elected member of the Provincial Congress.

The departure of Laurens from London was unfortunate for South Carolina and for the wider American interest, as Charles Garth, the Member of Parliament who was the agent for the colony, 'seems to have swung towards the ministry some time around 1774,' according to Bernard Donoughue, who added: 'He was definitely receiving a pension from 1777, and possibly earlier. Whether because of a change of convictions or because of financial exigencies, Charles Garth ceased to work for the colonists at the time when they needed him most, and in January 1775 was advising the use of military force against them.'[9]

The apparent change of mind by Garth draws attention to one increasing difficulty facing the colonists in London. They had many friends, especially among Opposition members and newspaper editors, who supported their cause in relation to taxation, representation and a number of other issues. However, some of the colonists' staunchest British friends drew the line at independence. Many wished the colonies well – but as members of the British Empire, and not as independent states. Even Edmund Burke, who was agent for the New York Assembly from 1771 to 1775, and the principal pro-American orator in the House of Commons, felt that way. He wrote to the Assembly on

---

[8] *Laurens Papers*, 16: 70n.; and see, chap.15.
[9] Donoughue, Bernard, *British Politics and the American Revolution: The Path to War 1773-75*, London: Macmillan, 1964, 159.

February 2, 1774, that he would obey any instructions sent to him, but gave his opinion that the public good lay in 'the proper subordination of America, as a fundamental, incontrovertible maxim, in the government of this Empire.'[10]

Laurens left all three sons in England when he went home at the end of 1774. The eldest, John, was just 20 and mature enough to be placed in charge of his two schoolboy brothers, but he could not be with them every minute of the day. The youngest of the boys, James, died in an accidental fall within a year, when trying to jump across the basement area to a ground floor window of John's lodgings. On the completion of his own school years, John had decided that he would like to be a barrister and started to read law at the Middle Temple with Charles Bicknell. John Adams and Thomas Jefferson had both qualified as lawyers before the Revolution in America, and John Quincy Adams was to do the same after Independence. However, before 1775, it was not at all unusual for young Americans to come to London to read for the Bar.

The Inn of Court which was most popular with such students – and particularly those from South Carolina – was the Middle Temple. As we have seen, as soon as Benjamin Franklin arrived in London in 1757, he entered his son, William, at that Inn, where John Dickinson had shortly before completed his studies, and where their associate, Arthur Lee, was to practise. Five of the signers of the Declaration of Independence were Middle Templars: Arthur Middleton, Edward Rutledge, Thomas Heyward, Thomas Lynch and Thomas McKean, all from South Carolina, apart from the last-named. Dickinson, decided against signing at the last minute, possibly influenced by his Quaker mother and wife, who were against war.[11]

---

[10] Donoughue, 133, 160.

[11] John Adams, who could make very waspish comments, later wrote of Dickinson, 'If I had such a mother and such a wife, I believe I should have shot myself.' In fairness to Dickinson, it must be added that he

It would be a mistake to regard the Inns of Court as places where only law was learned. As well as barring entry to anyone not a member of the Established Protestant Church, the English universities of the time had a very restricted choice of topics, so many parents sent their sons to an Inn of Court to learn law, together with other subjects, such as history, politics, logic and debating skills. Although there were no formal lessons at the Inn – not even in law – students were encouraged to undertake a broad education. John Dickinson, whose father was also a member of the Middle Temple, wrote home at the beginning of his three-year period in London, on March 8, 1754. Of Westminster Hall, the ancient building housing the Common Law courts, he wrote, 'When I view a Hall where the most important questions have been debated, I am filled with awe and reverence.' Florence Scull pointed out, 'In addition to studying law, Dickinson read history, for he was eager to understand how Englishmen in the past had acquired the freedoms guaranteed by the British Constitution. His study at the Middle Temple laid the foundation for a life-long love of history.'[12]

John Rutledge from South Carolina studied at the Middle Temple from 1757 to 1760. When he started to practise in Charleston at the age of twenty-one, he was an immediate success, one of his regular clients being Henry Laurens. By 1764, he was already the Royal Attorney-General of the Colony, though he only kept the job for ten months. As his father had died, he personally first sent his brother Hugh to the Middle Temple and then his youngest brother, Edward. When Edward was embarking on his legal studies, John Rutledge, who owned a

---

served in the Pennsylvania militia. Somewhat confusingly, Adams described Edward Rutledge as 'a swallow, a sparrow, a peacock': a rare bird, indeed. McCullough, David, *John Adams*, New York: Simon & Schuster, 2001, 94, 93.

[12] Scull, Florence Doughty, *John Dickinson Sounds the Alarm*, Philadelphia: Auerbach, 1972, 28, 32. See also, Jacobson, David L., *John Dickinson and the Revolution in Pennsylvania 1764-1776*, Berkeley: U. of California P., 1965.

copy of *Letters to his Son from Lord Chesterfield*, gave him advice on
similar lines, in a letter dated July 30, 1769.[13]

John made some good points about the wider aspects of the
education available, the first of which was rather surprising. He
counselled his young brother to learn to write shorthand, 'which
you will find of infinite advantage in your profession'. He added
that he should perfect it by taking down 'every public discourse,
either at the bar or at the pulpit'. That advice reminded John to
add that his brother should attend the Temple Church on a
Sunday: 'It will be more to your credit to spend a few hours of
that day there, than as it is generally spent in London, especially
by the Templars.' He not only advised him to attend the courts
assiduously, but also the House of Commons, with the help of
Charles Garth. He counselled him to perfect both his French
and his Latin, and advised, 'The history of England should be
read with great care and attention.'[14] It is not clear how faithfully
the younger brother accepted all that advice, but he certainly had
a successful career after returning home.

When dining in the Middle Temple Hall, the students regularly rubbed shoulders not only with other students, but also
with some of the senior practitioners and judges who were
members of the Inn. For instance, during the week commencing
November 6, 1769, Edward Rutledge and Thomas Heyward,
later signers of the Declaration of Independence, dined in Hall
with the great William Blackstone. He had just completed his
four-volume *Commentaries on the Laws of England*, which was to be
their indispensable companion as lawyers in America.[15] It is
apparent from the letters that John Laurens sent home, that a
consideration of the political situation played an important part

---

[13] Barry, Richard, *Mr Rutledge of South Carolina*, New York: Duell, Sloan and
Pearce, 1942, 70, 74, 75, 131.
[14] Adams, J., *Laws of Success and Failure in Life*, Charleston: A. E. Miller,
1833, 50.
[15] Middle Temple 7/BUB/2; I am grateful to the Inn's archivist, Lesley
Whitelaw, for drawing my attention to this entry.

in his life when at the Middle Temple, but he also made a point of trying to obtain a broader views of matters and to round off the schooling he had received in Geneva.

Some of the American students in London were loyalists, but many of them were patriots and argued the colonists' case with anyone prepared to listen. They had a significant number of English supporters in the legal fraternity, such as William 'Oriental' Jones, who was friendly with Benjamin Franklin and Arthur Lee; Richard Lovell Edgeworth and his life-long friend, Thomas Day; and the latter's friend, John Laurens Bicknell, whose name intrigued John Laurens from Charleston. John Bicknell was the brother of Charles Bicknell, the barrister who took John Laurens under his wing. Jones and Day had been at Oxford together and for a time shared chambers in the Middle Temple. The friendship that developed between young Laurens and Thomas Day, who was some six years older, is crucial to our story, as it was Day who led Henry Laurens to John Stockdale's shop as a place to stay, and that connection which in turn led to the Adamses and Jefferson getting to know the bookseller well.

The attachment of many colonial students – before the war – to the places where they had been educated in England was noted by Benjamin Franklin, when he wrote about the colonists to the *Public Advertiser* on February 5, 1770, posing once more as an Englishman: 'Their sending constantly their children home (for that was the affectionate term they always used when speaking of England) for education, was both a very convincing proof of their respect for the principles and manners of the mother country, and was likewise a powerful means of attaching them to us from generation to generation. For there is no stronger attraction than to the place where we pass our most innocent and happiest days; nor are any friendships stronger than those contracted at places of education.'[16] Franklin might have added

---

[16] Crane, Verner W., *Benjamin Franklin's Letters to the Press 1758-1775*, Chapel Hill: U. North Carolina P., 1950, 196.

that after his return home, such a student might well continue to buy his books from the London booksellers he had patronised.

Thomas Day practised very little as a lawyer: he had private means and increasingly saw himself as an author. He was interested in scientific developments and became a member of the Lunar Society (as it was later known), which so impressed Franklin that he recommended it to Thomas Jefferson's former teacher at The College of William and Mary in Williamsburg, Rev. Dr. William Small. Small not only joined, but found a potential wife for Day in due course: Esther Milnes, an heiress. Day protested that the lady in question had a fortune: he had always wished to bestow his own fortune on his chosen partner. Small very sensibly asked, 'What prevents you from despising the fortune, and taking the lady?' Miss Milnes and Day were duly married.[17]

Day originally – in both senses of the word – had other plans for marriage and is now remembered as the eccentric who thought that he could educate a young girl, carefully selected by him from an orphanage, to become the perfect wife – with a second as a reserve. The girl who played Galatea to his Pygmalion did not marry Day but in due course married his friend, John Bicknell. As an author Day is remembered now principally for the book which made his name and contributed significantly to the success of Stockdale, his publisher, *History of Sandford and Merton*, but his first published work was a joint one with Bicknell.

One of the questions that arose during discussions about freedom for the colonies, was the vexed one, does that freedom include everyone living there, even the slaves? Fortunately for their friendship, Day and John Laurens were agreed about the iniquity of slavery. John Bicknell and Day were both much affected by the sad story in the London press about a servant of

---

[17] Uglow, Jenny, *The Lunar Men*, London: Faber and Faber, 2002, 225, and generally.

African origin who had committed suicide in the city. Bicknell suggested that they should jointly compose a poem on the subject. The result was *The Dying Negro*, which was immediately brought out by William Flexney, who had published Charles Churchill's poems. The work was well received, especially by the growing number of opponents of slavery, and it was to be republished by Stockdale once he had his own bookshop, with Day's name an early entry on his list of authors. The success of the poem was the more remarkable for having been the product of two pens: Day wrote 250 lines and Bicknell 186 of the total.[18]

On August 14, 1776, Henry Laurens, despite owning slaves, wrote to his son: 'You know, my dear sir, I abhor slavery. I am not the man who enslaved them; they are indebted to English men for that favour, nevertheless I am devising means for manumitting many of them and for cutting off the entail of slavery. You are apparently deeply interested in this affair but as I have no doubts concerning your concurrence and approbation, I most sincerely wish for your advice and assistance and hope to receive both in good time.'[19]

On September 30, John Laurens wrote to Francis Kinloch, a fellow Carolinian, studying at Lincoln's Inn: 'I think that we Americans, at least in the Southern colonies, cannot contend with *a good grace* for liberty, until we shall have enfranchised our slaves. How can we, whose jealousy has been alarmed more at the name of oppression than at the reality, reconcile to our spirited assertions of the rights of mankind, the galling abject slavery of our negroes?'[20]

John Laurens introduced Day to a fellow-American who, prompted by the poem, challenged the Englishman to

---

[18] See, Stockdale's advertisement in the back of his publication, Keir, James, *An Account of the Life and Writings of Thomas Day Esq.*, 1791.

[19] *Laurens Papers*, 11: 224.

[20] Wallace, 475; *A South Carolina Protest against Slavery*, New York: Putnam, 1861.

reconsider his views on slavery. Day drafted a long and careful reply in 1776, but this did not appear in print until Stockdale published it eight years later, with the title *Fragment of an Original Letter on the Slavery of the Negroes – Written in the year 1776.*

In his introduction to that piece, written in 1784, Day made plain where he had stood during the war, writing that enlightened Americans 'may perhaps respect an Englishman, who after daring to assert their cause through all the varied events of the late revolution, dares now with equal intrepidity assert the cause of truth and justice, and of that part of the human species whose wrongs are yet unredressed, and almost unpitied.' He continued, 'If there be an object truly ridiculous in Nature, it is an American patriot signing resolutions of independency with the one hand, and with the other brandishing a whip over his affrighted slaves.'

Day's latest biographer has suggested that the American who had challenged him was none other than Henry Laurens, but this seems unlikely, having regard to the Carolinian's agreement with his own son and with Day on the principal issue.[21] Furthermore, John's introduction to his new friends at the Middle Temple largely occurred after his father's departure for home. Keir's account of the matter, in his biography of his friend Day, also makes it unlikely that Henry Laurens was the slave-owner in question: 'This letter had been actually written without any view of publication to an American gentleman, who being possessed of many slaves had requested Mr. Day to give his sentiments on the subject of slavery, having received the highest opinion of his wisdom and virtue from their common friend, Mr. Laurens, son to the President of Congress. Mr. Day had been well acquainted with him in London, and entertained a very high opinion of his worth.'[22]

---

[21] Rowland, Peter, *The Life and Times of Thomas Day 1748-1789*, Lampeter: Edwin Mellen Press, 1996, 81.
[22] Keir, 40, 113.

Many Americans agreed with those views expressed about slavery, including Thomas Jefferson. However, Jefferson's failure to do anything about freeing his own slaves, coupled with DNA testing in 1998, suggests that his views on that topic may not deserve the respect earlier accorded to them. The tests, when combined with other evidence, show that he was almost certainly abusing one of his own young slaves, Sally Hemings, and was the father of at least one of her children.[23] Incidentally, as Washington and John Adams both have impeccable private records, Jefferson now has the dubious distinction of being the first President to have had problems with his trouser fastenings – albeit before assuming office. The argument that other slave owners did likewise is, of course, no excuse whatsoever, but in some slight mitigation it may be added that Jefferson was a widower and that there is no similar evidence against him relating to his eight years as President.

In June 1775, John Almon began to publish a monthly magazine called *The Remembrancer, or Impartial Repository of Public Events*, at a shilling a time. At the end of the following year he advertised it as follows:[24] 'This work began in June 1775, with the commencement of hostilities at Lexington in New England, and has been continued monthly to the present time; containing from time to time the accounts, as given by both sides, of every public transaction.' His reference to publishing both sides is worth noting in view of the criticism sometimes levelled at him that he was not always faithful to the Americans, in that he

---

[23] O'Brien, Conor Cruise, *The Long Affair: Thomas Jefferson and the French Revolution, 1785-1800*, London: Sinclair-Stevenson, 1996, chap.7; Ellis, Joseph J., *Founding Brothers – The Revolutionary Generation*, London: Faber and Faber, 2000, 201; see also articles by Ellis and others in *William and Mary Quarterly*, 2000, 57: 121-210; Ferling, John, *Setting the World* Ablaze, Oxford U.P., 2000, 291; Wallach, Jennifer Jensen, 'The Vindication of Fawn Brodie', *Massachusetts Review*, Summer 2002, 277.

[24] e.g. in the back of his publication, *A Letter to the Rev. Josiah Tucker, Dean of Gloucester*.

sometimes published contrary views. Almon continued, 'Seventeen numbers have been published, which makes three volumes;
to each volume is a copious index, the whole half bound and
lettered, 18s.6d.' The first issue included a reprint of letters
written by John Adams to the Boston *Gazette* with the pen-name
Novanglus, and subsequent issues also contained a great deal of
material from America. As a source for materials on the dispute
it was, and still is, invaluable.

In the first year of publication the *Remembrancer* carried a
considerable number of items from South Carolina, including
some relating to the activity of Henry Laurens as President of
the colony's Council of Safety. Some of this information may
well have been supplied to Almon by the young law student,
John Laurens.[25] There is some support for this view to be found
in the letter that the father wrote to his son on August 14, 1776.
In it he recounted how a British fleet had appeared north of
Charleston Town Bar, and continued: 'For the history of this
fleet I refer you to Jack Wells's paper of the 2d inst. and to certain notes which I have added. His account although true in
general substance, is the most bungling and inaccurate of anything I have seen from him. I wish you or somebody else would
publish a fair and honest compilation from his Gazette and my
papers – you know me too well to suppose I would in a tittle
exaggerate or suppress. You may add as much of what follows
as may appear to be necessary, but let the whole be cleverly
done and introduced by such declaration of candor as these
accounts are well entitled to – nothing more abhorrent to me
than publications of falsehood for truth.' After giving details of
the fifty-five British ships, Henry Laurens informed John that he
had become 'Vice-President of the Colony (now State observe).'
The new President was John Rutledge. South Carolina, under his
leadership, had broken away from the Crown and become a

---

[25] I am obliged to the late George C. Rogers, a former editor of the
Laurens Papers, for this suggestion in a letter to me.

republic a hundred days before the Declaration of Independence.[26]

In July 1775, John Dickinson drafted a conciliatory document in which the colonies made one last attempt to assure the King of their basic loyalty, and to avert a war. The document, known as the Olive Branch Petition, was signed by John Adams and Thomas Jefferson among others, and was presented by Arthur Lee and Richard Penn to the Earl of Dartmouth, the Secretary of State for the Colonies. Almon, as usual, was one of the first to know about this move, having heard about it from one of his many sources, probably Lee. Almon at once notified Edmund Burke, who replied on August 6: 'I am obliged to you for your early communication of the intelligence you have, and wish most ardently that this opening towards a reconciliation on the part of America may be approved by the ministry here, and prove the means of a lasting peace to this empire.'[27]

The approach was not approved by the ministry and the King ignored the Petition, ruling out a reconciliation. On August 25, 1775, before news of the failure of the attempt had been received, Jefferson wrote to his loyalist cousin, John Randolph, the Royal Attorney-General of Virginia, who was returning to England: 'Looking with fondness towards a reconciliation with Great Britain, I cannot help hoping you may be able to contribute towards expediting this good work.' A postscript confirmed that Jefferson was as opportunistic as the next bibliophile: 'My collection of classics is not so complete as I could wish. As you are going to the land of literature and of books, you may be willing to dispose of some of yours here and replace them there

---

[26] *Laurens Papers*, 11: 222; Barry, 193. The Jack Wells paper referred to was presumably the *South Carolina and American General Gazette*, started by Robert Wells, printer and bookseller in 1764. For Robert Wells, see, Raven, James, *London Booksellers and American Customers*, Columbia: U. of South Carolina P., 2002, 426, n.32.

[27] Almon, *Memoirs*, 93.

in better editions.' It's an ill wind that does not blow good for some book collector or other.[28]

Shortly before Christmas 1775, Parliament passed the Prohibitory Act, which forbade any trade with the colonies. David Hartley, a good friend of Franklin's and of America, warned the Commons that they would live to regret the Act. He spoke repeatedly in favour of the American cause and produced a number of pamphlets pressing the colonists' case. Almon later wrote: 'The impartial historian of this period, if ever such a person should arise, will receive an invaluable fund of materials from the gentleman's writings.'[29] Writing of a later period, when Henry Laurens was one of the American Peace Commissioners, Almon added to his comments on Hartley, 'His thorough knowledge of the American subject, and his intimacy with Dr. Franklin, pointed him out as the most proper person to negotiate the treaty of peace with America in the year 1783.'

At the beginning of 1776, Almon published Day's first pro-American contribution, an *Ode for the New Year, 1776*. This was immediately followed by Day's satirical piece, called *The Devoted Legions*, which he addressed 'to Lord George Germaine and the Commanders of the Forces against America'. His friend and chambers colleague, William Jones, wrote to his former pupil, Lord Althorp, on February 23: 'A poem called *The Devoted Legions* is just published and I like it extremely, not only because I know and esteem the author, but because I begin to be as warm as your friend the Bishop of St. Asaph in condemning the American War.'[30]

In January 1776, Thomas Paine, a recently arrived, and very disgruntled English immigrant, published the pamphlet in

---

[28] *Jefferson Papers*, 1: 241. Randolph and his brother Peyton were both Middle Templars but were on opposite sides. Peyton Randolph was the first President of Continental Congress.

[29] Almon, *Anecdotes*, 2: 149.

[30] Cannon, Garland, *The Letters of Sir William Jones*, Oxford U.P., 1970, 1: 213.

Philadelphia which was to inspire most American patriots and to break all records as a publication: *Common Sense*. One of the reasons for this success is that Paine followed John Bunyan's hundred-year-old example and wrote in a plain English that could be understood by all. He asserted that reconciliation was a fallacious dream. ''Tis time to part', wrote Paine, and thousands of his readers in America agreed with him. As we have seen, Almon published an English edition. He based it on the third American one, but he decided to play safe, and omitted some of the more pungent criticisms of his sovereign. Unfortunately, his crude editing left odd gaps in his edition.[31]

Henry Laurens did not approve of Paine's pamphlet, but nevertheless decided to send his son John a copy. John had earlier obtained one of Almon's copies, probably from his Piccadilly bookshop. He strongly approved of the stirring call for independence and informed his father that he had already read it 'more than once'.[32]

In America, hostilities had started with the shots fired at Lexington and Concord in April 1775, and the subsequent siege of Boston by the colonists, commanded by General George Washington. John Adams proposed the General to Congress as a suitable commander-in-chief and his colleagues agreed with him. Although they demonstrated their valour at Bunker's Hill, hard by the city, the Americans were unable to take Boston until March 1776. When they did so, it was in part due to the sterling efforts of a former bookseller of the city, Henry Knox, who had hauled all the guns captured from the British at Fort Ticonderoga and placed them on the heights overlooking the British positions, making them untenable. The guns of the new colonel of Continental artillery, together with some dummy

---

[31] Bonwick, Colin, *English Radicals and the American Revolution*, Chapel Hill: U. of North Carolina P., 1977, 41.

[32] Massey, Gregory D., *John Laurens and the American Revolution*, Columbia: U. of South Carolina P., 2000, 59.

barrels, achieved that which his pamphlets had failed to do: the departure of the British forces to Halifax, Nova Scotia.

The British returned on July 2, 1776, the very day on which Continental Congress at Philadelphia voted for independence. They landed in force near New York, under the command of General Sir William Howe, whose army had been carried from Halifax by a large fleet commanded by his brother, Admiral Lord Howe. Two days later Congress finally approved the Declaration of Independence, largely the work of Jefferson, though he was assisted by Benjamin Franklin and John Adams, In his letter of August 14, to his 21-year-old son John in London, Henry Laurens dealt with the reading of the Declaration in Charleston in a most moving way. Laurens expressed the feelings of many people on both sides of the Atlantic, and showed that he regarded the conflict as a civil war:

'The scene was serious, important and awful. Even at this moment I feel a tear of affection for the good old country and for the people in it, whom in general I love dearly. I say even at this moment my heart is full of the lively sensations of a dutiful son, thrust by the hand of violence out of a father's house into the wide world. What I have often with truth averred in London and Westminster, I dare still aver: not a sober man, and scarcely a single man in America wished for separation from Great Britain. I am glad you continue with Mr Bicknell and your brother with Mr Henderson; frugality is essential to you both. Consider I cannot supply you while the sword of Britain remains unsheathed. May God protect and guide you all, and may he still give peace and mutual friendship to the divided family of Britain, and promote the happiness, equally of the ancient root and the transplanted branches.'[33]

---

[33] *Laurens Papers*, 11: 225.

Illus. 6. John Laurens by Charles Fraser

4

President Laurens and Colonel Laurens

A brief glance at this chapter might suggest that it is about the progress of the Revolutionary War – and so it is – but it also about Almon's part in it. It will be remembered that John Stockdale was working for him during the years covered by this chapter, doubtless learning all that he could about the American links of his master's bookshop. It is also about Henry and John Laurens, for without them Stockdale would never have made the crucial close contacts with the Adamses or Jefferson, or been introduced to David Ramsay and Jedidiah Morse, two of the first American authors of note. Just like the speeches of Burke and Wilkes in Parliament, the book and the pamphlet had failed to obtain a reasonable outcome for the colonies. The courage of Washington's small army could not achieve it speedily either, and French military help at first achieved little. Perhaps the diplomatic endeavours of Henry and John Laurens in Europe could achieve more than the bravery of John and his fellow soldiers on the battlefield. For our story, the significance of Henry Laurens's diplomatic posting was that it brought him – albeit as a prisoner – back to London where, after his release, he was to get well-acquainted with Stockdale and his new bookshop.

John Laurens found it impossible to concentrate on his legal studies in London after the Declaration of Independence and obtained the consent of his father to return to America. He left England in January 1777, and travelled home via Paris, where he visited Benjamin Franklin. They were to meet there again four years later, by which time the law student would be representing

Congress and the Commander-in-Chief. Shortly before his departure from London, Laurens married Martha, the daughter of his father's English business associate, William Manning. Martha was pregnant by John at the time of the marriage, and he apologised to his father for marrying in haste without his consent.

After he left England the young couple were never to meet again before Martha died in 1781, and John Laurens was to lose his life in the following year. He never saw the child his wife was carrying at the time they made their farewells. He also took his leave of his friends at the Middle Temple, including John Bicknell and Thomas Day, but it seems likely that he asked them to make arrangements for future correspondence. The Virginian Arthur Lee, a pastmaster of the science and art of covert communications, wrote to Henry Laurens on April 4, 1778, 'I have settled the means of receiving from time to time Mrs Laurens's letters for your son; and intelligence from different persons, that may be useful to the public.'[1] It may safely be assumed that it was not the British public that Lee had in mind.

Franklin had arrived in Paris in December 1776, as his country's principal Commissioner. He had been preceded by Silas Deane, whose main task was to obtain supplies for the Continental army. In view of the importance of French assistance, Thomas Jefferson had been requested to go to Paris with Franklin, but had declined for family reasons – which some, including Richard Henry Lee, Arthur Lee's brother and Jefferson's replacement in Congress, found spurious.[2] In the event, Jefferson stayed out of national politics for seven years. Arthur Lee was appointed in his stead, while another of his brothers, William, together with Henry Laurens's friend from South Carolina, Ralph Izard, were also appointed to represent the infant United States on the Continent of Europe. Arthur Lee's

---

[1] Lee, R. H., *Life of Arthur Lee*, Boston: Wells & Lilly, 1829, 2: 141.
[2] Ferling, John, *Setting the World Ablaze*, Oxford U.P., 2000, 151.

appointment in place of Jefferson has been called by the Henry Laurens's biographer, 'One of the most unfortunate occurrences in the history of the Revolution'. He added that Lee was of 'such a high degree of the low order of talent necessary for writing interestingly unscrupulous slander as to have earned the soubriquet of the American Junius.'[3] Lee caused a great deal of trouble because he distrusted Deane and later took up a great deal of the valuable time of the Congress with his complaints about him – and of the time of the then President of that body, Henry Laurens.

It is clear that the move of Arthur and William Lee and of Izard to France did not deprive John Almon of information from those sources, nor did it prevent him from keeping his American contacts informed with such news from England as might prove useful to their cause. Before departing for France, Izard wrote to Almon from Richmond in Surrey, on August 4, 1776: 'Montezuma did not appear in the last *Remembrancer*; if it does in the next it will do as well. I thank you for the news of the capture of the West Indiamen, but I am sorry to have had so sudden a damper as the total evacuation of Canada.' Izard went on to give Almon news about Lord Dunmore's hostile cruise off the coast of Virginia, and continued, 'Let me hear from you if you can convey any intelligence to us before it finds its way into the papers. There are two stage coaches that come from town every evening; anything of consequence might be conveyed to me that way sooner than by post. I am under the greatest anxiety about the operations of the two armies under Washington and Howe; for as to an accommodation, that is I think quite out of the question. The accounts from Canada make me uneasy. I had no thoughts of it being possible to carry around vessels by means of machines called 'camels' over the rapids of the River Richelieu or Sorel. What have you been able to learn on this subject? Have you consulted your friend Mr Masares? I am so

---

[3] Wallace, 305.

well pleased with the production of Valens in the last *Remem-brancer* that I think you should reprint them all.'[4]

The letter has been quoted extensively because a question which inevitably arises when one reads a document such as this is, What was the nature of the relationship between the writer and the recipient? One interpretation is that Almon was merely passing on items already in the public domain, and was being asked to do better than that. Another is that he was acting as a spy, paid or unpaid. Possibly he regarded information supplied in return as a sufficient reward; or perhaps his devotion to the cause of liberty in both England and America made any reward unnecessary. Though sometimes accused of venality, he may even have believed in the maxim, Virtue is its own reward.

Izard's letter to Almon from Paris, dated October 16, 1777, certainly reads more like that of a spymaster than that of a cus-tomer to his bookseller: 'I left London without giving you such a direction as would conduct your letters to my hands unopened. I should be very glad to receive your communications as often as possible, and the fuller they are, the more acceptable they will be to me.' The use of the word 'communications' rather than 'publications' – which one usually receives from a bookshop – will have been noted. Izard continued: 'Frequent and authentic information on the state of affairs will be of greater importance to me than I was aware of when I left England; it will not only be a gratification to me, but may put it in my power to be of service to the cause, which if I am not much mistaken in you, you have very much at heart, as well as myself. The greatest part of the news that we ever have here is brought from England. Despatches from the Congress do not arrive very frequently – I send you this by a private hand, who has promised to deliver it safely to you. I beg that you will on no account let anybody know that I have written to you, as there are good reasons for secrecy.'

---

[4] British Library Add. MSS 20,733, f.57. The next letter quoted is at f.59.

The letter concluded with peremptory words which read like instructions rather than a request. 'The last *Remembrancer* that I have is No. 4; contrive to send them regularly to me if possible. By this opportunity I send you the Constitution of South Carolina, which you will print in your next *Remembrancer*.'

It must have been difficult for Almon to keep all the communications secret. However, although prosecuted for contempt, Almon was never charged with treason, so he seems to have succeeded in obeying Izard's injunction about the need for secrecy. Whether his employee, John Stockdale, was unaware of his master's communications with the enemy, or whether he knew and kept quiet about them, is not clear. He clearly never betrayed Almon's secrets and certainly later managed to give Henry Laurens the impression that he had always been on the side of the Americans. In addition, as will be seen later, Stockdale was certainly prepared to pass on letters sent to England during the war by John Adams, using a cipher.

Later in the war Almon heard from another American in Paris. He was Samuel Wharton, who before independence had been active in London in the formation of the Walpole or Grand Ohio Company, with a view to developing the land to the west of the thirteen colonies. He had been closely associated in that venture with Franklin, Temple, Camden, Pownall, Strahan and others. Almon had been interested in the project and in 1772, had published the *Report of the Lords Commissioners for Trade and Plantations on the Petition of the Hon. Thomas Walpole, Benjamin Franklin &c.* Wharton sent some items to Almon for insertion in the *Remembrancer*, and made a request for news of importance. He added, 'You may depend on my forwarding the American newspapers as soon as I can get them, and always upon my friendship. You may fully rely upon my exerting my utmost interest in your behalf in America, for I am very sensible of your obliging accommodation in several instances. I shall take proper care of your son's interests in Indiana.'[5]

Young Almon can only have been seventeen years old at the most, but presumably his father had managed to get him a stake in America's westward expansion, contingent on a British victory. In parenthesis – and jumping ahead to 1782-3 – it should be noted that Franklin 'traded with the enemy' throughout the hostilities by keeping his interest in a British company and staying involved with Thomas Walpole. Richard Morris, the historian of Franklin, Laurens and the other Peacemakers, has pointed out this blemish on the good Doctor's record: 'Franklin was the one member of the peace delegation about whom there might be a suspicion of conflict of interest. Throughout the war Franklin remained a secret member of the Vandalia syndicate, a land company with a huge potential stake in the Old Northwest. Because his name was anathema to the law officers of the Crown, Franklin on the eve of the Revolution turned in a bogus resignation of his interest in the company, but he had a secret understanding with Thomas Walpole protecting his shares.'[6]

On the same day that Wharton wrote to Almon, Thomas Bradford sent him a letter from Philadelphia to suggest an exchange of information – another example of 'business as usual', despite the war. Bradford had been one of the booksellers involved in the scramble to publish Paine's *Common Sense*, and will have known that Almon was the publisher of several English editions of the work. Bradford wrote: 'As a printer, I need not expatiate on the mutual benefit of an exchange of newspapers. I have therefore taken the liberty to send you a number of mine, and request the favour of yours, by such opportunities as may offer. I shall continue to send you my papers, and if you think they are not adequate to yours, please to

---

[5] Letter dated March 20, 1779, British Library Add. MSS 20,733, f.141.
[6] Morris, Richard B., *The Peacemakers – The Great Powers and American Independence*, New York: Harper & Row, 1965, 249.

open an account against me, and it shall be punctually paid, as soon as a communication is open between England and America.'[7]

We must go back to the British invasion, launched from Halifax, in July 1776. General Howe eventually took New York, gaining access to New Jersey and the road to Philadelphia, the seat of Congress. However, he failed to press on and ordered his troops into winter quarters. This halt by the British enabled Washington, at the end of the year, to turn his exhausted troops round, and to gain a limited victory at Trenton and, shortly afterwards, at Princeton also. These two successes provided a much needed tonic for Washington and his men, and for their supporters.

We have already seen that Henry Laurens and John Laurens were showing potential as a remarkable father and son combination. The year 1777 confirmed that they were indeed so. In January, Henry Laurens was elected to the Continental Congress as a representative of South Carolina, although he did not take his seat in Philadelphia until July 22. By August 17, he had so impressed John Adams that he wrote to his wife Abigail about him: 'This last gentleman is a great acquisition – of the first rank in his State. He has hitherto appeared as good a member as any we ever had in Congress. I wish that all the States would imitate this example and send their best men.'[8]

John Laurens arrived in America in April 1777, and with the help of a recommendation from John Rutledge, his fellow Middle Templar, by then President of their State, was accepted by Washington as a member of his official family on August 9. Alexander Hamilton, an artillery captain, had been appointed as an aide-de-camp by the General a few weeks earlier, and was joined as such not only by John Laurens, but also by the

---

[7] Almon, *Memoirs*, 111.
[8] Butterfield, L. H. (ed.), *Adams Family Correspondence*, Cambridge: Harvard U.P., 1963, 2: 318.

Marquis de Lafayette, a young French nobleman, serving as a volunteer. Laurens and those two fellow aides became firm friends and were regarded by Washington almost like sons. Laurens did not have much time to settle in at the headquarters, for Howe began his attack on Philadelphia at the end of the month, giving the new recruit a crash course in soldiering. He fought at Brandywine Creek and, later, at Germantown, and both he and Lafayette were wounded.

Philadelphia fell on September 26. Congress moved out hastily, but Henry Laurens refused to be panicked. 'After many thousands had passed by me, I made my breakfast, filled my pipe, and soberly entered my carriage; drove gently on to Bristol, took on the wounded Marquis de Lafayette and proceeded to [Lancaster and York].' Laurens left the young Frenchman to be treated by Moravians in Bethlehem on the way.[9] After this unusual journey, Lafayette was not only a good friend of John, but also of Henry Laurens, offering to help him when he was a prisoner in the Tower of London.

On November 1, Henry Laurens was unanimously elected as President of Congress, as successor to John Hancock, for one year. At the expiry of that year he was asked to stay on and held that prestigious and important appointment until December 9, 1778, when he resigned because he felt he was not receiving sufficient support from his colleagues over the Deane issue. One of his first, and very onerous tasks was to deal with the aftermath of the important surrender of General Burgoyne's British army at Saratoga, two weeks before his Presidency commenced. Burgoyne had been given generous terms by General Horatio Gates, one of the many former British officers serving with the Americans. The Saratoga Convention was soon regarded by many Americans as far too generous. Gates was criticised for his

---

[9] *Laurens Papers*, 11: 570. Though they probably never knew it about each other, Laurens and John Stockdale shared a life-long interest in the Moravian Church.

generosity toward his beaten foe, but praised for his generalship. It was felt that if Burgoyne's men were all allowed back to England on condition that they did not return to America, they could all be replaced by the troops they could relieve elsewhere. Burgoyne himself was allowed back to England on parole, as were some of his men. Almon was soon at work.

On January 3, 1778, Sir George Yonge, later to be Shelburne's Secretary-at-War, wrote to Almon: 'I suppose Burgoyne is amongst you by this time. Some of the poor fellows that composed his army passed by here this week; others landed at Lyme [in Dorset]. There cannot be a stronger mark of the wretched service they were sent upon, or of what they have gone through, than their expressions. Some of them burst into tears of joy at landing; others, prostrate on the ground, thanked God for being restored to their country. All spoke of the *humanity* of their *enemies*.'[10]

After his return to England, Burgoyne went to great lengths to clear his name, pointing out that he had not had the support that his invasion from Canada had deserved. As a Member of Parliament he defended himself vigorously by speaking in the Commons; as a playwright and poet he elaborated with his pen. Almon published the resultant pamphlets and eventually also Burgoyne's book, containing copies of many relevant documents and entitled *State of the Expedition from Canada*. On November 27, 1779, Almon apologised in his *Courant* for the delay in production, explaining, 'This publication has been hitherto postponed for the purpose of inserting several plans explanatory to his actions, which it has taken a considerable time to engrave.' Burgoyne was upset by the hold-up, but Edmund Burke assured him, 'Since your vindication could not come out when the

---

[10] British Library Add. MSS 20,733, f.148. The bulk of Burgoyne's army ended up on parole near Jefferson's home in Virginia, earning a living at various trades, and merging with the local population as much as possible.

matter of the enquiry was warm, nothing has been lost by the delay.'[11]

The book only appeared in 1780, but the care taken over the text and maps made it a useful work of reference, which is still used by military historians. Almon also sold the vindications of their conduct in America by both Admiral Howe and his brother, the General. They were *A Candid and Impartial Narrative of the Transactions of the Fleet under the Command of Lord Howe* and *Narrative of Lieutenant-General Sir William Howe*, The publication date of the latter was September 14, 1780, and the imprint included the statement, 'Sold by Almon and Debrett in Piccadilly'. In his defence, the soldier brother made an important point of general application, when answering the criticism that he had not pressed his attack in 1776 sufficiently. 'On the other hand, the most essential duty I had to observe was, not wantonly to commit his Majesty's troops where the object was inadequate. I knew well that any considerable loss sustained by the army could not speedily, nor easily, be repaired.' That last point almost shouted out that the war could not be won.

Almon did not merely publish and put on sale the three military men's self-vindications because he thought they would sell well: he clearly personally resented the attacks which the ministry made on those commanders, who happened to be Whigs. Signing himself An Independent Whig, he wrote *A Letter to the Rt. Hon. Charles Jenkinson* (the Secretary-at-War), which Debrett, 'Successor to Mr. Almon', published at the end of 1781. In this he claimed, 'When a temporary advantage has been obtained, by the spirit of the officers and innate bravery of the troops, the ministers have always claimed the merit of it. But if the commander has been misled by false information, or overpowered by numbers, the blame is fixed entirely and exclusively upon him. The fair name and well-earned reputation

---

[11] de Fonblanque, E. B., *Political and Military Episodes … of Burgoyne*, London: Macmillan, 1876, 376.

of the commander are wounded and traduced, through all the public prints in handbills, and in pamphlets; and it is upon strong suspicion that ministers are charged with giving their assistance, besides countenance and circulation, to the wicked and artful fraud upon the public.'

To find Almon, a dedicated pamphleteer, complaining about pamphlets, is somewhat novel, but he was making a fair point of general application. In America, General Washington was also finding that things can be made very unpleasant for commanders who do not deliver the victories expected of them by military colleagues, politicians or the general public.

The principal results of the victory at Saratoga were that it gave heart to the Americans at a time when things were not going well for them and persuaded the French to come out openly in their support. On February 6, 1778, Franklin's efforts in France were rewarded by a Treaty of Commerce and a Treaty of Amity and Alliance. Almon had shrewdly foreseen this major change in the fortunes of the Americans. At the end of 1776, John Lloyd, a political writer, had asked him for his views on the war and on Franklin's mission to Paris.

In a remarkably astute forecast, Almon had replied on December 28, 1776: 'The war will go on. Much will depend upon who can best winter. Respecting Dr Franklin – he will doubtless try to persuade France to acknowledge the independence of America. My opinion has always been that France will not declare *openly* until 1778, at which time our treaties with Brunswick and Hesse will expire, and our finances pretty well exhausted. But she will assist the Americans *privately*, by permitting her merchants, and all her subjects to do it, in whatever way they find most advantageous to themselves; and by making all her ports in Europe and America so many asylums for the American privateers.'[12]

---

[12] Almon, *Memoirs*, 97.

In his open letter to Jenkinson, Almon made the additional point: 'It was obvious to every man that a civil war in the British empire must be an invitation to France to revenge the losses and disgraces she suffered in the last war.' He went on to criticise the government for forgetting about the balance of power. Referring back to the French and Indian, or Seven Years' War, he pointed out that Britain and America had jointly held the balance. He then added a most remarkable statement, much in vogue in the twentieth-century after two World Wars, but possibly never used before Almon's comment: '*It was America that turned the scale so triumphantly in our favour in the last war.*'

A further result of Saratoga was that critics of Washington were able to point to the success of General Gates, and to suggest that perhaps someone else might make a better Commander-in-Chief than the Virginian. Gates was mentioned as a possible successor for the top military post, as was General Thomas Conway. The movement to oust Washington, known as the Conway Cabal, made some progress. John Laurens was with Washington and the army in the appalling winter quarters at Valley Forge and was able to communicate with his father, the President of Congress. That link proved to be a useful tool for helping to defeat the Conway Cabal. Henry Laurens first learned of the plot when his son wrote to him, giving details, on January 3, 1778: 'By this day's courier you will be informed of a base insult offered to the Commander-in-Chief which will raise your indignation.' Five days later Henry Laurens replied that Washington's ruin would involve the ruin of the cause, adding, 'On the other hand his magnanimity, his patience, will save his country and confound his enemies.'[13] The aide doubtless felt obliged, most respectfully, to pass on the views of the President of Congress to his general, who seems to have followed, or at any rate agreed with the hint dropped by Henry Laurens.

---

[13] *Laurens Papers*, 12: 244, 272.

It need scarcely be added that the Cabal was defeated and that Washington, thanks to his many friends, remained in his post until the end of the war. That was some way off, but the news of Saratoga had alarmed the British as much as it had delighted the French, and peace feelers were put out by Lord North's ministry. On March 25, 1778, North wrote to the King that England's condition was so deplorable that, 'It is totally unequal to a war with Spain, France and America. Peace with America, and a change in the Ministry are the only steps which can save the country.' After quoting that letter, Lutnick added the shrewd comment: 'The Prime Minister's words might have been written by John Almon, William Parker, or by any of a number of London propagandists for the Opposition.'[14]

Once in America, the British delegation under Lord Carlisle wrote to President Laurens of their 'most earnest desire to re-establish, on the basis of equal freedom and mutual safety, the tranquillity of the once happy empire'. On June 17, 1778, the President replied that Congress inclined towards peace, but would only consider a treaty of peace and commerce, 'when the King of Great Britain shall demonstrate a sincere disposition for that purpose. The only solid proof of this disposition will be an explicit acknowledgement of the independence of these states, or the withdrawing his fleets and armies.' Only ten days earlier, the busy President of Congress had written to his son in terms that will ring a bell with many a reader, but are no less startling for that: 'You asked me some time ago why I did not employ a secretary. I'll tell you: I don't know where to get a good one.'[15]

It was in June also, that the British withdrew from Philadelphia to New York, which remained their principal base to the end. On June 28, the last important land battle outside the Southern Colonies was fought; it also turned out to be

---

[14] Lutnick, Solomon, *The American Revolution and the British Press 1775-1783*, Columbia: U. Missouri P., 1967, 152.
[15] *Laurens Papers*, 13: 471, 413.

Washington's last personal one for over three years. If Washington had defeated General Clinton there, the war might well have been over, as a second Saratoga would then have proved too much even for the King. As it was, General Charles Lee, another former British officer, attacked the enemy rearguard at Monmouth Court House so incompetently that he was easily repulsed, and then pursued. John Laurens witnessed Lee's failure to stand his ground and urged Washington to save the situation personally. This he managed to do, but the chance of winning the war had been thrown away by Lee.

The former law student then made what was probably his only court-room appearance as a participant: Laurens gave evidence against Lee at his immediate court-martial. Although convicted, Lee continued to make disparaging remarks about Washington. This was too much for Laurens, who challenged Lee to a duel in which he wounded him. Alexander Hamilton acted as Laurens's second, but that experience was not enough to deter him from duelling himself. He was to be killed in 1804, in a duel with Jefferson's first Vice-President, Aaron Burr.[16]

In August 1778, John Laurens participated with distinction in the first – but unsuccessful – combined Franco-American operation at Newport, Rhode Island. Washington had sent him as his representative as he spoke French, having learned it when at school in Geneva. A few days earlier, on July 27, and some three thousand miles to the east, the French and British fleets had met off Ushant in an inconclusive engagement. The failure to defeat the enemy there was important for the British because of the real danger of an invasion of England by the French.

---

[16] For an interesting detailed recent account of that duel, see, Ellis, Joseph J., *Founding Brothers – The Revolutionary Generation*, London: Faber and Faber, 2000, chap.1. For the opinion that Washington was as much to blame for the Monmouth Court House debacle as Lee, see, Ferling, John, *Setting the World Ablaze*, Oxford U.P., 2000, 195.

The encounter was followed by an acrimonious political dispute involving the two senior admirals concerned, the Hon. Augustus Keppel and Sir Hugh Palliser, who were supported by the Whigs and the ministry respectively. On December 22, Almon wrote to a friend, possibly Edmund Burke: 'You little imagined the other day when you was here that your friend, the brave and worthy Admiral Keppel, would be brought to a court-martial, but it is another mark of the unbounded baseness of the Ministers. I would have the people go to the King and demand exemplary justice on Sandwich. Something of this sort is become more than necessary. No officer of character will venture to take command.'[17]

In January 1779, the court-martial acquitted Keppel of any neglect of duty. He, better than anyone else, knew the danger he had faced, as he had been a member of the court-martial that had ordered Admiral Byng to be shot, *'pour encourager les autres'*. The result also came as a relief to his many Whig supporters who were present, including Charles James Fox, Edmund Burke, and Keppel's junior counsel, a young former naval officer called Thomas Erskine. It was only Erskine's second case at the Bar but his contribution to its successful outcome was so signal that the Admiral sent him two notes to express his gratitude. Each was for £500. Almon asked Burke, who had assisted Keppel with his defence, if he could help him to obtain a copy of the transcript of the trial. Burke made inquiries and replied, 'I find that the Admiral leaves the publication of the trial, with all the emoluments which arise from it, entirely to the shorthand writer.'[18] Almon persuaded the shorthand writer, William Blanchard, to let him have the transcript, and so was able to add yet another Whig military man's exculpatory account to his list by publishing *The Proceedings at Large of the Court Martial on the Trial of the Hon. Augustus Keppel* before the end of the year. This

---

[17] Draft letter in John Almon Papers, New-York Historical Society.
[18] Almon, *Memoirs*, 111.

was the most successful exoneration of all, as it was a very distinguished court of senior naval officers that had found the charge brought by Palliser to be 'malicious and ill-founded'.

On December 29, 1779, Almon published an advertisement in the *Courant*, which he had launched on November 25, calling for subscriptions 'in favour of Walter Parker, a printer of the *General Advertiser*, now suffering in Newgate under a rigorous and unprecedented sentence of the Court of King's Bench upon the prosecution of his Majesty's Attorney-General for having joined himself and encouraged others to join in the general joy upon the honourable acquittal of Admiral Keppel and in the great indignation against Sir Hugh Palliser for having preferred a malicious and groundless charge against his Commander-in-Chief.' The wording sounds like that of Almon himself. The notice concluded by expressing the hope that a healthy response to the appeal would 'convince the world that the man who dare be honest in the worst of times and boldly assert the birthright freedom of an Englishman, never will be permitted to fall the sacrifice of ministerial vengeance'.

On December 13, 1779, Almon included a letter in his *Courant* in which the writer complained that insufficient attention was being paid to the extravagant spending of public money. This cry was taken up in Parliament by John Wilkes and others, and throughout the country. In Yorkshire the Rev. Christopher Wyvill galvanized the opposition to the government's spending and called for 'economical' reform, adding that the Crown had acquired too great an influence.

On January 4, 1780, Almon's paper printed a call – probably drafted by him – for 'a grand national association to act by the deputies of the respective counties and towns'. The plea continued: 'The British Empire, so lately the envy and admiration of the world, seems now to be upon the very brink of ruin. The people would rather see America independent than desolated. The -- would prefer the desolation of America to its independence. By acknowledging the independence of America, the blessing of peace would immediately be restored to this much impoverished country, and the trade of the western world return to our ports.' On January 27, the Wiltshire county meeting was urged by Charles James Fox to bear in mind the need for the people to demand their rights. Thomas Day's friend, William Jones, warned the assembly that 'the nation's grievances would not be redressed until Parliament was reformed'.[19]

Although Almon's interest in politics was usually that of a writer or publisher, he became slightly more involved at the beginning of 1780, when he attended some of the meetings of his local committee. On February 2, he attended a general assembly of the inhabitants of Westminster in Westminster Hall, which was attended by Earl Temple, his original patron, and by Fox, Wilkes, Burke, Sheridan, Dr John Jebb and George Greive, one of the proprietors of the *Courant*.[20]

Almon's interest in domestic matters did not diminish his concern about America. He was conscious of that fact that a number of American prisoners, mostly captured at sea, were languishing in prisons in Hampshire and Devon. In February, he took the unusual step of publishing, jointly with Charles Dilly, the other main pro-American bookseller, a portrait of Washington, with the proceeds destined for the relief of the prisoners.

After the assembly on February 2, Almon does not appear to have attended many meetings, but he turned up at one on December 3, 1781, when Dr. Jebb, probably at his request, proposed Mr. Debrett of Piccadilly as a committee member. When the Society for Constitutional Information was set up in April 1780, Almon did not join it, despite the fact that it had ideals and membership similar to that of the Westminster committee, and despite the fact that it was 'the heir to the Wilkite Society

---

[19] Norris, John, *Shelburne and Reform*, London: Macmillan, 1963, 126.
[20] British Library, Add. MSS 38, 593 and 4. Burke and Sheridan were both Middle Temple members.

for the Supporters of the Bill of Rights', of which he had been a stalwart.[21]

The war in America had switched to the south at the end of December 1778, when a British force took Savannah in Georgia. A Franco-American force attempted to retake the city, but was heavily repulsed. This encouraged the British to press on to Charleston, South Carolina, which fell in May 1780, after a six weeks' siege. John Laurens fought both at Savannah and at Charleston, and was taken captive in the latter, his home town. Another American prisoner taken there was the historian David Ramsay, who was to marry Laurens's sister, and who used his time in captivity to plan a book that Stockdale was to handle in due course. Fortunately for Laurens, he was soon paroled, and then exchanged.

Almon's *Courant* for August 3, 1780, carried the official item: 'Mr Washington's army does not at this time consist of above three thousand effective men, and even these are most of them dissatisfied, being half naked, badly paid, and half starved for want of provisions, so that there is no doubt, when Sir Henry Clinton gets on their backs, they will instantly surrender.' Almon made his opinion plain by heading the item *Ministerial Puffs!* Washington, on the other hand, would probably have conceded that this description was uncomfortably close to the truth. He was desperate for further help from Europe. Congress decided, at different times, to dispatch two of the best men available, as ministers, to seek assistance from the Netherlands and France, respectively. The two men chosen were father and son: ex-President Henry Laurens and Colonel John Laurens.

---

[21] Black, Eugene C., *The Association*, Cambridge: Harvard U.P., 1963, 175.

5

The Ending of the War

In this chapter we shall see how Thomas Jefferson had to flee from his beloved Monticello to avoid capture by Col. Banastre Tarleton's loyalist dragoons, and how that gave him the opportunity to write his only book, which John Stockdale was to publish for him. We shall also see how, after his son had negotiated the surrender of the British at Yorktown, Henry Laurens came to be Stockdale's lodger and how John Adams noticed that his colleague Laurens had an eye for reasonably priced accommodation.

In August 1780, Henry Laurens set sail for the Netherlands, but had the misfortune to be captured by the Royal Navy off Newfoundland on September 3. His papers were fairly innocuous but were nevertheless thrown overboard, only to be recovered by a British sailor armed with a boathook. One of the documents was a privately drafted proposed treaty between the Netherlands and the United States, but it had no official backing. Despite that it was speedily used by the British to justify a commencement of hostilities against the Netherlands, which then joined the alliance of France, Spain and the United States – a formidable combination, and one difficult, if not impossible for the British to defeat. John Almon criticised the government's decision to add yet another nation to its list of enemies, as 'impolitic, unnecessary and unnatural'.[1]

---

[1] An Independent Whig, *A Letter to the Rt. Hon. Charles Jenkinson*, London: J. Debrett (Successor to Almon), 1781, 7.

It is one of the ironies of history that thanks to the bellicose response of the British government to his documents, Laurens achieved far more by being captured than he could have done as an envoy, namely, the speedy alliance of the Dutch.

Laurens was taken to London, charged with 'Treason at Philadelphia' and lodged as a prisoner in the Tower of London, where he was to remain for some fifteen months. British opinion was divided about what to do with this unusual marine catch. Lutnick guessed that Laurens probably received 'no small satisfaction from reading in the Ministry's new and most trusted journal that, "Such is the distraction of the times, that while one party sentences him to the scaffold, the other would vote him into Parliament".'[2]

The fact that one party – and friends of America such as Edmund Burke – were well-disposed towards him, gave Laurens some comfort. The fact that he was the highest-ranking and most distinguished American prisoner of the whole war, was of limited help to him: he was treated poorly, save in one respect. He was able to enlist the aid of the principal warder by whom he was guarded, James Futterell, and of his wife. Catherine Futterell not only nursed him when he was ill – as he was for much of the time – but also carried messages for him.

Several of the messages sent out by Laurens were used by the press, especially the *Courant*, published by Almon during the first part of his period in the Tower, and by John Stockdale during the later part. The authorities must have known that messages were being smuggled out, but seem to have made little or no effort to stop that traffic. For example, Stockdale's *Courant* twice published a prediction by Laurens that Cornwallis would be forced to surrender in the South. On the second occasion there could be no doubt about the source, in view of the wording:

---

[2] Lutnick, Solomon, *The American Revolution and the British Press 1775-1783*, Columbia: U. Missouri P., 1967, 163; the paper was the *Morning Herald*, Nov. 2, 1780.

'A *certain* gentleman, confined in a state prison, has declared it to be his opinion, that Lord Cornwallis, from the peculiar danger of his situation, *must inevitably be captured*.'[3]

The ministry did its best to try and persuade Laurens to abandon his rebellious views, and to return to the loyal fold. This was not an unusual step, for whenever the British army retook territory in America, it gave the colonists the opportunity of swearing allegiance to the Crown – unless they had been very actively engaged against the British interests. Some supporters of independence were persuaded to change sides, others pretended to do so and kept their original, or their second loyalty. The British had even succeeded in getting one of the signers of the Declaration of Independence to disown his signature. Persuading President Laurens to recant would have been regarded as something of a propaganda coup, although it could have made no difference to the outcome of the war. The ministry used two of Laurens's old friends and business associates to sound him out and try to persuade him to change sides: Richard Oswald and William Manning, by then John Laurens's father-in-law. Manning was able to bring along his daughter, John's wife Martha, and the little granddaughter the two merchants had in common. What a place for a man, his daughter-in-law and grandchild to meet for the first time! Despite his physical suffering, Henry Laurens refused to change his allegiance and so remained a prisoner in the Tower from October 6, 1780 to December 31, 1781.

---

[3] *Laurens Papers*, 15: 375n. It was typical of Laurens that he never forgot the kindness of the Futterells and helped the family in different ways. He also advised John Miller, the printer of the *Courant*, about emigrating. As a result, in 1783, Miller set up a newspaper in Charleston and was appointed State Printer. *Ibid.*, 16: 4n. Stockdale is reported to have helped his 'kinsman' Miller's family, who were left behind in England. Granger, William, *New, Original and Complete Wonderful Museum and Magazine*, London: Alex. Hogg, 1807, 5: 2470.

Although Laurens was very ill, he retained both his powerful personality, as indicated by the way he received help from his warder, and his sense of humour. When presented with a bill for his lodgings and the services of the men detaining him, he protested that he had half a mind to take his custom elsewhere.

John Adams had been notified in November 1777, by President Laurens, of his appointment by Congress as a Commissioner and had been in Europe since April 1778, with one short trip home only, in 1779. After Laurens's capture, Adams, who was originally intended to join Laurens for his negotiations with the Dutch, managed very successfully in the Netherlands on his own.

During his father's enforced period of inactivity, John Laurens was able to further the American cause significantly. In February 1781, the veteran twenty-six year old colonel sailed for France, arriving there in just under six weeks. He had little doubt about the importance of his mission to get speedy help from the French, for he had been appointed a minister by Congress for that purpose, had seen the shortages with his own eyes, and had been informed by Washington: 'If France delays a timely and powerful aid in the critical posture of our affairs, it will avail us nothing, should she attempt it hereafter. Why need I run into the details, when it may be declared in a word that we are at the end of our tether, and that now or never deliverance must come.' Washington commended the young man to Franklin, who had met young Laurens three times in Paris, when he was hurrying home from London to join in the war. 'Justice to the character of this gentleman conspiring with motives of friendship will not permit me to let him depart without testifying to you the high opinion I entertain of his worth as a citizen and as a soldier. You will find him a man of abilities.'[4]

---

[4] Fitzpatrick, John C., *Writings of George Washington,* Washington: Government Printing Office, 1939, 21: 439, 100.

On May 8, John Adams wrote a very friendly note to John Laurens from Amsterdam: 'I am much mortified that I am not to have an opportunity of shewing you, in person, the respect which I have for your character, as well as that affection which I feel for the son of one of the worthiest friends I ever had. Alas! When will he be able to obtain his own liberty, who has so nobly contended for that of others?'[5] Adams had a very high regard for Henry Laurens, but three years later Laurens, by then a very sick man, was to break up their friendship for no good reason.

In Paris, Franklin, who had earlier feared that Adams might offend the French with his manner, thought that John Laurens succeeded in doing so with his forceful insistence on immediate aid. On August 24, Franklin wrote to William Carmichael, who assisted the American Commissioners in Europe, about Laurens: 'He was indefatigable, while he stayed, and took true pains, but he brusqued the ministers too much, and I found after he was gone that he had thereby given more offence than I could have imagined.'[6] Despite his soldier's brusqueness, his pleas had some success, so Laurens sailed home at the end of May 1781, with substantial French financial and military support. Edmund Morgan has recently asserted that Franklin deserved a large part of the credit usually given to Laurens: the Doctor had been working away steadily at obtaining help from the French. Indeed, Morgan went so far as to write, 'Laurens's mission was little short of a disaster.'[7]

The consequences of the mission for John Laurens's family were less happy. The existence of his mission was known to the British government, and Henry Laurens felt that had counted

----

[5] *Adams Papers*, 11: 311.

[6] Middlekauf, Robert, *Benjamin Franklin and his Enemies,* Berkeley: U. California P., 1998, 194; Labaree, Leonard W. et al. (eds.), *The Papers of Benjamin Franklin,* New Haven: Yale U.P., 1959-, 35: 399.

[7] Morgan, Edmund S., *Benjamin Franklin,* New Haven: Yale U.P., 2002, 267. Morgan is highly qualified to make such a comment, and gives his reasons, which we need not pursue here.

against him. Also, hearing of her husband's presence in France, Martha Manning Laurens took her daughter across the Channel to meet her father for the first time, but it appears she missed him, and died soon afterwards in Lille. Fortunately, John's sister, also called Martha, raised the child.[8]

While John Laurens was in France and sailing home, the war in Virginia was in a state of flux. In June 1781, the Americans had little cause for optimism: large numbers of British troops were marauding in that State with impunity, partly because the governor of the previous two years, Thomas Jefferson, had done little to prepare for invasion – though some apologists say there is little he could have done effectively in a war of constant movement.

On June 2, Jefferson narrowly avoided being captured at his home at Monticello by the dreaded Col. Tarleton's loyalist dragoons. He fled just in time and attained safety at a plantation he owned some ninety miles away. Shortly after his arrival he was thrown by his horse and immobilised for six weeks. Fortunately, he had been far-sighted enough to pack up some notes when he left home hurriedly and he then had the opportunity to work on them.

Jefferson later gave a short account of how his project had come about: 'In the year 1781 I had received a letter from M. de Marbois, of the French legation in Philadelphia, informing me he had been instructed by his government to obtain such statistical accounts of the different states of our Union as might be useful for their information; and addressing to me a number of queries relative to the state of Virginia. I had always made it a practice, whenever an opportunity occurred, of obtaining any

---

[8] For John Laurens generally, see Appendix 1 of the biography of his father by Wallace; also Massey, Gregory D., *John Laurens and the American Revolution*, Columbia: U. of South Carolina P., 2000; Stockdale, Eric, 'The Middle Templar at Washington's Side', South Carolina Hist. Soc's *Carologue*, 2003, 19: 20.

information of our country which might be of use to me in any
station, public or private, to commit it to writing. These
memoranda were on loose papers, bundled up without order
and difficult of recurrence [retrieval?] when I had occasion for a
particular one. I thought this a good occasion to embody their
substances, which I did in the order of M. de Marbois' queries,
so as to answer his wish, and to arrange them for my own use.'[9]
The outcome of Jefferson's rearrangement of his scraps of paper
became his only book, *Notes on the State of Virginia*.

By the Autumn, the situation in Virginia had improved significantly for the Americans, thanks largely to the arrival of a
French fleet from the West Indies, with additional troops to
reinforce the French army already there under the Comte de
Rochambeau. The British and Hessians (a term used to cover all
the Germans troops) under Earl Cornwallis were bottled up on
the coast at Yorktown and nearby Gloucester. The senior British
commander, General Clinton, felt unable to send adequate
reinforcements from New York, as he feared an attack by Washington there, whereas the American commander was in fact
marching south into Virginia. On his return to America, John
Laurens reported to Congress, and hurried south so as not to
miss the coming battle. According to Almon, before arriving at
Yorktown, John Laurens had played a significant part in Washington's deception of the enemy. In his open letter to Jenkinson
(the Secretary-at-War), Almon wrote:

'But the manoeuvre of young Laurens (son to the state
prisoner in the Tower) disguised Mr. Washington's movements
from before New York so effectually, that the true reason was
not suspected until some time after the American chief had
begun his march to the southward, to co-operate with the
French admiral. The new deception was entrusted to young
Laurens, who completely executed it. He circulated a report in

---

[9] Randolph, T. J., *Memoirs, Correspondence and Private Papers of Thomas
Jefferson,* London: Henry Colburn and Richard Bentley, 1829, 1: 52.

Jersey, in order that it might be conveyed to New York, of circumstances having happened in Europe which were unfavourable to the French and American interests. The bait answered. In New York it was instantly credited, and propagated by authority. Instead of the French *coming to* America with greater force, they were here represented to be *going from* America, with all they had there. The inference is obvious, viz. that Lord Cornwallis could want no assistance.'

At the battle of Yorktown, Laurens distinguished himself once more, fighting alongside his old friends Hamilton and Lafayette. On October 17, 1781, Cornwallis requested surrender terms. Washington invited Rochambeau to nominate a French officer and appointed his own delegate to negotiate the surrender. The American chosen for this historic task was John Laurens. Washington insisted that the British surrender on humiliating terms, similar to those imposed by them on the American garrison at Charleston. When Major Alexander Ross, the British representative, protested that Cornwallis had not been there, Laurens pointed out that he himself had been one of the humiliated prisoners of the British, but remembering his role, gave the well-known impersonal answer, 'It is not the individual that is considered. It is the nation.'[10]

After the surrender, Washington placed Laurens in charge of all the prisoners, including Cornwallis, the Constable of the Tower of London, where Henry Laurens was still detained. Edmund Burke gleefully drew attention to this twist of fate in the House of Commons. Washington knew and respected Henry Laurens, having worked with him, and having stayed with him in Philadelphia for six weeks, immediately after Laurens's term as President had ended in December 1778.[11] He was probably delighted to approve the suggestion made by John Laurens, that the Constable of the Tower might like to consider being

---

[10] Emery, Noemie, *Washington: A Biography*, London: Cassell, 1977, 280.
[11] *Laurens Papers*, 15: 61n.

exchanged for one of the prisoners there. After some months that exchanged was effected.

The news of Yorktown reached London on November 25. Lord North's reasonable response was to say, repeatedly, 'O God! It is all over!'[12] The King's first reaction was probably, 'What? What?' His second, and more foolish response, was to say that the defeat at Yorktown made no difference and that the war should continue. Fortunately, wiser counsel was – agonisingly slowly – to prevail. Almon's letter to the Secretary-at-War had earlier stated, in words that were certainly approved by Edmund Burke, Thomas Day and all the other British opponents of the war: 'The success of the last campaign in America, as well as of every other campaign since 1775, ought to convince us that the conquest of the vast country is hopeless; that the attempt is impracticable; and that the great promises of future success, which year after year have been held out to us, and are now made to us for the next year, are like all the past, delusive, irrational and wicked.' After giving the account of John Laurens's part, quoted above, Almon added, 'I do not know whether the stratagem of young Laurens may not fall heavy upon his father.' Fortunately, it did not: on the last day of the year 1781, five weeks after the arrival of the news of Yorktown, Henry Laurens was at last released on bail by the Chief Justice, Lord Mansfield.

Some further comments must be made about Almon's letter. He dated it November 26. If he did indeed write it on that day – rather than giving it that date later – that was remarkable, as Lord North only had the news of Yorktown on the day before. He was clearly receiving details of Washington's plan very quickly, and from a source close to the centre. It looks as though John Laurens himself may have communicated directly with Almon – there was scarcely time for a roundabout route.

---

[12] Morris, Richard B., *The Peacemakers – The Great Powers and American Independence*, New York: Harper & Row, 1965, 251.

Another possibility is that the information came via a friend, such as Thomas Day, who could have read a letter from Laurens to his father, and then passed the contents on at once to the nearby Almon.

The writer has not seen any other reference to Laurens's participation in Washington's deception plan, but it is hard to believe that Almon, even though not wholly reliable, would have invented it. There was insufficient time for Laurens to be in on the plan at an early stage: he reported to Congress on September 2, nearly two weeks after Washington had set off for the south.[13] He may have spread false news to support the cover story, and then exaggerated his role in a letter. This was, of course, neither the first nor the last time that such a cover plan was used to prevent an enemy from moving his forces to the actual point of attack. Until the attack commences, and sometimes after that, there is a need for a continuous stream of misinformation. Another American general and future President was to use a similar ruse in 1944. Then, fortunately for all of mankind, not only the French but also the British and the Russians, were on the same side as the Americans, while the Hessians were once more on the losing side.

In January 1782, Almon fired a last broadside at Sandwich, the First Lord of the Admiralty. In *An Address to the Interior Cabinet*, writing as An Independent Whig again, he dealt with recent naval history: 'If America is lost, as most certainly it is, as far as relates to the subjection of it, that loss is to be ascribed to Lord Sandwich. The fleet in America has never been adequate to the service. The surrender of Lord Cornwallis is entirely owing to this insufficiency of the fleet. If the sea had been kept open, Lord Cornwallis could have been in no danger.' There was a great deal of truth in this observation, although defence of the homeland had to be a priority for the Royal Navy. Almon then

---

[13] I am indebted to C. James Taylor, formerly editor of the *Laurens Papers* and now of the *Adams Papers*, for this point.

turned to the advantages enjoyed by France, and included a passage that must have delighted the enemies of the notorious rake, Jemmy Twitcher (Sandwich): 'Her marine ministers have not been men of debauched, profligate lives, whose nights have been spent in brothels, bawling an obscene catch, beating a drum, or contriving a blasphemous burlesque on the rites of religion.'

While Sandwich could not very well reply to the last barbs, he did at one point attempt to defend the Admiralty against the charge of operational misconduct, writing, somewhat lamely: 'These charges are not so easily answered, because there is no demonstrative evidence that the orders given have been right; the event certainly does not decide the question; but those who mean to find fault, wait the event, and then adopt whichever side of the question best suits their purposes.'[14]

In March, Lord North and his colleagues finally surrendered their offices, and in April the Independent Whig gave North a similar send-off, with *The Revolution in 1782 Impartially Considered*. Almon wrote: 'The revolution in the government of Great Britain, or, as it is commonly called, the change of the British ministers in the month of March 1782, is one of the most splendid epochs in the history of these islands. When Lord North came to the head of the Treasury, we were in perfect peace with all the world. The disputes with America, which a few years before had threatened such violence to the mother country, were happily adjusted by the wise and critical repeal of the Stamp Act. When his Lordship was removed from his post of minister, he left the nation engaged, without an ally, in a quadruple war, of his own making and approving, with America, France, Spain and Holland.'

Immediately after his release from the Tower, Henry Laurens, who felt very ill, went to Bath, for the treatment of his

---

[14] Mackesy, Piers, *The War for America 1775-1783*, London: Longmans, 1964, xv.

gout and other ailments. He was soon approached by his son's friend from the Middle Temple, the pro-American lawyer and writer, Thomas Day. Peter Rowland concluded that the two men entered into such a warm friendship that they enjoyed a father and son relationship. That may be an over-statement, but Laurens was certainly on very good terms both with Day and his wife. On December 23, 1782, Laurens wrote to Day, calling him his 'very dear friend' and referring to 'my good friend Mrs Day'. He added, 'Although you are not my secretary, or if you are, I pay no salary....' Henry Laurens had at last got close to finding a good secretary.[15]

Day's close companion at the Inn, William Jones, also befriended Laurens. Jones was a pro-American who felt very uncomfortable living in England; greatly impressed by Laurens, he was happy to take his advice about America. As he was not only a good lawyer but also a great authority on oriental languages, he was hoping for a judgeship in India. Failing that, he seriously contemplated emigrating to America, especially after visiting Franklin in Paris in 1779, and again in 1780, and then speaking to Laurens. On March 1, 1782, Jones wrote to his former pupil, Viscount Althorp: 'Mr. Laurens was with me yesterday for two hours: he talks divinely. Did you know that the Americans had settlements *seven hundred* miles from the coast? Every man among them is a soldier, a *patriot* – subdue such a people! The King may as easily conquer the moon or wear it in his sleeve.'

Four days later, Jones wrote to Franklin in Paris to tell him that he might be travelling to America via France with a friend, John Paradise, whose wife had some property and legal problems in Virginia. He added, 'I have no wish to grow old in

---

[15] Rowland, Peter, *The Life and Times of Thomas Day 1748-1789*, Lampeter: Edwin Mellen, 1996, 180, 188; *Laurens Papers*, 16: 94. Laurens received some clerical help from his son Henry, or Harry, and also from his daughter, Martha, once she got free of a romantic entanglement in France.

England; for, believe me, I would rather be a peasant with freedom than a prince in an enslaved country.' In France, Jones met Franklin and we shall see later how his further thoughts on the peasant's rights led to an important prosecution involving the Dean of St. Asaph's, Bishop Shipley's son. He decided to return to England on receiving some favourable news, abandoning the idea of practising law in America, an idea Laurens had encouraged. He also gave up trying to help Paradise and his wife. Thomas Jefferson was later to be burdened by them and their problems for many years.[16]

During his time in London, Laurens sat for a portrait by one of the American painters living in the city, John Singleton Copley. This established a fortunate precedent: John Adams and John Quincy Adams were both to have their portraits painted by him in London in due course. On October 1, 1782, John Stockdale published copies of the Laurens portrait, with his permission, engraved by V. Green, 'Mezzotint Engraver to His Majesty'. In the following February, he also published an engraving of Washington. Laurens made it one of his first tasks to visit American prisoners and tried to alleviate their conditions; the proceeds of that Washington print later went to that cause. The American prisoners were mainly seamen and most of them were held in prison in the naval ports of Portsmouth and Plymouth; Day accompanied Laurens on at least one of his prison visits. According to Gignilliat, Laurens and his younger son, Henry junior, 'had frequent and friendly associations with Day and his wife', so they may well have met John Stockdale on a social visit to the Days, for Day and Stockdale had become increasingly friendly.[17]

---

[16] Cannon, Garland, *The Letters of Sir William Jones,* Oxford U.P., 1970, 2: 515, 517; Malone, Dumas, *Jefferson and the Rights of Man*, Boston: Little, Brown, 1951, 61. For Paradise and Jefferson, see, *John Paradise and Lucy Ludwell*, Shepperson, Archibald Bollings, Richmond: Dietz Press, 1992.
[17] Gignilliat, G. W., *The Author of Sandford and Merton*, New York: Columbia U.P., 1932, 195, 194. For the Day-Stockdale friendship, see chap.10.

One of the principal contributions Laurens made to the peace process when in London, was to make it clear that there were three non-negotiable conditions. The first was an immediate cessation of all hostilities; the second that there could be no separate peace without France, a condition that proved to be flexible; and the third that there should be absolute independence for all thirteen colonies – for the British had from time to time had wicked thoughts about keeping Georgia or South Carolina.

Day was clearly agreed with Laurens about important questions relating to America, and wrote a pamphlet for Stockdale, *Reflections Upon the Present State of England, and the Independence of America,* in which he stated Laurens's main points with emphasis.

In Paris, Benjamin Franklin was encouraged by an English visitor to communicate with Lord Shelburne, who was said to have a great regard for the Doctor. Franklin duly wrote to Shelburne, mentioning a general peace. The historian of the Peacemakers, Richard B. Morris, continued the story: 'When Franklin penned these lines he had not yet learned that Lord North had resigned the seals of office two days before, and that Shelburne had come into the Rockingham Ministry as Colonial Secretary. Now affairs moved quickly. An old friend and former London neighbour of Franklin's named Caleb Whitefoord appeared at Passy and introduced the Scottish merchant, Richard Oswald, bearing letters from both Shelburne and Henry Laurens. And so, from this odd chain of circumstances the negotiations for peace began.'[18]

In his letter to Franklin from London, dated April 7, 1782, Laurens gave Oswald the strongest reference possible, based on 'an experience little short of thirty years'. Franklin replied to Laurens on April 12, enclosing a copy of the commission,

---

[18] Morris, 250. Whitefoord was Oswald's secretary until David Hartley took over as the British negotiator.

naming the two of them, plus John Adams, Thomas Jefferson and John Jay (Laurens's successor as President of Congress) as Commissioners to negotiate the peace.[19] Jefferson's trip was cancelled by Congress. Laurens was reluctant to act, writing to Adams from Nantes on August 27, to say that three Commissioners were quite enough: a fourth one would be surplus to requirements, adding, 'The business is in very good hands.' There was further evidence of his modesty in his postscript: 'The next time a packet from you comes directed to his Excellency Henry Laurens &c., *Mr.* Laurens will disclaim it.'

However, on November 12, Laurens received a letter from Adams (dated November 6) informing him of the wish of Congress that he should continue as a Commissioner, and adding his own wish for his 'judgment and advice'. Adams included the terrible news that John Laurens had been killed in South Carolina during a skirmish with a British foraging party.[20] Laurens dragged himself to Paris, too late to be able to contribute much to the polishing of the Preliminary Treaty of Peace, which was signed shortly after his arrival. Franklin had not been very well either, so most of the negotiations at the end had been conducted by the two lawyers: Jay, with the help of Adams. However, Franklin's overall contribution had been invaluable, partly because 'he had established with the principal British negotiators an accord that is rare in international diplomacy, since it rested not only on respect for his learning and his

---

[19] *Laurens Papers*, 15: 478, 482. At least one author has referred to Laurens writing the Oswald recommendation 'from his cell'. He had, of course, been freed, albeit conditionally, at the end of 1781. The error may have been caused by other writers referring inaccurately to his being in the Tower for nearly two years, instead of just under fifteen months. For Oswald, see also, Hancock, David, *Citizens of the World*, Cambridge U.P., 1995.

[20] *Laurens Papers,* 16: 52.

wisdom, but on a friendship for the man himself, built up over twenty-five years.'[21]

The Preliminary Treaty was signed on November 30, 1782. Adams wrote the following tribute to Laurens in his diary entry for that day: 'I was very happy that Mr Laurens came in, although it was the last day of the conference, and wish he could have been sooner. His apprehension, notwithstanding his affliction under the recent loss of so excellent a son, is as quick, his judgment as sound, and his heart as firm as ever. He had the opportunity of examining the whole, and judging, and approving, and the article which he caused to be inserted at the very last – that no property should be carried off – which would most probably in the multiplicity and hurry of affairs have escaped us, was worth a longer journey, if that had been all. But his name and weight is added which is of much greater consequence.'[22]

Laurens wrote to Thomas Day to inform him of John's death, and to ask him to write some suitable memorial lines for his young friend – which he did. He also invited him to join him in Paris, but Day did not take him up on the offer.

John Adams, who did not have the solid financial background that Laurens had (until his wartime losses, at any rate), noted in his diary for December 6: 'Mr Laurens's apartments at the hotel de York are better than mine at the hotel de Roi, on Carousel. Yet he gives but twelve louis and I am obliged to give eighteen.' Thereafter he seems to have borne in mind that Laurens had a good nose for reasonably priced accommodation.

Laurens spent another eighteen months in Europe, but did not travel to Paris to sign the Final Treaty on September 3, 1783,

---

[21] Wright, Esmond, 'The Peace Treaties of 1782 and 1783: Diplomacy by Affection', in Lemay, J. A. Leo, (ed.), *Reappraising Benjamin Franklin*, Newark: U. of Delaware P., 1993, 169.
[22] Butterfield, L. H., (ed.) *Diary and Autobiography of John Adams*, Cambridge: Harvard U.P., 1961, 3: 83.

as he was in England on behalf of the Peace Commissioners at the time. One of the points he was discussing with Fox and the Duke of Portland (of Burlington House, Piccadilly), the titular head of government since Shelburne's fall in April, was the future appointment of the first official United States minister.[23]

For some time Laurens worried unnecessarily about being captured by the British on the way home without an adequate passport, but received the help and reassurance of Thomas Day and other friends on that score. Despite his continuing indifferent health, he did his best to represent his country and to look after its citizens, prisoners and freemen alike. Wallace has fairly summed up his contribution: 'Laurens's services during 1782-3-4, terminating only with his departure for America, were of great importance and entitle him in a very true sense to be considered the first minister of the United States to England.'[24]

After his release from the Tower, Laurens got to know Stockdale very well. It was almost certainly Day who made the introduction to the bookseller who, as we shall see in detail in the next chapter, had set up on his own in 1780. It is possible that at first he merely introduced Stockdale as his own publisher, whose new bookshop he could recommend. It is also a possibility that Laurens recognised Stockdale from his earlier visits to Almon's shop, before the war. As Day became more friendly with Stockdale, he will have learned that he had accommodation to spare over the shop. Laurens, who had spent several years in London before the war in long-term lodgings, seems not to have wanted anything resembling permanent accommodation after his release from the Tower. He was always anxious to move on: to Bath for his health; to Holland or France on official business, despite his health; to see his daughters in France; or to return home to South Carolina. As a result of his restlessness he had

---

[23] *Laurens Papers*, 15: 403.
[24] Wallace, 412.

different lodgings, but he stayed with Stockdale over his book-shop in Piccadilly on at least four occasions.

In view of the Laurens-Day-Stockdale friendship, the first stay could have been in 1782, but there is no supporting evidence relating to that year. The earliest extant letter from Laurens to Stockdale is from Bath and dated February 6, 1783, but it is neutral on the point, for it merely states: 'Mr. Laurens presents his compliments to Mr. Stockdale: he expects to be in London in four or five days therefore requests a cessation of newspapers to Bath.'[25] The first time that Laurens lodged over the bookshop was almost certainly before April 7, 1783, when he felt able to recommend him to his business associate, John Lewis Gervais, in terms which suggest that he knew him better than merely as a customer of the shop. 'I also recommend to the public of South Carolina, the public library, and to my friends in particular, Mr. John Stockdale, Bookseller in Piccadilly. He is an honest industrious man, and has been uniformly our friend, and an active friend too, from the beginning of the Persecution. He will serve his customers upon as good terms as any man, from these considerations, I think he deserves a preference by every virtuous American.' It is possible that Stockdale, in conver-sation, had claimed credit for some of Almon's efforts from 'the beginning of the Persecution' until 1780 or so.[26]

On July 3, 1783, Laurens wrote to Stockdale from Bath once more, asking him to forward a package for him. He ended his note by sending his compliments to Mrs. Stockdale, whom he presumably knew by then as a landlady.[27] On August 4, Laurens, just back from Paris, wrote to Thomas Day from Piccadilly, 'I

---

[25] Henry Laurens Papers, South Carolina Hist. Soc.

[26] *Laurens Papers*, 16: 181. For Stockdale's later connections with the Charleston library, see, Raven, James, *London Booksellers and American Cus-tomers*, Columbia: U. of South Carolina P., 2002, generally; and for Gervais, 423, n.93. See also, chap.14, below.

[27] Henry Laurens Papers, South Carolina Hist. Soc.

returned to London at a very late hour last night and put in at Stockdale's, whose apartments happened to be empty.' It is clear from the wording that Laurens had stayed there earlier: he would not have called at a bookshop late at night for accommodation on the off-chance, without knowing about it. His affection for the Days is apparent from his closing remarks: 'Every good wish of my heart attend you and Mrs. Day.'[28]

Laurens spent the second half of August in Bath, but on September 10, wrote from Piccadilly again. This would appear to have been his third time in the accommodation over the book-shop. He may well have kept his rooms on in August, when going off to Bath for a short period of further treatment.

When Laurens returned to London from France on November 21, the Stockdale lodgings were no longer available for him, as they were then occupied by John Adams and his son, John Quincy, so he had to make do with less satisfactory accom-modation in nearby Leicester Fields instead.[29]

On April 27, 1784, Franklin wrote to Laurens to say that he wished he could come to Paris, using terms which indicate how poorly he and Adams got on: 'Mr. Jay will probably be gone, and I shall be left alone, or with Mr. A., and I can have no favour-able opinion of what may be the offspring of a coalition between my ignorance and his positiveness.'[30] Paris lacked the charms of home for Laurens, so he was not tempted by Franklin's friendly words.

He must have been content staying with the Stockdales, for John Quincy Adams found him lodging with them again in May 1784, shortly before Laurens's final departure from England in June.[31] Laurens probably felt at ease with the bluff, plain-

---

[28] *Laurens Papers*, 16: 246.

[29] *Laurens Papers*, 16: 335, 354; for the Adams's two-month stay with Stockdale, see chap.7.

[30] Brands, H. W., *The First American*, New York: Doubleday, 2000, 638.

[31] Butterfield, L. H. (ed.), *Adams Family Correspondence*, Cambridge: Harvard U.P., 1963-, 5: 329.

speaking bookseller, whom he will have compared favourably
with some of his more polished compatriots. Very much the
loving family man, Laurens doubtless appreciated having
children around the place. By the time he left the country he had
spent, willingly and unwillingly, about nine years of his life in
England. It is a moot point whether the worst months were
those spent in the Tower, or those at liberty, burdened by his
resultant ill health and the loss of his son.

Laurens never returned to public life; had his health been
better, Washington might well have made him a member of his
first administration. However, he enjoyed having time for his
own affairs and his three surviving children. He lived to see all
three married into the families of political colleagues and friends.
In 1787, his elder daughter, Martha, married Dr. David Ramsay,
whose connections with Stockdale we shall consider in Chapter
14. The younger girl, Mary, married Charles Pinckney in the following year. He had been busy at the Constitutional Convention
as a delegate from South Carolina and was to be a Governor of
the State on four occasions. Laurens's only surviving son,
Henry, married Eliza, the daughter of his lawyer, close friend
and political colleague, John Rutledge, the first President of the
State, who had played an important part at the Convention.[32]

It is almost as though that third wedding made Henry
Laurens feel that his work was done. His son was married in
May 1792 and Laurens died in the December. Before his death
he must often have thought about his first-born, John, and how
his promising life had been cut short so unnecessarily. It is
certain that he thought of him when Washington appointed
John's fellow aide and friend, Alexander Hamilton, to be his first
Secretary of the Treasury. By the spring of 1790, Hamilton 'was
already the young lion of the administration'.[33] Laurens must

---

[32] Wallace, 430.
[33] Peterson, Merrill D., *Thomas Jefferson and the New Nation*, Oxford U.P.,
1975, 396.

have wondered what post Washington would have found for John, his own young lion, had he survived.

Henry Laurens's last traced letter to John Stockdale from South Carolina is dated April 20, 1787, and indicates that he had warm memories of his time recuperating at his address. 'I feel a pleasure from having occasion to write to my good old landlord,' he began, concluding his letter, 'With affection and respect to yourself, Mrs. Stockdale and the children.'[34] He meant what he wrote and at some stage, probably in the late summer of 1783, he undoubtedly recommended the lodgings to the man who had envied him his bargain accommodation in Paris, John Adams. That recommendation by Henry Laurens turned out to be one of the most important events in Stockdale's life as a publisher.

---

[34] Henry Laurens Papers, South Carolina Hist. Soc.

Illus. 7. John Stockdale by Thomas Rowlandson

6

John Stockdale Opens his Bookshop

John Stockdale's origins are not entirely clear, but he was almost certainly born at Cotbeck in Cumberland on March 25, 1750, to Joseph and Priscilla Stockdale. His father was a blacksmith and in 1784, Stockdale was depicted in a cartoon by Thomas Rowlandson as a smith, but as far as one can tell now, he himself was never apprenticed as such. At most, he helped his father, or someone else in that trade. At the age of seventeen he moved to Mottram-in-Longdendale in Cheshire and near Manchester, where he met a local girl at the Dukinfield Moravian chapel.

The minutes of the chapel elders for March 16, 1770, refer to Brother Parminster's concern about J. Stockdale: 'He cannot be brought to work and earn his bread.' The chapel diary records that on November 7, 1771, Brother Parminster heard John Stockdale admit that he had 'formed an acquaintance together with Mary Ridgway'. Mary had confessed to someone a year earlier 'that she was in love with him'. Stockdale's departure was noted in the congregational diary on November 11, 1771: 'Today by our permission he set off to his parents at London.' Mary Ridgway followed him at some time and they were married, either in Cheshire or in London.[1]

By 1774, Stockdale was working for John Almon as his shopman or porter. What made him choose to work for a

---

[1] I am indebted to Brian Hugh Stockdale, who is a direct descendant of both John Stockdale and James Ridgway, for this information; see also, *The Intrepid Magazine*, William Hamilton (ed.), London: James Ridgway, 1784, 1: 53.

bookseller? William Granger, who was not the most reliable source, stated that the introduction to Almon was effected by John Miller, 'the notorious printer of the *London Evening Post*', whom he described as Stockdale's kinsman. Another explanation is to be found in his younger brother Joseph's choice of trade. The Stationer's Company apprentice register shows that Joseph, the son of Joseph Stockdale, smith, of Gray's Inn Lane, Holborn, London, was apprenticed for seven years, from 1770 to 1777, when he obtained his 'freedom'.[2]

Joseph, who was born in 1754, was still an apprentice in 1774, but may well have been able to put in a word for his brother with Almon. At the very least, he could have pointed out to John that the book world was expanding and that there were opportunities for bright young men. Joseph was so promising as a printer that in 1783, a mere six years out of his apprenticeship, he was invited by the House of Assembly of the island to emigrate to Bermuda, complete with his Gutenberg machine, to set up a printing press there. He was doubly lucky to get the offer, in that not only was he a comparative novice, but also because the vacancy might well have been filled earlier by the Boston printer, Isaiah Thomas, later famous for his *History of Printing in America*, published in 1810, by his son. Back in 1772, Thomas had thought about moving to Bermuda, for the interesting reason that 'one of my profession here [Boston, Mass.] must be either of one party or the other; he cannot please both.'[3]

In 1784, Joseph Stockdale started the first newspaper, the *Bermuda Gazette*, and a postal service to deliver it. In 1984, in a

---

[2] Granger, William, *The New, Original and Complete Wonderful Museum and Magazine*, London: Alex. Hogg, 1807, 5: 2470. The late D. F. McKenzie drew my attention to the entry in his *Stationers' Company Apprentices, 1701-1800*, Oxford: Bib. Soc. Publs. N.S. 1978, 19, 5472.

[3] Amory, Hugh, 'The New England Book Trade, 1713-1790', in Amory, Hugh and Hall, David D. (eds.), *The Colonial Book in the Atlantic World*, Cambridge U.P., 2000, 335.

rare tribute to a printer, Bermuda celebrated the bicentenary of his innovations with a commemorative set of three postage stamps, showing Joseph, his Gutenberg press, the newspaper and his postal service.[4]

John Stockdale was certainly with Almon at the time hostilities broke out in Massachusetts in April 1775, and must early on have appreciated the publishing potential, both of the dispute and of the American market. He was bright enough to learn from Almon how to run a bookshop, both as a place where books, papers and pamphlets were sold, and as one where manuscripts were selected for publication. Although Stockdale is sometimes referred to as a printer, he never qualified or practised as such. Indeed, he may only have learned to read and write during his years with Almon. Even Almon seems never to have worked as a printer once he was set up in Piccadilly, so both men had printing work done for them by outside printers using their own premises elsewhere. Once the printers had done their job for Almon, Stockdale had the task of carrying some of the finished products to the shop for sale, and for that that task he had a sling, or porter's knot. He was also responsible for getting the binding of the many loose parts done by outside binders. Doubtless a cart of some sort was used to carry the heaviest loads.

---

[4] I am grateful to Gwenlliam M. Davies and Barbara S. McCrimmon for drawing my attention to Joseph Stockdale in Bermuda. After Joseph's death in 1803, his three daughters continued his business for thirteen years, see, Lent, John A., 'Pioneer Woman Editors – The Stockdale Sisters of Bermuda', *Printing History*, 1988, 10: 36. There were also several Dublin booksellers named Stockdale, but they had no detectable connection with Piccadilly John and Bermuda Joseph – save that their forebears presumably also came from the North of England. Percy Bysshe Shelley managed to suggest a link by being published early on by John Joseph Stockdale (John's son) in London and later by other Stockdales in Dublin, but that seems to have been coincidental only.

We have seen what a good journalist and pamphleteer Almon was. He clearly did not sit in the shop for long hours, thinking up topics – although he later referred to his having 'a sedentary situation'. That was probably a reference to the time spent at his desk, in the shop or above it, writing his own articles and pamphlets, and reading those by other authors. Although some of his contacts will have called in at the shop, he was probably out and about regularly, meeting politicians in search of publicity, sacked generals wanting to explain away their defeats, disgruntled merchants, dissenting ministers and others, in coffee shops like the Carolina and elsewhere. Almon was a writer and a political creature with strong views on subjects such as the American fiasco, so he was probably quite glad to be out of his shop. During his absences he increasingly relied on Stockdale and other employees.

Almon started the *Courant* (later the *London Courant*) in November 1779, with George Greive, who was a part proprietor and was possibly also employed 'to superintend the printing'.[5] We have seen how the paper backed the reform movement from the start, and how Almon was not afraid to use it for the expression of views hostile to the King and his ministers.

In June 1780, the *Courant* was full of the news of the Gordon riots, which started as an anti-Catholic demonstration but descended into a drunken series of indiscriminate mob attacks on people and on buildings, with a number of dead and injured. Much to his dismay, it was Lord George Gordon, the leader of the Protestant Association, whose name became attached to the disturbances: he had in fact tried, without success, to restrain his supporters.

On June 7, the *Courant* reported the release by the mob of Walter Parker, the pro-Keppel printer, and of the other prisoners in Newgate. On the following day it announced that Lord

---

[5] Letter J. H. Trumbull to Robert C. Winthrop, *Massachusetts Hist. Soc. Procs.*,1869-1870, 11: 5.

Mansfield's town house had been razed to the ground by the rioters, and that after the King's Bench prison had been stormed, 'the whole pile of buildings was in a few hours reduced to ashes'. The editor of the pro-ministry *Morning Post*, Henry Bate, who shortly before the riots had been successfully prosecuted for calling the Duke of Richmond a rebel and a traitor, obtained a dubious benefit from the destruction of the prisons. He was sentenced to twelve months' imprisonment, but was asked if he would kindly mind waiting for a cell: the prisons had first to be rebuilt.[6]

The Lord Chief Justice may have lost his house in Bloomsbury (fortunately he had a spare one, Caen Wood, or Kenwood, on Hampstead Heath) but the Inns of Court were successfully defended by the barristers, attorneys and their clerks. The defenders included the Whig lawyers, Thomas Erskine (the ex-naval officer, complete with cannon), Samuel Romilly and William 'Oriental' Jones. On July 4, Almon celebrated this unique bit of military history – which would have interested the ex-student, Col. Laurens – by publishing in his paper 'An *ex tempore* Soliloquy by an Attorney's Clerk in the Temple'.

> In vain old *latitat* may storm and swear,
> And bid me in a plea of debt declare;
> Pleas, declarations, bonds and writs may sleep,
> While I at Temple-gate my post will keep.
> There under valiant Erskine I will stand,
> And learn the pond'rous musket to command,
> There all protesting rebels I'll defy,
> And none the gates shall enter, but to die.
> What tho' my fortune, as a Clerk be marr'd
> I'll live and die a loyal, true Blackguard.

To avoid any understandable confusion, a note explained, 'The gentlemen of the Inns of Court, who took up arms on a late

---

[6] Lutnick, Solomon, *The American Revolution and the British Press 1775-1783*, Columbia: U. Missouri P., 1967, 30.]

occasion, were called Black-guards from the colour of their regimentals.'

On June 10, the arrest of Lord George Gordon was reported. He was committed to the Tower, where Henry Laurens was to join him later in the year. They were kept separated there, partly because Benjamin Franklin and his compatriots were wrongly suspected by some of having fomented the riot.[7] Gordon and Laurens had one brief unauthorised meeting in the Tower. That led to Laurens, but not Gordon, being punished by the Governor for his unwitting offence. On June 13, the paper praised the City Chamberlain, John Wilkes – a new member of the establishment – for his part in saving the Bank of England from the rioters.[8] The riot was eventually suppressed because the King, having consulted Franklin's old opponent, Alexander Wedderburn, by then promoted to Attorney-General, was prepared to use the troops. The King and Lord North regained some of their lost support as a result of this firm line.

Of more immediate interest to the present story, is an advertisement that appeared among the items of riot news on June 5 and 6: 'To be let, the shop of a bookseller and stationer, at the west end of town, in an undeniable situation. Want of health is the only reason of the present occupier wishing to retire, therefore ready money is not wanted for the stock, goodwill &c., but good security will be expected. It will suit a young man bred to the business, and of good connections.' Although the address given for replies was that of Curtis, a stationer in Fleet Street, the advertiser was Almon.

As early as June 14, another notice in the *Courant* announced: 'John Debrett begs leave most respectfully to acquaint the

---

[7] Hibbert, Christopher, *King Mob*, London: Longmans, Green, 1958, chaps.10 and 11.

[8] Despite this and his other public services, until recently there was no statue of Wilkes in London; he now stands in Fetter Lane, opposite the site of the Moravian chapel attended by the Stockdales, permanently gazing down towards the Temple.

nobility and gentry, and his friends in general, that he is removed from the late Mr. William Davis's, the corner of Sackville Street, to Mr. Almon's, bookseller and stationer, opposite Burlington House in Piccadilly, where he hopes he shall be honoured with their commands as long as he shall be found by a diligent and faithful attention, to deserve the favour of their countenance and protection.'[9]

On the following day, Debrett advertised to ask all creditors and debtors of the estate of William Davis to deal with him. This led to an indignant announcement in the issue of August 1: 'Miss Davis, residuary legatee of W. Davis, will carry on business with her father, Robert Davis, at the corner of Sackville Street, Piccadilly. Mr. and Miss Davis being informed that certain interested and designing persons have insinuated that the trade of their house is given up, and have made a personal and written application for the favours of the nobility and gentry to another house, beg leave to caution their friends from paying attention to such insinuations, which are fabricated only to deceive.' Debrett chose not to reply. This was not a happy beginning for a business that was going to have to meet stiff opposition from Almon's former employee.

If it was true, as Almon stated, 'ready money is not wanted for the stock, goodwill &c.', why had he not offered his business to Stockdale? The sad answer is that he felt he had been cheated by him and some of his unidentified colleagues in the shop. This is what Almon wrote of himself later: 'Naturally attached to a sedentary situation, his greatest fault was giving his confidence to unworthy servants, and permitting them to exercise that power which he ought to have kept in his own hands. Nor had he firmness to withstand their solicitations for favours. He was therefore duped, betrayed, plundered and abused by them,

---

[9] Debrett's name has been variously spelled as Debret, de Brett and, at least once, Dr Brett, but the writer will stick to the spelling still used today.

according as it suited their occasional views. At length ill health obliged him to seek for ease and recovery in retirement, which he flattered himself he should there obtain. With this view he quitted his business in favour of a very worthy and respectable young man (Mr. Debrett) and went into the country.'[10]

Some confirmation of the charge that Stockdale was a rogue came in 1784, from James Ridgway, a fellow publisher, who was Mrs. Stockdale's brother. Ridgway had fallen out with his brother-in-law and made a vicious attack on him in his own short-lived *The Intrepid Magazine*, which was edited for him by Rev. William Hamilton. In the first issue he included the cartoon by Thomas Rowlandson, showing Stockdale at an anvil, hammering a book. The caption read: 'John Stockdale – The Bookselling Blacksmith, one of the King's New Friends.' If the cartoon was intended as a hammer blow, it missed its mark, but the article probably contained more than a grain of truth, even though some of its contents are highly suspect. If the object of the cartoon was to make the point that Stockdale had humble origins, it was an extremely foolish one. Apart from anything else, so had Ridgway. In any event, as James Raven has pointed out: 'The meteoric rise of a few self-made booksellers became the stuff of legend: Robert Dodsley the footman, Thomas and James Harrison the sons of a Reading basket-weaver, Thomas Wright the son of a Wolverhampton buckle-maker, Ralph Griffiths the watchmaker, and William Lane the poultryman's son.'[11]

'Almon had entrusted to Stockdale the employ of persons for serving out the newspapers ordered from his shop,' the magazine article stated. 'Instead of employing others on his

---

[10] Almon, *Memoirs*, 121. The increase in the number of his employees is some measure of Almon's success. In 1770, he had only one servant, Thomas Adams. Public Record Office, TS 11/177, 765.

[11] Raven, James, 'The Book Trades', in Rivers, Isabel (ed.), *Books and their Readers: New Essays*, Leicester U.P., 2001, 28.

master's account, he takes the serving of the papers all to himself. Almon had entrusted him also to procure the binding of his books; and on this he takes a profit to himself; but his master finding out his intrigues, resolves to dismiss him and make an arrangement with Debrett; upon which Stockdale accuses Almon of treachery, but having for some time laid the plan now ready for execution, and by this pitiful means mentioned, scraped together about forty pounds, he takes to himself a wife, not caring whether she had one eye or two as long as she had got fifty or sixty pounds in money.'

The reference to Mrs. Stockdale indicates that Ridgway was not the author himself, despite being the source of much of the information contained in the article. It was not only an unflattering picture of his own sister but incorrect: the Stockdales had been married for several years at the time. Ridgway cannot have read the manuscript carefully before he published it, or he would have corrected it. The article gave no reason for their breach. The writer also referred to the Almon's *Courant*, adding, 'on Stockdale's leaving him, the paper was also taken away from Almon and given to Stockdale.' Somebody seems to have approved of him in 1780.

It would certainly have been difficult for Stockdale to save very much from his pay. There is no record of what Almon paid him, but we know that when John Hatchard set up his first shop in Piccadilly in 1797, he paid his man, George, two-and-a-half guineas a month, or just under thirteen shillings a week. Stockdale possibly started at a similar wage but by 1780, Almon probably paid him, as an experienced shopman, often left in charge, about £1 a week. Altick has pointed out that shopmen, who had completed their apprenticeship, earned between 4 and 16 shillings a week plus board, while clerks in merchants' offices made about £1 (20 shillings) a week. Stockdale had not been an apprentice but he doubtless lived out with his family and did not board with his employer. Altick also drew attention to the fairly obvious fact that the working man's wage at this time virtually ruled out book-buying. 'If a man in the lower bracket of the white-neckcloth class – an usher at a school, for instance, or a merchant's clerk – had a taste for owning books, he would have had to choose between buying a newly published quarto volume and a good pair of breeches (each cost from 10s. to 12s.), or between a volume of essays and month's supply of tea and sugar for his family of six (2s.6d.).'[12]

Setting up as a bookseller in London probably required less capital than setting up in America, where the booksellers were almost without exception still printers at this stage.[13] Stockdale, like Almon before him, could publish and sell books which had been printed for him by one or more of the many London printers: neither of them needed the significant amount of capital required to buy a press and type. It is also possible that just as Almon had been encouraged by Earl Temple to set up as an opposition bookseller, Stockdale had been given an advance indication that he would receive government work, for he was soon known to be 'one of the King's New Friends'. Someone may have hinted that Almon's days were numbered and that a move might be advisable.

Stockdale was lucky enough to obtain the tenancy of the shop three doors away from the Almon-Debrett premises (at a rental of £75 a year) and started his own business at 181 Piccadilly, at the corner of Duke Street, justifying the same address and imprint as Almon's at no. 178, namely, 'Piccadilly – opposite Burlington House'. Stockdale's shop was immediately opposite the entrance gateway. Among the many illustrations showing different views of Piccadilly, the writer has been unable to find a single one showing no. 181, despite a search by the Royal Academy staff, but John Tallis (son of a bookseller of that

---

[12] Humphreys, Arthur. L., *Piccadilly Bookmen: Memorials of the House of Hatchard*, London: Hatchard, 1893, 33; Altick, Richard D., *The English Common Reader*, 2nd ed., Columbus: Ohio State U.P., 1998, 53.

[13] Amory, Hugh, 'Reinventing the Colonial Book', in Amory and Hall, 45.

name) made a sketch of it for his *London Street Views 1838-1840*.[14]

The house, together with its immediate neighbours to the west, is shown as four storeys tall, the windows of the upper storeys becoming progressively smaller, as was customary. While the building was only wide enough for two windows on each of the upper floors on the Piccadilly frontage, the return frontage on Duke Street was considerably longer and Tallis shows four windows on each floor there. It seems likely that there were four rooms on each of the three residential floors, so that Stockdale was able to accommodate his family above the shop and still have three or four rooms available for letting to past and future Presidents. There is, incidentally, no evidence to suggest that he ever rented rooms out to any lesser mortals, but he may well have done so.

Tallis also shows that by 1838, the booksellers had nearly all gone from this section of Piccadilly and been replaced by suppliers to Royalty: a poor exchange for book-lovers. Hatchards remained at 187 as 'Booksellers to The Royal Family', but Stockdale's former corner shop was occupied by 'Bit and Spur Makers to Her Majesty', while 185 boasted 'Whip Manufacturers to the Queen'. One might be forgiven for concluding that the Queen preferred horses to books.

By 1780, Stockdale had worked for Almon for about six years, so had obtained considerable experience. If Ridgway's own magazine is correct, he himself was sent for by Stockdale from Cheshire once he had set up on his own, presumably in 1780 or 1781. They fell out before long but Ridgway soon thought himself experienced enough to set up on his own at 196 Piccadilly, shortly before the appearance of *The Intrepid Magazine* in 1784. Shortly after that he moved around the corner to York Street, St. James's Square, but eventually returned to Piccadilly (to no. 170) in 1806.

---

[14] London Topographical Society, 2nd ed., 2002, 86.

During the first few months after Almon handed over to Debrett, their names appeared jointly on the imprint of the business, but Almon was clearly easing Debrett in and played only a minimal part in it himself. At some time in 1781, he dropped out of the picture completely, although he had still not accounted in full for all royalties due from him. Thomas Pownall had earlier arranged with Almon that Amelia Barry, the daughter of Lewis Evans, the American explorer, should receive the royalties on a work which had used her father's maps and other information. Almon had not paid them, and Franklin was asked for his help. Franklin received a letter from John McGill from London, dated August 20, 1781: 'In consequence of your esteemed commands, soon after my arrival here I waited upon the house of your friend Mr Almon in Piccadilly, in order to obtain from him what you requested for our mutual friend Mrs Barry of Leghorn, but to my disappointment, was informed by Mr. Debrett, his successor, that he was retired some distance into the country, and that he very seldom came to town.' The reference to 'your friend' is interesting. By that time Franklin must have known Almon for the best part of eighteen years.[15]

We shall see later that Almon made a comeback, albeit not to Piccadilly. Before continuing with Stockdale's story, we should look at Almon's long career up to 1780. We have seen that he was an extremely shrewd writer, and that he had succeeded in persuading many members of the opposition that his shop should be a first resort, whether for purchases, or for discussing the possibility of his publishing a speech or pamphlet. It was the constant wearing-down of the British troops, coupled with the victories at Saratoga and Yorktown, that principally secured American independence. However, Almon, like Burke, Price, Day and many others, had helped by asserting that the colonists had a just cause, and by emphasising that, though they might be

---

[15] *Franklin Papers*, 35: 331, 388; Almon was not far away: he lived at Boxmoor in Hertfordshire.

defeated time and again, they could never be conquered. Eventually the message got through to Lord North's administration and, some time later, even to the King.

Not everyone regarded Almon as a reliable pro-American. We have already seen the dismay he caused when he published a reply to Dickinson's *Farmer's Letters*. Similarly, on June 20, 1779, William Lee, one of the distinguished Virginian brothers, expressed his misgivings in the strongest terms in a letter to Ralph Izard, the South Carolina friend of Henry Laurens: 'Don't you think that everything relative to America had better be sent in the first instance to Miller, for the *London Evening*, than to Almon? This man, besides that he is not in my opinion friendly to our cause, plays so many tricks as a publisher, that the intelligence is seldom so public as it ought to be.' The suggestion that Almon was not friendly to the cause of America is a startling one.[16]

A post-war critic of Almon's was Rev. William Jackson, who claimed in the *Morning Post* on October 16, 1784, that he had merely pretended to sympathise with the Americans, so that he could sell their information to the newspapers. Some of the information, it was claimed, he had first obtained from the American newspapers in the coffee-houses. A modern critic, who called Almon 'a thoroughgoing rogue', was Lucyle Werkmeister, who worked on the assumption that Jackson's allegations were true – as they may have been.[17]

Although Almon on more than one occasion felt disenchanted with both the administration and the opposition, the writer has been unable to detect any wavering by him from his support for the American cause. Even if he did occasionally

---

[16] Ford, Worthington Chauncey, *Letters of William Lee*, Brooklyn: Historical Printing Club, 1891, 2: 676.
[17] Werkmeister, Lucyle, *The London Daily Press 1772-1792*, Lincoln: U. of Nebraska P., 1963, 114.

publish answers to pro-American pamphlets, he personally consistently *wrote* only pro-American sentiments.

Two other writers were critical of Almon. Horace Walpole called him a 'rogue' in a letter to William Mason; and George Woodfall, the son of Henry Sampson Woodfall, who had published the Junius letters, made the comment, 'Remember Almon was the most notorious liar of his day.'[18]

From the criticisms referred to, it is clear that Almon had made some enemies, but it is difficult to discover exactly what he did that was wrong, or what significant lies he told. The fact that ministers found him a thorn in their side is, of course, no ground for doubting his integrity. Having regard to the poor standard of Lord North and his colleagues, one might say that the converse is true. If he was indeed a liar, then perhaps some of his complaints about Stockdale and his colleagues were also untrue, or exaggerated. It seems tolerably clear that, unlike Stockdale, Almon was never accused of piracy – at least, not in a court. So too, unlike Stockdale's brother-in-law, Ridgway, and his son, John Joseph Stockdale, Almon was never accused of being a blackmailer.

It took Stockdale a little while to get going: he clearly did not have a list of best-sellers up his sleeve when he parted company with Almon, and probably had to be careful with his limited funds. The *Monthly Review* dealt in classic critic's style with one of his few publications to appear in 1780: *A Satire on the Present Times*, 'the second edition'. 'There cannot be a severer satire on the times than that such a dull rhapsody as this should run, as the title page asserts, to a second edition. We suspect, however, that this is not only the first, but will in all probability be the last edition of this very insipid performance.' Stockdale was not showing any originality if it was indeed only the first edition. 'It was a basic ploy of the advertising publisher to boast of perhaps

---

[18] Rea, Robert R., 'Mason, Walpole and that Rogue Almon', *Huntingdon Library Quarterly*, 1960, 23: 23; British Library, Add. MSS 27,783, f.20.

fourth or fifth editions which were in fact reissues of the second or even first. It appears, for example, that James Lackington issued a 'seventh' edition of his infamous *Memoirs* in succession to the 'third'.[19]

Werkmeister was satisfied that the real reason that Almon retired, or pretended to retire was not ill-health, but to avoid a prosecution for a libel on the Russian ambassador, contained in his *Courant* at the beginning of 1781. If he really was scared off by the government, as she maintained, it is difficult to understand her claim that he almost immediately resumed his activities, including the conduct of the *Courant*, a course he knew to be dangerous. It also has to be borne in mind that Almon had advertised his business for sale in the previous summer, referring then to his 'want of health'.[20]

On February 5, 1781, the masthead of the *Courant* still announced: 'All information, letters, orders and advertisements for this paper, are desired to be sent to J. Almon, bookseller.' That issue, somewhat surprisingly, having regard to Almon's bitter remarks about his former servant, contained an advertisement for the seventh edition of David Hartley's *Letters on the American War*, 'printed for J. Stockdale (from Mr Almon's), No. 181 Piccadilly.'

On the following day the paper came out with Stockdale's name on the masthead in place of Almon's. The printing of the paper must have been done during the course of the day for an evening edition, for the whole issue was taken up with a report of the trial for treason of Lord George Gordon, which had ended only that morning. He was defended by Lloyd Kenyon and Thomas Erskine, and it was Erskine's final speech, delivered during the night, that helped to secure an acquittal. Lord Campbell, a later Chief Justice and Lord Chancellor commented

---

[19] Raven, James, *Judging New Wealth – Popular Publishing and Responses to Commerce in England, 1750-1800*, Oxford U.P., 1992, 37.

[20] Werkmeister, 121-123.

in the following century: 'Luckily for him, he was defended by
an advocate who on this occasion first gave full proof of those
wonderful powers which afterwards rendered his name so
illustrious.' Stockdale was to benefit from Erskine's 'wonderful
powers' a few years later, when being tried before Lloyd
Kenyon, by then Chief Justice.[21]

Stockdale's first issue of the *Courant* concluded the account
of the trial with the passage, 'Judge Willes then informed Lord
George that he was discharged, and of course at liberty to
depart, and his Lordship AT NEAR SIX O'CLOCK THIS
MORNING went from the Hall, attended by his brothers.' We
talk nowadays of the desirability of night courts. In eighteenth-
century England there were *day and night* courts: once a trial
started, the judge usually sat on until it was finished, with short
breaks only. Such trials were often finished quite quickly, as the
defendant was as a rule not permitted to give evidence in his
own defence, and as evidence for the defence from others was
generally regarded as a waste of time. If necessary, as in
Gordon's case, the trial continued through the night.

When Almon handed over to Debrett, and Stockdale set up
almost next door, his former customers had the choice of pat-
ronising Debrett, whom they cannot have known very well, or
Stockdale – or of going elsewhere. Inevitably, some preferred
the devil they knew. Fortunately for Stockdale, Thomas Day,
who was only two years older than him, but had been published
by Almon since the beginning of 1776, had taken a liking to him.
He decided to let Stockdale publish his work, despite the fact
that many of his own author friends were content with Joseph
Johnson.[22] In 1783, Day gave Stockdale the first volume of his
three-volume book for children, *History of Sandford and Merton.*

---

[21] Campbell, John Lord, *The Lives of the Chief Justices of England,* London:
John Murray, 1849, 2: 531.
[22] Tyson, Gerald P., *Joseph Johnson – A Liberal Publisher,* Iowa City: U. of
Iowa P., 1979.

He was also happy to let him republish some of his earlier works. According to Ridgway's *Intrepid Magazine* article, Day read his drafts over to Stockdale: 'Does Mr Day, whose talents as well as integrity entitle him to respect, know this contemptible book-seller, with whom he is intimate enough to read to him his performances previous to publication?' The answer, clearly, was Yes. The connection with Day was a close one and turned out to be extremely important for the new bookseller.

Stockdale and Debrett had a healthy rivalry from the start, despite the fact that they supported different political factions and so inevitably published opposing views on some topics. Ian Christie, when undertaking research for his book on the end of North's government, drew heavily on the printed parliamentary division lists published by the two rivals in their first months in business on their own account. The lists have discrepancies in them, and Christie came to the conclusion that Debrett's lists were slightly more reliable than Stockdale's, at any rate when dealing with the opposition vote.[23] Stockdale's alignment with the government became clear at an early date, as did Debrett's with the opposition. However, whereas Debrett followed in Almon's shoes in the political sense, Stockdale undoubtedly took over much of Almon's business.

John Cartwright, the well-known radical, had asked Almon in 1776, to publish his call for annual elections and other reforms, with the title *Take Your Choice!*. Almon's second edition bore the altered title *The Legislative Rights of the Commonalty Vindicated, or, Take Your Choice!*. In 1782, Dilly and Stockdale jointly published Cartwright's *Give us our Rights!*, but he then seems to have realised that Stockdale's political affinities were hostile to reform. As a result, *A Letter from John Cartwright to a Friend at Boston* was put out by the new opposition publisher, Ridgway, though why he was chosen in preference to Debrett is not clear.

---

[23] Christie, Ian, *The End of North's Ministry 1780-1782*, London: Macmillan, 1958, 378.

At least three active members of the Society for Constitutional Information, who might have been expected to follow Cartwright's decision and abandon Stockdale once his political leanings became apparent, continued to patronise him. The most important one was Day, the second was Dr. John Jebb, and the third was Capel Lofft. Day and Jebb thought alike on many important topics. In 1784, Stockdale published Day's *Letters of Marius*, which contained his views on a number of political topics. The first three letters were addressed to Jebb, and the next two to John Dalrymple, Earl of Stair, a former author of Almon's, several of whose pamphlets Stockdale was also publishing.

Day's principal biographer has written that the dedication of the letters to Jebb was most appropriate, 'for hardly any reformer held so many opinions which coincided with Day's. He had opposed the American war and advocated the peace; he had urged a parliamentary reform which included annual parliaments, universal suffrage, and equal representation; he attacked the coalition and the East India bill; he upheld the rights of juries to hand in a general verdict; and he opposed the slave trade.'[24] Day's opposition to slavery and his support of America were, as recorded earlier, two of the main points that had been a feature of his friendship with the young law student from South Carolina, John Laurens. Jebb's views were to appeal greatly to John Adams.

Day made his opposition to the American war clear once again in his *Reflections upon the Present State of England and the Independence of America*, which Stockdale put out in 1782, after the virtual end of hostilities. Day made a very good point about the lot of the English opponents to the war. 'A very considerable portion of this nation has been long in avowed opposition to public measures; because they believed those measures, with

---

[24] Gignilliat, G. W., *The Author of Sandford and Merton*, New York: Columbia U.P., 1932, 216.

whatever success attended, adverse to the interests and liberties of their country. These men have been reviled with every odious epithet which slander, falsehood, and malice could invent.' Twentieth-century British opponents of the Suez adventure, and Americans against the Vietnam war, will readily understand how Day felt.

Day's pamphlet contained a stinging attack on British complacency and then dealt with the views of the American Peace Commissioners, 'amongst whom are included Dr. Franklin, Mr. Adams, and Mr. Laurens'. Day had been provided with them in detail by his friend Henry Laurens. Gignilliat wrote of Day's important pamphlet, 'In his writing he upheld practically all the ideas which Laurens had been urging on the British ministry; a prompt termination of the war, no peace separate from France, absolute independence of the colonies.'

Once the war was over, Stockdale could concentrate on more peaceful subjects, such as books for children and geographical works. Fortunately for him, the American contacts initiated by Almon were not only to prosper and grow, but also to help him with those other lines.

Illus. 8. John Adams by John Singleton Copley

7

John Adams Stays with John Stockdale

It is difficult to think of anyone, other than George Washington, who served the infant – and adolescent – United States better than John Adams. Although he is best remembered for his part in the Declaration of Independence and his later four-year term as the second President of the United States, his ten years' service in Europe made a major contribution to the recognition of the new nation and to the peace process. However, we shall concentrate on Adams as a bibliophile and author, and on his relationship with the similarly inclined Thomas Jefferson – and also, obviously, on his links with John Stockdale. Adams wrote on April 1, 1778, to Henry Laurens, as President of Congress, to report his safe arrival at Bordeaux after a dangerous crossing of the Atlantic. But for one very short trip home in 1779, he was to remain in Europe for ten years as one of his country's principal and most effective representatives.

Adams joined Benjamin Franklin in Paris on April 9, 1778, and on the very next day the shrewd old public relations expert took the new arrival to dine with a most distinguished company, including Anne-Robert-Jacquest Turgot, the former Comptroller of Finances in France. Turgot and several of his pro-American friends had been involved with Franklin in the production of a periodical, *Affaires de l'Angleterre et de l'Amerique,* and they soon had Adams writing for it as well.[1] Turgot, like Franklin, was a firm believer in the efficacy of a single chamber for a legislature,

---

[1] Haraszti, Zoltan, *John Adams and the Prophets of Progress,* Cambridge: Harvard U.P., 1952, 140.

and said as much, forcibly, in a letter to his friend Dr Richard
Price, which he had written on March 22, a few days before
meeting Adams. Price only published the letter in 1784, after
Turgot's death, in his pamphlet, *The Importance of the American
Revolution*, but Turgot and Adams doubtless discussed the topic
when they met, for Adams held equally strong views about the
need for a bicameral system. He accordingly disagreed strongly
with both Turgot and Franklin on the point, and when in
London was to write his most important work, a three-volume
work on constitutions, to demolish their arguments. Stockdale
was to publish it.

In 1778, the year of Adams's arrival, Franklin was appointed
as the sole minister in France, so Adams found himself without
a job. Nobody complained about his work and nobody thanked
him for it. In the following year, Adams returned home but after
a few weeks was requested by Congress to return to Europe, as
minister plenipotentiary, to negotiate peace and trade with
Britain in due course. He still felt aggrieved about the ending of
his earlier mission, but was mollified on receiving a letter from
President Laurens, apologising for the fact that he had been so
badly treated by Congress, and 'dismissed without censure or
applause'.[2]

After his return to Europe, Adams tried to keep himself
informed about English matters, and also to keep the British
informed about the American point of view. One of his contacts
in London was the American, Thomas Digges, who arranged for
a supply of newspapers. Almon's paper clearly met with
approval, for on May 13, 1780, Adams wrote to Digges: 'You
may stop the *Evening Post* and the London *Packet* for the future,
but send on the *Courant*, if you please.' As the war was still
raging, Digges on December 22 warned Adams to be careful:
'When you write to Mr W. S. C. you are requested not to *direct*

---

[2] McCullough, David, *John Adams*, New York: Simon & Schuster, 2001,
226.

but only mark the letter thus, X on the seal part, and put it under a cover directed to Mr. Stockdale, Bookseller, Piccadilly, London.' This could well have been the first time that Adams saw the name of the newly-established bookseller. Unfortunately, Digges disappeared in the following year, taking with him the £400 that Benjamin Franklin had sent to him for the relief of American prisoners.[3]

Rather better as a contact in London was Edmund Jenings, who travelled a great deal in Europe, and who dropped in from time to time at Almon's shop, and later at Stockdale's. Adams made a note about him in his dairy on November 3, 1782: 'He is related to several principal families in America, and to several great families in England; was bred to the law in the Temple, and practised as chamber counsel, but not otherwise.'[4] It was probably Arthur Lee, the Virginian, who introduced Adams to Jenings, for during 1777 and 1778, using different cover names, Jenings had often communicated with Lee from London. For example, on April 26, 1778, he had written to Lee: 'I do not know whether you have a collection of treaties, published by Almon; if you have not, the bearer hereof will present them to you. If you think they may be of use to any of your friends, I will send other sets over.'[5]

Adams was very concerned about the pro-British articles being produced in London by the loyalist, Joseph Galloway, and decided to counter them in the English press, with 'the assistance of friends in London'. He was far-sighted enough to include a discussion of the post-war relationship of the two

---

[3] Taylor, Robert J. and others (eds.), *Papers of John Adams*, Cambridge: Harvard U.P., 1977-, 9: 307; 10: 907, hereafter cited as *Adams Papers*; Brands, H. W., *The First American*, New York: Doubleday, 2000, 586.

[4] Butterfield, L. H. (ed.), *Diary and Autobiography of John Adams*, Cambridge: Harvard U.P., 1961, 3: 44.

[5] Lee, R. H., *Life of Arthur Lee*, Boston: Wells and Lilly, 1829, 2: 91.

countries, and to try and reassure his British readers about the future goodwill of the independent United States.[6]

While in Paris, Adams asked Jenings for his help in connection with his *Dissertation on the Canon and Feudal Law*, 'a kind of philosophical and political rhapsody, written when I was not very old, and when I had certainly seen very little of this world, and knew but little of men or things'.[7] We have seen how Almon produced the dissertation, with other Massachusetts documents, under the title *The True Sentiments of America*. Adams asked Jenings to obtain a copy of the Almon publication for him, and also to get Almon to republish it once again, this time in his *Remembrancer*, the value of which Adams clearly appreciated. Jenings failed with the latter commission, but seems to have succeeded with the former, for John Quincy Adams later had a copy of *The True Sentiments* in his superb library. Like his father and Jefferson, he also collected thousands of books – apart from the ones he acquired from his father.[8]

Adams disagreed with Franklin on many matters, including the Doctor's lifestyle in Paris, and he was often critical of him in his letters home. Eventually Adams expressed a hatred of Franklin, though the Doctor never responded in similar terms.[9] The lawyer and the printer were certainly agreed on the value of the printed word: Adams was quite as publicity-conscious as Franklin and appreciated the worth of the written works of the pro-American former governor of Massachusetts, Thomas Pownall. In England, before the war, Pownall's wife had 'encouraged him in his writings, stimulated his interest in

---

[6] Ferling, John, *Setting the World Ablaze*, Oxford U.P., 2000, 215. Galloway had been a fellow-member of Congress, but Adams had not trusted him even then. McCullough, 86.

[7] *Adams Papers*, 9: 221.

[8] Ford, W. C., *A Catalogue of the Books of J. Q. Adams*, Boston: Athenaeum, 1938.

[9] Middlekauff, Robert, *Benjamin Franklin and his Enemies*, Berkeley: U. of California P., 1998.

politics, brought important people to their home for dinner and evenings of conversation, and helped entertain weekend guests like Benjamin Franklin, William Samuel Johnson, John Almon and Horace Walpole'. In 1780, Almon published, anonymously, Pownall's *Memorial Addressed to the Sovereigns of Europe*, which 'was immediately successful and gained unusually wide publicity … its authorship was easily discovered'.[10]

Adams recognised the potential value of many of Pownall's remarks and arranged for the work to be translated into French by John Luzac, the editor of the Leiden *Gazette*. On September 23, 1780, Adams wrote to Jenings from Amsterdam, where he was hard at work enlisting the support of the Dutch, 'I wish the translation might appear as soon as possible, because it may have some effects here.' Adams's grandson, Charles Francis, later wrote: 'He set before the Dutch nation an abridged French translation of Governor Pownall's *Memorial*, which he justly regarded as effective testimony from a good quarter of the character of the Americans, and likewise translations of the narratives of Generals Howe and Burgoyne, calculated, as coming from enemies, to give a strong impression of their means of resistance.'[11]

In his letter to Jenings, Adams not only stated his conviction, 'that English will be the most respectable language in the world, and the most universally read and spoken in the next century, if not before the close of this', but also made clear his great love of the language. 'I have written to Congress a serious request, that they would appoint an academy for refining, correcting, improving, and ascertaining the English language.' This, at the height of a war for survival. Adams was impressed by the contents of Pownall's book, but did not care for the style at all and so,

---

[10] Schutz, John A., *Thomas Pownall*, Glendale, Calif.: Arthur H. Clarke, 1951, 200, 255; Johnson was to become President of Columbia College.
[11] Adams, Charles Francis, *The Works of John Adams*, Boston: Little, Brown, 1856, hereafter cited as C. F. Adams, 7: 248, 9: 509, 1: 330.

spurred on by his love of good English, and unconcerned about any copyright considerations, decided to 'translate' it into a more readable form.[12]

By the time the Adams version was ready for the press, Almon had handed over his business to Debrett and Stockdale had set up on his own. Adams clearly knew Almon as a bookseller and publisher, but he cannot have known much about either Debrett or Stockdale at that stage. It is not clear who suggested Stockdale as a suitable publisher to Adams. Jenings had probably met Stockdale on different visits to his master's shop. He may also have consulted his fellow-barrister, Thomas Day, about Stockdale's abilities. However, in a letter that he wrote to Adams from Brussels on January 31, 1781, Jenings seems to disclaim any credit for choosing him, while praising Stockdale's qualities, 'his integrity, principles and knowledge.'[13] In any event, it was Stockdale who published Adams's *A Translation of the Memorial … into Common Sense and Intelligible English* in January 1781, as one of his first productions.

This publication demonstrated that Stockdale was able to benefit from his employer's departure, even though Almon's former shop was still competing, in the hands of Debrett, and despite the fact that he personally had decided to support the government rather than the opposition – a point that may not have been readily apparent, especially from a distance, in the early days of the business. This publication also marked the beginning of the direct Adams-Stockdale link, which was to have important consequences for the young bookseller. There cannot be many publishers – even in America – who in their very first months in business, manage to land a future President of the United States as one of their authors – especially one who

---

[12] C. F. Adams, 7: 332. Governor Pownall, an Englishman and a Member of Parliament, must have had mixed feelings on learning that an American lawyer-politician thought that his English required translation.

[13] *Adams Papers*, 11: 93.

will speedily introduce two more future Presidents to the business.

In his preface to the work – which he had slimmed down to 45 pages from the original 127 – Adams gave his reason for producing a second English language version, explaining that the original contained 'so many quaint words and dark expressions, intermixed with so many good thoughts and so much knowledge of America, that it seems worth translating'. Many years later he was blunter about Pownall as an author, while still praising him as a man: 'A reader who has patience to search for good sense, in an uncouth and disgusting style, will find in these writings proof of a thinking mind, and more sagacity than in any thing that remains of his two more celebrated successors [as Governor of Massachusetts], Bernard or Hutchinson. Pownall was a Whig, a friend of liberty, and a lover of his country, and he considered North America a part of his country as much as England, Scotland or Ireland.' He added, 'In 1783 he made me repeated visits with his lady at Auteuil near Paris, and dined with us more than once. Near the end of the same year he visited me again at Stockdale's in Piccadilly.'[14]

It would be difficult to overestimate the importance of this work of an English Whig which, according the editors of the *Adams Papers*, 'influenced John Adams' views of foreign policy more than any other published work, and Adams' revision of Pownall's pamphlet constituted a clear, focused exposition of the principles that guided his diplomacy for the remainder of his career.'[15]

While acting as minister in the Netherlands after the capture of Henry Laurens, Adams was asked many questions about America by a leading Amsterdam lawyer, Dr. Calkoen. Adams found that giving adequate answers through an interpreter was unsatisfactory and so asked the Dutchman to submit his

---

[14] C. F. Adams, 10: 241.

[15] *Adams Papers*, 11: ix.

questions in writing. He produced twenty-six questions, which Adams answered in a series of letters. Calkoen was so impressed that he used them for lecture purposes. When Adams eventually had his answers printed privately at the end of 1786, he concluded his introduction with the comment, 'These papers are now printed in order to preserve them, but by no means to be made public for the present'. He added proudly that the letters had helped to win Dutch opinion over in favour of the American cause. Although Adams is known to have overstated his own contribution to some historic events, that claim was probably justified.[16]

A Frenchman's questions led to Jefferson producing his *Notes on the State of Virginia*; a Dutchman's queries led to Adams writing his *Letters to Dr. Calkoen*. While the former work was to become world famous after Stockdale had republished Jefferson's privately printed version, Adams's work shared the fate of most privately produced works.

Shortly before signing the Peace Treaty in Paris on September 3, 1783, Adams decided that he was entitled to a vacation, especially as he had suffered from serious ill-health. On September 1, he wrote to his wife, 'I propose a tour of three weeks to England and shall take my son with me, whose company is the greatest pleasure of my life.' By the time he wrote to Abigail on October 14, he had decided to increase the visit to six weeks, but he in fact stayed for just over two months.[17]

Adams was clearly delighted to have his son's company, and one can understand why: despite his youth, the boy had been away from his father in Europe for the best part of two years. He had 'lent' John Quincy to Francis Dana, his own secretary, when he had been despatched to St. Petersburg to obtain the recognition of the United States by Catherine the Great. Dana

---

[16] C. F. Adams, 10: 241.
[17] Butterfield, L. H. and others (eds.), *Adams Family Correspondence*, Cambridge: Harvard U.P., 1963, 5: 231, 255.

needed John Quincy as a French interpreter, and the two of them had set off for Russia on July 7, 1781, four days before the boy's *fourteenth* birthday. In St. Petersburg John Quincy 'haunted the booksellers, the start of a lifelong hobby, buying many volumes for shipment home'. On his journey back to his father, on his own at fifteen, he found that there were other interesting things in this world: books were all very well, but he discovered the joys of feminine company, and the pleasure of being lionised. The fifteen-year-old lingered so long in Stockholm, Copenhagen and Hamburg, that his journey back to his father took six months: from October 1782 to April 1783, a period that could not be wholly blamed on the bad weather. During that time, like many a modern parent with a backpacking teenager, 'a frantic John Adams was asking everyone who had been in northern Europe if they had seen his wandering son, for Johnny made little effort to keep his father apprised of his whereabouts.'[18]

When father and son landed at Dover on October 24, 1783, it was the first occasion on which either of them had set foot in the land of their forefathers, but it was by no means to be the last for either of them. John Adams must have had some feelings of apprehension, if he really meant what he had written to John Jay about the British in the previous August – after the effective end of hostilities: 'They hate us, universally, from the throne to the footstool, and would annihilate us, if in their power.' He was soon to have that assessment challenged.[19]

On October 26, the Adamses arrived in London, and checked in at Osborne's hotel in the Adelphi, a new development, just off the Strand and very close to Franklin's old lodgings in Craven Street. The Adelphi was the work of the

---

[18] Nagel, Paul C., *John Quincy Adams: A Public Life, a Private Life*, New York: Knopf, 1997, 29. Jenings was originally meant to accompany Dana, but John Quincy replaced him when he withdrew.

[19] C. F. Adams, 7: 610.

Illus. 9. John Jay by Gilbert Stuart

Adam brothers, and John Adams was delighted to find himself in John Street, Adam Street and John Adam Street. Later, when writing of the coincidence, he could not resist the temptation to add an 's' to the name of the Adam family. Although Mr. Osborne was a fellow-American, his charges proved too steep for Adams, who complained in his diary: 'I am obliged here to give thirteen shillings a day for a parlor, a bedchamber and another bedchamber over it for my son, without any dining-room or ante-chamber. This is dearer than my lodgings at the Hotel de Roi in Paris.'[20]

Because of the cost, Adams decided to change his lodgings after only three days, but before he did so, on his second day in London, he went to see his fellow Peace Commissioner, John Jay, with whom he had enjoyed working in Paris. Jay, who was staying in Harley Street with William Bingham, a future United States Senator, had also come to England to visit Bath, in view of his bad health.[21] All four of the American Peace Commissioners suffered from ill health at the end of 1783. Henry Laurens was the first to use the waters of Bath, with some success, and may have persuaded both Adams and Jay to follow him there. Jay's brother, Sir James Jay, was Adams's physician and also recommended the spa waters.[22] The only one of the quartet who did not feel the need to go there, despite his poor health, was the oldest, Franklin, just coming up to his 78th. birthday. He was a great swimmer, who in younger days used to swim in the Thames. Had he not been so ill, he would probably just as soon have tried the River Seine as the Roman bath in Bath.

Both Adams and Jay favoured the resumption of trade between Britain and America and almost certainly discussed that

---

[20] Butterfield, *Diary*, 3: 148. Extracts from the letter to the *Boston Patriot*, quoted below, start at 149.
[21] Pellew, George, *John Jay*, Boston: Houghton Mifflin, 1890, 224.
[22] McCullough, 300.

topic at Bingham's lodgings. Early in the following year, Stockdale published an anonymous pamphlet, *A Letter from an American now Resident in London*, making the excellent point, 'The United States, stretching through such a variety of climates, abounding in such various productions, and affording such a vast field for the consumption of European manufactures, most naturally have a very intimate and active commerce with the different states of Europe. From adventitious circumstances, peculiarly favourable to Great Britain, no nation possesses opportunities of so effectually promoting this connection.'

Although the author's name did not appear, the letter bore the dateline 'Harley Street, Cavendish Square, December 16, 1783'. The author was Bingham and not his distinguished guest, John Jay, who was to return to London years later to negotiate the controversial trade treaty bearing his name. It is clear that Adams was the one who thought of Stockdale as an appropriate publisher, for by that date he was lodging with him and his family over his bookshop.

After October 27, 1783, there is an eight months' gap in Adams's diary, so that it contains no entry at all for the two months during which he made Stockdale's shop and home his base. Fortunately, on February 17, 1812, Adams wrote a letter to the *Boston Patriot* which dealt with this period. 'I was not long at the Adelphi, but soon removed to private lodgings, which by the way were ten times more public, and took apartments at Mr. Stockdale's, in Piccadilly, where Mr. Laurens had lately lodged before me. Here I had a great opportunity of learning, for Debrett was at the next door, the state of the current literature of London. I will not enlarge upon this subject at present, if ever. I found it exactly similar to what I had seen in Paris. The newspapers, the magazines, the reviews, the daily pamphlets, were all in the hands of hirelings, men of no character.'

Adams went on to quote the words of a leading printer and bookseller, possibly Strahan, without identifying him: 'The men of learning are all stark mad. There are in this city at least one hundred men of the best education, the best classical students, the most accomplished writers, any one of whom I can hire for one guinea a day to go into my closet and write for me whatever I please, for or against any man or any cause.'

Adams moved to Stockdale's address at 181 Piccadilly, on October 29. It is almost certain that he had earlier asked Laurens to recommend good, but reasonably priced lodgings in London, or that Laurens had strongly recommended Stockdale without being asked. As early as November 8, John Adams wrote two letters to his wife from Stockdale's address, expressing his satisfaction with the visit. 'My son and I have been here this fortnight and have been very civilly and obligingly treated by some private gentlemen. (*But this Government?*) It is a fine country; but it is undone by prosperity.' 'I have met with an agreeable reception here, as agreeable as I wish. In short I have been received here exactly as I wished to be.'[23]

On November 9, Adams wrote a letter to the President of Congress, justifying his decision to leave his post and to visit England. He stated that he had been seized in Paris in mid-September with a dangerous fever, and that he had come to London on the advice of his friends. The journey had already paid off: 'My health is so much improved that I am persuaded the last sickness has been of service to me, having never enjoyed, since my great sickness at Amsterdam, so good health as at present.' He added that as he had come in a private capacity, he had not called on any of the ministers, but he gave his assessment of the Fox-North coalition, which was on the point of collapse. 'The Whig part of the present administration are much embarrassed with the Tory part and their refugees, so that the spirit of the present administration, I must in duty say, is not so friendly to the United States as it might be.' Once again, he confirmed that there was little evidence of hatred on the part of the British, by writing, 'Mr. Jay had set off for London about

---

[23] Butterfield, *Adams Family Correspondence*, 5: 264, 266.

ten days before me, and, since my arrival we have been much together, and have found everything agreeable, notwithstanding the innumerable and incessant lies and nonsense of the newspapers.'[24]

After the improvement in his health, Adams may have had a relapse – or else a later lapse of memory – for in his letter to the *Boston Patriot* he continued: 'My health was very little improved by the exercise I had taken in and about London; nor did the entertainments and delights assist me much more. The change of air and diet from which I had entertained some hopes, had produced little effect. I continued feeble, low and drooping. The waters of Bath were still represented to me as an almost certain resource.'

Adams found that his lodgings were 'ten times more public' than Osborne's hotel. The principal reason for this was that Stockdale's bookshop was already a popular resort, both for those interested in browsing in, or even buying books, and for those interested in discussing politics or other topics. Among the callers Adams met was Dr. John Jebb, for whom he had a healthy respect and on November 9, the Adamses were invited to dinner at Jebb's house.[25] One can readily appreciate why Adams admired his host of that evening: Jebb was both a friend of the American cause and strongly in favour of constitutional reform. He was also one of that select band of men who were qualified in medicine and theology, as well as being a Fellow of the Royal Society. In 1782, Stockdale had published Jebb's *Select Cases of the Disorder Commonly Termed Paralysis of the Lower Extremities* and in 1783, some of his political writings. Earlier in the year a request had come from Ireland for the views of

---

[24] C. F. Adams, 8: 156.

[25] Allen, David Grayson et al. (eds), *The Diary of John Quincy Adams*, Cambridge: Harvard U.P., 1981, 1: 202. John Quincy kept a note of most of their engagements, without details. However, in a letter to his cousin, Elizabeth Cranch, dated April 18, 1784, he gave a lengthy account of the English visit. Butterfield, *Adams Family Correspondence*, 5: 322.

several constitutional reformers, on the proposals that had been made for the reform of the Irish parliament. Among those approached were Jebb, Price, Cartwright and Wyvill. Stockdale published both Jebb's and Wyvill's response. Jebb died in 1786; in the following year Stockdale, together with Thomas Cadell, Joseph Johnson and the Merrills of Cambridge, published *The Works of John Jebb* in three volumes, together with a biographical essay by Dr. John Disney.

Adams and Jebb hit it off so well together, that Colin Bonwick commented, 'Of all Adams's English friends, three stand out: Brand Hollis, Jebb, and especially Price.' Bonwick felt sure that Adams had discussions with other radicals as well, commenting: 'Although almost all record of Adams's political discussions with radicals has vanished, the hints and scraps that remain are sufficient to suggest that they were extensive.' He added that the most substantial fragment still in existence was the correspondence between Adams and Jebb.[26]

The Adamses next dined with an American businessman, Joshua Johnson, and his English wife, whom they had met earlier in France. The eight-year old girl in the house, Louisa Catherine, was understandably not mentioned in his diary by the sixteen-year-old John Quincy, but she was to become the First Lady of the United States in due course, as his wife. Later in November, the Adamses were invited to dinner by both Hartley and Oswald, their friendly British negotiating opponents. As well as accepting numerous dinner invitations, they also had plenty of time for visits to the theatre and for sightseeing.

On November 24, Adams wrote to J. G. Holtzhey, a medallist in Amsterdam, suggesting a way in which Stockdale might benefit from further sales. He claimed that since he had

---

[26] Bonwick, Colin, *English Radicals and the American Revolution*, Chapel Hill: U. of North Carolina P., 1977, 173, 175. For Adams and Jebb, see also, Page, Anthony, 'Liberty has an Asylum: John Jebb, British Radicalism and the American Revolution', *History*, 2002, 87: 204.

been in London, a number of gentlemen had 'expressed a desire
to have the medal struck by you in commemoration of the connection between your country and mine.' He asked for three of
each sort to be sent to Stockdale and added, 'The sooner they
arrive here the better – I fancy Mr. Stockdale would be able to
sell a great number of them here, if you should think proper to
send them to him for sale.'[27]

As noted earlier, one of Adams's visitors at the bookshop
was Governor Pownall – presumably without any interpreter.
On December 5, another visitor, the American naval hero, John
Paul Jones, who had attacked the British mainland during the
war, called in on his way to Paris. On December 14, Adams
reported to the President of Congress, 'On the fifth of this
month Capt. Jones arrived at my lodgings in Piccadilly with
dispatches.' As Marjorie Bowen, using the pseudonym George
R. Preedy, pointed out, 'The object of these was that overtures
should be made for a commercial treaty between the new
Republic and Great Britain. Mr. Adams received Paul Jones
cordially and directed that the dispatches should be taken to Dr.
Franklin.' Jones, a renegade Briton, had been concerned about
his safety in England, but Bowen added, 'Paul Jones found that
he had nothing to fear in London; his treatment was that which
a vain man finds the hardest to endure – he was ignored.' The
latter comment may safely be ignored, as Jones only made a
flying visit: he arrived in London at 9 p.m. and left it again, for
Paris, six hours later.[28]

While staying in Piccadilly, Adams saw a great deal of the two
most distinguished American painters resident in the city, Benjamin West and his student, John Singleton Copley, who had

---

[27] Adams Papers, Reel 107.
[28] Adams Papers, Reel 107; Preedy, George R., *The Life of Rear-Admiral
John Paul Jones*, London: Herbert Jenkins, 1940, 153; Mackay, James, *I have
not yet begun to fight: A Life of John Paul Jones*, Edinburgh: Mainstream, 1998,
249. Jones had named his ship *Bon Homme Richard*, in honour of Franklin's
sage 'source' of wise sayings.

already painted a portrait of Henry Laurens in 1782, after his release from the Tower (now in the National Portrait Gallery in Washington). Copley painted the splendid portrait of Adams, which Stockdale was to use as a book illustration in due course, and which is now in the Harvard University Portrait Collection. West made a study of Adams for his even more famous, though unfinished, painting of the four American Peace Commissioners in Paris, together with their secretary, William Temple Franklin, which is now in the Henry Francis du Pont Winterthur Museum in Delaware.

In his letter to the Boston newspaper Adams also wrote, in terms which scarcely hint at serious ill-health, 'Curiosity prompted me to trot about London as fast as good horses in a decent carriage could carry me'. Both painters helped to satisfy that curiosity. West obtained the King's permission to show Adams over Buckingham House (as it then was), where the book-loving tourist cast envious eyes over the library, which was to become the nucleus of the collection in the British Museum, and later, of the British Library. 'The King's library struck me with admiration; I wished for a week's time, but had but a few hours. The books were in perfect order, elegant in their editions, paper, binding, &c. but gaudy and extravagant in nothing. They were chosen with perfect taste and judgment; every book that a king ought to have always at hand, and as far as I could examine, and could be supposed capable of judging, none other.'

Copley obtained permission from Lord Mansfield to bring Adams to the Opening of Parliament and to witness the introduction of the Prince of Wales, who had just attained his majority. Standing in the lobby of the Lords, Adams heard Black Rod calling out, 'Where is Mr. Adams, Lord Mansfield's friend?' Someone pointed out to Adams that is was not all that long since he had heard Mansfield warning the Lords about him, 'My Lords, if you do not kill him, he will kill you.'

At some time in November or December, Stockdale must have discussed with his guest the possibility of further reprints of his earlier work. Stockdale liked to reprint anything that would sell: Adams liked to see his own work in print, or back in print. Nine years earlier, in November 1774, on his return to Boston from Congress, he had found the *Massachusetts Gazette* to be 'teeming with political speculations, and Massachusettensis shining like the moon among the lesser stars. I instantly resolved to enter the lists with him.'[29] In his second letter to the newspaper Adams, using the pen-name Novanglus, had included a reference to Governor Pownall: 'Mr. Pownall seems to have been a friend to liberty and to our constitution, and to have had an aversion to all plots against either.' In his third letter he shrewdly referred to other British friends: 'But we know that the people of Great Britain are not united against us. We know that many of the most virtuous and independent of the nobility and gentry are for us, and among them the best bishop that adorns the bench, as great a judge as the nation can boast, and the greatest statesman it ever saw,' He was clearly referring to Shipley, Camden and Chatham. Years later, when making jaded comments about the British, Adams seems to have forgotten about the many British friends.

The last letter in the series was published two days before the shots rang out at Lexington in April 1775. Someone brought the letters to the attention of Almon and later in that year he published them in London in his *Remembrancer*. They next appeared in a Dutch translation for which Adams was responsible. This was published in Amsterdam by Walter Holtrop in 1782, as part of Adams's plan to increase the support of the Dutch – a plan which was largely successful. In 1784, Stockdale published the *Novanglus* letters once more, using the title that Almon had chosen for them in his own periodical: *History of the Dispute with America: from its Origin in 1754*. In the same year, probably also at the suggestion of Adams, he put out two

---

[29] Preface by Adams in *Novanglus and Massachusettensis*, Boston: Hews and Goss, 1819.

pamphlets by Franklin, the second of which had been written that January. They were *Remarks Concerning the Savages of North America* and *Information to Those who would Remove to America.*

At Christmas 1783, Adams finally made it to Bath, but he had no sooner reached the healing waters than he was required to come back to London and dash off to Holland to deal with a financial crisis that had arisen. On January 3, 1784, his English vacation ended: he and John Quincy left London for Harwich, reaching their Dutch destination only after an icy long journey.

On January 20, a present arrived at the bookshop for Adams from his wife's relatives by marriage, the Cranch family, who lived in the county of Devon. Stockdale at once wrote to Adams in The Hague. The tone of his letter and of the reply from Adams gives an indication of the good relationship of the two men.

'Domestic News

'I have received by the packet some medals enclosed in a letter and directed for you, for which I paid 16/8d, and shall not open till I receive your instructions. I this day received a basket sealed up and directed for you. As I suspected it was some sort of game I resolved, in the presence of Dr. John Jebb, to commit an act of felony and broke the seals, with an intent for Dr. Jebb to seal it up again with his seal, should it prove to be anything else. But as it appeared to be two fine hares unaccompanied with any letter, I took the liberty to offer one to Dr. Jebb in your name, which he very politely refused, desiring me at the same time to remember him to you in the strongest terms. I am now left in the distressed situation of being obliged to eat (with the assistance of my little family) both the hares. We shall do ourselves the pleasure after dinner of drinking your, your son's and family's good health in a glass of fine old Madeira which I had from a *friend.*

'Political News

'Mr. Wm. Pitt rises every day higher in the estimation of the people and no doubt will be minister many years. This night four of Mr. Fox's friends in the House of Commons got up and begged for a coalition of parties, which in fact is nothing less than Mr Fox's coming upon his knees to Mr. Pitt, but you may rely upon it Mr. Pitt will never join Lord North.'[30]

Stockdale's comments about the Whigs and Pitt are interesting. If he had looked out of his front window at about this time, he would have seen the Whig leaders going in and out of the Duke of Portland's Burlington House on the other side of Piccadilly.[31]

Adams replied on January 31: 'Your favour of the 20th was sent me last night and put me in a fit of good humour which continues to this moment. The letter containing the medals I beg you to open and deliver one set to Mr. West and another to Mr. Whitefoord in my name – you will please to make a minute of the postage you pay for me, which I will remit you. The hares were well disposed of and I hope they gave pleasure to the little family – you could not have offered one of them more properly than to Dr. Jebb, for whom I have the highest esteem, as one of the best citizens of the little Commonwealth of the just upon Earth. If I did not know that the burthen of the State lies so heavily upon your shoulders I would invite you to take a trip to The Hague.' Adams added, 'and drink a glass of finer old Madeira than that you had from your friend', but then crossed out those words. He clearly did not want Stockdale to get the impression that he had made him a present of an inferior Madeira before his departure.

Adams continued: 'I would not advise you to come in this season, to travel in iceboats and boors' waggons as I did. It gives me great pleasure to hear that Mr. Pitt rises in the esteem of the People, because he has a fair character and promises great things; nevertheless a friend to Old England would wish for a coalition. But Mr. Fox is of so peremptory a cast, and not always

---

[30] Adams Papers, Reel 362.
[31] Lascelles, Edward, *The Life of Charles James Fox*, Oxford U.P., 1939, 138.

in the right, that I fancy it will be difficult to form any coalition in which he is not the essence. It will ever give me pleasure to know of your welfare and to receive a spice of the politics of the day.'[32]

On July 21, 1784, Abigail Adams and her daughter, also Abigail but known as Nabby in the family, arrived in London from Massachusetts to stay at Osborne's in the Adelphi, until her husband or son could come over from Holland to collect them. John Quincy had already been in London to meet them in May, but had been two months too early and had left again after a month. With time on his hands he had done the usual Adams thing: he had gone into a bookshop he knew well, and had discussed an order for books for his father. John Stockdale was out of the shop when John Quincy first called, probably on the evening of May 20, but he encountered Henry Laurens there. Laurens had spent some twelve fruitless hours that day 'exploring the Thames' for a ship to carry him home, and had resolved to sail from the western port of Falmouth instead. Young Adams wrote to his father that evening: 'I have not seen Mr. Stockdale yet, nor our books, but tomorrow morning I shall go and see in what state things are. Mr. Laurens is in the lodgings at present, but intends to sail for America in about a fortnight. He is chosen member of Congress for South Carolina with [four others].' This was probably Laurens's fourth, and certainly his last stay with Stockdale and may well have included his very last days in London.

Adams wrote to his son on June 6, from The Hague: 'You say nothing of our books at Stockdale's, have you shipped them? And by whom? I am impatient to collect together here all the little things which belong to me, that I too may be in a condition to return home, upon occasion. My best respects to Mr.

---

[32] Adams Papers, Reel 107. In November 1784, Stockdale published one of the first of his many maps: one of Zealand and the River Scheldt. Perhaps he was thinking of taking Adams up on the suggestion of a visit.

Laurens. Happy Mr. Jay! Happy Mr. Laurens! in their prospects of seeing home.' Adams seems to have been more concerned to see his books than his eldest son, for he followed that letter up with another: 'You may embark with the books for Rotterdam or come by way of Harwich as you please. Get the books on their way at all events.' Adams also advised his son that he should attend Parliament, enlisting the help, to that end, of 'Mr Copley, Mr West, Mr Oswald or Mr Stockdale.'[33]

In his letter Adams sent his best respects to Laurens, but they had fallen out and exchanged their last letters (which both referred to Stockdale) in the February. It is possible that Laurens had suffered a temporary breakdown as a result of his various burdens, and that this had led to the intemperate language of the letter he wrote to Adams on February 3, 1784. Wallace, Laurens's biographer, did not mention the rift between the two men, but noted that Laurens, in January, 'being taken violently ill, was confined seven weeks in London.' He had obviously not got over his son John's recent death, but in addition, he had concerns about the other members of his family and about his return to South Carolina. On top of all that, he had been heavily engaged in an ill-advised pamphlet duel with Edmund Jenings and, infuriatingly for him, Adams continued to trust Jenings despite all of Laurens's suspicions. Finally, he was unreasonably peeved with Adams for reading some of his official correspondence while he was in the Tower of London. Adams concluded his reply of February 11 by affirming, 'I have most certainly never injured you to my knowledge, in thought, word or deed.' It was a miserable end to an association that had started at the Continental Congress in 1777, shortly before Laurens had been elected its President, with the firm approval of Adams.[34]

---

[33] *Laurens Papers*, 16: 453; Butterfield, *Adams Family Correspondence*, 5: 329, 338, 341.
[34] *Laurens Papers*, 16: 379, 384.

On August 7, John Adams arrived in London from Holland and went to the Adelphi to have a happy reunion with his wife and daughter. Instead of returning to The Hague, Adams at once took them to Paris, where Thomas Jefferson had just arrived. In the next nine months, until Adams was appointed as the first official minister to London, the Adams family saw a great deal of the Virginian and became very close to him. Jefferson spent a small fortune on books in Paris: he and Adams must have loved talking about their various finds. Adams passed on Stockdale's name to Jefferson almost immediately. That introduction was to be another important factor in Stockdale's business career.

Illus. 10. Thomas Jefferson by Gilbert Stuart

8

Thomas Jefferson and John Stockdale

Thomas Jefferson finally made it to France, at the third request of Congress, arriving in Paris on August 6, 1784. He was to stay until 1789, the year in which he witnessed the start of the French Revolution. 'For anyone with an historical imagination,' Max Beloff commented, 'the five years which Jefferson spent in Europe must make a stronger appeal as a subject of study than any other phase of his career.'[1] For anyone interested in him as an author and book collector, those years are particularly appealing.

In his letter to his wife dated October 14, 1783, John Adams made the interesting comment: 'It is not very material whether you arrive in Nantes, Amsterdam or London – the distance from Paris is about the same,' so she had ample choice. Before setting off for the Old World, Jefferson had suggested to Abigail Adams that they might make their first trans-Atlantic voyage together but she had already finalised her arrangements and travelled separately, arriving in England shortly before he landed in France. Their first experiences in Europe were, however, remarkably similar and may – just conceivably – ring a bell with later American travellers. Mrs. Adams and her companions landed at Deal in Kent on July 20 with seven cases, which needed to be carried a few paces across to the customs house. They were promptly seized by seven porters who managed to carry them to the customs but when a further journey was

---

[1] Beloff, Max, *Thomas Jefferson and American Democracy*, Harmondsworth: Penguin, 1972, 72.

needed to cross the street to an inn, another seven porters undertook that onerous task. Abigail wrote in disgust that she and her companions had 'fourteen of those rascals to pay; three Americans could have done the whole business'. Jefferson landed at Le Havre ten days later and was cheated by the porters who dealt with his bags. His daughter Patsy wrote, 'It cost Papa as much to have the luggage brought from the shore to the house, which was about half a square apart, as the bringing it from Philadelphia to Boston.'[2]

In Paris, Jefferson initially replaced John Jay, who went home to be Secretary for Foreign Affairs, but he later took over as minister from Franklin, the original – and unique – American in Paris. John Adams and his family arrived there from London a week after Jefferson. As early as September 1, 1784, and undoubtedly on the recommendation of Adams, Jefferson wrote the first of many letters to Stockdale in London, referring to William Temple Franklin, Benjamin's grandson, who had acted as secretary to the American Peace Commissioners. 'I asked the favor of Mr. Franklin, who lately went from hence to London, to send me a book or two which you had published. As he will not have left London when you receive this, I will beg the favor of you to procure for me a copy of the small 12mo. edition of Blackstone's *Commentaries*, published I believe in Ireland. I would choose it unbound, because I can then have it bound into one or more volumes whichever may best suit me as a traveller. Mr. Franklin will be so good as to pay you for it; and should there still remain in his hands any balance of the small sum I troubled him with, after he shall have had the articles he undertook to procure for me, I shall be glad if it is convenient for you to

---

[2] Smith, Page, *John Adams*, Garden City, N.Y.: Doubleday, 1962, 1: 596; Brodie, Fawn M., *Thomas Jefferson – An Intimate History*, London: Eyre Methuen, 1974, 186.

receive it, and answer any little calls I may have for things in your way while I am here.'[3]

The request for the Irish edition may have been prompted by Benjamin Franklin, for on April 21,1785, he was to write to his friend Benjamin Vaughan, 'If books can be had much cheaper from Ireland (which I believe, for I bought Blackstone there for 24 shillings when it was sold in England at four guineas [84 shillings], is not this an advantage, not to English booksellers, indeed, but to English readers, and to learning?'[4]

William Blackstone's work was that of an English judge on English law, but was regarded as indispensable by many generations of American lawyers, as English law continued to apply after Independence unless a new legislature decreed otherwise. When Robert Bell of Philadelphia had invited subscriptions in 1770, for the first American edition of Blackstone, to be published in 1771 and 1772, he had received the startling total of 1600 orders. Bell put forward a neat defence to the suggestion that he was guilty of pirating Blackstone's work, which was protected in England by the Copyright Act. He relied on what the jurist had written in the book in question, namely, that an Act could have no effect in Ireland or America unless Parliament had expressly so provided.[5]

When placing his order for the book, it is possible that Jefferson was thinking of returning to a legal practice after his diplomatic career was ended, but more likely that he felt that he could not be without his own copy of Blackstone, even in Europe. In his letter to Stockdale, Jefferson also mentioned that

---

[3] Boyd, Julian P. and others (eds.), *The Papers of Thomas Jefferson*, Princeton: Princeton U.P., 1950-, 15: 615; hereafter cited as *Jefferson Papers*.

[4] Sparks, Jared, *The Works of Benjamin Franklin*, Boston: Tappan, Whittemore and Mason, 1840, 10:161.

[5] Hall, David D., 'Learned Culture in the Eighteenth Century', in Amory, Hugh and Hall, David D. (eds.) *The Colonial Book in the Atlantic World*, Cambridge U.P., 2000, 416; Green, James N.. 'English Books and Printing in the Age of Franklin', *ibid.* 287.

young Franklin was to be found 'at Govr. Franklin's, Norton street, London'. Behind those few words lies the tragic falling out of the three Franklins, mentioned earlier. Young Temple was prepared to be reconciled with his loyalist father and had come to England to be with him, but Benjamin Franklin could never forgive his own son.

In the event, the money Jefferson had provided, at the beginning of his five-year European shopping spree, to young Franklin, did not go far enough to benefit Stockdale at this stage. On September 26, Franklin wrote to his grandfather that he had sent Jefferson's letterpress to Rouen, adding, 'What remains of the sum he entrusted me with, shall be left as he desired, with Mr. Stockdale, subject to his orders.' However, by October 13, he was obliged to add that he had spent so much for Jefferson, that there was nothing left for Stockdale.[6]

While still in America, Jefferson had been asked by several friends for a copy of his Notes on his home State, and so had thought of having them privately printed. He was dismayed by the prices he was quoted there, and was delighted to find that he could get the work done in France 'for a fourth of what I had been asked here [in America]'. He had two hundred copies printed for him, anonymously, in Paris and gave some to friends in Europe, including John Adams, sending most of the rest to friends back home. Jefferson clearly authorised the French translation which appeared in 1786: not only did the translator refer to his consent, but he borrowed Jefferson's map plate. Jefferson was not happy with the finished product.[7]

In his autobiographical notes, written many years later, he described how Stockdale had come to publish the first English language edition: 'A London bookseller, on seeing the

---

[6] American Philosophical Society, Philadelphia BF 85. I am obliged to Claude-Anne Lopez, consulting editor of the *Franklin Papers*, for drawing these two letters to my attention in a personal note.

[7] *Observations sur la Virginie, par Mr. J*****, Paris: Barrois, 1786.

translation, requested me to permit him to print it in the English original. I thought it best to do so to let the world see that it was not really so bad as the French translation had made it appear. And this is the true story of that publication.'[8]

True, but rather brief. We can fill in some of the matters omitted by Jefferson in his short account. The French printer had completed his work on the English language version on May 10, 1785. Ten days later, Adams left Paris with his two Abigails to take up his post as the first official resident American minister in London. John Quincy was making his own way home to study at Harvard, so did not return to London with his parents. On their journey to Calais they and their daughter read Jefferson's *Notes on Virginia*. On May 22, Adams wrote to the author from Montreuil-sur-Mer, somewhat extravagantly: 'I thank you kindly for your book. It is our meditation all the day long. I cannot now say much about it, but I think it will do its author and his country great honour. The passages upon slavery are worth diamonds. They will have more effect than volumes written by mere philosophers.'[9]

At the conclusion of his note on the population of Virginia, Jefferson had written: 'In the very first session held under the republican government, the assembly passed a law for the per-petual prohibition of the importation of slaves. This will in some measure stop the increase of this great political and moral evil, while the minds of our citizens may be ripening for a complete emancipation of human nature.'

Jefferson was a slave owner himself and appreciated that emancipation of all slaves was a long way off: the ripening of some minds was to take much longer than that of others. He replied to Adams on May 25, commenting on his praise for the

---

[8] Randolph, T. J., *Memoirs, Correspondence and Private Papers of Thomas Jeffer-son*, London: Henry Colburn and Richard Bentley, 1829, 1: 52, 53.
[9] *Jefferson Papers*, 8: 160.

passages on slavery, 'My country will probably estimate them differently.'[10]

Adams arrived in London on the next day and moved into accommodation in Piccadilly once more. This time he had a larger party and a different status, so he chose the Bath hotel, rather than the friendly nearby bookshop. Adams and Jefferson shared three great loves: the United States, books and wine, but Jefferson was the acknowledged expert on French wines.[11] On his second day in London, Adams wrote to Jefferson about that most important topic, mentioning Stockdale. 'Upon enquiry I find that I cannot be exempted from paying duties upon my wines,' wrote the distressed minister, who clearly had a gentleman's sense of priorities, 'because no foreign minister is, except for a less quantity than I have of the best qualities in my cellar at The Hague, so that I must stop all that I have in France, if I can.' He suggested alternative ways for Jefferson to help him out and concluded with interesting financial proposals. 'Let Petit dispose of it as he will, give you an account of proceeds and give me credit, and then order me to pay Stockdale or anybody else here for you to the amount.'[12]

The idea of using a London bookseller for the settlement of debts was finding increasing favour with travellers and others. Gosling, a bookseller in Fleet Street, found himself helping clients so much with their financial transfers, that he gave up selling books and shrewdly became a full-time banker. His bank is still there in Fleet Street although, inevitably, swallowed up by a large banking chain. American booksellers, who tended to stock even more non-book items than their English counterparts and were frequently offered goods in exchange for

[10] *Jefferson Papers*, 8: 164. By 'my country', Jefferson clearly meant Virginia, rather than the United States as a whole.

[11] 'Both Washington and John Adams depended on Jefferson's taste in wines to secure their supplies.' Adams, James Truslow, *The Living Jefferson*, New York: Charles Scribner's Sons, 1936, 176.

[12] *Jefferson Papers*, 8: 166.

books, were more likely to turn into general merchants than bankers.[13]

On June 1, Adams had his historic meeting with George III, at which both expressed themselves in conciliatory terms.[14] On the following day, Jefferson wrote to Adams further about the really important matters – the wine and publications. 'Either retain the money in your hands or put it into Stockdale's as most convenient. Can you take the trouble of ordering me the two best of the London papers (that is to say, one of each party) and by any channel which will save me postage and the search of government?' On June 22, he added that the Duke of Dorset, the British minister in Paris, who had been helpful to Adams before his departure, had given him leave to use his London address for the onward transmission of papers. Jefferson also asked, 'Will Mr. Stockdale undertake to have these papers sent regularly, or is this out of his line of business? Pray order me also any really good pamphlets which come out from time to time, which he will charge to me.' In July, Adams moved into his new official residence in Grosvenor Square, but still found the time to reply on the 18th., 'I shall go this morning to Stockdale to talk with him about sending you the newspaper and pamphlets.'[15]

On July 28, Jefferson wrote to Stockdale that he would have occasion for books and pamphlets to be sent either to him in Paris or to America, adding, 'which will render a correspondent

---

[13] Amory, Hugh, 'Reinventing the Colonial Book', in Amory and Hall, 45.

[14] One of the ways in which the Bicentenary of Independence was celebrated in England in 1976 was by the '1776' Exhibition at the National Maritime Museum in historic Greenwich. The words of George III and Adams were specially recorded for the exhibition by Prince Charles and the United States ambassador, Elliott Richardson. The exhibition also displayed a book from George Washington's collection, John Abercrombie's *The hot-house gardener and the general culture of the pine-apple*, published by John Stockdale in 1789.

[15] *Jefferson Papers*, 8: 172, 247, 301.

in London in your way convenient.' He included his first large order to Stockdale, and it gives some indication of the trouble and expense a bookseller might have to incur for a customer with international connections: 'For the present I will ask the favour of you to have the underwritten books packed in a very tight box, directed to James Madison, president of the College in Williamsburg, Virginia, and to furnish me with the cost. I must further desire you to find some opportunity of sending the box by some vessel bound from London to James or York river in Virginia.'[16] David Hall has pointed out, 'When warfare ended in 1781 and the colleges began to rebuild or restore collections that had been dispersed or damaged, Americans turned anew to the London trade.' Jefferson was clearly not the only one buying for American colleges, their faculties or their students.[17]

The books ordered by Jefferson included works by Herodotus, Xenophon and Cicero, which Stockdale had to find and buy at other bookshops, before beginning to comply with the complex packing and shipping requirements. (Jefferson later asked a friend to take the books home to Virginia with him, but Stockdale still had to attend to the packing for the sea voyage.) In a subsequent letter, Jefferson showed that he appreciated that Stockdale had taken considerable trouble to find some of the books, writing, 'I remember you had to get some of them from Scotland.' Later still, Jefferson asked Stockdale to send a number of specified books to Paris for him and added, 'Besides this I wish to receive from Lackington, Chiswell Street, those stated on the next leaf, so far as they remain unsold. As my friend, Colo. Smith is absent from London and Lackington gives no credit, will you be so good as to procure from him the books, send them with the others, and pay him for them, for which I will duly account with you.'

---

[16] *Jefferson Papers*, 8: 322.
[17] Hall, 420.

James Lackington had built up a very successful business. The full explanation for his success is to be found in his auto-biography but the second part of his catalogue for 1785 gave two clues. It listed twenty thousand titles and carried the warning: 'N.B. Not an hour's credit will be given to any person, nor any book sent on board ships, or into the country, before they are paid for.' Lackington gave no credit to Jefferson but did not lose a single sale, as Stockdale was prepared to provide it in his stead. With a system like that, it is scarcely surprising that Lackington succeeded.[18]

James Raven, in his account of the ordering of books by the Charleston Library Society, pointed out: 'From other correspondence of the period it is clear that many London booksellers found it hard to satisfy demanding overseas customers.' The best account of such difficulties were contained in a letter from Stockdale, dated September 14, 1792, which Raven found in the Society's records, and which will be considered later, but his letter to Jefferson, dated August 31, 1787, also illustrates how much running around a London bookseller might do for a customer abroad. 'I have sent to Mr. Richardson at the Royal Exchange, I believe at least a dozen times by his appointment for the *Remarks on the Taxation of Free States*, and though he is sensible he has got many copies, he has not yet been able to find one.'[19]

The James Madison mentioned in his first large order was the president of Jefferson's own college, The College of William and Mary, and must not be confused with his cousin, the Virginian politician of the same name, co-author with Alexander Hamilton and John Jay of *The Federalist Papers*, who was to succeed

---

[18] *Jefferson Papers*, 11: 85, 522; Lackington, James, *Memoirs of the First Forty-Five Years*, 1791.

[19] Raven, James, *London Booksellers and American Customers*, Columbia: U. South Carolina P., 2002, 109, 288, and see, *post*, chap.14; *Jefferson Papers*, 12: 73.

Jefferson as the fourth President of the United States. Jefferson's nephews were attending the college, and the cost of the books that he sent over to Madison were credited against the young men's tuition fees.[20]

On August 19, 1785, Jefferson wrote to his fifteen-year-old nephew and ward, Peter Carr, to advise him on the order in which he should read the various books Stockdale was sending. He added Juvenal's advice, 'A strong body makes the mind strong,' and counselled him to walk for exercise, rather than resorting to the horse. 'Walking is the best possible exercise. Habituate yourself to walk very far. The Europeans value themselves on having subdued the horse to the uses of man. But I doubt whether we have not lost more than we have gained by the use of this animal. No one has occasioned so much the degeneracy of the human body.'[21]

From their letters to John Quincy in America it is clear that his mother and his sister, like both John Adams and Nabby's future husband, Col. William Stephens Smith (the secretary of the legation), were also customers of Stockdale's bookshop. On September 12, Abigail wrote to her son: 'Your old acquaintance Stockdale is bought up by the Ministry and receives a pension of four hundred per year. It is said he is quite a different man from what he was when you knew him. Not a single paragraph can be published in favour of America, suppose it is only six lines, under three or four guineas.'[22]

---

[20] Peterson, Merrill. D. *Thomas Jefferson and the New Nation*, Oxford U.P., 1975, 336.

[21] *Jefferson Papers*, 8: 407. Peter Carr and his brother were later to be falsely accused by Jefferson's family of fathering the children of Sally Hemings. Brodie, 296, 493.

[22] Butterfield, *Adams Family Correspondence*, 6: 360. An editorial note on p.361 states, 'If the Pitt ministry did try to buy Stockdale's support in 1785, the arrangement did not endure.' The reason given is the prosecution of Stockdale by the ministry in 1789, which is discussed in chap.11. In fact, though much offended, Stockdale stayed 'bought'.

On September 26, Jefferson, the son of a map-making surveyor and something of a surveyor himself, revealed his own interest in maps by ordering a number produced by Stockdale as a result of Captain Cook's voyages. We shall see later how important geographical books became for the bookseller, and how well Jefferson's work on Virginia fitted in with them. Jefferson's interest in that topic was so great that Carl Cannon made the following comment about his library: 'It is under the heading of American Geography, rather than under History, that some of the most interesting books in the collection are to be found. Here, for example, are the earliest works of the travellers and explorers of the American interior: Cortez, La Salle, Vespucci, and later, Lewis and Clark, Pike, Bartram, Burnaby and Ellicott.' With all his geographical knowledge, it is no wonder that Jefferson, the compulsive buyer, later jumped at the opportunity to double the size of the United States with his bargain price Louisiana Purchase.[23]

Jefferson continued his letter of September 26, with some specific requests, and stressed that the only pamphlets he wanted in future were 'those which relate to America, and which have also some degree of merit'. Jefferson was wise to rule out other pamphlets, few of which were cheap. Stockdale published his fair share of rubbishy ones – many, doubtless, at the request and expense of their proud authors.[24]

Benjamin Franklin, who may well be regarded as an expert witness on the subject, had continued his letter to Vaughan, cited above, by complaining about English publications: 'And of all the complainants, perhaps these booksellers are least worthy

---

[23] *Jefferson Papers*, 8: 544; Cannon, Carl L., *American Book Collectors and Collecting*, New York: H. W. Wilson, 1941, 42. The offer came through the French Finance Minister Marbois, who had asked the questions that led to Jefferson writing his *Notes on the State of Virginia*.

[24] On the topic of payment generally, see, Belanger, Terry, 'Publishers and writers in eighteenth-century England', in Rivers, Isabel, *Books and their Readers in Eighteenth-Century England*, Leicester U.P., 1982, 5.

of consideration. The last catalogue you sent me amazes me by the high prices (said to be the lowest) affixed to each article. And one can scarce see a new book, without observing the excessive artifices made use of to puff up a paper of verses into a pamphlet, a pamphlet into an octavo, and an octavo into a quarto, with scab-boardings, white-lines, sparse tittles of chapters, and exorbitant margins, to a degree, that the selling of paper now seems the object, and printing on it only the pretence. You have a law, I think, against butchers blowing of veal to make it look fatter; why not one against booksellers' blowing of books to make them look bigger?'

On November 20, Jefferson wrote to Abigail Adams, stating that he would like to have a trip to London, 'of which the pleasure of seeing your family would make a great part'. He added, 'But I foresee no circumstances which would justify, much less call for, such an excursion.'[25] Abigail probably suggested to her husband that he really must try and find some reason to justify a visit by Jefferson to London. Ever anxious to please his wife, and close as he was to Jefferson at that time, it did not take long for Adams to find an excuse to send for their friend. The United States, like other maritime nations, was suffering from the depredations of pirates in the Mediterranean. Also, there was still the outstanding question of a trade treaty with Britain to be concluded. In February 1786, Adams sent Col. Smith to fetch Jefferson from Paris, so that he could help with both problems. Jefferson made no protest and arrived in London on March 11, leaving it for Paris only at the end of April. As one might have guessed, the Mediterranean question and trade treaties combined did not occupy him for the whole of the seven weeks – though the piracy was still to trouble him when he assumed the Presidency after Adams, until he sent his Marines 'to the shores of Tripoli'.

---

[25] *Jefferson Papers*, 9: 48.

Adams and Jefferson enjoyed a tour of some of England's finest countryside and several famous gardens. William Howard Adams was doubtless correct when he stated, 'Jefferson's garden tour with the Adamses, a trip to Windsor Castle and shopping expeditions for books and other supplies no doubt helped ease his official frustrations in England.'[26]

In London, Adams introduced his colleague to some of his literary and political friends. On April 15, for example, the two men were invited out, together with Col. Smith. The host at the dinner party was Thomas Brand Hollis, one of the stalwarts of the Society for Constitutional Information. The other guests included the Rev. Dr. Richard Price, whose Sunday services the Adams family attended in the village of Hackney, Dr. Andrew Kippis, the well-known biographer, and Samuel Romilly, the Whig law reformer, later Solicitor-General. Adams also made a point of showing Jefferson some of the improvements that would appeal to the scientist in him, including a large steam engine at Blackfriars bridge, between St. Paul's Cathedral and the Temple. This was the work of Matthew Boulton and James Watt, two of Thomas Day's colleagues in the Lunar Society, which was so admired by Franklin that he had persuaded William Small, Jefferson's own teacher, to join. Had Jefferson stayed in England, he would probably also have wanted to become a member. Their visit to the Court was less successful, for the King gave the impression that he did not want to meet Jefferson.

During his stay, Jefferson met the American painters in London, Benjamin West, Mather Brown and John Trumbull, all three of whom were to paint him, then or later. Adams was very keen to have a portrait of Jefferson, and he of Adams, so Brown painted two portraits of each of them, so that they could each have a pair. Brown's is the first known portrait of Jefferson.

---

[26] William Howard Adams, *The Paris Years of Thomas Jefferson*, New Haven: Yale U.P., 1997, 210.

That of Adams is of interest because it contains a compliment to Jefferson: it includes a representation of the copy of the *Notes on Virginia* that the proud author had given him, hot from the press in Paris.[27] It also indicates that Adams's fulsome letter of praise, written on the journey to London, was a genuine comment on his friend's book. Furthermore, Adams gave his good opinion of the work to Stockdale on at least one of his visits to the shop. Jefferson at some stage presented a copy of his privately printed version to Col. Smith (bearing the misleading date of 1782, instead of 1785, on the title page), probably when the young man collected him from Paris. Despite the fact that he and Jefferson got on very well, Smith seems to have parted with his inscribed copy while in England, for it is now in the British Library, the British Museum having bought it from the well known bookseller, Bernard Quaritch, in 1886. The colonel had at any rate read the book, or some of it, for he also recommended it to Stockdale.

A week before Jefferson's departure for Paris, Adams noted in his diary, 'I walked to the booksellers, Stockdale, Cadell, Dilly, Almon.'[28] The reference to Almon was in error, but he knew that Debrett's shop had formerly been that of Almon. He did not write that Jefferson had gone with him, but it is highly likely that the two men visited different bookshops together. Jefferson was staying in lodgings in Golden Square, very close to Piccadilly, and certainly called in on Stockdale at least once. One would expect the booklover to call at the shop from which he was buying books, and two letters and an entry in his account book make it clear that he did so.

On June 26, Jefferson wrote to Thomas Elder from Paris, asking him to take some of the books that he had ordered for his nephew Peter Carr, via Madison, to Virginia. 'They are some

---

[27] There is a good colour reproduction of both portraits in McCullough, David, *John Adams*, New York: Simon & Schuster, 2001.
[28] Butterfield, *Diary*, 3: 189.

which I desired Mr. Stockdale to send to him the last year,' he explained, 'but when I was in London he had not yet done it.' In a letter in September of the following year, Jefferson referred to Stockdale having replaced some books for him 'when I was in England'.[29] On April 25, the day before he finally left London, Jefferson noted in his account book, 'Paid Stockdale for books £40.10.6.' However, it is clear from what followed, that he did not discuss the possibility of Stockdale publishing his *Notes* for him at any time during his seven weeks in England.

Although Jefferson's letter to Elder made no complaint about Stockdale's delay in sending the books to his nephew, he was probably irritated by it sufficiently for it to contribute to their ultimate breach. A very similar delay by Stockdale in dealing with a large order from South Carolina was to lead to great resentment on the part of his customer there, the Charleston Library Society.[30]

After his return to Paris, Jefferson ordered some more books; Stockdale's acknowledgment on August 8, contained his first written mention of the *Notes*. 'I have had some thoughts of printing your book in England, which is highly spoke of, except those parts that relate to our country, but I had some doubts whether it would sell sufficient to defray the expense. At a convenient opportunity shall be glad to have your opinion on it.'[31] There were two reasons why London booksellers, such as Stockdale and Dilly, were careful about publishing American authors without any pruning. Apart from the fact that they had no wish to annoy their English customers with what they might regard as unfair comments by such authors, they had a more specific reason for caution. Some American authors were very precise with their charges of atrocities by named British officers,

---

[29] *Jefferson Papers*, 10: 72; 12: 115.
[30] Raven, 97.
[31] *Jefferson Papers*, 10: 201.

and the London booksellers were anxious to avoid being sued for libel by their compatriots.[32]

Jefferson did not deal with Stockdale's letter at once, but the timing of his request, although the bookseller could not have known it, was just right. Jefferson had been agonising for some months over the idea of a public edition to be produced in England, in English. On February 8, shortly before his trip to London, he had informed Madison, the academic, about the bad French translation and his fear that it might be re-translated into English and re-published by someone else. 'I am now at a loss what to do as to England. I rather believe it will be most eligible to let the original come out in that country; but I am not yet decided.' On May 12, Madison firmly advised Jefferson to 'give out the original'.[33]

Stockdale returned to the *Notes* in a letter on November 20, and also, for the first time, asked Jefferson to obtain a book for him in Paris. Jefferson's help with this and later similar requests, was reflected in due course in the publications issuing from the Piccadilly shop. 'I shall esteem it a great favour if you'll be so kind as to send me *History of Sandford and Merton* in French, which I am this instant informed is just translated by Mr. Berquin, the author of the *Children's Friend*. I beg pardon for the liberty taken, as I am anxious for a copy (the original being my own publication), having no friend in Paris beside the Duke of Dorset, Mr. Stone, his secretary, and yourself.'[34]

The reference to the translation of Thomas Day's book into French may only have stirred unpleasant memories in Jefferson,

---

[32] For Dilly's objection to some of David Ramsay's text, and American indignation about 'inaccurate' British histories, see chap.14.

[33] *Jefferson Papers*, 9: 265, 517.

[34] *Jefferson Papers*, 10: 545. The Duke was clearly the friendly type. He has been described as 'that great seducer the Duke of Dorset', and among his closest 'friends' were Lady Derby and the Duchess of Devonshire. Foreman, Amanda, *Georgiana, Duchess of Devonshire*, London: HarperCollins, 1998, 109n.

but the alarm bells certainly rang when he read on: 'Some time past two French gentlemen called upon me, with a copy of your Minutes on Virginia, with a view to have it printed, but I informed them that I had some reason to believe that a new edition was coming out, with corrections by the author, and Col. Smith informed me that a large map was engraving for the work. I have some doubts whether it would pay the expense, at same time have a wish to publish it, with your name, as I am convinced it is a work of great merit. I have spoken to Mr. Adams and Col. Smith on the subject, who much wish to see the work published in England.' The recommendation of the book by John Adams must have carried considerable weight with the bookseller.

Two matters delayed the final go-ahead for Stockdale. The first was a technical one: Jefferson, always interested in scientific advances, was exploring the possibility of producing his own English language edition in France, obtaining a quotation for the cost of printing by Francois Hoffman's new Polytype method. The other was an affair of the heart, which caused the widower Jefferson much anguish. While in London he had invited John Trumbull to visit him in Paris and, once there, the painter, with Jefferson's assistance, started to compose his famous painting of the Declaration of Independence, now in the Capitol in Washington. Trumbull also introduced him to two fellow-artists, Richard Cosway and his wife Maria. Jefferson immediately fell in love with Maria Cosway and on October 12, wrote his celebrated love letter for her. Because of the form it took – that of a debate within the anguished lover – it is known as 'My Head and my Heart'. The first lines of the letter show how smitten Jefferson was. 'Having performed the last sad office of handing you into your carriage at the Pavillon de St. Denis, and seen the wheels get actually into motion, I turned on my heel and walked, more dead than alive, to the opposite door, where my own was awaiting me.'[35]

Rather more than Jefferson's heart was broken. In trying to impress Maria with his virility, the 43-year-old widower leapt over an obstacle and landed on his right hand. For a while, he had to use his left hand for writing, or an amanuensis.[36]

While Jefferson was mooning over Mrs. Cosway, Col. Banastre Tarleton, who had put Jefferson to flight and given him the opportunity to work on his Notes, was disporting himself in Paris with his permanent companion. She was none other than the former actress, Mary 'Perdita' Robinson, the discarded mistress of the Prince of Wales, who had already been painted by Richard Cosway at his request. With some help from Mary Robinson, herself an author and a poet, Tarleton had also written about Virginia and his book was shortly to be published by Cadell. In his *History of the Campaigns in 1780 and 1781*, Tarleton described (at p.297) how Jefferson had narrowly evaded capture by his Legion of loyalists. On July 1, 1787, Jefferson was to order a copy of the book from Stockdale; this doubtless proved to be one of his more interesting purchases.[37]

Despite his work, his preoccupation with Maria Cosway, and his concern about his *Notes* being pirated, Jefferson still took the trouble to obtain various children's books for Stockdale in Paris. He first sent him the parts of *Sandford and Merton* that were available in French, and then other works, especially those of Arnaud Berquin, a well-known French author of books for children.

Eventually, in January 1787, Jefferson decided to let Stockdale publish his book. On February 1, he wrote the letter

---

[35] Peterson, Merrill D., *The Portable Thomas Jefferson*, London: Penguin, 1977, 400.

[36] Peterson, *Thomas Jefferson and the New Nation*, 349.

[37] Davenport, Hester, *The Prince's Mistress – A Life of Mary Robinson*, Stroud: Sutton, 2004, 158; *Jefferson Papers*, 11: 521.

which was one of the most important ever received by the bookseller: 'You have two or three times proposed to me the printing of my *Notes on Virginia*. I never did intend to have them made public, because they are little interesting to the rest of the world.' One is bound to wonder whether Jefferson really believed this, or whether it was a case of mock modesty. He continued: 'But as a translation of them is coming out, I have concluded to let the original appear also. I have therefore corrected a copy, and made some additions. I have moreover had a map engraved, which is worth more than the book. If you choose to print the work I will send you the corrected copy, and when it shall be nearly printed I will send the plate of the map. It is not necessary to observe that as I have been at the expense of engraving the large map, I should expect to be paid for those you should have occasion for, a shilling a piece.' His private edition, unlike the French translation, had not included the map.[38]

On February 13, the delighted Stockdale replied, agreeing to publish the book. He claimed that as he would 'not be above three weeks in printing the work' – despite its 382 eventual pages – it would be as well for him to have the plate at the same time. He added, 'I intend to print 500 copies, which from the merit of the work and the advantage of your name, I hope will be sold, but all things are uncertain.'[39]

Jefferson replied on February 27, giving his publisher detailed instructions, much as Shakespeare's Hamlet had commanded the player king: 'By the diligence of tomorrow I will send you a corrected copy of my *Notes*, which I will pray you to print precisely as they are, without additions, alterations, preface, or any thing else but what is there. They will require a very accurate corrector of the press.' Jefferson had clearly failed to spot that his own edition ended with his last two last answers bearing the same number: XXII. Stockdale and his printer duly obeyed his

---

[38] *Jefferson Papers*, 11: 107.
[39] *Jefferson Papers*, 11: 143.

instructions and copied the two identical numbers 'exactly as they are'. In his letter Jefferson then turned to the plate, which was causing problems. It had been engraved in London, with 'a prodigious number of orthographical errors', which he was having corrected. Jefferson thought highly of the map itself, partly because it was based on an original for which his father, Peter Jefferson, was jointly responsible. It showed not only Virginia, but also Maryland, Delaware and Pennsylvania.[40]

Stockdale was as good as his word about the printing of the text, but he was then held up by the absence of the map plate. On May 15, he wrote to William Short, Jefferson's secretary, asking for its immediate dispatch, 'as I have had his book printed and waiting for publishing for some time. The season for sale of books is now far advanced.' The letter continued with a reference to a new book by John Adams, which Stockdale was publishing and which will be considered in detail in the next chapter. Stockdale stated that his 'man' had just informed him that Jefferson's copy of the book, ordered by him, had not been dispatched, 'as we find it is not entered in his account.' He added, 'There will be very soon another volume of Mr. Adams's.'[41]

Jefferson explained how he had been badly let down by the Frenchman who had kept the plate instead of forwarding it to London, and that it had been necessary for him to threaten to go to the police. Stockdale acknowledged receipt of the plate on July 10, pointing out the 'detriment to the sale of the book, London now being nearly empty of book buyers.' He complained that the plate was so badly worn that it looked as though 1500 copies of the map must already have been run off.[42] Stockdale added that he was sending an advertisement for the book 'to every paper in England and Scotland, to be inserted, which I

---

[40] *Jefferson Papers*, 11: 183.
[41] *Jefferson Papers*, 11: 364.
[42] *Jefferson Papers*, 11: 521, 577.

believe are between 70 and 80 in number, and which will cost me upwards of £30, but I hope the book will repay me.'

Stockdale then turned to the question of children's books, thanking Jefferson for continuing to send Berquin's works, and promising to credit his customer's account with the costs incurred in Paris. Jefferson took his job as Stockdale's unpaid Parisian scout for children's books seriously. He replied on July 17, sending Father Berenger's *A Complete Course of Instructions and Anecdotes*, and commenting: 'Having little time to read I have been able to peruse only about 30 or 40 pages, and so far it appears to me one of the best things I have ever seen of the kind. If it does not correspond with your view you will easily get this single volume off your hands.'[43]

Stockdale often mentioned the cost of advertising to his authors, but much of it was included in the front or back of his own books. While the cost of newspaper advertising was not cheap, advertising in his own works cannot have cost much. If one ignores street-sellers cries and posters urging 'Vote for Snubbins!', the booksellers were among the first to use advertising on a large scale.[44]

With the map plate in his possession Stockdale was able to complete and publish the book, with the slightly longer title, *Notes on the State of Virginia*. The finished work contained two dates that betrayed the delay. Jefferson's preface concluded, 'They are now offered to the public in their original form and language. Feb. 27, 1787.' The large folded map in the front bore the legend, 'Published as the Act directs, 13 July 1787 by John Stockdale in Piccadilly. Engraved by S. J. Neele, no.332 Strand.' Jefferson's private edition had included two appendices: the first

---

[43] *Jefferson Papers*, 11: 597.

[44] For an interesting article on this topic, see, Tierney, James, 'Book advertisements in mid-18th-century newspapers: the example of Robert Dodsley', in Myers, Robin and Harris, Michael (eds.), *A Genius for Letters*, Winchester: St. Paul's Bibliographies, 1995, 103.

contained comments made on his draft by Charles Thomson, the Secretary of Congress; the second was Jefferson's draft Constitution for Virginia. For Stockdale's edition the author added a third appendix: the short historic work of which he was most proud, his Act for establishing religious freedom in his home State, which the Virginia Assembly had passed in the previous year. One of Thomson's comments (at p.336) seems on a first reading to refer to the famous battle: 'I am informed that at York town in Virginia, in the bank of York river, there are different strata of shells and earth, one above another, which seem to point out that the country there has undergone several changes.'

In later letters the bookseller informed the author that the book was selling well in London at seven shillings in boards, retail, and 'it is well spoke of in London.' He also informed him, 'I have sent a small number to Dr. Ramsay and Mr. Laurens at Charleston.' There was no subscription list for the book but one can guess who else, or what type of reader, would have been interested. The three copies of the Stockdale edition of the book in the British Library bear marks showing that they came from the libraries of George III, Joseph Banks (President of the Royal Society) and Thomas Grenville. Grenville, the son of George Grenville, had been Rockingham and Fox's peace delegate in Paris in 1782, and was a great book collector. On his death he left his collection of over twenty thousand volumes to the British Museum, of which he was a trustee.

It was now Stockdale's turn to exasperate Jefferson in connection with his map plate, for he failed to return it despite several requests. Jefferson even asked John Trumbull, the painter, to call in at the shop about it. Eventually, on February 22, 1788, Stockdale provided an excuse of sorts: 'I duly received your three letters, but owing to the alterations I have been making in my house, by enlarging the shop &c. has prevented me for this two months past of paying that respect to you, and attention to my business that it required. But I have now got the shop in excellent order and my business in a proper train, though I am a little discomposed by having been complained of by the House of Commons for having published what they deem a libel; they have ordered me to be prosecuted. I have sent your copper plate this day and next week I hope to send you all the books ordered.'[45]

There is no further mention of the enlargement of the shop, so one can only guess that Stockdale had extended it backwards into the yard or, possibly, upwards onto the next floor. He could certainly not have extended it to either side of no.181. The reference to the prosecution on the orders of the House of Commons had nothing to do with any American book: it was in connection with Stockdale's pamphlet which criticised the House for its handling of the impeachment of Warren Hastings.[46]

Despite his promise, Stockdale delayed the dispatch of the ordered books so long that he lost Jefferson's custom. Trumbull had been asked to help again and reported to Jefferson on June 20: 'The books from Lackington are at Stockdale's as well as the paper &c. &c. from Woodmason's, to go with his books. He has promised so often that they should go by the next diligence that I don't believe his promises of sending them tomorrow,' The books were in fact dispatched, but before their arrival in Paris, the disappointed customer wrote to Trumbull, 'No news from Stockdale. I am done with him irrevocably.'[47]

---

[45] *Jefferson Papers*, 12: 621. For Trumbull's background and his friendship with Jefferson, see, *The Autobiography of Colonel John Trumbull*, ed. by Sizer, Theodore, New York: Yale U.P., 1953. Of his historical paintings, that of the Yorktown Surrender is of particular interest: apart from all the other main characters, it includes a posthumous representation of John Laurens. One of many books containing a copy is Whitridge, Arnold, *Rochambeau*, New York: Macmillan, 1965, for Rochambeau and some of his officers had posed for Trumbull at Jefferson's house in Paris in 1787.
[46] See chap.11.
[47] *Jefferson Papers*, 13: 280, 301. Jefferson may well have patronised James

Jefferson ordered no more books from his publisher after this letter, but there was a final exchange between them about the *Notes*. On July 14, Jefferson wrote that he wished that Stockdale had sent all the copies of the book to Charleston, Richmond, Philadelphia and Boston, as they could all have been sold there immediately. He added, 'As the work could not be bought there, the periodical papers retailed it out to the public piecemeal till at length (as I am informed) a bad edition is printed.' The publisher replied on August 15, mentioning his American connections and pointing out the important commercial distinction between selling and being paid for the sales in question.

Stockdale wrote: 'From letters which I have received from different gentlemen in America, I am convinced that the whole of the impression of your book would have been sold immediately had they been sent there, but I have my doubts whether I should have been able to have got remittances for them, having not yet received any, or even answers to my letters, for several years past, excepting Dr. Ramsay. But I sincerely hope that the new Constitution will have the desired effect and put them upon a better footing.' This was a vain hope, as the Constitution merely gave Congress power 'to promote the progress of science and useful arts by securing for limited times to authors and inventors the exclusive right to their respective writings and discoveries'. Not surprisingly, there was nothing in it designed to protect British publishers.[48]

Although Jefferson was 'done with him irrevocably', Stockdale was not done with his distinguished customer. We shall see in chap. 15 how Jefferson's support of Thomas Paine, and his bitter disagreement with John Adams over the French

---

Woodmason because he was the son of a well-known South Carolinian, Charles Woodmason. *Laurens Papers*, 16: 340n.

[48] *Jefferson Papers*, 13: 375, 518. For Ramsay, see chap.14.

Revolution, enabled Stockdale to publish yet another book – one which involved all three of the future Presidents he knew.

On October 2, 1788, Jefferson appointed Thomas Payne the Elder as his new London bookseller. Trumbull had made inquiries after Jefferson asked him to find 'the best classical bookseller', and had reported back that he had been assured that Payne was 'as good as any, if not the best'. Jefferson was clearly determined to ensure that his dealings with Payne would be smoother than those with Stockdale, for he gave him the clearest possible instructions, including the following: 'When I name a particular edition of a book, send me that edition and no other. When I do not name the edition, never send a folio or quarto if there exists an 8vo. or smaller edition. I like books of a handy size. Where a book costs much higher than the common price of books of that size do not send it, though I write for it, till you shall have advised me of the price. I disclaim all pompous editions and all typographical luxury; but I like a fine white paper, neat type, and neat binding, gilt and lettered in the modern stile. But while I remain in Europe it will be better to send my books in boards, as I have found that scarcely any method of packing preserves them from rubbing in a land transportation.' He enclosed a large order for books, including, 'Indian vocabulary. 12mo. Stockdale.' On January 28, 1789, Jefferson gave a further direction, which indicates that he was buying books for other people, not just in Paris but also in London. He asked Payne to note the price in each book 'because the books I write for are often for friends here.'[49]

Probably the last that Jefferson heard of Stockdale, rather than of his books, was in a letter which he received in October 1790, by which time he was Washington's Secretary of State, Adams having become Vice-President. Col. David Humphreys, who had been another of Washington's aides and then served under Jefferson in Paris, wrote to him, 'Stockdale, the political

---

[49] *Jefferson Papers*, 13: 434, 650; 14: 511.

bookseller, however, informed me today that he had just been assured by a person very high in office, that no war would happen.'[50]

Some of the books which Jefferson bought from Stockdale went to a most suitable resting place. After British troops had set fire to Congress and the White House in Washington in 1814, Jefferson's library was bought to form the nucleus of the new Library of Congress collection. Jefferson at once started to build up a new collection for his own library, but without Stockdale, who died in that year. On June 10, 1815, Jefferson wrote to John Adams, with whom he was once again on good terms, to thank him for introducing two young men. He continued: 'Mr. [George] Ticknor is particularly the best bibliograph I have met with, and very kindly and opportunely offered me the means of re-procuring some part of the library treasures which I have ceded to Congress to replace the devastation of British vandalism at Washington. I cannot live without books; but fewer will suffice where amusement, and not use, is the only future object.'[51]

Of the 6500 or so books that Jefferson sold to Congress in 1815, only some 2000 are still in existence, the remainder having been destroyed in a fire in 1851, for which the British cannot be blamed. Some of those survivors will have started their journey in Piccadilly, opposite Burlington House. Jefferson's own annotated copy of Stockdale's edition of *Notes on the State of Virginia* is, most appropriately, in the Alderman Library of the University of Virginia, which Jefferson designed. He never wrote another book, but it was enough on its own to ensure Jefferson

---

[50] *Jefferson Papers* 17: 605. Humphreys, like Barlow and Trumbull, was one of the patriotic literary circle known as the Hartford Wits. Peterson, *Thomas Jefferson and the New Nation*, 296.

[51] Cappon, Lester J., *The Adams-Jefferson Letters*, Chapel Hill: U. of North Carolina P., 1959, 2: 443.

'a scientific and literary reputation to accompany his reputation as a political philosopher and statesman.'[52]

The book has never been out of the public eye in America. An excerpt is carved into the Jefferson Memorial in Washington, albeit in a drastically edited version, which makes Jefferson's views on slavery and emancipation appear more liberal than they were in his full texts.[53] It has been republished many times, the last occasion being in 1999, by Penguin. Jefferson's work is still studied in the United States, not only by historians, but by students of American literature and others. The only other book published by Stockdale which may be said to come close in distinction to that of Jefferson, is John Adams's three-volume work, which we must now consider.

---

[52] Peterson, *Thomas Jefferson and the New Nation*, 264.

[53] O'Brien, Conor Cruise, *Memoir – My Life and Themes*, London: Profile Books, 1998, 388.

9

John Adams's Defence

The year 1787 was of great importance to both Jefferson and Adams as authors, but in the greater scheme of things it was the year of the Constitutional Convention, which both men missed because they were representing their country in France and England, respectively. They were by then, incidentally, the only two ministers serving the United States abroad. In this chapter we shall consider briefly how the two absentees were able to have an influence, by virtue of their pen, on the deliberations of their fifty-five compatriots who met in Philadelphia in May to hammer out a new Constitution. We shall also consider the book by Adams, which was his main work and highly relevant to the discussions, but which appeared too late to be of much help. The outcome of the deliberations at the end of the summer was the new Constitution, which, apart from anything else, made it possible for Washington, Adams and Jefferson to become President of the United States in turn. Before that, as discussed earlier, there was no President of the whole country, but merely the President of Congress and of some individual States.

The Convention was convened because the Articles of Confederation of 1781 were outdated and quite inadequate for the new country. One of their many shortcomings, of which Adams was very critical, was the fact that they made provision for only a single-chamber legislature, which was powerless, whereas he and many others regarded a bicameral institution, with adequate powers, as essential. Eleven States had already made their agreement on the main point clear, by instituting two houses for each

of their separate legislatures. Among other important issues to
be considered was the question of how the membership of the
two separate chambers was to be made up, so as to ensure that
the larger States did not swamp the smaller ones. It was once
more a crucial time for the country: 'The American Revolution
thus entered a second phase and the constitutional settlement of
1787-1788 became a second "founding moment", alongside the
original occasion of 1776.'[1]

Fortunately, Jefferson and Adams were not missed too
much, because there was a wealth of talent in Philadelphia when
the fifty-five framers assembled from the thirteen States.
Washington represented Virginia and presided over the Convention, while his former aide, Alexander Hamilton, soon to be his
first Secretary of the Treasury, came as one of the delegates of
New York. James Madison, Jefferson's friend and ally, who was
to play the leading role, also came from Virginia. Benjamin
Franklin, having made his final crossing of the Atlantic, was one
of the 1776 stalwarts attending. So, too, was John Dickinson,
'the Penman of the Revolution', who had declined to sign the
Declaration of Independence and so had muffed his chance to
sign both seminal documents.

Henry Laurens had been chosen to be a delegate for South
Carolina, but had turned the honour down in view of his ill-
health. He was not replaced but his State's delegation was still
exceptionally strong, being made up of future national person-
alities, led by Laurens's friend and former lawyer, John Rutledge.
The other three members were Charles Pinckney, shortly to
become Laurens's son-in-law and a later United States Senator;
Charles Cotesworth Pinckney, who had studied law with Blackstone at Oxford and at the Middle Temple and was to be sent
on an important mission to France by President Adams; and
Pierce Butler, soon to be his State's first United States Senator.

---

[1] Ellis, Joseph J., *Founding Brothers: The Revolutionary Generation*, London:
Faber and Faber, 2002, 9.

Rutledge's younger brother Edward had been one of the five signers of the Declaration who were members of the Middle Temple. The thirty-nine eventual signers of the draft Constitution included seven members of the Inn, among them the elder Rutledge, the two Pinckneys and Dickinson.[2]

As more than half the delegates were lawyers educated either in England or in America, or both, there was an ample collective memory of the strengths and weaknesses of the English Constitution and legal system. Constitutional battles fought in the Old Country, such as the efforts of Wilkes and Almon to obtain freedom of speech and of the press, formed a part of their background. Those delegates will also have been readers of Blackstone's *Commentaries on the Laws of England*, which was cited during the Convention.

The relationship with Britain was a matter which was discussed at the Convention. Franklin made a point which the present writer has been attempting to make – and one that Adams would have been reluctant to concede: 'Even in the country with which we have been lately at war, we have now and had during the war a great many friends not only among the people at large but in both Houses of Parliament.'[3]

The issue of slavery was one which was – once more – effectively shelved until the Civil War, as at the Convention it had again threatened to split the thirteen States. This was scarcely surprising, as more than half the delegates were slave owners, some of whom asserted their agreement, in principle,

---

[2] Bradford, M. E., *Founding Fathers*, Lawrence: U. of Kansas P., 2nd ed., 1994, 188. The other three were William Livingston from New Jersey, Jared Ingersoll, Jr. from Pennsylvania and John Blair, Jr. from Virginia.
[3] Brands, H. W., *The First American*, New York: Doubleday, 2000, 688. Franklin also later made the oft-quoted and typical comment: 'Our Constitution is in actual operation; everything appears to promise that it will last; but in this world nothing is certain but death and taxes.'

with abolition, but who found spurious reasons for adding that the time was not ripe for such a step.[4]

The absent Jefferson's contribution was three-fold. First, his previous written work, including his privately printed *Notes on Virginia*, influenced some of the framers directly. Secondly, he had an additional indirect effect on the discussions. His friend and former colleague in the Virginia legislature, James Madison, had a great influence at the Convention, mainly because he was well informed about different political systems. He was extremely well read, partly because Jefferson had shipped him – to use Madison's own expression – a 'literary cargo', which had 'a great and immediate effect on Madison's constitutional studies'.[5] Jefferson's third and probably most important contribution, came after the Constitution had been signed. The Convention delegates had decided, for differing reasons, that there was no need for any Bill of Rights. Jefferson disagreed most strongly and wrote to Madison from Paris on December 20, 1787: 'I will now add what I do not like. First, the omission of a bill of rights providing clearly and without sophisms for freedom of religion, freedom of the press, protection against standing armies....'[6] Madison was prepared to change his mind and in 1789, as a member of the first United States Congress, helped to get the first twelve amendments to the ratified Constitution passed. The first ten became known collectively as the Bill of Rights. The First Amendment Freedom of Speech and Freedom of the Press owed a debt to the efforts of Almon and Wilkes, while the Fourth Amendment protection against unreasonable searches and seizures was largely inspired by other battles of Wilkes.

---

[4] Bradford, xvi.

[5] Malone, Dumas, *Jefferson and the Rights of Man*, Boston: Little, Brown, 1951, 87, 162; Bradford, 135.

[6] *Jefferson Papers*, 12: 440.

In parenthesis it should be added that the new Congress obviously replaced the earlier Continental Congress. It seems somehow appropriate for the present work that the last President of Congress, Cyrus Griffin, like the first one, Peyton Randolph, was a member of the Middle Temple.

The value of the contribution of Adams was similar to that of Jefferson. He had written a great deal about relevant topics over the years and so his greatest influence was on those framers who had read and agreed with his earlier published thoughts. On February 4, 1787, Adams wrote to his friend, Dr. Price: 'In the beginning of 1776 I wrote, at the desire of several gentlemen in Congress, a short sketch of a government which they caused to be printed under the title *Thoughts on Government in a Letter from a Gentleman to his Friend*, in which three independent branches were insisted on. This pamphlet was scattered through the States and was known to be mine.'[7] That pamphlet, together with the Massachusetts Constitution, which he had drafted in 1779, during his brief return to America, helped the framers to opt for the bicameral legislature and the separation of powers[8] As soon as the first volume of the new book by Adams, discussed below, appeared early in 1787, he sent copies to Jefferson and to his friends in America and received some compliments in return. His old friend, Dr. Benjamin Rush, wrote from the Convention to say that it had 'diffused such excellent principles among us, that there is little doubt of our adopting a vigorous and compound federal legislature.'[9]

Jefferson clearly appreciated that he had missed out by not being at the Convention, for he described it in a letter to Adams as 'an assembly of demi-gods'.[10] While anxious to return to

---

[7] *Mass. Hist. Soc. Procs.*, 2nd Series, 1903, 17: 364.

[8] I am obliged to Gregg Lint, former editor of the *Adams Papers*, for this point in a communication to me.

[9] McCullough, David, *John Adams*, New York: Simon & Schuster, 2001, 378.

[10] *Jefferson Papers*, 12: 69.

America as soon as possible, Adams does not seem to have minded being absent from the discussions in Philadelphia on this occasion: his principal points were covered satisfactorily in his absence, and before long he was to be runner-up to Washington in the first Presidential election. However, before we meet Adams as Vice-President, we must return to the three-volume book he wrote in 1786 and 1787.

In June 1776, Congress had entrusted the drafting of the Declaration of Independence to Adams, Jefferson, Franklin and two others. Jefferson is the acknowledged author of the document and Adams later recollected that it was he who had suggested to his colleague that he should draft it. The main reason he gave his friend was simple: 'You can write ten times better than I can.'[11] The admiration Adams expressed for Jefferson's *Notes on the State of Virginia* was a genuine one, but it may also have been tinged with envy. Although the two men were friends and allies on many issues, there was always a rivalry as well. Leaving aside the Presidential elections in which they ran against one another, each winning one, Adams and Jefferson were in competition at other times. Adams, while admiring Jefferson's landmark book, may well have had it in the back of his mind – or possibly the front – that it would be rather satisfying to produce a book that would be equally important, one by which he would be remembered. He often felt that he was not given enough credit for his contributions and was very conscious of the view that posterity would take of his life's work – hence, apart from anything else, his early useful decision that all his correspondence should be preserved. In any event, while Jefferson was arranging with Stockdale for the publication of his book in 1786 and 1787, Adams was hard at work on his own major work, the three-volume *A Defence of the Constitutions of Government of the United States of America.*

---

[11] McCullough, 119.

Although Adams detected some hostility to America while in England, especially from a few newspapers and from the more vociferous loyalists, he certainly had some good English friends, and he liked a number of English institutions, both political, such as the basic constitutional structure, and non-political, such as the bookshops, theatres and gardens. It will be seen later that after his return to America, while sharing Washington's desire for neutrality, he had little difficulty in preferring a trade agreement with Britain to one with France. One of his friends in England was Thomas Brand Hollis, who had inherited the estate of his rich friend, Thomas Hollis, the benefactor of the library at Harvard. His original surname was Brand but he added that of his friend to his own. As mentioned earlier, it was Hollis who had worked closely with Almon to get American pamphlets published in England.

In July 1786, Adams and his family paid a visit to Brand Hollis at his house, The Hyde, in Essex, where Adams was able to take a critical look at the library. Brand Hollis made Adams a present of a book: Marchamont Nedham's *The Excellencie of a Free State*. This had originally appeared in different issues of the *Mercurius Politicus* in 1651 and 1652, during the Commonwealth (England's taste of the republic), and in book form in 1656. A century later, in 1767, Thomas Hollis had recognised the worth of Nedham's ideas and arranged for a re-publication.[12]

The gift to Adams bore the inscription, 'Mr. Brand Hollis requests the favour of his friend Mr. Adams to accept benevolently this book, to be deposited among his republican tracts, which after the pomp and pageantry of monarchy, "the trappings of which would maintain a moderate republic", he will relish well.' Haraszti concluded: 'Undoubtedly, it was the receipt of this volume that prompted Adams to write his review.'

---

[12] Haraszti, Zoltan, *John Adams and the Prophets of Progress*, Cambridge: Harvard U.P., 1952, 162. It will soon be apparent how much I am indebted to this learned author and librarian in this chapter.

In the autumn of 1786, Adams visited Holland once again and on his return to Grosvenor Square concentrated nearly all his efforts on the first volume of his *Defence*. His expressed reasons for embarking on the work appear in later letters but vary a little. Many years afterwards, when both he and Jefferson had been President, and after they had disagreed bitterly about the French Revolution, Adams wrote to his friend that his fundamental political tenet was the proposition that 'despotism, or unlimited sovereignty, or absolute power is the same in a majority of a popular assembly, an aristocratical council, an oligarchical junto, and a single emperor. Equally arbitrary, cruel, bloody, and in every respect diabolical.'[13]

Adams's own remedy was the separation of powers, although Haraszti emphasized that his idea of separation was different from the more generally accepted one. 'What mattered for him was not the separation of the legislative, executive, and judiciary functions but the equilibrium of the democratic, aristocratic, and monarchic elements.' In particular, as we have already seen, he was devoted to the bicameral legislature with a passion bordering on monomania. It was largely to counter the arguments of Turgot in favour of a single chamber (which were set out in his letter to Dr. Price), that Adams decided to start work on his *Defence*. He virtually locked himself away with a large pile of books on history and politics, and wrote so fast that the first volume was ready in January and published by Charles Dilly in February 1787.

On January 15, 1787, Adams gave the following reasons for his new venture in a letter to his brother-in-law, Richard Cranch. 'I lament that it is so hasty a production. It is only since my return from Holland in September that I began to collect the materials. But the disturbances in New England made it necessary to publish immediately in order to do any good. My friends in Holland were much employed in revolutions. In several

---

[13] Haraszti, 26, 30.

conversations there I had occasion to mention some things respecting governments which some of these gentlemen wished to see on paper. Their desire, falling in with the seditious meetings in Massachusetts, determined me to write.'[14]

The disturbances in his home State were the ones collectively known as Shays's rebellion. Adams mentioned that he was partly writing to satisfy his Dutch friends: it was a similar situation to that which had led to his *Letters to Dr. Calkoen*. The first volume of the *Defence*, like the Calkoen letters, was at first intended for the eyes of only a few. On January 17, Abigail Adams wrote to their son, John Quincy, at Harvard, 'The seditions in Massachusetts induced your pappa to give the world a book which at first he designed only for a few friends.'[15] That last minute change of mind on the part of Adams, converting the project from a private limited edition into a publicly issued book, may explain why Dilly published that first volume on his own. The author seems to have realised that he could do better if he were to make use of Stockdale's location, clientele and American contacts. As a result he got Dilly and Stockdale to publish the second and third volumes jointly.

That Adams bought a large number of books while working on the *Defence* is clear from the contents of the three volumes. Quite a number must have come from the nearby bookshop he knew well. The proximity of Stockdale's shop probably explains the absence of any correspondence between him and Adams at this stage: Adams no doubt called in regularly to buy books in stock and to place orders for others. A letter of February 5, 1788, confirms that he was a frequent visitor there, as well as confirming the fact that the bookshop was used as a meeting place. Herbert Croft, a lexicographer, who had become aware of Adams's views about the importance of the English language, wrote to him: 'If Mr. Adams would condescend so far as to

---

[14] C. F. Adams, 1: 432.
[15] Adams Papers, Reel 369.

afford Mr. C. an opportunity of explaining the new dictionary, on which he is employed, of the language spoken in Great Britain and America, Mr. C. would be happy in the honour of waiting upon Mr. Adams or of meeting him any day at Mr. Stockdale's.'[16]

Unfortunately, Adams used the various books he had bought by extracting large chunks from them, some in their original language. He often failed to give the source of the quotations and sometimes even failed to make it clear that he was quoting, but he was not unique as an eighteenth-century author in writing like this. It will be seen later that Dr. David Ramsay, the first American historian of note, was guilty of similar neglect. Haraszti carefully checked the sources quoted by Adams and found that the major part of both first two volumes were extracts from commentators on different republican experiments. The third volume was better, in that only half the work was made up of quotes. Nedham's book provided the principal inspiration for the third volume, which Haraszti considered the best of the three.[17]

In 1789, Adams was appalled by the excesses of the French revolution. Partly because of that, in the following year, while serving as Vice-President, Adams began to write a series of discourses on Enrico Caterino Davila's *Historia delle Guerre Civile di Francia*, spread over a year, for the *Gazette of the United States*, edited by John Fenno. It is clear from what occurred later that Jefferson, the Francophile, read them with distaste.[18] The *Discourses on Davila* appeared in book form only in 1805, and may be regarded, according to Adams himself, as a supplement to his three-volume *Defence*. Haraszti made the point that the four volumes together, which are not easy to read, led to Adams having the reputation as 'a dull and ponderous writer', despite

---

[16] Adams Papers, Reel 371.

[17] Haraszti, 87.

[18] See chapter 15.

the fact that in his other works, he 'wrote a powerful and trenchant English'.

In recent times his *Defence* and other writings have been reassessed by a number of Adams experts. Richard Ryerson drew attention to two important effects of his work. First, Adams was a great influence on the small number of important revolutionary leaders. 'The second effect of his heavily documented prose has been to reveal to posterity with an exceptional clarity the intellectual underpinnings of the American Revolution.'[19]

The jury is still out on the quality of Adams's books. There is some suggestion that his style was possibly affected by a recurring bout of illness caused by a hyperactive thyroid, or Graves' disease, which made him ramble on when writing, without much self-control.[20] Despite that possible medical condition, Bradley Thompson thought that the *Defence* 'may very well be one of the most important reformulations of the theory of mixed and balanced government since Aristotle's *Politics*.' He added: 'In Europe, the *Defence* was praised rather lavishly. Dr. Richard Price was ecstatic about the treatise. He thought that Adams had made a genuine and important contribution to the science of politics. The subject of government, he wrote, was now "better understood than ever it was".'[21]

Adams always found it difficult to accept criticism. He knew very well that he had not devoted sufficient time to the writing of the *Defence*. Despite that, 'When offered the opportunity to revise the entire work in 1794, however, he declined.'[22] It was

---

[19] Ryerson, Richard Alan (ed.), *John Adams and the Founding of the Republic*, Boston: Mass. Hist. Soc., 2001, 23,24.

[20] Ellis, *Founding Brothers*, 218. Having read of that theory, the present writer decided to make an urgent appointment to see his own physician.

[21] Thompson, C. Bradley, 'John Adams and the Science of Politics', in Ryerson, 257, 258.

[22] Ellis, Joseph J., *Passionate Sage – The Character and Legacy of John Adams*, New York: Norton, 1994, 147.

Stockdale who gave him that opportunity; Adams's negative response to his proposal will be discussed later. In the meantime, Stockdale was prompted by Adams to consider publishing, or at any rate, selling the works of other American authors. This turned out to be a difficult task, as is clear from the letters passing between the bookseller and two of those authors, David Ramsay and Jedidiah Morse.[23]

By the time John Adams left London for the last time on March 30,1788, four-and-a-half years after visiting it for the first time, he must have appreciated that his view about the British hating all Americans was wildly incorrect. It is true that some of the press had been fairly hostile. This was an unfortunate change from the strong support accorded to the American cause by most of the newspapers in earlier times, and may perhaps be attributable in part to the venom of some unhappy loyalists in London, and to a lesser extent by the loss of British lives – which had been amply forecast. However, the *Whitehall Evening Post* was one of the papers that was friendly to Adams on his departure, pointing out, 'That gentleman settled all his concerns with great honour; and whatever his political tenets may have been, he was much respected and esteemed in this country.'[24]

Adams had met many fair-minded and polite Britons, including, somewhat to his surprise, the King himself. Thomas Brand Hollis was one of the closest of the friends that he had made in England. On December 3, 1788, Adams wrote to him from Massachusetts, 'I regret the loss of the booksellers' shops, and the society of the few men of letters that I knew in London.' One can certainly accept that he missed the bookshops of London: Boston could hardly compete. It had taken John

---

[23] See chaps.14 and 16. The layman's distinction between publishing and merely selling is used here. However, as a matter of law, even selling on its own constitutes publication for the purposes of libel, whether criminal or civil.

[24] McCullough, 348, 383.

Quincy Adams three days to unpack the books his father had brought home in June, admittedly not all from London.[25]

His wife Abigail probably gave a much fairer picture of their three-year stay in Grosvenor Square, when she wrote to that same English friend on September 6, 1790, from New York: 'I place the hours spent at the Hyde amongst some of the most pleasurable of my days, and I esteem your friendship as one of the most valuable acquisitions that I made in your country: a country that I should most sincerely rejoice to visit again, if I could do it without crossing the ocean. I have sometimes been suspected of partiality for the preference given to England, but were I to live out of America, that country would have been my choice.' Abigail Adams went on to give the news that her daughter, Nabby, 'respecting the name of the great literary benefactor of her native state, and in grateful remembrance of the friendly attention, and patriotic character of its present possessor, has named her new-born son Thomas-Hollis.'[26]

---

[25] Haraszti, 15.
[26] Disney, John, *Memoirs of Thomas Brand-Hollis*, London: T. Gillet, 1808, 35, 39.

Illus. 11. Thomas Day by Joseph Wright of Derby

10

Thomas Day and Stockdale's Children's Books

Thomas Day's greatest personal friend was his fellow Middle Temple barrister, Richard Lovell Edgeworth, better known as an inventor. That talent probably increased Day's regard for him, for they both became members of the group of friends eventually known as the Lunar Society, made up mainly of men with a scientific bent, such as Joseph Priestley, Erasmus Darwin, Josiah Wedgwood, Matthew Boulton and James Watt. Edgeworth had a large number of children, so he became interested in the question of education generally, but more particularly in the shortage of suitable books for children. His eldest daughter, who was considerably influenced by Day in her youth, was the novelist Maria Edgeworth. Her first book, which she wrote in 1787 but withheld until after Day's death, was based on conversations of her father with Day. It was published in 1789, by Joseph Johnson, as *Letters to Literary Ladies*.[1]

As Roy Porter has pointed out, 'The Edgeworths and others in late Enlightenment circles made a religion of education.' Day was clearly one of their co-religionists.[2] After her father's death, Maria completed his memoirs, describing how he had started to write for children, and how Day had joined in the venture. The style of their work was greatly influenced by Jean-Jacques

---

[1] Tyson, Gerald P., *Joseph Johnson: A Liberal Publisher*, Iowa City: U. Iowa P., 1979, 144.
[2] Porter, Roy, *Enlightenment*, London: Penguin, 2000, 345.

Rousseau, who had gained a reputation for his educational approach to children. 'Were all the books in the world to be destroyed, except scientific books (which I except, not to affront you),' Day had earlier written to Edgeworth, 'the second book I should wish to save, after the Bible, would be Rousseau's *Emilius*. It is indeed a most extraordinary work – the more I read, the more I admire. Rousseau alone, with a perspicuity more than mortal, has been able at once to look through the human heart, and discover the secret sources and combinations of the passions. Every page is big with important truth.'[3]

Maria described how her father and stepmother, Honora, had begun to write a suitable book for their first child, after they had 'found the want of something to follow Mrs. Barbauld's lessons and felt the difficulty of explaining the language of the books of children which were then in use.' [4]Together they wrote a piece called *The History of Harry and Lucy*, which they intended to continue as a series. 'Mr. Day, who was very pleased with my father's plan, offered to assist him, and with this intention began 'Sandford and Merton', which was first designed for a short story to be inserted in *Harry and Lucy*. The illness of Mrs. Honora Edgeworth interrupted the progress of that little volume and, after her death, the ideas associated with it were so painful to my father that it was not at the time continued. Meanwhile, Mr. Day wrote on rapidly, and finished and published his delightful book. Often, with pride and pleasure, my father used to say that the public owed *Sandford and Merton* to him, since it was he who first turned his friend's attention to the subject of education, and excited him to write that popular and useful work.'

---

[3] Edgeworth, Maria, *Memoirs of R. L. Edgeworth*, London: Hunter and Baldwin, Cradock and Joy, 1820, 1: 221.

[4] Edgeworth, 2: 312. The reference was to Anna Laetitia Barbauld's books for the very young that Johnson had published in 1778. Barbauld had also embarked on her books because unable to find anything suitable for her son. Tyson, 83.

Stockdale, who had known Day for all or most of his six years at Almon's shop, published the first volume of his *History of Sandford and Merton* in 1783, and it was an immediate success. The second followed in 1786, and the third and final volume was completed by Day shortly before his premature death, after a riding accident, on September 28, 1789. Porter has commented that Day, 'that omnipresent enlightened man', had championed animals and believed in treating them with kindness. He tried that idea out on his colt, which threw him. 'He had no more success than he did with Rousseau's theories on how to train a wife; the humanitarian died from his injuries, the English Enlightenment's authentic martyr.'[5]

Two months before his death, on July 28, Day had written a rebuke to his publisher and friend, using his didactic style. 'If you manage your affairs with other people as ill as you some-times do with me, I think it must tend very considerably to your own loss. I have bought one of Dixon's *Voyage* some time ago; not contented with this, you sent me a second: I told you of this last time you were down here, and should have sent it back, had I not been unexpectedly seized with the ague. Not contented with this, you have now sent me a third copy of the same dull book. As a little lesson I have taken the liberty of sending them all three back, and will now take neither of them. I have also to remind you that you have now had my account for several months, if not for some years, and you have made no progress in settling it; which is disagreeable to me, a man of method and regularity, though an author. My second lesson will therefore be this, that though I have finished the third volume ready for printing, I will not send the conclusion until you let me know, by a letter signed by your wife (for I will not take your word) that

---

[5] Porter, 350.

all our accounts are exactly balanced. I am your affectionate friend, Thos. Day.'[6]

Day had a point. Although a mere author, he was more efficient than his publisher at this time. However, Stockdale had some mitigation: his mother, Priscilla, had died after an illness, four days before the date of Day's letter, which probably arrived on the day of her funeral, July 29, and he must have been worried about his impending trial for publishing Logan's Warren Hastings pamphlet.[7]

Day's completed three-volume work was one of Stockdale's standard books and best-sellers, despite the fact that it was regularly pirated by different publishers. Incidentally, in a letter of March 17, 1794, to one of his American authors, Jedidiah Morse, Stockdale explained how he used retaliation as a weapon against one of the pirates of Day's book.[8] In 1795, Stockdale increased the popularity of the book by compressing it into one volume and reducing the price from nine shillings to three shillings and sixpence. The work became popular abroad as well as in England: we have seen from Stockdale's request to Jefferson, for a copy of the French version, how quickly the first volume had been translated into French after he had published it in English. Jenny Uglow has stated: 'Saccharine though it seems today, *Sandford and Merton* fed the imagination of the coming Romantic generation, and of the Victorians – running through a

---

[6] Bodleian, MS Montague, d 12, f.206; Gignilliat, G. W., *The Author of Sandford and Merton*, New York: Columbia U.P., 1932, 307.

[7] *Gentleman's Magazine*, 59: 763; Moravian Church Archives and Library, Muswell Hill, London. Stockdale's father, Joseph, had died in 1781 and after that his mother probably lived with his brother, Jeremiah, who had a mill-maker's business in Newton Street, High Holborn. As she was a member of the Moravian congregation at the nearby Fetter Lane chapel, she was buried in the Moravian burial ground in Chelsea, in the presence of six of her children.

[8] See chap.16.

hundred and forty editions before 1870.' Not many authors achieve figures of that order.[9]

The only other book that Day wrote for children was *The History of Little Jack*. This first appeared as one of the stories in *The Children's Miscellany* in 1788. Day's principal biographer, G. W. Gignilliat, was fairly certain that Day was also the author of the preface of that miscellany, pointing out, 'The publication was infused with Day's ideas. Pride is reformed by disastrous experience. Love of finery is rebuked. Virtue, especially generosity, is rewarded. A hardy, useful education is recommended.' He added that some of the stories were 'remarkably like those in *Sandford and Merton*'.[10]

Writing some thirty years after his death, Maria Edgeworth commented that it was 'remarkable' that Day's fame would probably rest on the works he personally regarded as the most perishable. 'He valued, in preference to his other writings, certain political tracts; but these, though finely written, full of manly spirit and classic eloquence, have passed away, and are heard of no more, while his *History of Sandford and Merton*, and even the story of *Little Jack*, are still popular. Wherever children are to be found, these will continue interesting and useful from generation to generation.'[11]

It is hardly surprising that the political pamphlets were not read by then: by their very nature they had a limited lifespan – even though we have considered some of them earlier. The last assertion by Maria Edgeworth certainly proved true for several decades, but Day's little heroes are scarcely known to the modern reader, save as characters who play a part in the history of children's literature. Michael Sadler commented, 'To read *The History of Sandford and Merton* is like looking into an eighteenth

---

[9] Gignilliat, 338; Uglow, Jenny, *The Lunar Men*, London: Faber and Faber, 2002, 322.

[10] Gignilliat, 300.

[11] Edgeworth, 2: 100.

century doll's house and finding the figures alive'; while Brian Doyle described Day's book as 'the greatest and most famous of what have become known as the "didactic" children's books of the eighteenth and early nineteenth centuries.'[12]

The poet and writer Leigh Hunt, who was born in 1783 (and whose father had earlier fled to England from Philadelphia as a loyalist), when writing his autobiography, had a clear recollection of the children's books available in his youth: 'Every good boy was to ride in his coach and be a lord mayor; and every bad boy was to be hung or eaten by lions. The gingerbread was gilt, and the books were gilt like the gingerbread. The pool of mercenary and time-serving ethics was first blown over by the fresh country breeze of Mr. Day's *Sandford and Merton* – a production that I well remember, and shall ever be grateful to. It came in aid of my mother's perplexities between delicacy and hardihood, between courage and conscientiousness. It assisted the cheerfulness I inherited from my father; showed me that circumstances were not to crush a healthy gaiety, or the most masculine self-respect.' Similarly, the publisher Charles Knight wrote, 'For myself, I cannot be sufficiently grateful to Thomas Day, who gave me *Little Jack* and *Sandford and Merton*.'[13]

Another of Stockdale's authors, Henry James Pye, who has a strong claim to the title of Worst Poet Laureate of all time, published an elegy after Day's death. 'His verses were pronounced to be the most beautiful of all the tributes to Day,' wrote S. H. Scott, another of his biographers, 'but Pye's verses invariably raised a smile from the sophisticated, in an age which could swallow a good deal without flicker of an eyelid. Even in

---

[12] Sadler, Michael, *Thomas Day, An English Disciple of Rousseau*, Cambridge U.P., 1928, 44; Doyle, Brian, *The Who's Who of Children's Literature*, London: Hugh Evelyn, 1968, 71.

[13] *The Autobiography of Leigh Hunt*, Oxford U.P., 1928, 70; Knight, Charles, *Shadows of the Old Booksellers*, London: Bell and Daldy, 1865, 243.

death Day was fated to appear slightly ridiculous.'[14] It was bad luck for Day that he should be the subject of an elegy by the man who was to produce, as Laureate, many a dreadful offering to George III, and of whom Byron wrote, in *The Vision of Judgment* :

> The monarch, mute till then, exclaim'd
> 'What! what!
> Pye come again? no more – no more of
> That!'

Anna Seward, a former friend, wrote a fairly cool appreciation of Day for the *Publisher's Advertiser* after his death. This upset Edgeworth so much that he immediately began to write a biography of Day; certainly nobody was better qualified for the task. With Maria acting as his secretary, Edgeworth worked on the project for a short while only, before discovering that the scientist, James Keir – another member of the Lunar Society – was also writing a life of their mutual friend. Edgeworth abandoned his own project and passed his notes over to Keir.

Day, who had only married his wife Esther late in life, had promised Edgeworth his library before that marriage. After his death Edgeworth very properly waived any claim that he might have had and received a moving letter of thanks from Mrs. Day: 'I will ingenuously own, that of all the bequests he could have made, the leaving his whole library from me would have mortified me the most, indeed more than if he had disposed of all his other property, and left me only that. My ideas of him are so much associated with his books, that to part with them would be, as it were, breaking some of the last ties which still connect me with so beloved an object. The being in the midst of books he has been accustomed to read, and which contain his marks and notes, will still give him a sort of *existence* with me. Unintelligible as such fond chimera may appear to many people, I am

---

[14] Scott, S. H., *The Exemplary Mr. Day*, London: Faber and Faber, 1935, 170.

persuaded they are not so to you.'[15] Unfortunately, the library and its contents did not console Mrs. Day for long: she survived her husband for less than three years.

Stockdale published James Keir's *An Account of the Life and Writings of Thomas Day* in 1791, but once again, problems with a plate delayed the work. In April, Keir wrote to Dr. Erasmus Darwin (grandfather of Charles Darwin) who was a also a member of the Lunar Society, 'My book has been ready for publication, printed &c., these two months, but waited for an engraving of Mr. Day, which was at last produced, but with such perfect destruction of the likeness, that it has been thought, by Mrs. Day and myself, better to destroy than publish a head in which no soul seems to reside.' Keir received a letter shortly after this which reported, 'Mrs. Day has been this morning with Stockdale and expressed a desire that your book should appear without the plate, and that the plate should be destroyed.' Day, like several other members of the Lunar Society, had been painted by the superb artist, Joseph Wright of Derby, so it looks as though the public may have been deprived of a copy of the portrait now in the National Portrait Gallery. In fact, the British Library copy of Keir's book has a perfectly acceptable portrait of Day as a frontispiece, but it is by G. Wood.[16]

Keir made a very neat distinction between Day and the Frenchman who had inspired him: 'We cannot avoid remarking the contrast of Mr. Day and of Rousseau. Mr. Day received two orphans under his protection; while the celebrated philosopher of Switzerland placed five of his own children in a foundling hospital at Paris.'[17]

On June 15, 1792, Stockdale wrote a letter to Keir, which indicates how much he had kept in touch with his friend's

---

[15] Edgeworth, 2: 91.

[16] Moilliet, Amelia, *Sketch of the Life of James Keir*, London: Printed by R. E. Taylor for private circulation, 1860, 112.

[17] Keir, 29.

widow, who had moved to London after her husband's death. 'Mrs. Day got up and drank coffee at 10 o'clock in the morning, was taken ill and expired immediately. I think with you that she died of a broken heart. I can say from my own knowledge that she has not enjoyed one day's comfort or health since our ever to be lamented friend's accident; I am very certain, from a long conversation that passed between her and me alone, that she wished death, preferable to life.'[18]

Stockdale, in the same letter, turned to business matters. Keir had floated the idea of a new edition of his Day biography, even though it had only been out for just over a year. Stockdale's comments show that Keir was financing the book, and also demonstrate his own affection for Day: 'How far it may be prudent to print a new edition of Mr. Day's Life I have my doubts, in point of profit, or without running some risk, as the present edition has been some time in going off. It has stood in catalogues that I have printed, not less than 30,000 in different forms, so that it has had every possible chance that I could give it; yet, was it my property instead of yours, it never should be out of print in one form or another while I lived. I mention this merely to show you my opinion, but I do not speak as a bookseller.'

The letter concluded: 'Mrs. Stockdale desires her kind respects; she and daughter are distressed at our second loss beyond description, as they were rather favourites, or at least vain enough to think themselves so.' The daughter mentioned was Stockdale's only daughter, Mary Ridgway Stockdale, who was by then grown up enough to consider herself a poet, inspired by Thomas Day and also – most unfortunately – by Henry James Pye.

We have now seen, in this chapter and earlier ones, that Day's interests ranged from the study of law, to essays on the American Revolution and slavery, and to books for children. Despite the breadth of his education and his interests he was, by

---

[18] Moilliet, 115.

no means uniquely, a male chauvinist. He may have given the impression, at times, of being a rather dull dog, but it would be a mistake to regard him as humourless. Keir wrote, 'To strangers he sometimes appeared rather too grave, whereas at home, with his familiar friends, he possessed not only an uniform cheerfulness, but also a singular gaiety of temper.' Maria Edgeworth wrote that Day 'had a horror of female authorship: at one time, he was nearly of Sir Anthony Absolute's opinion, that the extent of a woman's erudition should consist in her knowing her simple letters, without their mischievous combinations.'[19]

The ironic letter which Day wrote for a newspaper on the subject of female authors – but may not have despatched – deserves a wider readership: 'I think it one of the peculiar blessings of the present age, that the fair sex have so far emancipated themselves from former restraints, as boldly to indulge their genius in the course of literature. How far these fair adventurers may enlarge the limits of science, I will not pretend to decide; but I hope to see the period, and even flatter myself that period is at no great distance, where there shall not be a town in England, and scarcely a private family without its authoress. The infinite advantages this will produce to the morals, the taste, and happiness of the world, are too evident to need enumeration. Every mother will then be enabled to instruct her children, and form their tender minds to the love of glory, by favouring them with a perusal of her own works; and every blooming virgin will enchant her lover, not by tender looks, or gracious smiles, or the common arts by which affections are subdued, but by giving him an order to her printer:

'Sir, Please to let Henry Languish, Esq., have on demand five copies of my Essay upon the National Debt; as also sixteen of my Critical Observations on the various readings of the Pentateuch, from, Sir, yours &c.
Arabella Tender.'

---

[19] Keir, 130; Edgeworth, 2: 320.

Day's letter continued in a wonderfully prophetic manner: he must have been one of the first to foresee the arrival of the house-husband. 'Can there be a more edifying spectacle conceived, than that of a husband performing all the duties of a good housewife, instructing the cook in the discharge of her culinary functions, weighing out the ingredients of a minced pie, or darning the stockings of the family? When little Master is to be dry-nursed, or little Miss has fouled her petticoat, should the servant by mistake apply to his mistress, she will answer, like the great Corneille, Why do you trouble me with these things, you know I never interfere in family matters? If on the contrary, a new coach-horse should be required in the stable, or the steward want to settle his accounts, or the postillion come to complain of the indecent behaviour of Mrs. Betty, who entertains designs against his vartue, the master will refer them to the study, where the delightful consort gives audience in dishabillé.'[20]

Day was Stockdale's principal author of children's books, even though his output was limited; his next most important one was the Frenchman, Arnaud Berquin. We have seen how Stockdale obtained some of his publications with Jefferson's help in Paris. Thereafter he did a good trade in translations of Berquin's books for children, even though he had to share most of them with other publishers. Berquin wrote *L'Ami des Enfants* in twenty-four parts in 1782 and 1783, and then *Lectures pour Enfants, L'Ami des Adolescents* and other works. As Stockdale had mentioned to Jefferson, Berquin had also translated Day's book, without permission, and so he may have been able to use that fact as a bargaining counter.

Stockdale published Berquin's first book, as *The Children's Friend*, in 1787, but as a member of an association. The names and addresses of those involved, shown on the title-page, provide a good cross-section of the bookselling world of the

[20] Lowndes, Thomas, *Select Miscellaneous Productions of Mrs. Day and Thomas Day Esq.*, London: Cadell and Davies, 1805, 111.

day: 'Printed for J. Stockdale, Piccadilly; J. Rivington & Sons, St. Paul's Churchyard; B. Law, Ave Maria Lane; J. Johnson, St. Paul's Churchyard; C. Dilly, Poultry; J. Murray, Fleet Street; J. Sewell, Cornhill, and W. Creech, Edinburgh.' St. Paul's Churchyard and Ave Maria Lane were at the heart of the old Paternoster Row booksellers' area; Poultry and Cornhill lay a little to the east from there, and Fleet Street to the west. Stockdale was the furthest west in St. James's – the only missing links in the chain of shops were a bookseller in the Strand or Covent Garden, and one in Holborn, all on the way to Piccadilly.[21]

Berquin translations which Stockdale published included *The Friend of Youth* in 1787, *The History of Little Grandison* in 1791, and *The Honest Farmer* and *The Family Book, or Children's Journal*, both of which appeared in 1798. The last-named is of interest because the title-page proclaimed that Berquin's stories in it were 'interspersed with poetical pieces written by the translator, Miss Stockdale, Author of *Effusions of the Heart*, Poems.'

Mary Ridgway Stockdale, a spinster all her life, whose collection of poems had been published by her proud father on the same day, clearly did not approve of some of the wicked ways of the French, for she primly announced in the preface of the Berquin book: 'Notwithstanding the deservedly allowed celebrity of the Author of this work, to whom the rising generation is greatly indebted, the Translator must have deemed herself highly culpable, had she permitted it to pass through her hands in its original state. She had, therefore, taken the liberty of altering different parts, for reasons very obvious to the French reader; and which, she is well assured, must meet with the general approbation of parents and others, who have the care of children.' Stockdale also sold Berquin's French version of Day's book, and the French original of *L'Ami des Enfants* – though,

---

[21] For a brief note on the change from the booksellers' conger to the association, see chap.19.

perhaps, only after his daughter had checked it for any naughty French ideas and had bowdlerised it where appropriate.

One suspects that Day, if still alive, would have been dismayed to find that the little Stockdale girl he had known, had turned out to be another Arabella Tender, producing poems inspired by Pye. Unfortunately, she also loved to write poems about death. Even in *The Family Book, or Children's Journal*, she could not resist including her verses on 'The Funeral', which, she informed her happy young readers, 'were occasioned by the melancholy sight of a funeral, where two poor female children followed as chief and only mourners, the eldest apparently not more than ten years old'.

In the following year, 1799, Stockdale also published a poem by his eldest son. John Joseph Stockdale had produced a piece that was the equal in merit to his sister's. It was entitled *Albio-Hibernia; or, the Isle of Erin*, and demonstrated his loyalty to the Crown. The advertisements in the back make rather better reading. The first lists John Stockdale's 'poetical works' and is headed, as may have been guessed by the reader, by Mary's *Effusions of the Heart*. It includes *Poems on various subjects*, by Henry James Pye, Joel Barlow's *The Vision of Columbus* and Gay's *Fables*. *The Dying Negro* is included but attributed to Day alone: Bicknell, his collaborator, is not mentioned. The advertisement on the reverse of the poetry list announces that Stockdale has bought up the remaining copies of Dr. Robert Anderson's *British Poets* from the assignees of Eglin and Pepys, bankrupts. He offers the thirteen volumes for six guineas instead of the original eight and points out that for that money the reader will obtain twice as much as is contained in Samuel Johnson's collection, at half the price.

Day was not the only author who was inspired by Rousseau. In 1788, Stockdale published a translation of Joachim Heinrich Campe's *Robinson der Jüngere*, as *The New Robinson Crusoe*, and the preface mentioned that Campe had been influenced by the following passage from Rousseau's *Emile*. 'Might there not be found means to bring together so many lessons of instruction that lie scattered in so many books. There is one that furnishes, in my opinion, the best imagined treatise upon natural education that can possibly be. The book shall be the first I will put into the hands of my Emilius. Well then, what is this wonderful book? Is it Aristotle, Pliny, Buffon? No: it is *Robinson Crusoe.*' One can now see what inspired the format and wording of Day's letter to Edgeworth, quoted at the beginning of this chapter.

Daniel Defoe's classic had been a runaway success when it had first appeared some seventy years earlier, making a small fortune for William Taylor, the bookseller. It had thereafter been a standard work, but Campe decided that he could improve on it. Defoe's work, Campe asserted, had contained one particular error: Crusoe had been allowed to have European tools on his island. The opportunity had thus been lost of teaching the young reader about 'the wants of man in a state of solitude'.[22]

Stockdale made a notable improvement to Campe's book by including thirty-two woodcuts by John Bewick, who over the years provided illustrations for a number of his publications. John Bewick had recently completed his apprenticeship with his more famous brother Thomas, and was new to London, so he was probably prepared to work for little reward at the beginning of his career. Austin Dobson pointed out that John Bewick's work was mainly on blocks for children's books, such as *The Children's Miscellany* and Campe's book. He added that these books were 'no doubt highly popular with "little Masters and Misses", in frill-collars and mob-caps, who resorted to Mr.

---

[22] For an interesting commentary on the publishing history of *Robinson Crusoe*, see, Rogers, Pat, 'Classics and chapbooks', in Rivers, Isabel (ed.), *Books and their Readers in Eighteenth-Century England*, Leicester U.P., 1982, 27.

Stockdale's in Piccadilly, or Mr. Newbery's at the "Bible and Sun" in St. Paul's Churchyard.'[23]

Dobson was right to couple Stockdale's name with that of Newbery, who is sometimes referred to as though he were the only provider of children's books. Even Richard Altick, in his great work, *The English Common Reader*, failed to mention either Stockdale or Day, writing, 'Apart from the praiseworthy efforts of John Newbery in the eighteenth century, little attempt was made to provide children with reading matter designed especially for them until Maria Edgeworth, Mrs. Sherwood, and the Sunday-school tract writers sharpened their pens early in the nineteenth century.'[24]

Campe had personally translated his book into English in 1781, with the title *Robinson the Younger*, but according to Harvey Darton, 'The English translation which held the market for a generation or more, however, was one published by Stockdale in 1788 and 1789, as *The New Robinson Crusoe*.'[25]

Stockdale was clearly pleased with the combination of the Crusoe story and good illustrations, so in 1790, he put out a beautifully illustrated edition of Defoe's *Robinson Crusoe*. The artist on this occasion was Thomas Stothard, whose biographer wrote: 'In his various illustrations for books there was none more truly beautiful than those he made for *Robinson Crusoe*. I speak of the octavo edition of the novel, published by Stockdale in 1790. Whoever has seen it can never forget the design of Crusoe bringing the things he saved from the ship to the shore on a raft, and the lovely and inviting sylvan scene in the

---

[23] Dobson, Austin, *Thomas Bewick and his Pupils*, London: Chatto and Windus, 1884, 72.

[24] Altick, Richard D., *The English Common Reader*, 2nd ed., Columbus: Ohio U.P., 1998.

[25] Darton, F. J. Harvey, *Children's Books in England*, Cambridge U.P., 1958, 115.

background.'[26] The time was right for books about long voyages and faraway islands, actual and mythical. Stockdale was also busy publishing books about the great voyages and illustrating them with maps.

Since many readers will be acquainted with *The Swiss Family Robinson*, it is only right to point out that this work is sometimes confused with *The New Robinson Crusoe*. The Swiss story was written by Johann David Rudolph Wyss in German, and was published in two parts in Zurich in 1812 and 1813. The English version was published by M.J.Godwin in London in 1816, possibly with some financial help from Percy Bysshe Shelley.[27]

In 1793, Stockdale published two very attractive two-volume works, with uniform printing and binding, which are usually listed among children's books, though such classification may be questioned. The two works were the classic *Fables* of Aesop and the more modern ones of John Gay. These works are probably the most attractive ones that Stockdale published in his thirty-four years as a publisher. In the Gay volumes he mentioned some of the care taken in the production by Thomas Bensley, the printer. 'This book has been carefully hot-pressed, and will be delivered in boards, with silver paper between each plate and the letter press, to prevent the one from injuring the beauty of the other.' Pressing with heat, a process developed by the great typographer, John Baskerville, ensured that the paper used for the plates was as smooth as possible. The Aesop volumes contained no less than 112 plates, and the Gay seventy. Gay's book included an advertisement for the Aesop 'published this day', and made the excellent selling point that the latter work contained plates 'engraved by Grainger, Audinet, Hazell, Lovegrove, Wilson &c.'

---

[26] Bray, Anna Eliza, *Life of Thomas Stothard*, London: John Murray, 1851, 120.

[27] Darton, 115; Newton, A. Edward, *This Book-Collecting Game*, Boston: Little, Brown, 1928, 60.

One of the artists Stockdale had not troubled to name was a man of 36, who ten years earlier had engraved one of the plates in a book that he had published with Dodsley and others: Lodovico Arioso's *Orlando Furioso*. He had also provided one of the engravings for Captain Hunter's book on Australia, which Stockdale had published earlier that year. He was William Blake, but Stockdale clearly did not appreciate that he was soon to be a leading artist, meriting rather more than a mere inclusion in an ampersand.

The second volume of the Gay work contained a note explaining that some of the fables were previously unknown ones that Gay had written shortly before his death. 'They are printed from the originals in the author's handwriting. We hope they will please equally with his former Fables, though mostly on subjects of a graver and more political turn.' Once again, it is hard to see that this indicates children's literature. On the other hand one can imagine older children appreciating 'The Elephant and the Bookseller', which Stockdale must have tried out on his own children. The elephant comments out loud on the book he is browsing through in the bookshop. Then

> The Bookseller, who heard him speak,
> And saw him turn a page of Greek,
> Thought, what a genius have I found!
> Then thus addrest, with bow profound –
> Learn'd sir, if you'd employ your pen
> Against the senseless sons of men,
> Or write the history of Siam,
> No man is better pay than I am;
> Or, since you're learned in Greek, let's see
> Something against the Trinity.....

Illus. 12. Thomas Erskine, 1st Baron Erskine by Thomas Lawrence

11

Thomas Erskine Defends John Stockdale

John Stockdale was quite right to be alarmed when he wrote to Jefferson on February 22, 1788, 'I am a little discomposed by having been complained of by the House of Commons: they have ordered me to be prosecuted.'[1] He was in serious trouble, thanks mainly to Fox and his fellow Whigs. For the background it is necessary to go back to 1783, when the opposition, encouraged by the man often said to be the writer Junius, stepped up its attack on the high and mighty East India Company and on Warren Hastings, the first Governor-General of Bengal. Fox's India Bill of 1783 was designed to curb the Company, and the failure of that Bill, largely due to Pitt's efforts, had contributed to the end of the Fox-North coalition at the end of that year.

Fox and his friends, by then in opposition to Pitt, concentrated their fire on Hastings after his return to England and their move to get him impeached was successful, partly because of the unexpected support of Pitt. As Steven Watson commented: 'Pitt had come to power by opposing Fox's India Bill; he might therefore be thought a friend to Hastings when the latter became the target for Fox's fusillade. This was not so, however. For Pitt, perhaps more than Fox, wished to discipline the East India Company. Hastings – many as his enemies among the factions of the Company were – was the greatest public figure the Company had ever produced. To snub him was to keep the Company in a properly subject spirit.'[2]

---

[1] *Jefferson Papers*, 12: 621.
[2] Watson, Steven, *The Reign of George III*, Oxford U.P., 1960, 320.

Numerous pamphlets appeared on the topic of Hastings and India. Stockdale, two of whose four sons were to go out to India to live, and to die, was in the forefront of publishers covering the accusations and counter-allegations. In 1786, he produced several pamphlets on the dispute, including *The Articles of Charge of High Crimes and Misdemeanours against Warren Hastings, The Defence of Warren Hastings at the Bar of the House of Commons* and *Observations on the Last Debate upon the Delhy Negociations and the Proposed Impeachment of Mr. Hastings*. In the same year, he twice produced *The Present State of the East Indies* by Hastings himself.

In his preface to the second version of the last-named pamphlet, Stockdale gave some of the background: 'The following memoirs, containing an account of the State of Bengal, were printed in London first by the present publisher, Mr. Stockdale, in March 1786.' Stockdale was not a printer: for the sake of accuracy he should have stated that the memoirs were printed for him, rather than by him. He continued, 'Mr. Hastings, the author, not intending to make them public, only sixty copies were struck off at that time merely for the private perusal and information of a few official gentlemen; but a copy having been procured without his knowledge or consent by a bookseller, who printed one edition of it, the present publisher has conceived himself at liberty to offer his correct edition to the public, with the addition of a few explanatory notes and remarks.' It looks as though Stockdale may not have bothered to seek permission from Hastings himself. His preface added, 'It is only necessary to observe that a right honourable member of the opposition (Mr. Sheridan) seems to have alluded to these memoirs in the House of Commons; when having quoted their authority he adds, "This pamphlet in question was written by Mr. Hastings, and suppressed by him on better recollection." The fact, however, is as above.'

A number of the Indian pamphlets were printed for Stockdale by Benjamin Franklin's friend, the printer and politician, William Strahan, whose account book is now in the

British Library.[3] The accounts give some indication of the success anticipated for those pamphlets, by showing the number of copies printed and the amount of overtime considered to be worthwhile.

1787 Dec. Hastings's *Answer to the Charges*
16½ sheets No. 1500 @ £1.8.0   23. 2. 0.
Saved by overrunning 5s. per sheet   4. 2. 6.   18.19.6.
Corrections, labels and nightwork   3. 5.0

Articles of Charge against Sir Elijah Impey
9 sheets No. 1000 @ £1.4.0   10.16.0
Nightwork and Sunday (17 men)   3.13.6.

1788 Feb. Hastings's *Answer to the Charges* 2nd. edit.
16½ sheets No. 1500 @ £1.8.0.   23. 2.0.

Articles of Impeachment against Hastings
7 sheets No, 1000 @ £1.14.0.   11.18.0.

Another entry related to the Regency Crisis, caused by the King's illness with porphyria – as it is now thought to have been, rather than insanity. In March 1789, Strahan printed a thousand copies of the *Report of the Physicians and the Regency Bill* for Stockdale. The printer's charges for these and other pamphlets, including five thousand copies of Stockdale's catalogue, came to the considerable sum of £237.7.0, which the publisher paid in April, 'by note at 6 months'.

When in 1787, Rev. John Logan wrote a pamphlet which was in favour of Hastings and critical of the House of Commons, entitled *A Review of the Principal Charges against Warren Hastings*, Stockdale was an obvious choice of publisher. However, from Stockdale's preface to the report of his own trial, which he put out in January 1790, it appears that Logan first approached someone else. This is his account of the publication, taken from his own book, *The Whole Proceedings on the Trial of ... John Stockdale*: 'The bookseller to whom Mr. Logan originally presented his

---

[3] Add. MSS. 48,815, ff.120, 132.

pamphlet, offered a sum for it, which he conceived so inadequate to its importance, that he carried it to Mr. Stockdale, to whom he gave it; taking for himself a few copies only, which were sent in his name to men of the first eminence in letters, both in London and Edinburgh. After it had been for some time in circulation, and read with great avidity, it was publicly complained of by Mr. Fox.'

In his preface, Stockdale gave some further details of the author of the pamphlet. The first fact – of some importance to Logan – was that he was dead by then. As the author of the most readable biography of Thomas Erskine put it, 'John Logan's name, therefore, departs from history; John Stockdale's still lives on.'[4] Stockdale also mentioned that Logan had been 'the principal author of that part of the *English Review*, which gives the general state of foreign and domestic politics'. He had written comments in that periodical on the impeachment 'with great force and elegance,' and those remarks had contained 'reflections infinitely more pointed, than any of those which Mr. Fox objected to in his pamphlet.' Logan had been diligent with his research and had asked a friend of Hastings to check his draft. It never occurred to that reader 'that after the torrent of abuse that had been poured out upon Mr. Hastings, for years, *any thing* said in reply could be deemed libellous, and therefore he merely examined whether Mr. Logan was correct in his statement of facts.'

The trial of Hastings started on February 13, 1788. It was to go on for seven years before ending in an acquittal, the case costing the unfortunate defendant some £100,000. One reason for the inordinate length was that the sittings could not be continuous – apart from anything, Parliament might have ground to a halt had they been uninterrupted. Another was the vast expanse of ground that was covered by the prosecution.

---

[4] Stryker, Lloyd Paul, *For the Defence – Thomas Erskine*, London: Staples Press, 1949, 153.

On the day after the trial started, while Edmund Burke was settling into his four-day opening speech for the prosecution in the adjoining Westminster Hall, Fox rose in the House of Commons to complain about Logan's pamphlet in favour of Hastings. He made the most of the fact that this time it was not a Whig about whom the complaint was made. In an attempt to get the support of the Tories, he craftily said that 'the House could never wish it to be understood that they were eager to punish libellers of one party, but unwilling to punish libellers of another.'[5]

Turning to the pamphlet itself, Fox pompously claimed that 'it contained a gross and scandalous libel on the committee appointed by the House to manage the prosecution of Mr. Hastings, as well as a libel upon the House itself, upon his Majesty, and upon the whole legislature.' Fox continued on such a high plane that one might be forgiven for thinking that he was complaining on behalf of the Archangels, rather than a collection of politicians, some of whom could scarcely claim to have been elected by the people. The pamphlet, he maintained, held up 'the whole legislature as acting upon base and improper motives on a subject in which, of all others, it behoved them to act on the purest principles, and with the strict regard to impartial justice.'

Fox then read extracts from Logan's pamphlet to the House. He chose them carefully – just as the Attorney-General was to do at Stockdale's trial. Pitt, who had not had the opportunity to read it himself, said that from what Fox had read out, it seemed to be 'a libel of a very heinous, though not a very dangerous nature'. Fox moved that the King should be asked to direct the Attorney-General to prosecute the author, printer and publisher. The motion was carried unanimously.

Although neither the beginning nor the end of Stockdale's trial was delayed as much as that of Hastings, he nevertheless

[5] *Parliamentary History*, London: T. C. Hansard and others, 1816, vol.7.

had to wait, in a 'discomposed' state, for nearly two years – until the December of the following year – to know his fate. As the author Logan was dead and the printer had been left untouched by the prosecution, Stockdale had to stand trial on his own. He must have been peeved that the ministry, which he was supporting with his publications, had joined with the opposition to attack him. Pitt must have known, as Abigail Adams did, that Stockdale was receiving payments from Secret Service funds, such as those in 1784, totalling £228, 'for various pamphlets and publications'.[6]

Stockdale fortunately made the wise decision to ask Thomas Erskine, the greatest advocate of the day – and possibly of all time – to defend him, regardless of expense. The trial of John Stockdale on December 9, 1789, marked the last of an important line of criminal libel cases, several of which had involved Erskine. The most important relevant case to have preceded it was that of the Dean of St. Asaph, William Davies Shipley. He was the son of Jonathan Shipley, the Bishop of St. Asaph, and Franklin's friend.

Once again, it is desirable to back-track, mainly to understand the background of the prosecution of the Dean, but also because that background includes some old friends. We met William 'Oriental' Jones as the brilliant Middle Temple barrister who was a friend of both Thomas Day and of young John Laurens, and who – like Day – befriended Henry Laurens after his release from the Tower. He met Franklin for the third time in Paris in 1782. Franklin introduced him to Vergennes, the French Foreign Minister, who challenged his assertion that the basic principles of government could be made intelligible even to illiterate people. Jones rose to the challenge by writing a dialogue, in French – one of his many languages – between a scholar and a peasant, containing a number of simple questions

---

[6] Aspinall, Arthur, *Politics and the Press, 1780-1850*, London: Home and Van Thal, 1949, 166.

about arbitrary power and resistance to such power. Franklin thought that Jones had proved his point, so the author felt justified in translating the exercise into English and publishing it in London. It was duly distributed as one of the free pamphlets of the Society for Constitutional Information, of which Jones was an active member, with the title *The Principles of Government, in a Dialogue between a Scholar and a Peasant.*

The Dean of St. Asaph liked the pamphlet so much that he arranged for a Welsh translation. This so angered one of his local critics, Thomas Fitzmaurice, who was both Shelburne's brother and the Sheriff of Flint, that he initiated a prosecution against the Dean. One can see from an excerpt why the pamphlet might appeal to friends of America but be anathema to opponents of colonial or other change. The scholar sets the scene of a village club with agreed rules, and then asks the peasant:

'What would you do, if any one member were to insist on becoming *perpetual* master, and on altering your rules at his arbitrary will and pleasure?'

Peasant: 'We should expel him.'

Scholar: 'What if he were to bring a serjeant's guard, when the militia are quartered in your neighbourhood, and insist on your obeying him?'

Peasant: 'We should resist if we could.'

The attack on Jones's pamphlet could not have come at a worse time for him in one sense, nor at a better one in another. On March 1, 1783, George III wrote to Lord Thurlow, the Lord Chancellor, who had been hostile to the idea of appointing Jones: 'Lord Shelburne will think himself unkindly treated if Mr. Jones is not sent to the East Indies on the vacancy of judge which has subsisted some years; I shall take it as a personal compliment to me if you will consent to it.'[7] The Lord Chancellor

---

[7] Cannon, Garland, *The Letters of Sir William Jones*, Oxford U.P., 1970, 2: 604.

found himself able to consent, so Jones was duly appointed and knighted on March 20.

On April 8, the new judge married Anna Maria Shipley, one of Bishop Shipley's daughters and so a sister of the Dean. Miss Shipley was one of the sisters who had enchanted Franklin during his time in England, and who had received from him a present of the squirrel, immortalised when he later wrote its epitaph for the girls: 'Here Skugg lies snug as a bug in a rug.' Franklin was delighted that his friend Jones had married one of his own favourites.[8] With literary inspiration from both Franklin and her husband, Anna Maria Jones eventually edited a collection of her distinguished husband's works. The first edition was published in 1799, five years after his death, by the Robinsons. The second was put out in 1807 in thirteen volumes by Stockdale, who had by then bought a major part of the Robinsons' stock.

The prosecution of the Dean was very embarrassing for Jones, his new brother-in-law, who was then virtually immune from prosecution. However, he distanced himself from the Dean and his problems when he sailed for India, where he further increased his reputation as a lawyer and as a scholar of oriental languages. Together with his friend, Warren Hastings, and others, he founded the Asiatic Society, remaining in India until his death in 1794.

The Society for Constitutional Information retained Thomas Erskine for the defence of the Dean. The trial eventually came on at Shrewsbury before Mr. Justice Buller, Erskine's former pupil-master, in August 1784. At the close of the evidence Erskine invited the jury to acquit the Dean, on the grounds that he had been charged with publishing a libel with a seditious intention, and that no such intention had been proved. In his summing up the judge instructed the jurors, in accordance with several precedents of Lord Mansfield and other judges, that it

---

[8] Van Doren, Carl, *Benjamin Franklin*, London: Putnam, 1930, 416.

was their duty merely to decide whether the Dean was guilty of publishing the pamphlet. Mansfield had laid it down that whether a publication was libellous or not was a question of law for the judge. The jury returned the verdict, 'Guilty of publishing only.' There followed a heated discussion between Buller and Erskine about the effect of the verdict, and after a while it was recorded as 'Guilty of publishing, but whether a libel or not we do not find.'[9]

Erskine then applied to the King's Bench Court, presided over by Mansfield, for a new trial. The application failed, but his later motion in arrest of judgment succeeded, as Mansfield and his brethren agreed that the pamphlet written by their brother judge, Sir William Jones (as he then was), contained no libel – a view held all along by its lawyer author.

John Almon later made an excellent point, when he wrote about the plight of the publisher bound over to keep the peace (as he himself had been): 'And if he complains, he is told there is no hardship in the case, for he is to take care to print *only what is lawful*, and then his sureties will not be forfeited. But how is he to distinguish what is lawful from what is unlawful? A special jury of gentlemen are told that they are not competent to decide upon any paper, whether it is a libel or not, that being a question of law; yet the culprit, who is commonly a man of inferior rank, as well as education, must, at his peril, be competent to understand what a special jury cannot. And this is called Law.'[10]

'Lord Mansfield is at Bath, sleeps everywhere but in bed, receives his quarter's salary, but does not resign,' General James Grant, a veteran of the American war, complained in April 1787. Fortunately for Stockdale, by the time his trial started, Mansfield had decided to retire after thirty-two years as Chief Justice. His

---

[9] *Speeches of the Hon. Thomas Erskine*, London: James Ridgway, 1810, 1: 213; Stryker, chap.10.

[10] Almon, *Memoirs*, 145. To use an American legal term, a bind over would have a 'chilling effect' on the freedom of the press.

successor, who was to preside at Stockdale's trial, was Lord Kenyon, who as a Member of Parliament had consistently supported Warren Hastings – possibly a good omen for the defendant.[11]

The prosecution team at the trial was a formidable one. The Attorney-General, Sir Archibald Macdonald, led the Solicitor-General, Sir John Scott and two others. Scott was to become Lord Eldon as Lord Chancellor, but at this time was another House of Commons supporter of Hastings. Stockdale was defended by Erskine, with Edmund Dayrell as his junior. Dayrell was a Buckinghamshire associate of Temple and Wilkes, and had a stake in the *Courant.*

The information, or charge, which launched the proceedings, was also formidable, not only because of its length, but because of its awesome language. The pro-government bookseller must have winced at the description of the defendant: 'John Stockdale, being a wicked, seditious, and ill-disposed person, and having no regard for the law of this realm, or for the public peace and tranquillity of this kingdom, and most unlawfully, wickedly, and maliciously devising, contriving, and intending to asperse, scandalize, and vilify the Commons…' and so on and on. Stockdale must have wondered if he were sitting in the wrong dock: the rascal he heard so fulsomely described clearly deserved to be instantly hanged.

By contrast, the Attorney-General's opening speech to the jury was quite short and restrained. Indeed, so was his conduct throughout the trial. It looks as though he did not have much enthusiasm for the case he was obliged to prosecute. At one point he told the jurors, 'Gentlemen, the particular passages which I shall put my finger upon in this libel, it will now be my duty to state. You know very well, that it is your duty to consider of the meaning that I have imputed to those passages in the

---

[11] Kenyon, George T., *The Life of Lloyd, First Lord Kenyon*, London: Longmans, Green, 1873, 166, 163.

information; if you agree with me in that meaning, you convict; if you disagree with me, of course you acquit.'

The Attorney-General then referred to various excerpts from the pamphlet, but made no attempt to suggest the powers of the jury were in any way limited. He made no suggestion that they were confined to deciding merely whether there had been a publication by the defendant. After his relatively short speech, the evidence for the Crown took a few more minutes only.

Erskine, who was known to be a supporter of Fox, Burke and Sheridan, started his speech to the jury with a reference to that fact. 'Gentlemen of the Jury, Mr. Stockdale, who is brought as a criminal before you for the publication of this book, has, by employing me as his advocate, reposed what must appear to many an extraordinary degree of confidence; since, although he well knows that I am personally connected in friendship with most of those whose conduct and opinions are principally arraigned by its author, he nevertheless commits to my hands his defence and justification.'

Erskine based his principal line of attack on the fact that his opponent – like Fox in the Commons in the previous year – had picked out selected passages for criticism. 'The defendant published – what?' Erskine asked rhetorically. '*Not* those latter ends of sentences, which the Attorney-General has read from his brief, as if they followed one another in order in this book. *Not* those scraps of passages which are patched together upon this record, and pronounced in one breath, as if they existed without intermediate matter in the same page, and without context anywhere.'

After inviting them to read the whole book once they retired, Erskine told the jurors that if they then came to the conclusion that the author wrote it with the wicked, seditious and corrupt intentions charged, they had his 'full permission to find the defendant guilty'. To help them he proposed to refer once again to the selection of the prosecution, which he contemptuously described as a 'miserable juggle'. 'I will then,' he added, 'by reading the interjacent matter which is studiously kept out of the fight, convince you of the true interpretation'.

Methodically, the great advocate made his points, starting with the comment that the prosecution had picked out odd frag- ments of sentences from three or four only of the 110 pages. 'In this manner the greatest works upon government, the most excellent books of science, the sacred scriptures themselves, might be distorted into libels, by forsaking the general context, and hanging a meaning upon selected parts. Thus, as in the text put by Algernon Sidney, "The fool has said in his heart there is no God." The Attorney-General on the principle of the present proceedings against this pamphlet, might indict the publisher of the Bible for blasphemously denying the existence of heaven, in printing "There is no God". For these words alone, without the context, would be selected by the information, and the Bible, like this book, would be *underscored* to meet it. Nor could the defendant in such a case have any possible defence, unless the jury were permitted to see, by the book itself, that the verse, instead of denying the existence of the Divinity, only imputed that imagination to a fool.'

At one stage Erskine said, 'I see around me those by whom, by and by, Mr. Hastings will be most ably defended.' The trial had indeed attracted a great deal of attention, and so did Erskine's speech. 'It was spoke in as crowded a court as ever appeared in the King's Bench,' Stockdale wrote in his book on the trial. Henry Brougham, who like Erskine was to be a Whig Lord Chancellor in the next century, later commented: 'Mr. Erskine then delivered the finest of all his orations, whether we regard the wonderful skill with which the argument is conducted, the soundness of the principles laid down, and their happy application to the case, or the exquisite fancy with which they are embellished and illustrated, and the powerful and touching language in which they are conveyed. It is justly regarded by all English lawyers as a consummate specimen of the art of addressing a jury.'[12]

The summing-up by the new Chief Justice showed a welcome new approach: 'In applying the innuendoes, I accede entirely to what was laid down by counsel for the defendant, and which was admitted yesterday by the Attorney-General, as counsel for the Crown, that you must, upon this information, make up your minds, that this was meant as an aspersion upon the House of Commons – and I admit also, that in forming your opinion, you are not bound to confine your enquiry to these detached passages which the Attorney-General has selected as offensive matter. You have a right to look at the whole book; and if you find that it has been garbled, and that the passages selected by the Attorney-General do not bear the sense imputed to them, the man has a right to be acquitted; and God forbid he should be convicted.'

The jury were out for about two hours, and then returned a verdict of Not Guilty. Stockdale, much relieved, had incurred 'a very heavy expense', and tried to recoup some of it by producing, with the help of Joseph Gurney's shorthand transcript, *The Whole Proceedings on the Trial of … John Stockdale.* He published the book in 1790, and included in it an account of the earlier trial of the Dean. The copy in the London Guildhall Library also has four printed letters added to it, written originally to the *Public Advertiser* by an unidentified observer who was present throughout the trial, and who signed himself A Briton.

In the first of his letters, the writer made a valid point about the original decision of the House to pursue Stockdale. 'Those who know anything of the House of Commons, or any other public body, need not be told how easy it is to carry a question, in which their privileges or dignity are stated to be involved. It is not, therefore, surprising that the Commons, *nemine contradicente*, voted *that* to be a gross libel, which twelve dispassionate

---

[12] *Works of Henry, Lord Brougham*, Edinburgh: Black, 1872, 7: 218.

gentlemen, upon their oaths, have declared *not to be one.*' He then shrewdly added a point that was to appeal to the legislature before long: 'But it is a very nice question, and ought to be well considered in future by the Member who shall propose it, whether a few detached sentences in an ingenious work, ought to be selected in order to institute a prosecution.'

The trial had some important after-effects – apart from the one foreseen by that writer. On May 21, 1790, General John Burgoyne, the loser at Saratoga, complained in the House of Commons about a letter by the agent for Warren Hastings, Major John Scott, a fellow Member of Parliament, in Woodfall's *Register*. Like the Logan pamphlet, it was critical of the House and its impeachment proceedings. In agreeing with the condemnation of Major Scott, Fox – conscious of the fact that the jury had acquitted him – modified his earlier extravagant attack on Stockdale. According to the *Parliamentary History*, he felt that, 'With regard to the degree of criminality between Mr. Stockdale, or the printer of a newspaper, and Major Scott, there was no comparison. A bookseller and newspaper printer could be supposed to have no personal view in the libel they published, and could only act in the way of their profession and trade; but Major Scott had no excuse of that kind.' However, Fox overlooked one major point when speaking of Stockdale's criminality: there was none, as the jury had acquitted. Had Fox repeated his remarks outside the House, without the protection of parliamentary privilege, he could have been sued for libel by the innocent Stockdale.

Stockdale, who in 1788, had published Scott's pamphlet, *Observations of Mr. Sheridan's Pamphlet*, now added to his Hastingsiana list *The Speech of Major Scott in the House of Commons on Friday 21 May 1790*. He needed every penny he could make, for he found himself in the unenviable position of many an English litigant who is also a parent. As well as having to find money to pay his lawyers, he also had to find the fees for his sons at William Wright's boarding-school at Apsley in Bedfordshire.

Erskine was one of the Whig members who lost his parliamentary seat in Pitt's sweeping election victory in 1784 – the group of unfortunates known as 'Fox's Martyrs'. He was re-elected in 1790 and in the following year seconded Fox's motion for leave to bring in the Bill which had been hanging fire since the Dean of St. Asaph's case and which became Fox's Libel Act of 1792. This enacted the point that Erskine had urged in Stockdale's case, and on which Kenyon had supported him, that the jury should judge any alleged libel 'upon the whole matter put in issue'. The Bill was, in fact, largely the work of Erskine, who persuaded Fox of the necessity for that reform of the law. Lord Campbell, a later Chief Justice and Lord Chancellor, commented on the trial and the Bill: 'According to the doctrine laid down by the judges in the House of Lords, the defendant ought certainly to have been convicted … the jury, with the consent of the judge, having exercised the power afterwards conferred on juries by Mr. Fox's Libel Bill.'[13]

Lord Campbell pointed out that shortly before he had presided over the trial as a newly appointed Chief Justice, Kenyon, as a politician, 'had strongly sided with the defenders of Hastings, and very much approved of the sentiments which the prosecuted pamphlet expressed, thinking that the House of Commons had been guilty of oppression and vexation in the manner in which they had instituted and conducted the impeachment.' He concluded with a comment of the kind one rarely sees when one Chief Justice is writing about a predecessor: 'Perhaps his wish for an acquittal might have unconsciously biased his judgment.' In all the circumstances, it might have been better if Kenyon had declined to hear the case, in view of his personal feelings.

---

[13] Campbell, Lord John, *The Lives of the Chief Justices of England*, London: John Murray, 1857, 3: 48.

Another result of Stockdale's acquittal was that it clearly dampened Edmund Burke's enthusiasm for the Hastings case, in which he was a leading 'prosecutor' or manager. He wrote to Philip Francis, the suspected Junius, who had encouraged the pursuit of Hastings, 'Now for one word on our affairs. The acquittal of Stockdale is likely to make a bad impression on them. I confess that at last I totally despair, and think of nothing but an honourable retreat from this business.'[14]

Another consequence of the trial was that Stockdale received praise from some contemporaries for his stand. William Granger, or one of his contributors, wrote years later: 'In this respect he deserves the thanks of every liberal-minded man, for venturing to defend the sacred rights of the public, at a time when everything was at stake, and even the rights of free discussion.' The writer possibly overlooked the fact that Stockdale did not choose to be prosecuted, but the bookseller, who was criticised often enough, will have appreciated the compliment anyway.[15]

Some *fifty* years later, his eldest son, John Joseph, chose to enter the lists against the House of Commons repeatedly. He kept suing Hansard, the printer to the House, for libel, until stopped by the Parliamentary Papers Act of 1840, passed to deal with the problems of breach of privilege his cases had revealed. It was extraordinary that the publisher father and son should both have had battles with the House of Commons and its lawyer, the Attorney-General, and that both incidents should have been followed by an Act of Parliament. The present book concentrates on the father, so an earlier brief history of the son and his legal struggles has been relegated to the Appendix.

---

[14] Cobban, A. and Smith, R. A., *The Correspondence of Edmund Burke*, Cambridge U.P., 1967, 6: 54. For a brief account of the above two cases and other cases of Erskine, see, Stryker; and Hostettler, John, *Thomas Erskine and Trial by Jury*, Chichester: Barry Rose, 1996.

[15] Granger, William, *The New, Original and Complete Wonderful Museum and Magazine Extraordinary*, London: Alex. Hogg, 1807, 5: 2485.

However, it is fair comment to point out here that the 1840 reform of the law might never have taken place, but for John Joseph being inspired by the part his father had played – albeit reluctantly – in the years 1789 to 1792 struggle to improve the law of libel, at a time when the government was ruthlessly restricting the freedom of speech and of the press.

Illus. 13. William Murray, 1st Earl of Mansfield by John Singleton Copley

12

John Almon's Final Years

By an extraordinary coincidence, the years 1788 and 1789 saw not only the prosecution of John Stockdale, but also that of John Almon, who had retired in 1781, when only about 53 but, like many another fighter, had made a comeback. Although Almon at the time of handing over to John Debrett had referred to his own ill-health, that of his wife must have been worse, for she died immediately after his retirement. She had borne him ten children, and the youngest were still with their father. In September 1784, Almon married again. His second wife was the widow of Walter Parker, the printer of the *General Advertiser*, who had been imprisoned for a year in 1779, for contempt in connection with his support of Admiral Keppel. Parker had some of the brass neck qualities of Wilkes. He had complained about the size of his cell, and when given a larger one, had carried on his business. 'After converting his cell into an editorial office, he managed the *General Advertiser* from Newgate.'[1] He was probably annoyed when interrupted at his work by the Gordon rioters, who captured the prison and insisted on releasing him with the other inmates.

Almon decided that he did not care much for retirement so, having taken on Parker's widow and house at 183 Fleet Street, he took over his newspaper as well. No doubt more from habit than anything else, he also published the odd pamphlet, but he never resumed publishing on the former scale. Sadly, as Almon

---

[1] Lutnick, Solomon, *The American Revolution and the British Press 1775-1783*, Columbia: U. Missouri P., 1967, 33.

himself recorded, 'In his new situation as printer of the *General Advertiser*, he was again the object of the enmity of the court. The first prosecution against him was brought by Mr. Pitt, for printing a paragraph, which it is more than probable, any other minister would have despised. It was singular that Mr. Pitt should be tempted to seize so trifling an occasion to commence a prosecution against the friend of his father.' In fact, Pitt had brought a civil case against him.[2]

The issue for October 20, 1785, had accused Pitt of stockjobbing. Thomas Erskine, who appeared for Almon when his case was heard in the following February, pointed out that this was almost a routine accusation for ministers to expect: 'This is a squib, an idle ridiculous squib, which has been played off; to use my learned friend's own expression, they have pelted every minister so, from the first institution of the funds. The famous Mr. Pelham, the Duke of Bedford, Mr. Charles Townsend and my Lord Bute, they were all pelted so, they were all spoke of except the great father of the present plaintiff.'

Lord Mansfield, who had at that stage not quite reached the end of his thirty-two years as Lord Chief Justice, corrected Erskine. 'I believe you are mistaken; I believe not one of the ministers you have mentioned was ever charged with stockjobbing. I am sure Mr. Pelham never was, and the Duke of Bedford never.'

'Perhaps not,' Erskine conceded, adding, somewhat ungraciously, 'Your Lordship must certainly know, having lived so long in those times.'

'You know very well they were charged with other things,' the Chief Justice retorted, 'but not with stockjobbing.'

'If they were not,' Erskine replied, determined to have the last word, 'they were charged with things which, God knows, were much worse.'

'That may be so,' Mansfield allowed.

---

[2] Almon, *Memoirs*, 126, 236.

In his closing speech to the jury, Erskine expressed his surprise that Almon should have been picked as a defendant, when Pitt had received so much abuse from others. He then allowed himself a great deal of advocate's licence, claiming that Almon 'was a friend and favourite of his great father, the Earl of Chatham, and I believe he suffered considerably in supporting his interest; he was often tried for libels wrote in his favour.' He also told the jury that when Pitt had still been at college, he had been so outraged by an attack on his father, that he 'published a vindication of his noble father and put the thing into Mr. Almon's hands.'

The jury were obviously impressed by Erskine's points. Although Pitt claimed £10,000 damages, they only awarded him £150, so that Almon could claim a moral victory. Pitt waived the damages and asked only for his costs.[3]

From the Almon papers now with the New-York Historical Society, it is clear that he was involved in a considerable amount of expense with lawyers at this time. On May 10, 1786, shortly after Pitt's case, Almon paid £55 on account to his attorney in respect of a case brought against him in the Court of Common Pleas by a man called Copping. Eight days later he paid for his own costs incurred in the Pitt case. On August 13, 1787, another lawyer gave him a receipt for £50, 'for which I undertake to defend him in all actions brought against him for twelve months from the date hereof respecting any advertisement in the *General Advertiser*.' On August 19, 1788, Pitt's lawyers wrote to express their surprise that he had not yet paid their costs. In order to persuade Almon to pay, they threatened to take 'the proper steps for compelling payment of the damages and costs'. Pitt had foregone his damages but doubtless on condition that Almon pay the costs speedily. Almon must have seriously

---

[3] John Almon Papers, New-York Hist. Soc.

wondered whether it had been worth his while to give up his retirement, just to keep a pack of lawyers in pocket.[4]

At the end of 1785, the Prince of Wales secretly married his mistress, Maria Fitzherbert. The marriage was secret mainly because the bride's Roman Catholicism ensured that the Prince could not legally succeed his father, whose consent to the marriage was required in any event. Rumours of the ceremony reached the House of Commons and questions were asked. The Prince's staunch supporter, Fox, who was not in on the secret, authoritatively denied the existence of such a marriage. In June 1788, the King had his first serious attack of what may have been porphyria, though at the time it was the general view that insanity had disabled him. The Prince and his friends saw their chance of gaining power, by way of a Regency being declared in his favour, and battle lines were drawn. The publishers were not slow to benefit.

Pitt was not feeling too well either. Richard Brinsley Sheridan, the Whig playwright and politician, wrote to Lord Palmerston: 'The King is certainly worse than ever. Pitt and Chancellor have both seen him: he abused Pitt like a dog.'[5] Despite their litigation, Pitt asked Almon to place some minor items in the newspapers for him. On June 14, 1788, he asked him to place an item without indicating its source, and on October 29, when he was justifiably worried that a Regency would cost him his job, Pitt sent Almon an open signed letter for publication. He asked him to place it in 'all the daily papers tomorrow.' Realising that this request might be a bit much even for Almon, he added, 'If you cannot get the letter into all the papers, let it be in as many as you can.'[6]

---

[4] The writer hopes that his former brethren in the legal profession will forgive this comment.

[5] Aspinall, Arthur, *The Correspondence of George, Prince of Wales 1770-1812*, London: Cassell, 1963, 1: 391.

[6] Almon, *Memoirs*, 107.

The Duchess of Devonshire, one of the main props of the Whigs, kept a diary during the Regency Crisis, and two of the entries are of interest. '20 November 1788: Sheridan, who is heartily tired of Hastings trial and fearful of Burke's impetuosity, says that he wishes Hastings would run away and Burke after him.' '2 January 1789: A handbill was sent to Mrs. Fitzherbert telling her that tomorrow 500 libels would be published declaring that the P. had forfeited his right to the Crown by marrying her. Sheridan called here at 2 on his way to the bookseller's to suppress it.'[7]

The bookseller in question was James Ridgway, Stockdale's brother-in-law, who had already published a number of pamphlets attacking Mrs. Fitzherbert. According to Bruce Gronbeck, Ridgway had taken to 'political blackmail to expand his financial base'. After leaving the Duchess, Sheridan did indeed call on him, for the Whigs were very keen to form a government. Sheridan knew that if the odious Prince were to become Regent, Fox and his friends would almost certainly replace the Pitt administration – and that he would be included in the new government. Ridgway's pamphlet constituted a dangerous threat to their hopes, so Sheridan tried to persuade him to drop it. At the same time the author of the pamphlet, Dr. Phillip Withers, was told it was a pity that he had written about the Prince, 'just on the point of his being chosen Regent'.[8]

Withers refused to re-write his pamphlet to suit the Prince's ambitious friends, but Ridgway was bought off and agreed to

---

[7] Sichel, Walter, *Sheridan*, London: Constable, 1909, 2: 404, 422. Sheridan was calling daily at Devonshire House, but the attraction was sex rather than politics: he was having an affair with the sister of the Duchess, Lady Duncannon. Foreman, Amanda, *Georgiana, Duchess of Devonshire*, London: HarperCollins, 1998, 213.

[8] Gronbeck, Bruce, in Baylen, John O., and Gossman, Norbert J., *Biographical Dictionary of Modern British Radicals*, Sussex: Harvester Press, 1979, 1: 17; Wardroper, John, *Kings, Lords and Wicked Libellers*, London: John Murray, 1973, 130.

cancel publication. Withers soon found another publisher for his
History of the Royal Malady, which recounted how the King had
his celebrated chat with an oak tree, thinking the while that his
courteous silent listener was the King of Prussia. There must
have been quite a few chuckles in America about the King's
plight, and many a comment on the lines of, 'I always told you
King George was mad.'

Almon published one of the many pieces on the Regency
Crisis. As might be expected, his contribution stated the case for
the opposition: for the Prince and his Whig friends. It was *The
Prospect Before Us*, and the author is thought to have been Denis
O'Bryan. Almon's advertisement in the front of the third edition
was dated December 15, 1788, and stated, 'The extraordinary
declaration of Mr. Pitt on the 11th. instant, "That the Prince of
Wales had no better right to administer the government during
his father's incapacity, than any other subject of the realm", calls
for and claims the repetition and dissemination of every thing
that may tend to enlighten the nation upon this momentous
question.'

Despite their all-out efforts, the Whigs failed to get their
Regent in 1788 or 1789. They were thwarted by a combination
of the time taken over the Regency Bill and the recovery of the
King in February 1789 – a recovery which distressed them not a
little. The indecent haste of Fox, Sheridan and their colleagues
to bury the unfortunate King was noticed by the cartoonists.
One cartoon showed Sheridan at his Drury Lane theatre, hissing
instructions to the pit orchestra, 'Don't play God Save the
King.' Another, by Rowlandson, showed the Prince and Sheridan bursting into the King's bedroom and interrupting the
prayers for his recovery. John Wardroper has pointed out that
the mood at Devonshire House, one of the Whig strongholds,
was 'revealed in one artless sentence in the diary of Lady Bess

Foster, the Duke of Devonshire's mistress: "Great anxiety on our side – Fox not well – King better".[9]

The Regency Crisis assuredly led to Almon feeling much worse, as it led to his being prosecuted once again. He was particularly unfortunate, as he was the only publisher dealing with the King's illness to be chosen for prosecution: not in respect of his pamphlet, *The Prospect Before Us*, but for his publication of a reference to the illness in his *General Advertiser* for November 18, 1788. He later gave the following account of the matter, referring to himself in the third person, as usual: 'Yet he forebore to print any anecdotes of the King's private conduct, though they were not unknown to him, or of the occurrences at Cheltenham, which were known to many more. But a short paragraph, which might have escaped almost any observation, sent to him in a handwriting that had made itself familiar for some weeks past, affecting to be that of a friend, but as now seems with the sole view of *ensnaring* him, was inserted in his paper on 18 November 1788; and for which he was immediately prosecuted by the King's Attorney-General. As soon as the paragraph was printed, the writer ceased his correspondence, and although the paragraph appeared in other papers, yet Mr. Almon alone was prosecuted.'[10]

Almon continued his account with wording that is probably substantially true, even if touched with a tinge of paranoia. It will be noted that he called himself a printer, rather than a bookseller or publisher, and that, with his reference to bait, he seemed to overlook that he was a thinking man with free will, rather than a fish or other prey. 'When a printer is marked for a victim, it is almost impossible to escape; for if one kind of snare does not succeed, another will be attempted: the bait will be

---

[9] Wardroper, 128. It will have been noted that the Duke had so arranged his love life, that he could rely on the political support of both his wife and his mistress.

[10] Almon, *Memoirs*, 136.

tried in all shapes, until the purpose is effected.' He added that the ministers seemed determined to get him, for 'they retained the flower of the Bar against him – no less than six of the most eminent counsel'. Somewhat surprisingly, Thomas Erskine was one of them. The reason for selecting him for the prosecution – a decision almost certainly taken by the Attorney-General – was no doubt the tactical one still sometimes used to this day: to stop the other side from engaging him.

The short paragraph which had landed Almon in trouble read: 'Old George the Second was very much against the alliance of his eldest son Frederick (father of the present King) with the House of Saxe-Gotha. He often said it would bring the evils of insanity into his family. Old Jeptha was right.'[11] At about this time Sir Godfrey Webster wrote to Captain John Payne, the Comptroller of the Household of the Prince of Wales: 'I suppose you observed the Shelburne gang were down yesterday. Almon, the printer of the *General Advertiser*, is a creature of Lord S's and that paper speaks the language of that party, as far as you can judge of such men by such language. He has inserted in the paper of this morn a dozen reasons for a sole Regent, seemingly above the production of a mere grub.'[12] Webster was right, of course, about Almon being a Whig 'creature': he had been making little secret of that fact over the preceding twenty years.

Almon was convicted but had to wait for his sentence to be pronounced on another day. While out on bail pending his return to court, he had a most remarkable encounter, which he recorded as follows: 'Mr. Almon happened to meet in the street one of the principal law officers of the Crown who, in the course of conversation that passed between them, assured Mr. Almon that he should press for the severest punishment, and in particular, the pillory.' The expression 'principal law officers of the Crown' usually refers only to the Attorney-General and the

---

[11] Public Record Office, TS 11/91, 293; KB 28/348.
[12] Aspinall, *ibid.*

Solicitor-General. In the context of the present case it looks as though it was the Attorney-General who, most improperly, spoke to the defendant awaiting sentence. He may have felt that it was only fair to Almon to give him the opportunity to make himself scarce – a strange attitude for a principal law officer to adopt. Alternatively, as a politician, he may have doing his best to rid the government of a thorn in its side.

The reference to the pillory must have struck a note of terror. Nowadays, some people have the picture of a jolly scene on the village green with, perhaps, the local scold being pelted with rotten eggs. In practice the experience could be deadly if, for example, a drunk or a paid villain threw rocks at the defendant, unable to move or to protect his head. Almon would have recalled that his friend, Edmund Burke, had on April 11, 1780, taken up in the House of Commons the case of William Smith, who had on the previous day been killed by the mob while in the pillory.[13]

He would certainly have remembered that in July 1781, Joseph Cooper, the printer of Almon's *Courant*, had been sentenced to a year's imprisonment, a fine of £100 and one hour in the pillory.[14] Cooper survived that experience. Almon, who can only have escaped prosecution on that occasion by a hair's breadth, may well have had the benefit of his printer's description of what it felt like to be pilloried. He was very realistic about what might happen to him if he were to receive such a sentence, writing later: 'Those who were in the habit of hiring mobs to disturb the Westminster election, would feel neither remorse nor difficulty in bringing a mob against an individual.' He added that he had received 'repeated information of the design.'[15]

---

[13] Woods, John A., *The Correspondence of Edmund Burke*, Cambridge U.P., 1963, 4: 230.

[14] Public Record Office, TS 11/939, 3369.

[15] Almon, *Memoirs*, 142.

Almon decided to take no chances: 'Under the advice of many of his friends, and even of some of the learned gentlemen who had been retained against him, he went to France; and there, as Mr. Wilkes says, "met with that protection which an innocent man has a right to expect, but could not find in his own country".' One of those 'learned gentleman' was probably Erskine, who had previously acted for him.

Almon's self-imposed exile meant the end of his days as a printer and publisher, but certainly not as an author. He was obliged virtually to give away his 'paper and printing materials with all possible expedition....he did not receive for his property, which had cost him several thousand pounds, one eighth part of the value.' He wrote, 'The treatment Mr. Almon has met with will no doubt operate as a warning to other printers and book-sellers, not to risk their persons and fortunes, in opposing any minister whatever.' John Stockdale had certainly taken heed of a similar warning, as we have seen, for he immediately allied himself with the ministry when setting up on his own.

Earlier in his *Memoirs* Almon had made similar bitter comments on the lot of the contemporary bookseller: 'But there are very few real friends to the liberty of the press. Men some-times *talk* of it as an inestimable privilege, but their friendship lasts no longer than the occasion. A man had better make his son a tinker than a printer or bookseller. The laws of tin he can understand, but the law of libels is unwritten, uncertain and indefinable. It is one thing today, and another tomorrow. No man can tell what it is. It is sometimes what the King and Queen pleases; sometimes what the minister pleases; and sometimes what the Attorney-General pleases.'[16]

In another passage he made a comment which accurately sums up the history of prosecutions in his time as a bookseller: 'There have been more informations against libels in the reign of George the Third than during the reign of any of his

---

[16] Almon, *Memoirs*, 35.

predecessors. From the accession in the year 1760 to the year 1790, the like number of informations against the press in the same number of years is not to be found in the history of Great Britain.'[17]

It is remarkable how closely Almon followed in the footsteps of his friend John Wilkes after his conviction. Like Wilkes, he decided that discretion was the better part of valour and fled to France, despite the turmoil caused by the recent Revolution there. Like Wilkes, he was outlawed when he initially failed to appear for sentence. While in France he also made good use of his pen and, like Wilkes, risked a secret return visit to England, while still outlawed. On March 7, 1791, he wrote to a friend, 'In my present situation it is not perhaps prudent that I should be publicly seen in London, therefore since my return to England I keep in the country.' That friend may have been the one who wrote to warn him, 'At nine this night I received intelligence that you are certainly to be taken by a *capias*. I came away instantly and desire you will not be visible tomorrow morning to any but yours sincerely, Charles Martyn.' The reference was to the writ of *capias utlagatum*, which gave the sheriff authority to arrest an outlaw.[18]

In March 1792, Almon began a period of fourteen months' imprisonment; like Wilkes, he had surrendered himself. It could well be that he gave himself up because France was no longer the congenial haven it had been some years earlier, and as living behind closed curtains in England had probably also lost its charm. In April of the following year, he was brought before the Chief Justice, Lord Kenyon, and his outlawry was set aside on the grounds of a technical error.[19]

---

[17] Almon, *Memoirs*, 139; see generally, Thomas, Donald, *A Long Time Burning*, New York: Praeger, 1969, chapter 8; Levy, Leonard W., *Emergence of a Free Press*, Oxford U.P., 1985.

[18] John Almon Papers, New-York Hist. Soc.

[19] *R. v. Almon, English Reports*, 101: 114; Public Record Office, TS 11/91, 293.

The Times of May 9, 1793, reported the final appearance of the prisoner. 'Mr. Attorney-General, with great candour, hoped the court might think some slight punishment sufficient. Lord Kenyon ordered the recognisance of the defendant to be taken for £100, that he would submit to the judgment of the court when called upon, and that he should be discharged.' The very next item in the newspaper was an account of the imprisoning of the publishers Ridgway and Symonds for a total of four years for their publication of the works of Thomas Paine and others. The government, which was apprehensive about the populace getting too interested in the French Revolution, was determined to keep Paine's influence to a minimum. At the same time, the administration confirmed all that Almon wrote about the extent of the curbing of free speech and a free press.

Almon's outlawry had affected the claim he was making against the Whigs in respect of their unpaid subsidy for his newspaper. Before his hasty departure he had submitted a bill for £900 arrears and £100 law charges to 'The Duke of Portland & Co.' George Reid replied on behalf of the Duke and his associates, asking Almon whether he had or had not disposed of his interest in the *General Advertiser*, adding, 'Mr. Downes has just been with me on a similar application and has offered to show me the deed by which you transferred the whole of the property. Till this is adjusted between you nothing can be done – as it cannot be paid to both.' Reid had a point: Downes might have bought all the debts due to Almon when he bought his newspaper.[20]

As long as he remained an outlaw, Almon could obviously not resort to the courts as a plaintiff, but after the reversal of his outlawry in 1793, he sought counsel's opinion about his chances of success in an action against the Whig party. The instructions to counsel, drafted by his attorney on the basis of Almon's information, fill in some of the gaps and assert that he had not

---

[20] John Almon Papers, New-York Hist. Soc.

transferred his property, but had merely abandoned it
temporarily when fleeing the jurisdiction. The instructions also
revealed that the links with the Whigs dated back to 1784, when
Sheridan, acting on behalf of the Duke of Portland, Earl
Fitzwilliam and other members of the Whig club, had entered
into an agreement with Almon. For a fee of £300 a year he had
agreed to publish in his newspaper 'certain essays and para-
graphs, which should be sent to him with a private mark, and to
keep his paper in the interest and service of that party.' The
party had been out of cash during the first two years, so nothing
was paid for 1785 or 1786. However, during the next three years
Lord Robert Spencer, the treasurer of the club, paid Almon the
annual sum of £200 for his services; the annual balances of £100
were to be paid later.

Counsel was further instructed that Almon had received
nothing after his prosecution at the end of 1789, 'although the
newspaper was continued in the line of politics, was printed
upon Almon's premises, and with Almon's types and presses;
and Almon was obliged to pay the debt contracted at the Stamp
Office. In the year 1791 the newspaper was purchased by Bell
and extinguished. In the year 1793 Almon's outlawry was
reversed, and the concluding words of the reversal are, *That he
shall be restored to all he has lost thereby.*'

Then followed his attorney's request for counsel's opinion:
'Question, Can Almon sustain an action against the Duke of
Portland, the Earl Fitzwilliam and Lord Robert Spencer, for the
continuation of the compensation from the year 1789 to the time
of the sale to Bell? And Question, As the Party or club paid the
law expenses of the first part of the prosecution against Almon,
has he not a right to make a charge to the Party of the remainder
of the law expenses, being the same cause?'

Counsel's opinion is not available, but he almost certainly
advised against legal proceedings, for in July 1794, when
Portland, the Whig leader, was taking office in Pitt's coalition as
Home Secretary, Almon made a direct appeal to him for

payment – though, obviously, not to him in his official capacity. Portland, no longer an opposition member, made the rather strange decision to lodge Almon's letter with the Home Office official papers, for it is still there. He was perhaps doing what politicians do from time to time, especially when changing sides or co-operating with traditional opponents: he was demonstrating that he was whiter than white.[21] Almon had concluded his letter with the assertion that Sheridan had accepted the accuracy of the claim, but it is unlikely that the new minister paid any of the debt. It is certain that Sheridan did not, for he had just opened his new theatre in Drury Lane. Poor Sherry had enough financial problems of his own, without paying off any of the old debts of his party.

In view of all that he had experienced at the hands of the government, and all that he written about the hazards of his earlier profession, it is hardly surprising that Almon did not make a second comeback to the publishing business. However, he edited collections of works and wrote a great deal. His *Memoirs* had been published for him in 1790. Deborah Rogers is of the view that he wrote them 'when he was being sought as an outlaw', but it is unlikely that he would have fled to France equipped with his correspondence files, from which he quoted copiously.[22] He may, of course, have started work on them from memory while in France. The autobiographical work was followed by his long-term project, *Anecdotes of the Life of the Right Honourable William Pitt, Earl of Chatham*, which J. S. Jordan first published in 1792. Robert Rea has said of this work, 'Almon presented in his *Anecdotes* a priceless collection of Chatham's speeches as well as biographical materials recognized as invaluable by modern scholars.'[23]

---

[21] Public Record Office, HO 42/32.

[22] Rogers, 99.

[23] Rea, Robert R., 'Bookseller as Historian', *Indiana Quarterly for Bookmen*, 1949, 5: 84.

In 1795, T. N. Longman and L. B. Seeley published Almon's very useful three-volume *Biographical, Literary and Political Anecdotes*. It is not clear what financial arrangement Almon managed to make with his publishers, but he clearly retained a financial interest in the Pitt biography, for he tried to interest Seeley in taking 750 copies of the fifth edition of that successful work. On December 19, 1796, Seeley declined the offer charmingly: 'I have been considering the necessity of declining the favour of Lord Chatham's intended visit – except you will take the chance of his fate upon yourself while under my roof. I hope Mr. Hodson will find apartments for him in his new residence – more worthy of such a guest.'

Richard Phillips, another of the many publishers imprisoned for publishing Paine, handled Almon's last books. In 1805, the year of Almon's death, he published his five volumes of Wilkes's correspondence and his collection of William Mason's poems. Almon's edition of the Junius Letters was published by Phillips only in the following year. Robert Rea has pointed out that, 'If students of the life of Chatham are indebted to Almon, far more so those who deal with the career of John Wilkes.' He added: 'It was only just that Almon should father the publication of Wilkes's letters. Their acquaintance of thirty-six years duration, their significant relationship as publisher and author, their common political interests pointed to a logical culmination.'[24]

The first volume of the Wilkes collection contained Almon's biography of his friend. His letter to Phillips about that work, dated September 21, 1804, contains some suitable last words: 'I thank you, sir, very sincerely, for the polite offer of residence at your house, but it is natural to me to prefer my daughter's house. On Wednesday next I shall send the fourth volume to London. The fifth I shall postpone until I have finished the first, which will require much attention and which I hope to bring

---

[24] Rea, 87.

with me. Pray order your printers to send me more proofs. The copy is clear enough for any blockhead to read.'[25]

Almon's success as a publisher and as a writer enabled him to die, on December 12, 1805, a man of property. By his will, which he had executed in 1800, with John Debrett as a witness, Almon left the Fleet Street house to a daughter, and a house in Jermyn Street, Piccadilly, and one at Boxmoor in Hertfordshire, to a son. The pamphlets and books he left behind constitute a substantial memorial for this remarkable writer and publisher, who had fought with John Wilkes, collaborated with Benjamin Franklin and his compatriots, had stood up to criticism until worn down by the government, and had made John Stockdale's successful career possible.[26]

---

[25] This letter and the Seeley letter are both in John Almon Papers, New-York Hist. Soc.

[26] Public Record Office PROB 11/1434 f.161. In her biography of Almon, Deborah Rogers included a useful list of Almon's publications. The present writer has not attempted a similar list of Stockdale's publications, as they number some 1500.

13

Stockdale's Books on Australia

When Captain James Cook sailed on his first great voyage to the southern seas, he was accompanied on board *Endeavour* by Joseph Banks, a young botanist, who had the advantage of being a friend and neighbour of the First Lord of the Admiralty, the Earl of Sandwich, and the distinction of having already undertaken a scientific journey to Newfoundland at an early age. Banks was with Cook when he discovered Botany Bay. Cook's untimely death in Hawaii on his third voyage in 1779 deprived the government of the benefit of his views on Australia, and its principal adviser on the 'new' continent from then on was Banks, who had just begun his forty-one year tenure as President of the Royal Society. Because of his advice in favour of a settlement there, he has been called 'the godfather and patron of New South Wales.'[1] He was also inevitably closely concerned with some of the earliest publications dealing with Australia and his own excellent library became a well-known resort of scholars. He took a personal interest in the production of several of Stockdale's books relating to travel.[2]

In 1781, Cook's widow asked Sandwich, as First Lord of the Admiralty, whether she and her children might be allowed to share in the proceeds of any published account of the first voyage of her late husband. With the help of Banks, an

---

[1] Mackaness, George, *Sir Joseph Banks*, Sydney: Angus and Robertson, 1936, 1, 2.

[2] I am indebted to the Banks scholar, Harold Carter, for this information, provided in a letter to me.

arrangement was entered into with George Nicol, a London bookseller, who duly published *A Voyage to the Pacific Ocean,* by Captains James Cook and James King. Half the proceeds were to go to Cook's family.[3]

Banks was personally concerned in the publication and was kept in the picture by the publisher. On October 1, 1783, Nicol wrote to Banks about the paper for the work, which the printers considered too thin. Nicol did not think much of their complaint, as they had been given the opportunity to examine every parcel. He went on, with some justification, to complain about the printers' slow progress, for it was not until June 1784, that the work appeared in London in three quarto volumes.[4]

So great was the interest of the public by then, that it sold out in three days. Nicol was unable to bring out his next edition until the following year, but in the meantime, at the end of 1784, Stockdale and some colleagues brought out a rival octavo edition in parts and in four bound volumes. Their edition was well illustrated, and attracted a long list of subscribers, among whom were customers as diverse as the Lords of the Admiralty, the Book Club at the 'Golden Lion' in Ipswich, and the Literary Societies at two Cambridge inns, the 'Hoop' and the 'Sun'. The subscription list also included, 'Nicol, Mr. George, Strand, Agent-seller of the Quarto Edition.' Having obtained his first subscription parts, Nicol responded with an application to a judge for an injunction (or temporary restraining order) against his book trade colleagues, without giving notice to any of the defendants in the first instance – a routine step in many such cases.

On January 1, 1785, the very first issue of the *Daily Universal Register,* which three years later became *The Times,* carried the defendants' indignant notice: 'Messrs. Stockdale, Scatcherd,

---

[3] Beaglehole, J. C., *The Life of Captain James Cook,* London: Black, 1974, 691.

[4] Grey MSS, Auckland Public Library.

Whitaker, and Fielding, proprietors of the octavo edition of *Cook's Voyages*, respectfully inform the subscribers, that a Mr. George Nicol, the agent-seller of the quarto edition, did on the 14th. inst. obtain, *ex parte*, an injunction, which arrests their sale till the merits of the case comes before the Court of Chancery, on the 15th. of January instant.'[5]

After complaining about the nature of an application without notice, the defendants asked: 'If his case be good, why did he not come forward, like a brother tradesman, and meet the defendants upon the merits before the Chancellor, from whom candor and impartial justice he must have been certain of receiving redress, if he had suffered injury? This injunction being obtained by surprise, the proprietors are prevented from delivering the few remaining numbers till after a hearing. The five subsequent numbers are printed and ornamented in the same style of elegance, which has marked the preceding ones, and which, by giving the work a superiority over the quarto edition, has stimulated the envy of Mr. Nicol, who, by putting an exorbitant price upon the edition partially vended by him, frustrates the intention of Parliament, which granted him a supply of public money for the purpose of disseminating nautical and philosophic knowledge among all classes, and who did not mean to confine it to the opulent, who bury it in dusty libraries to which the public have no access.'

The reference to his 'exorbitant price' must have infuriated Nicol, who had a relatively low price imposed on him, as will be seen. Furthermore, his rivals could scarcely claim to be publishing at prices which could be afforded by 'all classes'. When the

---

[5] The *Register/Times* was a latecomer on the newspaper scene, and did not attain prime status for some time. S. H. Steinberg wrote of the *Daily Advertiser*, founded in 1730, that it 'soon became, and remained until its demise in 1807, what one might call *The Times* of the eighteenth century'. *Five Hundred Years of Printing*, Harmondsworth: Penguin, 1974, 3rd. ed., rev. by Moran, J., 252. This passage has been omitted from p.125 of the 2001 edition.

hearing on notice came before the Lord Chancellor, Lord Thurlow, Stockdale and his colleagues were represented by John Scott, who four years later, as related earlier, was to be part of the formidable team prosecuting Stockdale on behalf of the House of Commons. Scott moved for a discharge of the injunction. He submitted that the plaintiff had no sufficient legal interest in the book he had published, since he, Nicol, had proved that the Lords of the Admiralty had appointed him to print it, but could not personally claim to be either the author or the assignee of the author. Furthermore, Scott argued, the book by his clients was only an abridgment of the original work and therefore an entirely new work. This argument had some merit, as Lord Hardwicke, the Lord Chancellor, had earlier held, in the case of *Gyles v. Wilcox* that a real and fair abridgment could be called a new book, rather than piracy.[6]

The Lord Chancellor accepted Scott's main argument. He referred to Nicol's evidence that his work had been published 'by direction of the Crown, for the benefit of the widows of the officers and men who had perished in the expedition'. As he had affirmatively proved that the Crown had *not* granted him any monopoly, he had no right to an injunction. Nicol could not claim any right under the Copyright Act of 1709, for that had given fourteen-year rights to *authors*, with a further fourteen years protection if they were alive at the end of the first period.[7]

When Nicol advertised a new edition of his work in the *Whitehall Evening-Post* for January 5-7, 1786, he added a warning of a kind that became familiar to Stockdale during his career. 'It

---

[6] Kaplan, Benjamin, *An Unhurried View of Copyright*, New York: Columbia U.P., 1967,10; see also, Feather, John, *Publishing, Piracy and Politics*, London: Mansell, 1994.

[7] *Swanston's Reports*, 3: 687. John Scott, Lord Eldon, was eventually succeeded as Lord Chancellor by Lord Lyndhurst. Before his elevation, he was John Singleton Copley the Younger, who had been born in Boston, Massachusetts and was the son of the American painter in London, who painted three of our Presidents while they were there.

has become necessary to caution the Public against the impo-
sition of all pretended abridgments, and spurious editions of this
work; such publications being made without the authority of the
Lords of the Admiralty, or any persons concerned in the
Voyages; and are incorrect as they are imperfect.'

Nicol did not do all that badly out of the work, despite the
rival edition, and the low price imposed on him by the authorities. On January 14, 1801, he wrote to Banks that the work
had netted £4000 for himself and the Cook family. 'I have often
calculated,' he added sadly, 'what the profits of the book would
have been, had it been published at such a price, as any fair
dealer could have put upon it, and I found they would have
amounted to about £12,000!!'[8] He was clearly one of those
unfortunates who torment themselves with thoughts beginning,
'If only ....' It is comforting to read, in the very last sentence of
Richard Hough's biography of the captain, that Mrs. Cook, who
survived her husband by fifty-six years, managed to live in comfort, partly thanks to 'her share in the profits of her husband's
publications'.[9]

Rather more important to Stockdale than the Cook book,
were his works specifically about Australia. The settlement of
New South Wales was brought about principally by the need of
the British government to find an alternative destination for the
convicts who, but for the American Revolution, would have
been shipped to Maryland or Virginia. (That practice, incidentally, used to infuriate Benjamin Franklin, who suggested
that the colonists might return the compliment by sending their
rattlesnakes to England, particularly to the ministers of the
Crown.) Banks strongly recommended Botany Bay as a suitable
area for a new colony, with ample natural resources, and the
government accepted his advice. Few people realised the

---

[8] Grey MSS, Auckland Public Library.
[9] Hough, Richard, *Captain James Cook*, London: Hodder and Stoughton,
1995.

potential of the continent, but Stockdale's publications, together
with those of his rival, John Debrett, were to make an important
contribution to increasing public awareness of what was available there.

The Australian historian, Eris O'Brien, commented that in
despatching the First Fleet of convicts in May 1787, Pitt 'seems
to have been entirely unconscious that he was authorising the
birth of a new nation, and to have paid no more attention to the
project than any Prime Minister does to an irritating and persist-
ent departmental problem. Indeed, only poets, such as Erasmus
Darwin, and other lesser and anonymous fry, seem to have had
any conception of the possibilities of the occasion. The *Annual
Register* did not mention the project until the First Fleet reached
the Cape, and the memoirs of contemporary statesmen are
singularly lacking in any reference to it. Several political pamphlets and *livres de circonstance* need to be noticed, however. Chief
among them is the anonymous *History of New Holland*.'[10]

Stockdale had published that *History* – but it had a fore-
runner. In 1786, Fielding, one of his associates in the Cook venture, put out a quarto edition of *An Historical Narrative of the
Discovery of New Holland and New South Wales*. It was a mere thirty-
three pages and had a folding frontispiece map. The British
Library copy is of the second edition: the map names Fielding as
its publisher and is dated November 4, 1786. Stockdale published a fifty-five page octavo version at about the same time,
probably with Fielding's approval. In order to squeeze the same
map, albeit with different colouring, into his edition, Stockdale
trimmed the bottom off it, thereby also cutting out the reference
to Fielding having published it. As these slim volumes were
published before the First Fleet set sail, it is clear that they could
not contain any information about the convict settlement. In the

---

[10] O'Brien, Eris, *The Foundation of Australia 1786-1800*, Sydney: Angus and
Robertson, 1950, 2nd ed., 127.

circumstances, all they could do was to whet the considerable appetite of the public.

Stockdale brought out an enlarged second quarto edition in 1787, shortly before the First Fleet sailed, with the shorter title, *History of New Holland*. The new edition contained some up-to-date material, probably provided by the administration. The preface included the following information: 'The expedition to New South Wales being expected to take place, it may not be unacceptable to the reader to be informed of the numbers and equipment of the fleet destined for that purpose, and the nature of the establishment with which it is proposed to commence the regular government of the colony.' The list of officers began with the name of 'Captain Arthur Phillip of the Navy, Governor and Commander-in-Chief of the territory of New South Wales and of his Majesty's ships and vessels employed on that coast'. He was also shown as the commander of *Sirius*, with Captain John Hunter as a second captain.

Some months after the arrival of the fleet at Botany Bay, reports started arriving in London. It was not long before Stockdale published a third book on the subject, his folio edition of *Governor Phillip's Voyage to Botany Bay*, copies of which are now very valuable. This was an enlargement of his earlier two books and in a different league. Having earlier collaborated with Fielding and a dubious bookseller called Forster, Stockdale had at last produced a bona fide book of his own on Australia. In his preface, Stockdale explained how he had been able to compile the work: 'The official papers of Governor Phillip, which were liberally communicated by the Government, formed at first our principal source of intelligence. These, from their nature, could contain but little information on subjects of natural history, and many other points, concerning which the curiosity of every reader would naturally be excited. The efforts of the publisher to give satisfaction to the public in these respects produced a gradual influx of materials; and the successive arrivals of different vessels from the Indian seas, occasioned additions to the work, which made it necessary to engrave new plates.'

Stockdale had not received any direct help from Phillip, but how much he had been helped by official sources is clear from his statement: 'The publisher thinks it his duty, in this place, to return thanks to the following gentlemen, for their kind assistance and free communications: The Marquess of Salisbury, Viscount Sydney, Lord Hood, Sir Joseph Banks, Bart., Mr. Rose, Mr. Nepean, Mr. Stephens, Sir Charles Middleton, Sir Andrew Snape Hammond, Mr. Dalrymple, and Mr. Chalmers.' That was quite a roll call of names figuring in Australia's early history: those of Banks and Chalmers are of particular interest to our story, and we shall meet Rose again later.

The work was first sold in 1789, in twenty-one weekly parts, at a shilling a time. It was profusely illustrated and included maps; an appendix contained the names of all the convicts transported by the First Fleet. The list of subscribers included the name of William Pitt, as well as those of the booksellers Lackington and Longman, who were put down for twenty-five and twenty copies respectively. The British Library copy of the Phillip book is bound in kangaroo skin and, like several of Stockdale's geographical books in that library, came from Banks's own collection. The book sold extremely well and was soon followed by a second and third edition, both in quarto and folio. Jonathan Wantrup, an authority on Australian rare books, has stated, 'The importance of Stockdale's Phillip must not be underestimated. If offers a full record of events both on land and on sea in the first months of the settlement, detailing early expeditions of Phillip and the other officers into the interior around Botany Bay and Port Jackson, the earliest coastal voyages of discovery and important discoveries in the surrounding seas.' He added that it was a 'a key work'.[11]

---

[11] Wantrup, Jonathan, *Australian Rare Books 1788-1900*, Sydney: Hordern House, 1987, 63, 64. I am greatly obliged to Jonathan Wantrup for his

There was clearly something of a race between London booksellers for works on the new settlement. Stockdale's important Phillip book had been beaten to the tape by the book published in April 1789, by John Debrett, who had shrewdly entered into an agreement with one of the officers of the First Fleet *before* he set sail. The work was *A Narrative of the Expedition to Botany Bay*, by Watkin Tench, a Captain of Marines, who had served in the American war as a subaltern. Stockdale seems to have got wind of the Debrett book before it appeared, for he allowed the rascally bookseller, Forster, to cobble together a bogus Voyage account, incorporating his fifty-five page *An Historical Narrative* and the trimmed map. This appeared three weeks before Tench's genuine account, but was speedily recognised as a fraud.[12]

In the same year Stockdale, together with George Goulding, published the *Voyage of Captain Portlock and Captain Dixon* in forty-two parts. This work was dedicated, 'by permission, to his Majesty, Sir Joseph Banks and the Lords of the Admiralty'. An advertisement claimed, 'The publishers have already expended, for the embellishment of this work, near £2000.' The engraving of the plates was probably the most costly part of this production, for the printer's bill was modest enough.. William Strahan's account book includes the following printing item for Stockdale:

> 1789 July. Portlock's Voyages 54½ sheets No. 2000 @ £1.16.0   98.2.0.
>   Corrections throughout and table 5 sheets   5.18.0.[13]

On January 1, 1793, Stockdale published *An Historical Journal of the Transactions at Port Jackson and Norfolk Island* by Captain John Hunter. This also contained a number of plates, including one engraved by William Blake. In the preparation of this work Stockdale had the help of Banks and of George Chalmers, who

---

advice on this chapter. His book should be consulted for a detailed account of all the relevant publications.

[12] Wantrup, 57.

[13] British Library Add. MSS 48,815, f.132.

wrote a large number of books for him and, later, for his son, John Joseph. As Chalmers was of considerable importance to the publisher, we must shortly consider some of his output, even though his reputation as an author was a modest one only.

Chalmers was a Scot, who had practised law in Maryland from 1763 until 1775, when his loyalty to the Crown brought him back across the Atlantic to London. For some time after his return he worked on a history of the American colonies and in March 1780, William Knox, by then an Under-Secretary, gave Chalmers access to official papers relating to America for research purposes.[14] Shortly afterwards, Chalmers abandoned his American history and concentrated on a work designed to show that Britain was still great, despite the recent loss of the thirteen colonies. The result was his *Estimate of the Comparative Strength of Britain during the Present and Four Preceding Reigns*, which was first published by Charles Dilly and J. Bowen in 1782. Stockdale put out a revised edition in 1786, with Dilly, and several further editions after that, each being brought up to date by the author. It was translated into several languages, including Russian.[15]

In March 1785, Pitt was anxious that his views on trade with Ireland should be broadcast, so the Treasury arranged with Stockdale for the publication of the official *Report of the Lords of the Committee of Council*.[16] This was followed by an anonymous pamphlet on the same lines, prepared by George Rose of the Treasury, entitled *The Proposed System of Trade with Ireland Explained*. Debrett answered this with *A Reply to the Treasury Pamphlet*, and Stockdale responded with *An Answer to the Reply of the Supposed Treasury Pamphlet*. This last one was the work of

---

[14] Cockroft, Grace Amelia, *The Public Life of George Chalmers*, New York: Columbia U.P., 1939, 55.

[15] Cockroft, 63.

[16] Ehrman, John, *The Younger Pitt: The Years of Acclaim*, London: Constable, 1969, 207.

Chalmers and so impressed Pitt that he appointed him to be Chief Clerk at the Office for Trade in 1786. After his appointment Chalmers, according to Ehrman, was one of the people to whom 'Pitt was inclined to pay attention'.[17] He kept his senior Civil Service post for many years, and the knowledge he acquired in the course of his duties proved extremely useful for the pro-government publisher.

In 1786, Stockdale produced no less than four works by Chalmers, who in the next year edited Samuel Johnson's *Debates in Parliament* for him. In 1790, Chalmers edited a two-volume *Collection of Treaties between Great Britain and other Powers* for Stockdale. This was clearly a copy of an earlier idea of Almon's: the last treaty included was that which John Adams had signed in Paris in 1783, immediately before he and his son, John Quincy, came to London and stayed with Stockdale. Once again, the British Library copy of this work, like that of several other works by Chalmers, came from the library of Joseph Banks. In 1791, Chalmers was elected a Fellow of the Royal Society, of which Banks was President, and Stockdale published his *Life of Thomas Pain*, which we shall look at later, in chapter 15. Chalmers built up a significant library of his own. When William Beloe wrote his *Anecdotes of Literature and Scarce Books* for publication by the Rivingtons in 1814, he thanked Chalmers in his preface not only for all his help, but also for 'the unreserved use of his valuable collection'.

We can now return to Captain Hunter's historical journal. On October 22, 1792, Chalmers wrote a charming letter to the naturalist Banks about Hunter's book, which he and Stockdale were preparing for the press. 'About the time that you and yours departed for Lincoln with the punctuality of the migratory birds, I wandered out upon the southern shores of England, and nestled at Cowes in the Isle of Wight, with no very determinate purpose.' Chalmers, who wrote many more books and

---

[17] Ehrman, 336n.

pamphlets than have been mentioned, added a comment which one can readily believe, 'Out of this unfortunate tour I could make a sizable octavo, which would be worth five shillings of any man's money, if I were not busy about other matters.' He continued, 'Before I set out on this foolish journey, Stockdale put into my hands Captain Hunter's Historical Journal to, and from Port Jackson; and Mr. Stephens entrusted me with Lieut. King's book, which I consider myself bound to return safe and sound.'[18]

Philip Gidley King's journal was used for part of the Hunter book. King had a poor opinion of Hunter's own account. He made that clear when thanking Banks for his help with the publication of 'what I may call my ill-wrote but faithful journal, with that bundle of jaundiced distractions which precedes it'.[19] The Stephens mentioned was the Secretary of the Admiralty, but there was no secret about his help, for Stockdale referred to the source, 'Official Papers', in his long title of the book.

Chalmers clearly did not think much of the skills of the printer Stockdale was using for Hunter's book, for his letter to Banks complained about his work and called him a 'carpenter'. The letter continued with a play on the name of the dreadful new Poet Laureate, Henry James Pye, who was published by Stockdale and, like Chalmers and Banks, was a regular caller at his shop. 'While engaged thus at Cowes, Stockdale wrote to me that you had sent for him, and wished to put your finger in the Pye of King. This gave me pleasure, as I knew that the pye would not be less savoury for your finger. Stockdale tells me that he has sent the work of his carpenter – who has a quality that every workman has not, that he will take advice – to you with King's original.'

---

[18] Dawson Turner Collection, British Museum (Natural History), 8: f.101; for a full list of works by Chalmers, see, Cockroft, 216.
[19] Mackaness, 57.

Hunter's book was published in 1793: its importance was acknowledged in 1968, when it was reproduced by Angus and Robertson, of Sydney, in association with the Royal Australian Historical Society. Stockdale's *Voyage of Governor Phillip* received similar recognition.

Shortly after the book by Hunter appeared, Banks and Pye were involved with the aftermath of an incident in Stockdale's shop, which throws some light on the degree of hysteria engendered by the French Revolution and by the war with France, which had been declared on February 1, 1793 – and which was to end only twenty-two years later. Dr. John Gillies, a historian and Fellow of the Royal Society, made some comment in the bookshop which seems to have been incorrectly relayed to Pye, who thereafter accused him of being a democrat. Clearly worried that he might be asked the dread question, 'Are you now, or have you ever been … ?', Gillies wrote to Banks on June 24, 1793, for his help. He referred to a request he had made to him that he should 'remove from the King's mind the absurd calumny of my being a Democrat. As I do answer to God, I never was a member, I never was once present, in any political club, any one time, in my whole life. My correspondence with France totally ceased from the time the affairs of that country took a republican turn.'

Two days later Gillies wrote to Banks again, enclosing a letter from Pye, who was also a lawyer and a stipendiary magistrate, accepting that his terrible accusation, that Gillies was a democrat, was not justified. Pye had written to Henry Dundas, the Secretary of State, with the assurance he was 'completely convinced that Dr. Gillies's conversation in Stockdale's shop had been grossly misrepresented and that the King had not a more loyal subject that the said Gillies.'[20] The *Dictionary of National Biography* may provide an explanation for the alarm displayed by Gillies. His entry shows that in that year,

---

[20] British Library Add. MSS 33,979, ff.209, 305.

presumably after his plea to Banks for help, he was appointed Historiographer Royal for Scotland.

One of Stockdale's first geographical books was his publication of Thomas Jefferson's *Notes on the State of Virginia*. That, and the success of his Australian books, coupled with the encouragement of Banks, doubtless played a part in his decision to put out *The History, civil and commercial, of the British Colonies in the West Indies*, in 1793. He may also have been influenced by the fact that his younger brother, Joseph, was the official – and only – printer on the nearby island of Bermuda. Chalmers was very interested in the West Indies by virtue of his post at the Office of Trade, for those islands had assumed an even greater importance for the British economy after the loss of the American colonies. It may well have been at his suggestion that the author, Bryan Edwards, came to Stockdale.[21]

The first edition contained a number of maps, and sold very quickly. Edwards started work at once on revisions for an early second edition, writing to Stockdale from Southampton on December 5, to promise his corrections and additions within a week. He added a comment about the critics. 'I hold myself greatly obliged to the author of the review of my work in the *British Critic*. He has treated me with great candour and politeness. As to the silence of the other reviewers, it is of no consequence, the public opinion having already stamped a value on my book which they cannot deprive me of.'[22]

Those comments on the critics may be compared with those made by another author of Stockdale's, James Pettit Andrew, four years earlier. Andrew, who like many of his contemporaries, may well have been a militiaman, wrote, in the preface to his *Anecdotes Antient and Modern*, of the hazards facing the author.

---

[21] Another possibility is that Henry Laurens had drawn Stockdale's attention to the pamphlet by Edwards on the West Indies trade, when Cadell published it in 1784. *Laurens Papers*, 16: 398.

[22] Folger Library, Washington, Y.c. 822 (1).

'Should he escape the regular batteries of *Monthly, Critical, English* and *Analytical Reviews*, and the bombs and howitzers of the *Gentleman's*, it is still likely that he may be mortally wounded by some irregular marksman in a daily newspaper. But suppose this danger is over, yet there remains, even at the legal distance of a year and a day, the strictures of an Old, and a New *Annual Register* to be dreaded. These, to keep up the metaphor, we may compare to mines, which sometimes take effect long after the appearance of danger is over.'

Edwards and his book on the West Indies survived the various hazards so well that in 1797, Stockdale also published his *A Historical Survey of the French Colony in the Island of St. Domingo*. It would not be safe to assume that a book was a success merely because it was pirated, but that fact is some indication of its popularity. On June 21, 1802, Stockdale wrote to the bookseller Becket to inform him that he was suing him for breach of copyright in respect of the new, 1801, third volume of the Edwards West Indies book – which was a version of the St. Domingo book coupled with a brief autobiographical note by the author, who knew that he was dying.[23] This threatened action was something of a rarity: Stockdale – like Almon before him – was usually at the receiving end of legal proceedings.

After our diversion to the Caribbean, we must return to the southern seas. It was not only the British government which was interested in that region of the world: the French also encouraged exploration there. Indeed, the British interest in the region was heightened by the concern about rival European powers with similar ideas.

In 1798, Stockdale published the *Voyage of La Pérouse round the World*, edited by M. L. A. Milet-Mureau, with 51 plates, which gave an account of the French expedition in the years 1785 to 1788. La Pérouse had disappeared and Admiral d'Entrecosteaux was sent to look for him. In 1800, Stockdale produced the

---

[23] Bodleian MS Add. C.89 f.340.

Voyage in Search of La Pérouse, by J. J. Houtou de la Billardière, with 46 plates. Both books were translated from the French for him, possibly by his son John Joseph and his daughter Mary, for they both translated other works for their father. Stockdale's translation of the Search volume was in quarto. An advertisement in the back of the book showed that Stockdale was publishing more maps.

In that notice, he boasted: 'Their Majesties and the whole of the Royal Family have been graciously pleased to patronise Mr. Stockdale's publication of Chaucard's maps of Germany, Italy &c.' The cost was five guineas to subscribers and eight for later purchasers. The income due from the subscribers at that time was over £12,000, but the production costs must have been higher than normal. We shall presently see that Stockdale was to let these large sums go to his head, and that he was to overreach himself financially. He kept complaining that the war was bad for business, but his business was good for the war. The Chaucard maps not only graced the royal apartments, but were used by Wellington's army to good effect.[24]

In the same year Debrett, who was also concentrating on Australian books, put out a different translation of the Search book in octavo. Debrett's translator dedicated his edition to Banks, while Stockdale, who in 1799, had published a speech by Robert Peel, the Elder, dedicated his 1800 volume to that statesman.

We shall see in the final chapter how Stockdale bought up the stock of the Robinsons. One of the books that he acquired in that way, and republished himself, was George Vancouver's *Voyage Round the World.* Vancouver had sailed with Cook on his first voyage as an able seaman, aged 15, but had climbed very successfully up the ladder after that. His book helped to confirm

---

[24] Longford, Elizabeth, *Wellington: The Years of the Sword,* London: Panther, 1971, 211.

Stockdale's shop as a suitable port of call for books on Australia and great voyages generally.[25]

Stockdale's translator of the Search book posed some far-sighted questions in his preface, which doubtless pleased Banks: 'Whether, as has hitherto generally happened, the advantages of civilisation may not, in the progress of events, be transferred from the Europeans, who have but too little prized them, to those remote countries which they have been so diligently exploring? If so, the period may arrive, when New Zealand may produce her Lockes, her Newtons, and her Montesquieu; and when great nations in the immense region of New Holland may send their navigators, philosophers, and antiquaries, to contemplate the ruins of *ancient* London and Paris, and to trace the languid remains of the arts and sciences in this quarter of the globe. Who can tell, whether the rudiments of some great future empire may not already exist at Botany Bay?'

---

[25] Hough, 230. Both Vancouver and the less deserving Lord Sydney have beautiful cities named after them; others, including Cook, have been less well rewarded. The islands named after Sandwich now have the better name of Hawaii.

Illus. 14. David Ramsay by Charles Fraser

14

The First American Historian

Both John Adams and Thomas Jefferson worked hard to get American authors published in England and France, and to get copies of books already published in America sold in those countries. When helping American authors they were fulfilling two functions. First, they were acting in a consular capacity, helping fellow-citizens and getting trade and publicity for their new country, of which they were justifiably proud. Secondly, they were doing what comes naturally to book lovers and collectors: they were enjoying anything to do with books. It was no great hardship for either Adams or Jefferson to stroll around the bookshops of London or Paris, inquiring about the chances of printing, of publishing or of selling any given book – or even buying one or two. When Jefferson gave considerable help to Stockdale by buying children's books for him in Paris, he was not acting in his consular capacity. He was helping an Englishman who had appealed to both his head and his heart: to his love of books, which played such an important part in the Virginian's life that, at times, it helped to get him into serious debt.

From time to time the two ministers complained that nothing American sold, and that English people were not interested in America or its authors. Some American authors also complained about the poor sales of their works in England. Stockdale was one of the booksellers about whom, and to whom complaints were made. How justified were those various complaints? It is quite instructive to study in a little detail the case of the first important American historian, Dr. David Ramsay. He is

of particular interest as he was introduced to Stockdale by his
father-in-law, Henry Laurens.

Robert Brunhouse, the historian who considered Ramsay's
work in two excellent pieces in 1945 and 1965, concluded the
first by referring to the difficulties of the early American
authors, which included, 'the quest for a satisfactory printer, the
primitive methods of marketing books, the fear of pirated editions, the hazards of foreign translations, and the hope that sales
might be sufficient to cover the costs of publication.' In his two
works, an article and a selection of his letters, Brunhouse demonstrated that Ramsay had his fair share of all those problems,
but it will be seen that the author contributed to some of his
own difficulties.[1]

David Ramsay was born in Pennsylvania and studied medicine there under Dr. Benjamin Rush, the political doctor, who
was also an author and was to sign the Declaration of Independence. It was Rush who, much later, encouraged his two friends,
Adams and Jefferson, to become reconciled after their long
breach. After qualifying, Ramsay moved to Charleston, South
Carolina, and lived and practised medicine there from then on.
Emulating Rush, he managed to combine medicine with politics
and writing. He soon became involved in South Carolina politics, being elected a member of the local legislature, and later, of
Congress. His first two marriages ended with the death of each
wife in the year following on her wedding, but then he married
Martha Laurens, Henry's daughter, who survived until 1811.
They had a number of children, but also gave a home to John
Laurens's daughter, Frances, who, as related earlier, had lost first
her English mother and then her American father during the
war, in a little over a single year.

---

[1] Brunhouse, Robert L., 'David Ramsay's Publication Problems 1784-
1808', *Papers Bib. Soc. of America*, 1945, 39: 51; 'David Ramsay, 1749-1815,
Selections from his Writings', *Transactions of the American Philosophical Society*,
N.S., 1965, 55: part 4; referred to hereafter as Brunhouse, Selections.

When Charleston fell to the British in May 1780, Ramsay, then serving as a doctor with a local artillery regiment, was taken prisoner, together with his future wife's brother, John Laurens. They were both paroled and we have seen that Laurens, very much a fighting man, was exchanged in time for him to be able to undertake his historic mission to France and to participate in the battle of Yorktown. The non-combatant medical man was less fortunate, as the British decided to make an example of some of their more distinguished captives, justifying the decision on the grounds of some suspicion of a resistance movement in South Carolina. Ramsay and several dozen others, who included Arthur Middleton and Edward Rutledge, two Middle Temple signers of the Declaration of Independence, were deported to St. Augustine in Florida, and detained there for the best part of a year.[2]

While in captivity Ramsay began to work on his first book, *The History of the Revolution in South Carolina*. After his release he was able to get on with his project, even though he was a South Carolina delegate to Congress in 1782-1783. He completed his draft by August 1784, and having decided to publish the work himself, asked Benjamin Rush for his advice about the better place to have it printed, London or Philadelphia. 'I incline to the latter,' he informed his old teacher, 'The accuracy of a London printer would make me less concerned about my own inaccuracies and yet I hate to be beholden to our late enemies.' He added that, among other topics, he intended writing about four named generals and one named colonel, John Laurens.

Rush advised Ramsay to use Charles Dilly in London. This was scarcely surprising, given that Dilly had first met Rush when on a pioneering trade trip to America in 1764, and that he had made him welcome at his bookshop in the City of London in 1768. Rush, who had just completed some medical studies in Edinburgh, later wrote: 'I was frequently and kindly entertained

---

[2] Brunhouse, Selections, 16.

by Messrs Edward and Charles Dilly, booksellers in London. At their hospitable table I met with many gentlemen of literary characters. Indeed their bookstore was a kind of coffee house for authors.'[3]

In September, 1784, Ramsay acknowledged the advice Rush had given him, indicating that he proposed following it. He intended sending the manuscript to London and hoped 'to have it back in America next summer neatly printed and finished for one half less than it would cost in this country and done twice as well.' However, for some reason he changed his mind, and instead chose an American printer, Isaac Collins of Trenton, New Jersey. Perhaps the 'late enemies' point and his captivity in Florida still rankled too much. Possibly it was his patriotism that made him give preference to the American printer.[4]

We must follow Ramsay's printing history through for a while. He was not at all satisfied with the work of Collins; despite that he decided to have his second book, *The History of the American Revolution*, printed in America as well. In 1788, he asked Robert Aitken, a Scottish printer working in Philadelphia, to produce the sheets for his new history. He was appalled by the results. Aitken had the advantage of a more legible manuscript than the one supplied to Collins for the earlier book, but still made many more errors. Ramsay complained, 'Aitken's work offends against every principle of good printing. The printing, the spelling, the rule, the form of the lines are in many cases execrable.' One cannot feel too much sympathy for Ramsay: he had asked Rush for his opinion, had received sound advice and had promptly ignored it.[5]

---

[3] When Rush's younger brother, Jacob, came to London to study law in 1770, the Dillys looked after him also. Butterfield, L. H., 'The American Interests of the Firm of E. and C. Dilly', *Papers Bib. Soc. of America*, 1951, 45: 290, 294, 305; Corner, George W., *The Autobiography of Benjamin Rush*, Princeton: Princeton U.P., 1948, 62.

[4] Brunhouse, Selections, 81-83.

[5] Brunhouse, Selections, 130.

The marketing history of the two works was also a tale of woe. Ramsay, like many an author before and after him, had great expectations for his first book. In January 1785, he wrote optimistically to John Witherspoon, the Scottish President of the College of New Jersey (Princeton) and his 'middle' father-in-law, who had also been published by Dilly: 'What would you think of sending the sheets to Mr. Dilly so as to prepare for giving him the copyright in England or that a thousand copies should be sent to him for binding and sale? The avidity is so great in Europe for American intelligence that perhaps some man may take it in hand to translate it into French or Dutch.'[6]

Quite where Ramsay had learned of such avidity is not clear. It may be added that the point sometimes made, that the British would not buy the works of American authors *because* they were their recent opponents in war, could hardly be made about the equally unenthusiastic French or Dutch allies. During the course of the year, Ramsay decided that a thousand copies of *The Revolution of South Carolina* would not be sufficient to satisfy the hungry British market, and on December 10, 1785, wrote to Jefferson that he was despatching 1600 copies to Dilly, exactly half of the total print run. It will be recalled that Stockdale, who was rather more experienced than Ramsay, had written to Jefferson in 1787, to say that he intended to produce only five hundred copies of his *Notes on the State of Virginia* – a more realistic figure, especially when one bears in mind that compared with Jefferson, Ramsay was a non-entity, both as a public figure and as an author. Besides, even in America, 'before the Revolution and for some years after, 500 copies of a book were thought a handsome edition.'[7]

---

[6] Butterfield, Dilly, 294; Brunhouse, Selections, 86.

[7] Isaiah Thomas, the American printer and historian of printing, quoted by Amory, Hugh, 'Reinventing the Colonial Book', in Amory, Hugh and Hall, David D. (eds.), *The Colonial Book in the Atlantic World*, Cambridge U.P., 2000, 51.

When Dilly saw that the book included several highly critical comments on the conduct of named British officers in South Carolina, he took legal advice and decided that it would not be safe to publish the book as printed, much as he would have liked to unmask some of them. 'The war being over, the hazard of publishing might enable the criminals, instead of receiving punishment (I mean Tarleton and others of his sanguinary cast) to call it down on the publisher.' Dilly may have been made aware of the fact that Col. Banastre Tarleton was yet another member of the Middle Temple.[8] According to Arthur Shaffer, Ramsay's biographer, American national pride was inflamed by Ramsay's publication problems in Great Britain. He pointed out that the American poet, Philip Freneau, had been spurred on to write a poem about the infamous British and their untrue versions of the war, containing the lines:

> They hired some historians to scribble and flatter,
> And foolishly thought they could hush up the matter.
> But Ramsay arose, and with Truth on his side,
> Has told the world what they labored to hide.[9]

Jefferson worked hard in Paris to make provision for copies in English to be sold there, and also for a French translation. His considerable efforts were in vain: the French allies did not want to buy Ramsay's book. Both Jefferson and Adams had been sent a copy by the proud author. Adams thanked Ramsay in February 1786, and reciprocated by sending him a copy of a newly published anonymous pamphlet, *An Address to the Landed,*

---

[8] Dilly to Rush, May 5, 1786, Butterfield, Dilly, 323. For a new look at the whole conflict, which apart from anything else, shows how both sides could be equally cruel, see, Bicheno, Hugh, *Rebels and Recoats*, London: HarperCollins, 2003.

[9] Shaffer, Arthur H., *To be an American*, Columbia: U. of South Carolina P., 1991, 102. Freneau was the pro-Jefferson editor, taken on by the Republicans to counter Hamilton's Federalist publisher, John Fenno. The principal weapons were the *National Gazette* and the *Gazette of the United States*, respectively.

Trading and Funded Interests of England. In thanking Adams for it in May, Ramsay also mentioned that Dilly had declined to sell his book. As he was wondering about an alternative bookseller, Ramsay must have noticed that the gift from Adams had been published by Stockdale.

On April 19, Stockdale was almost certainly made aware of Ramsay's homeless book. Adams noted in his diary that day: 'I walked to the booksellers, Stockdale, Cadell, Dilly, Almon, and met Dr. Priestley for the first time. *The Conquest of Canaan, The Vision of Columbus,* and the *History of the Revolution in S. Carolina* were the subject. Seeds were sown this day which will grow.'[10] Adams was clearly referring to Debrett's shop when mentioning Almon.

Nothing much seems to have happened to further the publication of the South Carolina book in England during the second half of 1786, but early in the following year, Ramsay's closer connection with Henry Laurens may have set the ball rolling again. It was on January 28, 1787, that Ramsay, who had treated Laurens as a patient, married his daughter Martha. Four weeks later he wrote to his new father-in-law, encouraging him to become one of the State's delegates to the Constitutional Convention. Laurens had no desire to re-enter public life, and declined to serve. At some time the two men, who had many interests in common, including the library in Charleston, must have discussed Laurens's time in London. It is clear that his stay with Stockdale over the bookshop on different occasions was mentioned. As a result of the discussions between the two men, on April 20, Laurens wrote to Stockdale, in the letter referred to earlier: 'Doctor Ramsay will apply to you to take possession of certain books which he has in London. I recommend his

---

[10] Butterfield, L. H. (ed.), *Diary and Autobiography of John Adams,* Cambridge: Harvard U.P., 1961, 3: 189.

correspondence not only as that of my son-in-law and particular friend, but as a man of honor in the truest sense.'[11]

Laurens added: 'I laboured to obtain your appointment of bookseller to our South Carolina Library, but the members have chosen to give the office to one of the most obnoxious, or one who was but very lately held the most obnoxious to my countrymen, Robert Wells; such things will happen, you have seen the same in your city.' The reason Wells was considered obnoxious was because he was a returned loyalist.[12]

Jefferson appears not have been informed by Ramsay of his request to Stockdale to sell his London stock of the South Carolina war history, for he wrote on August 4, 1787, 'I observe Stockdale in London has printed your book and advertised it for sale.' Jefferson may have assumed, not unreasonably, that Stockdale had pirated the book. On November 30, Ramsay wrote to Jedidiah Morse, informing him that Stockdale had indeed undertaken to sell his book and that he had advertised it in London. He added a note which confirmed the continued importance of Stockdale as a supplier, 'He has also sent me a number of new publications which will be of great use to me in my new work.' That first book sold very slowly on both sides of the Atlantic, and Ramsay made a large loss on it.[13]

Ramsay managed to work on his 'new work', *History of the American Revolution*, while attending Congress in the 1785-1786 session. John Hancock, who had been Laurens's predecessor as President, had been elected to preside once again, but like many other members, did not attend the virtually powerless, and therefore half-hearted assembly. Ramsay acted in his stead, gaining exemption from committee duties, so that he had ample

---

[11] South Carolina Hist. Soc., Henry Laurens Papers.

[12] The letter appointing Wells, dated April 14, 1787, is contained in Raven, James, *London Booksellers and American Customers*, Columbia: U. of South Carolina P., 2002, 277.

[13] Brunhouse, Selections, 112, 118; for Morse, see chap.6.

time to ferret in the archives when undertaking research for his second historical book. He also sensibly picked the brains of those with personal recollections of the historic days, including John Adams and Henry Laurens.

In the light of his bad experiences with his first work, Ramsay decided to sell the second by subscription. As we have seen, he once again chose to have the work printed, badly, in America, rather than in London. He had three hundred copies sent to Benjamin Vaughan, in London, with a request that he place them. Vaughan was an obvious choice for him. Not only had he been Franklin's friend for years, but he had also been responsible for the first collection of his assorted works, *Political, Philosophical and Miscellaneous Pieces by Benjamin Franklin*, which Joseph Johnson had published in 1779. Furthermore, in 1781, Vaughan had married Sarah Manning, the sister of John Laurens's late wife, whose child Ramsay was bringing up with his own wife, John's sister. By letter dated May 14, 1790, he informed Vaughan's brother, another John, that he had asked Aitken to dispatch the books to London, and added a revealing home truth: 'We have but few readers in America at least in these southern states. I am therefore anxious to hear of its reception in England.'[14]

Ramsay sent more copies for Stockdale to sell. On February 22, 1792, Stockdale wrote to the first American geographer, Jedidiah Morse, who had been introduced by Ramsay, 'There seems to be a general dislike in purchasing American printed books.' He added that he had tried to sell eleven hundred copies of Ramsay's second book at auction, but 'the highest bidder was eightpence per set [of sheets], though there were sixty-three booksellers present, and the selling price twelve shillings in boards.'[15]

---

[14] Brunhouse, Selections, 127.
[15] Jedidiah Morse Papers, New-York Hist. Soc.

In mentioning the London public's reluctance to buy 'American printed books', rather than 'American books' or 'books by American authors', Stockdale may have been referring to the quality of the printing done in America, as opposed to the contents of the books written by authors there. Potential customers picking up Ramsay's second work might well have noticed some of the atrocious misprints complained of by the author, and put it down again. Stockdale chose a drastic remedy. Without consulting the author, he had a revised edition printed. On April 12, 1793, Ramsay wrote to his friend John Eliot in Boston, to whom he had earlier sent two hundred copies of the first print, for him to place with 'some honest bookseller': 'You say Thomas and Andrews [Boston printers] wish to print an edition of my history of the American Revolution. Stockdale has printed one in London without my consent and many of the copies of Aitken's edition are yet on hand. The errors and blunders of Aitken's edition are many and cannot be corrected. Stockdale assigned this to me as the reason of his reprinting the work in London. The American printers may be assured that I knew nothing of the London edition till Mr. Stockdale wrote me an apologetic letter for making so free with my work.'[16]

As an author, Ramsay was clearly highly dissatisfied with booksellers who could not sell the hundreds of books that he had himself had printed. In the light of Stockdale's similar remarks, Ramsay was right to some extent about American books not selling in England, but went too far when he wrote to Morse bitterly: 'They affect a contempt of every production that is American, and a total indifference to what is going on, on this side of the Atlantic. Even Mr. Jefferson's book does not sell. The truth is, they do not wish to encourage literature or manufacture among us. Their unmerited and severe strictures on the literary performances of American have made me more American than ever. I have escaped pretty well; but you have doubtless

---

[16] Brunhouse, Selections, 135.

seen what they have said of Mr. Adams's, Mr. Jefferson's and Mr. Dwight's performances.' When Ramsay produced his next major work, *History of South Carolina*, in 1809, he did not even bother to send it to Stockdale.[17]

We have seen already what Ramsay had said about the failure of southerners to buy books. When Joel Barlow had invited him to sell copies of his *Vision of Columbus: A Poem in Nine Books*, Ramsay had replied: 'I rather think that twenty-four copies will satisfy our people.' It is distinctly possible that he not only grossly over-estimated the number of likely purchasers of his two histories in England and France, but also in America – even in his home State, South Carolina.

Ramsay bought a number of books from Stockdale for his own library, and on March 18, 1791, placed an order on behalf of the Senate of South Carolina, of which he had just been made President. Stockdale was asked to see to it that 'the letters S.S.C. be added on the back and the words "Senate of South Carolina" be in gold letters at full length on the outside of one of the covers'. Ramsay concluded, 'As in procuring the above books I act for a public body, I beg that you do not blend the account of it with my private account.'[18]

In the same year, Ramsay's recommendation of Stockdale to the Charleston Library Society, following on the earlier one of Henry Laurens, succeeded: he was appointed its official book-seller. However, he was sacked in the following year, and wrote to protest about the decision. He need not have bothered, for he was in excellent company. The Library Society, which could be extremely unreasonable with its demands, had already appointed, and then sacked, the flower of London booksellers, including Strahan, Rivington, Durham, Wilson, Dodsley, Fletcher and Nicoll, leading James Raven to make the fair

---

[17] Sprague, W. B., *The Life of Jedidiah Morse*, New York: Anson D. F. Randolph, 1874, 202.
[18] William L. Clements Library, U. of Michigan.

comment: 'One of the greatest honours to be avoided in the 18th.-century book trade was appointment as London Book-seller to the Charleston Library Society.'[19]

In his full history of the Library Society, Raven has pointed out that Stockdale's letter of protest, though ineffective for him, is extremely important for historians. He rightly asserts that 'very few business records and correspondence of eighteenth-century booksellers survive,' and adds that Stockdale's letter 'offers an important and unique testimony.'[20]

The Society, in a letter of November 2, 1791, signed by Ramsay as its Vice-President, had placed a very large order with Stockdale, worth £436: 'by far the largest and most valuable of the known book cargoes sent to the society'. As the order was for many books emanating from different booksellers and published over a number of years, it took Stockdale a consider-able time to assemble and carefully pack the precious cargo. Despite this, before his despatch of the books, he was dismissed by a letter dated July 18, 1792, for not responding quickly enough. In his letter of protest, dated September 14, Stockdale wrote: 'Many of the articles though trifling in price were the most difficult to procure and were only to be got by accident as they came into the trade from private persons. For this reason my clerks and myself have traversed the streets of London from bookseller to bookseller, I firmly believe an hundred times over at least, which is no trifling trouble considering that there are near two hundred, which cannot be gone through in less than two days, they lying at so great a distance from each other.'

Stockdale was clearly most anxious to please his South Carolina contacts. He stated that if he had included any

---

[19] Raven, James, 'Gentlemen, pirates, and really respectable booksellers', in Hunt, Arnold, Mandelbrote, Giles, and Shell, Alison (eds.), *The Book Trade and its Customers 1450-1900*, Historical Essays for Robin Myers, Win-chester: St. Paul's Bibliography, 1997, 247, 248.

[20] Raven, James, *London Booksellers and American Customers*, 86, 109.

overpriced book in his consignment, they were at liberty to sell them at auction. He would cheerfully bear any attendant loss rather 'than that the Gentlemen should think I wished to land them with books that they did not want, or that I had been imprudent in my selection'. Stockdale clearly made this point because he was aware that some of his colleagues, including even William Strahan, 'used the colonies as a dumping ground for unwanted remainders and poor sellers'. Raven has commented that it was extraordinary that, in the same letter, Stockdale, though 'bruised and rejected', should have offered to continue to supply books as required, with payments to be made 'as it is convenient to the Society'.

Stockdale was eventually paid the balance owed to him for the books sent in execution of the first and only order, but was not re-appointed. In fact, no other bookseller was appointed to replace him: the Society decided that its commercial agents would do just as well, and probably cost less in terms of mark up for services rendered. The agents were Bird, Savage and Bird; Henry Bird had been trained by Henry Laurens's old business associate, William Manning and, like John Laurens and Benjamin Vaughan, had married one of Manning's daughters. However, the Society's choice was not a brilliant one. The Bird agency failed a few years later, almost ruining John Adams, who had invested heavily in it and had to be rescued by his son, John Quincy.[21]

Brunhouse, a historian himself, has pointed out that although Ramsay's work was generally admired as that of one of the first American historians, his reputation has been tarnished ever since 1902, when Orin G. Libby was the first of several writers to

---

[21] Raven, James, *London Booksellers and American Customers*, 97, 115, 118, 280, 288. One of Manning's sons fathered the famous Cardinal Manning. The 'dumping' quote is also from James Raven, but from his 'The Importation of Books in the Eighteenth Century', in Amory and Hall, 187. Nagel, Paul C., *John Quincy Adams: A Public Life, a Private Life*, New York, Knopf, 1997, 141.

demonstrate that he had been a serious plagiarist.[22] Like John Adams in his *Defence*, and indeed other authors of the time, Ramsay used large sections of other writers' works without acknowledging their authorship. His works are still, however, at the very least, used for reference purposes. Arthur M. Schlesinger, Sr., began his book on American newspapers, in the crucial years 1764-1776, with a quote from Ramsay's second book that is relevant to the present work: 'In establishing American independence, the pen and the press had a merit equal to that of the sword.'[23]

Despite his plagiarism, Ramsay remains a writer of historical importance. Arthur Shaffer has stated, perhaps a little extravagantly: 'It is no exaggeration to say that David Ramsay created American history.' He added that he became 'a leading intellectual spokesman; he was attempting to do for historical writing what Benjamin Rush was doing for medicine … and Jedidiah Morse for geography.'[24]

One reason why Ramsay expressed so much concern about the progress of sales was because he had invested his own money in his first two major books – and because he was a very bad financial manager. Henry Laurens and his son, John, had been very careful about money. John Laurens never drew any Army pay, because his father supported him throughout the war. Henry Laurens was for a long time reluctant to claim any expenses from Congress for himself and was almost forced to accept some partial reimbursement. He nobly felt that his country had sufficient financial problems without his family adding to them. When Henry Laurens died in 1792, his daughter

---

[22] Libby, Orin G., 'Ramsay as a Plagiarist', *American Historical Review*, 1902, 7: 697.

[23] Schlesinger, Arthur M., *Prelude to Independence: The Newspaper War on Britain 1764-1776*, New York: Knopf, 1958. It is arguable that the sword or the gun was the decisive weapon, because the publications that really make the difference are the casualty lists.

[24] Shaffer, 1, 3.

Martha inherited a small fortune. Ramsay managed to get through it all in a few years and in 1798, asked for relief under the provisions of the Insolvent Debtors Act.[25] That fact did not inhibit him from writing in his *History of South Carolina* in 1809, 'A disposition to contract debts is one of the vices of the Carolinians.'[26]

Before he spent it, Mrs. Ramsay's inheritance almost got her husband a seat in the United States Senate. The biographer of Robert Goodloe Harper, a South Carolina Congressman, made the following unattractive comment about the 1796 election: 'Harper also pressed for the selection of a candidate to stand for [Pierce] Butler's Senate seat and thought the irascible Dr. David B. Ramsay might prove a good choice. Dr. Ramsay had previously irritated South Carolinians with his anti-slavery views, but Harper had heard that he [*sic*] had recently become a large slaveholder in Georgia and thought that that had likely brought the doctor to a right view of the matter.'[27]

As this chapter has been partly concerned with printing errors, it is interesting to note that in his selection of Ramsay's letters, Brunhouse included one from him to Henry Laurens in 1787, the year of his marriage to his daughter. The printed text records Ramsay as closing his letter, 'Gold [*sic*] bless you.' Perhaps that slip was in the original, as Father Laurens's prosperity may well have been on Ramsay's mind.

Ramsay came to an unfortunate end in 1815, four years after his wife's death. He had certified a tailor as insane and fit to be detained. After his release from detention, the resentful man exercised his Second Amendment right to bear arms,

---

[25] Wallace, 351; Brunhouse, *Selections*, 26.

[26] Quoted in Boorstin, Daniel J., *The National Experience*, London: Phoenix Press, 2000, 175.

[27] Cox, Joseph W., *Champion of Southern Federalism: Robert Goodloe Harper of South Carolina*, Port Washington, N.Y.: Kennikat Press, 1972, 74. One of Harper's pamphlets was to occasion serious strife between Stockdale and his rival, John Wright, see chap.18.

encountered Ramsay in the street and shot him. He died two days later.

We should look briefly at the other two authors and their poems, mentioned by Adams, together with Ramsay's name, to the different booksellers during his grand tour of the London bookshops on April 19, 1786. They were Timothy Dwight and *The Conquest of Canaan*, and Joel Barlow and *The Vision of Columbus: A Poem in Nine Books*, a later version of which was called *The Columbiad*. Stockdale did not really need Adams's introduction to either of them. The poem by Dwight, who was to become President of Yale in 1795, and that by Barlow, a future American minister in Paris, had both been seen by Stockdale before the date of Adams's tour.

On April 8, eleven days before the visit by Adams to the bookshops, Thomas Day, Stockdale's principal author, had written to Dr. Richard Price about Barlow's *The Vision of Columbus*. Price had clearly asked Stockdale to obtain the views of Day, a recognised poet as well as prose writer, on the merits of the poem. Day expressed his regret to Price that he had thought it 'necessary to consult any judgment but your own.' He nevertheless promised, reluctantly, 'to express an opinion upon so invidious a subject as an author's poetical merit' He had an open mind, for he added, 'I know nothing of the author and have not yet received the poem from Stockdale.'[28]

Day, who could hardly be accused of being anti-American, continued his letter to Dr. Price with some critical remarks about the American poetry he had already seen. 'All the attempts I have hitherto seen in that way from that country are certainly not above mediocrity. The poem of Col. Humphreys is but indifferent; and Stockdale for my entertainment has sent me down another extraordinary performance called *The Conquest of Canaan*, which is also intended for an epic poem. I defy the most resolute reader to wade through it without yawning an hundred

---

[28] *Mass. Hist. Society Procs.*, 2nd Series, 1903, 17: 340.

times.' Col. David Humphreys, as mentioned earlier, was the former Washington aide who served as Jefferson's secretary of the Commission in Paris: his 'attempt' was *A Poem on the Happiness of America*.

With Day's strong views on the subject of Dwight's poem, it is hardly surprising that Stockdale – obviously no authority on poetry himself – declined it. It did find a publisher two years later: Joseph Johnson took a chance with it.

In his letter, Day also included a warning to Price about Barlow's poem: 'Should your good nature think of printing it yourself, though I would not wish to stint your bounty, you will pardon me, who from being a brother author am alive to all the misfortunes of the trade, if I suggest the possibility of your being considerably out of pocket.' Price took Day's advice and suggested to Barlow that as his poem contained criticism of England, it was 'improper to be published in this country', and that America or France would be a more suitable outlet. Barlow managed to get it published in 1787, in Hartford, Connecticut.[29]

Stockdale seems then to have obtained some more favourable views of Barlow's work, for in the same year he published it after all, jointly with Dilly. However, as Butterfield pointed out, 'This work was not calculated to please English readers, and it did not sell.'[30] John Adams was so keen to obtain the views of Day at about this time, that he offered to go and see him about one of his compatriot's poems. Although Day offered to put him up for the night, Adams appears not to have found time for a visit. He did, however, have one success. It was probably on his recommendation that Dilly, in 1787, published the *Political Sketches*, written by another American student at the Middle Temple, William Vans Murray, from Maryland. John Quincy Adams had met and become friendly with Murray, when on his

---

[29] Cone, Carl B., *Torchbearer of Freedom*, Lexington: U. of Kentucky P., 1952, 173.
[30] Butterfield, Dilly, 298.

abortive trip to London to collect his mother and sister in 1784. They became close friends and were to follow similar paths for a while, Murray in due course succeeding young Adams as minister in The Hague.

Day turned out to be a better judge of the English market than Adams. On Christmas Day, 1787, Adams wrote to his friend, Mercy Warren: 'In short nothing American sells here. Ramsay's history, Dwight and Barlow's poems are not sold. There is a universal desire and endeavour to forget America, and an unanimous resolution to read nothing which shall bring it back to their thoughts. They cannot recollect it without pain.'[31] Adams, like Ramsay, may have overlooked the fact that customers were not only limited in number, but also looked carefully both at the subject-matter and the quality of printing before parting with their money.

---

[31] Butterfield, Dilly, 298; *Warren-Adams Letters, Mass. Hist. Soc. Colls.*, Vol.73, 1925, ii, 301.

Illus. 15. Thomas Paine by George Romney

15

Tom Paine and John Quincy Adams

'Tis time to rejoin Tom Paine and catch up with John Quincy Adams, before considering how they both managed to contribute to the breakdown of relations between Thomas Jefferson and John Adams, and John Stockdale's part in the saga.

Paine's *Common Sense* was one of the great successes of 1776, published in vast numbers in America, printed five times for Almon in London and translated for different European publishers. Not all Americans agreed with it but George Washington read it and wrote for the first time of independence, referring to 'the sound doctrine and unanswerable reasoning in the pamphlet *Common Sense*'.[1] In South Carolina both Henry Laurens and John Rutledge strongly disapproved of it, mainly because in early 1776, they still hoped that a separation from the old country was avoidable. According to one account Laurens, who was to become quite friendly with Paine, called him --------! in the Assembly.[2]

John Adams disagreed with many of Paine's views, but agreed with him about the need to part. He published in reply his very influential pamphlet, *Thoughts on Government*, but remained on relatively good terms with him for a time, helping him to get the job of secretary to the Congressional Committee for Foreign Affairs in April 1777. Much later on, Paine was to

---

[1] Flexner, James Thomas, *George Washington, Vol.II, In the American Revolution,1775-1783*, Boston: Little, Brown, 1967, 67.
[2] Keane, John, *Tom Paine – A Political Life*, London: Bloomsbury, 1996, 124 and generally.

infuriate Adams by suggesting that he had been hostile to Washington during the Conway Cabal period – during which John Laurens had been at his general's side and had kept his father, President of Congress at the time, fed with information that was helpful to the Commander-in-Chief. Paine's unjustified allegation led Adams, in his autobiography, to call him 'that insolent blasphemer of things sacred and transcendent libeller of all that is good'. There was only one other man who made Adams more angry, and that was Alexander Hamilton, who had changed from being a reliable aide to being an unscrupulous politician. Paine lost many more admirers by making an outrageous attack on Washington when he was retiring.

In December 1776, Paine produced the pamphlet which ranks with his *Common Sense*, namely, *The American Crisis*. This came out just in time for it to be read to Washington's exhausted men before they crossed the Delaware to attack the Hessians at Trenton. 'These are the times that try men's souls. The summer soldier and the sunshine patriot will, in this crisis, shrink from the service of their country; but he that stands it *now* deserves the love and thanks of man and woman.'[3]

Late in 1777, Paine visited Washington at his winter quarters at Valley Forge and befriended the general's new aide, John Laurens. Paine described the troops there as resembling 'a family of beavers, everybody busy; some carrying logs, others mud, and the rest fastening them together'.[4]

Once back with Congress, Paine was largely in agreement with Henry Laurens on the issues raised by the Silas Deane affair – the investigation into the alleged financial juggling by Deane, the first purchasing agent of the United States in France. Paine was so vociferous with his allegations that he made a number of enemies in Congress and eventually resigned his post before he could be dismissed. Henry Laurens, by then no longer President,

---

[3] Keane, 145.
[4] Flexner, 261.

was obliged to admit to Congress that he had informed his friend Paine of what had occurred in a private session. That was perhaps Laurens's greatest mistake during his time in Congress. After losing his job, Paine had great difficulty in making a living in America and often thought of returning to Europe, especially once the war was finally over. He continued to write articles and pamphlets but they made little or no money for him, even though they sometimes benefited others.

When young John Laurens was asked by Congress and Washington to go on his historic mission to France to raise urgently needed help, he felt under-qualified in political matters and asked Paine to accompany him as his secretary. Paine agreed but realised that it would be better if he were to travel in a private capacity, so Laurens had a fellow-officer, Major William Jackson, appointed as his official secretary instead. Jackson had been captured with him at Charleston and was later to be the secretary of the Constitutional Convention. Despite the major's appointment, in February 1781, Paine sailed to France with John Laurens as his unofficial secretary, returning with him after their successful mission in August. As we have seen, John Laurens rejoined Washington in time for the decisive battle at Yorktown, but for Paine there was no such glory, only unemployment and poverty.

The French Revolution in 1789, attracted Paine as much as it repelled others. In March 1790, he was back in London, inquiring about the awaited attack on the French by Edmund Burke, with his *Reflections on the Revolution in France*. He called in at Debrett's bookshop and was told by him that while he was not publishing it, he understood that, 'Mr Burke was much at a loss how to go on; that he had revised some of the sheets six, seven, and one nine times!'[5]

One matter that was regularly in Burke's mind when considering the Parisian scenes of violence, was his memory of the

---

[5] Keane, 288.

Gordon Riots in 1780, and that influenced his writing. After Burke's book had eventually appeared on November 1, he was challenged to reconcile his enthusiasm for the American Revolution with his distaste for the French version. The report of his speech in the House of Commons, answering Charles James Fox, is revealing: 'With a view to showing his inconsistency, allusions had been made to his conduct in 1780 [and over] the American War. If he thought, in 1780, that the influence of the Crown ought to be reduced to a limited standard, and with which Mr Fox himself at the time seemed to be satisfied, it did not follow that the French were right in reducing it with them to nothing. He was favourable to the Americans because he supposed they were fighting not to acquire absolute speculative liberty, but to keep what they had under the English constitution.'[6]

As soon as he had obtained a copy of Burke's book, Paine settled in at the Angel Inn, Islington, and dashed off his response. His *Rights of Man; being an answer to Mr Burke's attack on the French Revolution*, appeared in March 1791. It was on the verge of publication by Joseph Johnson when he got cold feet, so it was put out by J.S.Jordan instead. It was followed up in February 1792, by the Second Part. The first work sold in huge numbers in London, so much so that the government became alarmed and commissioned a civil servant to write a book designed to dent Paine's reputation.

The man selected for this hatchet job was George Chalmers, some of whose books for John Stockdale were considered briefly in chap. 13. As related earlier, he had lived in America, but was no friend of the colonists and, thanks largely to Pitt, was employed as the Chief Clerk at the Office of Trade. Using the pen-name Francis Oldys, he speedily wrote a book with the title *The Life of Thomas Pain: The Author of Rights of Men* [*sic*]. The spelling of the surname without an 'e' was deliberate as the

---

[6] O'Brien, Conor Cruise, *Edmund Burke*, London: Vintage, 2002, 211, 237.

author suggested that 'Pain' had added the extra letter to his name for sinister reasons. Some of the other criticisms were on a similar low plane. Stockdale published the book in 1791, with an engraving of Paine as a frontispiece, and it sold very well. He had obtained the engraving from a nearby rival, for the note underneath it reads: 'Published as the Act directs July 25, 1791, for J. Ridgway, York Street, St. James's Square.' The brothers-in-law seem to have made up their differences sufficiently to come to some agreement.

Simon Maccoby has rightly stated that the Oldys book 'was obviously written for the purpose of ending the influence of the author of the *Rights of Man*.' It need hardly be added that, like most such governmental dirty tricks, it failed to achieve its purpose. Oldys also attempted to blacken the names of other critics of the government, by claiming that 'Brand Hollis and a committee of democrats' had revised Paine's work for him. John Disney, Brand Hollis's friend and biographer, pointed out that he had denied helping Paine. Disney added , 'Besides which, it is highly improbable from the internal evidence of the tenor of Paine's writings, that he would have been disposed to receive the revisions and alterations of any person, however qualified or disposed to assist him.'[7]

We last encountered John Quincy Adams as a 16-year-old, when he re-visited Stockdale's bookshop in 1784, during his unsuccessful attempt to meet his mother and sister before their arrival from America. John Quincy stayed in Europe with his family only until the following year, when he returned home, studied at Harvard and – like his father – became a member of the Bar. While he was a student, his mother counselled humility: 'Reflect that you have had greater opportunities of seeing the world, and obtaining a knowledge of mankind than

---

[7] Maccoby, Simon, *English Radicalism 1786-1832*, London: Allen and Unwin, 1955, p.51; Disney, John, *Memoirs of Thomas Brand-Hollis*, London: printed by T. Gillet, 1808, 19; Oldys, 95, 106.

Illus. 16. John Quincy Adams by John Singleton Copley

any of your contemporaries. That you have never wanted a book but it has been supplied to you, that your whole time has been spent in the company of men of literature and science.'[8]

By the time Paine's *Rights of Man* reached America, John Adams was Vice-President and Jefferson was Washington's first Secretary of State. A rift was already opening up between the two old friends, partly because Adams tended to consider friendship and trade with Britain as desirable, whereas Jefferson favoured all things French. As Max Beloff wrote of Jefferson, 'His affection for France was constant, and his seven weeks' visit to England in the spring of 1786, had done little to alter his preference.'[9] Burke's criticisms of France were likely to anger those who thought like Jefferson, and Paine's views were likely to be welcomed by them. Adams had been prompted by his disapproval of the French Revolution to write the series of articles for the *Gazette of the United States*, which subsequently became his book, *Discourses on Davila*. Partly because of mis-understandings, partly because Adams in his writings and in the Senate had made one or two ill-chosen remarks, he was accused of wishing to become a king, with John Quincy as his successor. Jefferson thought of his views as heretical and contrary to the spirit of '76.

One of those agreeing with Jefferson about France was John Beckley, Clerk of the House of Representatives, who supported both him and James Madison, later fourth President of the United States. Beckley decided to get Paine's work reprinted and sent his own copy to Madison, who passed it on to Jefferson. Beckley called on him before he had finished reading it, so Jefferson promised to pass it on to the printer as soon as he had read it all. In a covering note to the printer, which he later

---

[8] McCullough, David, *John Adams*, New York: Simon & Schuster, 2001, 365.

[9] Beloff, Max, *Thomas Jefferson and American Democracy*, Harmondsworth: Penguin, 1972, 81.

asserted he did not expect to be included in the new publication, Jefferson praised Paine's work, adding his delight that 'something was at length to be publicly said against the political heresies which have sprung up among us. I have no doubt but that our citizens will rally a second time round the standard of COMMON SENSE'. Jefferson claimed to be 'thunderstruck' when the American edition appeared with his letter included, immediately after a note that ended, '… the printer hopes the distinguished writer will excuse its present appearance.'[10]

It was clear to most readers that the Secretary of State's reference to political heresies was to the views of the Vice-President, many of which had been published over the years by Stockdale, and some of which had been repeated in Adams's later writings. Politicians and the press were keen to see what the reply from John Adams would be. The initial response came in a series of eleven letters in the *Columbian Centinel*, starting in June 1791, sent to the editor by someone signing himself Publicola. Many, including Jefferson, thought that John Adams had written them, but it eventually transpired that the extremely learned and fluent author was his son, John Quincy.

In his first letter, young Adams wrote to the editor: 'I confess, Sir, I am somewhat at a loss to determine what this very respectable gentleman means by *political heresies*. Does he consider this pamphlet of Mr. Paine's as the canonical book of political scripture?' He went on to say: 'If, however, Mr. Paine is to be adopted as the holy father of our political faith, and this pamphlet is to be considered as his Papal Bull of infallible virtue, let us at least examine what it contains.' In his eleven letters he did just that and also defended his father's published views.

Jefferson realised that he had caused his old friend, John Adams, considerable distress and sought to repair some of the damage he had done, by writing him a friendly letter, which

---

[10] *Jefferson Papers*, 20: after p.384; Peterson, Merrill D., *Thomas Jefferson and the New Nation*, Oxford U.P., 1970, 438-441.

included the assurance that his reference to 'political heresies' had not referred to him. 'This little piece of mendacity,' Peterson remarked, 'aimed at closing the wound had the opposite effect. Jefferson protested too much, as Adams suspected. He made no answer, nor did the old friends correspond again for several years.' Jefferson had made matters worse by trying to blame Publicola for all the trouble. Dumas Malone has suggested that during their discussions, Adams was less than frank in not identifying his son as Publicola and that he sought to shield John Quincy.[11] However, when one reads Adams's letter to Stockdale, dated May 12, 1793 (below), it becomes clear that he was not seeking to hide the identity of Publicola but merely respecting his son's right to decide for himself whether he wished to remain anonymous. The fact that Jefferson and John Quincy had been on extremely good terms in Paris, did not give John Adams the right to invade his son's privacy.

Not everyone accepts Jefferson's protestation that his comments were published contrary to his wishes. Conor Cruise O'Brien, for example, has commented: 'In the literal sense, but only in the literal sense, the publication of the excerpt *was* unauthorized. Nobody will ever find a smoking gun in the shape of a letter from Jefferson, telling Jonathan Bayard Smith he could publish. But Jefferson was a man of the world, who knew the world of books. He was not the kind of innocent who would dash off a few lines to a publisher, which would make a marvellous blurb for the book he is about to publish, and then be "thunderstruck," as Jefferson affected to be, when the publisher actually published the blurb.'[12]

---

[11] Malone, Dumas, *Jefferson and the Rights of Man*, Boston: Little, Brown, 1951, 366.

[12] O'Brien, Conor Cruise, *The Long Affair: Thomas Jefferson and the French Revolution, 1785-1800*, London: Sinclair-Stevenson, 1996, 110. O'Brien is extremely critical of Jefferson's reaction to that Revolution and provides detailed reasons for accusing him of duplicity on this and other occasions.

In London, the administration was delighted to find that an American author had done such a good dissection of Paine's arguments, and suggested to Stockdale that he might like to publish the letters in a more permanent form, for circulation in England. (As in Almon's case, it is difficult to tell when a suggestion or a request became an instruction, as he who pays the piper tends to call the tune.) Stockdale agreed and early in 1793, published the Publicola letters in book form, with the title *An Answer to Pain's Rights of Man:* the author was wrongly stated to be John Adams. Presumably Stockdale thought that he was stuck with the misspelling of Paine's name used by him for the book by Oldys/Chalmers. As a result he managed to publish a book getting wrong, in one fell swoop, both the name of the author and of the author named in the title – a rare achievement.

On March 16, Stockdale wrote to his former lodger, John Adams: 'You have probably heard long before this that I have printed *Letters to Pain* by your son. A copy was given to me by a gentleman high in government to print as your production with your name affixed, and I actually advertised it as such, but fortunately had information of its being written by your son and, of course, cancelled the title before a copy was seen by anyone except the printer and myself. The work does the highest honour to the writer, be he who he may. The Attorney-General assured me that it was the ablest work of the kind he had ever read. The Speaker of the House of Commons, Mr Pitt and many other gentlemen of the first abilities spoke of it in the same terms. It was printed as your work several times in Scotland before it came into my hands.'

The gentleman high in government may have been a minister, but was probably Chalmers, a senior civil servant. The heavy dose of name-dropping by the bookseller makes it clear how much Stockdale had turned his back on Almon's opposition stance. In 1793, Alexander Wedderburn, who as Solicitor-General had abused Franklin in front of the Privy

Council, was appointed Lord Chancellor, as Lord Lough-borough. Stockdale in that year published an excellent book Wedderburn had written earlier, *Observations on the State of the English Prisons*. Franklin had died three years earlier, so Stockdale doubtless felt that this specialist book, which stressed the need for prisons to be properly inspected, could please the ministry, without offending his American contacts. From time to time, Stockdale must have been faced with similar delicate balancing exercises, when considering a manuscript that might offend one or other class of regular customer.

Stockdale had not waited for either Adams to point out the error in the author's name on the *Publicola* book to him: he made the first mention of it himself. However, he may not have been completely frank about the speedy correction of the error, as neither of the copies of the book in the British Library and the London Library mention Quincy: in both instances the work is stated to be by John Adams.

The Vice-President replied on May 12: 'My son's name is John Quincy Adams, which you know very well, so that by ushering the pamphlet into the world in the name of John Adams Esq. it still might pass for mine. I understand all this very well. Bookseller's policy! All I have to say is that I did not write Publicola nor any part of it; if you wish to know whether my son wrote it or not, you must write to him, who is a counsellor-at-law in Boston and, as he has been taught to read and write, is capable of corresponding with you concerning his own affairs.'[13] It is worth noting that neither John Adams nor John Quincy Adams at any time suggested that it was wrong of Stockdale to re-publish the *Publicola* letters without the express consent of the author.

Stockdale's letter of March 16, had continued with a request to his former author: 'Your work on Government has never yet

---

[13] The two letters are in Adams Papers, Reel 376, and BL, Add. MSS 24329, f.2, respectively.

had fair play. I wish you would give me a corrected copy with any additions that you may have, and at the same time an order upon Mr Copley for your picture to engrave a frontispiece. I would with pleasure risk any sum in bringing out an edition of the work, and that in a much more reputable style than the former.' Stockdale was aware of the Copley portrait, as Adams had sat for it during his stay with him. The letter closed with a family note, 'Mrs Stockdale desires her kind respects.'

In the same answering letter, Adams, the wounded author, wrote: 'My "work on Government", as you are pleased to call it, has been so much neglected by Britons and so much insulted by Frenchmen, Irishmen and Americans, that it shall now either be consigned to everlasting oblivion or be transmitted to posterity exactly as it is. If you think you can make your fortune by printing it you are very welcome to do it, but without any corrections, additions or subtractions, except literary or grammatical ones. I don't mean to insist that you should print again *capital* for *capitol* and all the other blunders of the press that a boy in the lowest form could correct. One alteration I would request in the title page and that is that it may be *A Defence of the Constitutions of Government of the United States against the Attack of Mr Turgot in his Letter to Dr Price dated the twenty-second day of March 1778*. This alteration will be a full answer to every sensible objection which I have ever read to the work. It is not and never was intended for a general Defence of the American Constitutions. It is a Defence on the point on which they were attacked, and that only.'

Adams then turned to the print of the painting. 'If Mr Copley is willing that the picture should be put into the hands of any artist you may name, I have no objection, and you may do as you please: but I own I should be mortified to see such a bijou affixed to those republican volumes.' This last comment may have been prompted by accusations that Adams was at heart a monarchist. Adams continued his letter with a bitter mention of Franklin, and of the tyranny and despotism in France, but concluded warmly enough: 'My kind regards to Mrs Stockdale and believe me to be, your hearty well-wisher and humble servant.'

On March 3, 1794, Stockdale wrote to the Vice-President, enclosing a copy of his new edition of the *Defence*, complete with an engraving of the author – the correct one. He enclosed six extra copies of the engraving from the book for 'any of your absent children'. Hall's engraving of the Copley portrait, at any rate, was very good, and 'is the source of many that followed and is a well-executed and faithful likeness'.[14] Stockdale apologised for the fact that he had produced the work in octavo and explained: 'War hurts my business much and prevented me printing it in quarto.' Great Britain had been at war with revolutionary France since the beginning of the preceding year – and it was not clear whether the United States would join in on one side or the other, or remain neutral. The letter continued, 'I was much pleased with your opinion relating to France, and so were several of our great men to whom in confidence I showed that part of your letter. There are some very bad ones on both sides of the Atlantic who would rejoice to see us at war again, but I trust and hope their hellish spirits will not be gratified, as it is in the interest of both countries to be on the most friendly terms.' Stockdale concluded by sending his regards to the whole of the Adams family and 'in particular to your eldest son, of whom I have the pleasure to hear a very favourable account'. Stockdale's view of the best interests of the two countries at this time was probably close to that of Adams, and sounder than that of Jefferson.

Washington also had very favourable accounts of John Quincy Adams and was impressed by the products of his pen in his Publicola and other articles. He was soon to make a further meeting between Stockdale and young Adams possible. At the end of May 1794, the Vice-President proudly announced to the

---

[14] Oliver, Andrew, *Portraits of John and Abigail Adams*, Cambridge: Harvard U.P. 1967, 3. Stockdale's letter is in Adams Papers, Reel 377.

Senate that the President had nominated his first-born, still only 26, to be the resident minister in the Netherlands – his own old job. In the same month, John Jay, his father's former colleague as a Peace Commissioner and the first Chief Justice of the United States, was despatched to England by Washington with instructions to avert a war between the two countries. He was to settle all outstanding disputes and, if possible, negotiate a trade agreement – quite a brief. John Quincy was duly appointed to the minister's post and was asked to travel to The Hague via London so that he could deliver a trunk of papers to Jay, who was already there.

He sailed from Boston to Deal in Kent, arriving on October 15, in the near record time of four weeks, and travelled by coach to the capital with his younger brother, Thomas Boylston Adams, following in his footsteps, as a young companion and secretary. On arrival in London after dark, Adams heard a bang and stopped his coach. He found that a thief had cut the ropes and leather straps securing the baggage, which had fallen onto the road. Had Adams not heard the contact with the ground, the State papers he was conveying might have made interesting reading for unauthorised eyes. A promising career might have been cut short by that thief's knife. As it was, Adams made a point of delivering them to Jay that same evening.

Adams stayed in London for about two weeks before taking up his post in The Hague. During that time he discussed with Jay the treaty he was negotiating and also had the opportunity of dining with John Singleton Copley, the painter, and his family. He was much taken by the elder Miss Copley and confided to his diary for October 27: 'There is something so fascinating in the women I meet with in this country, that it is well for me I am obliged immediately to leave it.'[15] He had already met his future wife in London and was to return there to court and

---

[15] Adams, Charles Francis (ed.), *Memoirs of John Quincy Adams*, Philadelphia: Lippincott, 1874, 54.

marry her. During this brief stay in the city he made a point of calling in at Stockdale's shop – ten years after his last visit. Apart from anything else, he could there have the author's satisfaction of seeing his own recent book on sale. On November 9, 1794, he wrote to his father from The Hague: 'I took the liberty of sending you from London a new publication strongly recommended to me by our friend Stockdale, but the character of which I do not know. He said it contained a great number of interesting particulars relative to our neighbours the Indian tribes, and I thought it would afford you some amusement at least.'

On November 17, the young minister wrote to Stockdale from Amsterdam: 'Agreeable to my promises on leaving London, I now enclose to you a draft for one hundred and fifty guineas to pay for the books you supplied me for my friend Mr Gardner of Boston, and also for a few which, as I mentioned to you, I shall have occasion for myself. With my best respects to Mrs Stockdale.' He followed that letter with another on December 6, to say that he should 'be glad to receive the critical and monthly reviews as they come out, and shall perhaps from time to time have occasion to write for pamphlets or single books'.[16]

Adams returned to London to help Jay and the resident minister, the South Carolinian, Thomas Pinckney (who had been educated in England) with the treaty negotiations, staying for many weeks in England. He found working with the Chief Justice and the minister to be a 'heady experience – only weeks before he had complained of being an obscure attorney'.[17] Jay's Treaty, which according to one recent commentator, 'buried the French alliance of 1778', inevitably infuriated Jefferson and the

---

[16] Ford, Worthington Chauncey (ed.), *The Writings of John Quincy Adams*, New York: Macmillan, 1913, 1: 201. The three letters are in Adams Papers, Reel 126.
[17] Nagel, Paul C., *John Quincy Adams: A Public Life, a Private Life*, New York: Knopf, 1997, 85.

pro-French lobby, as it favoured Anglo-American trade. It even led to riots in some American cities in July 1795 and to criticisms not only of Jay, but also of Washington.[18]

The treaty was another point on which Jefferson inevitably disagreed with John Adams. Jefferson had a number of good reasons to dislike Britain and was entitled to worry about a reintroduction of British ideas that were contrary to the principles of the Republic. However, Adams felt that Jefferson 'was so deeply in debt to British creditors that his judgment of European affairs was tinged with a virulent form of Anglophobia that rendered him incapable of a detached assessment of American's interests abroad.'[19] One could feel a little more sympathy for Jefferson and his debt problems, had they all been incurred on books, and had one not seen from his accounts how much he spent on luxuries and on furnishing his Virginian version of the Petit Trianon.

During this visit to London, John Quincy followed the precedent set by Henry Laurens and followed by his father: he had his portrait painted by Copley. He also met and became engaged to the grown-up Louisa Catherine Johnson, the English-born daughter of Joshua Johnson and his wife, with whom he had dined in London back in 1783.

In the 1797 election, John Adams narrowly beat Jefferson to the Presidency. The Virginian, as runner-up, under the provisions of the Constitution in its un-amended form, automatically took over his unsatisfying job of Vice-President, which involved presiding over the Senate and little else. The new second President of the United States decided to switch his son from The Hague to Prussia as minister. John Quincy was not pleased about this new appointment, as the outgoing President

---

[18] Bicheno, Hugh, *Rebels and Redcoats*, London: HarperCollins, 2003, 256; O'Brien, *The Long Affair*, 223.

[19] Ellis, Joseph J., *Founding Brothers: The Revolutionary Generation*, London: Faber and Faber, 2002, 170.

had already named him for Lisbon. He was all set to go to Portugal as the nominee of Washington, who could not be accused of nepotism – an accusation which inevitably followed on his father appointing him a minister as soon as he took office. John Quincy Adams made a trip back to London before heading for Berlin, and was married on July 26, at All Hallows by the Tower, to Louisa Johnson, a spinster of that parish. The nearby Tower was, of course, Henry Laurens's former place of confinement.

John Quincy's sister Abigail (Nabby) had been married in London while her father was the first minister there. As a result, John Adams had the slightly unusual experience, for a revolutionary American father, of two of his four children being married in the capital of the former enemy. Shortly after his marriage, John Quincy was greatly embarrassed when his new father-in-law fled his creditors and returned to the United States, without even paying his daughter's agreed dowry. The embarrassment was increased by the fact that Johnson was at the time the first consul of the United States in London. Shamefully, President Adams later appointed Johnson as postmaster for the District of Columbia.[20]

John Quincy Adams returned home in 1801, after Thomas Jefferson had defeated his father in the Presidential election. In 1809, he went back to St. Petersburg, this time as minister, staying there until 1814, when he was sent to Ghent. There young Adams took on another old job of his father's: on behalf of the United States he negotiated the peace treaty with Britain to end an unfortunate War, this time that of 1812, fervently hoping that it would be the last occasion on which anyone would be obliged to undertake such a task. He was then appointed minister to London and reunited with his wife and all their children. In London, 'they spent two idyllic years before

---

[20] McCullough, 563. There is a long editorial note on Johnson as consul in the *Jefferson Papers*, 20: 482.

returning to America so that John Quincy could accept the post of Secretary of State under President James Monroe.'[21] Stockdale died in 1814, so was not able to provide the American minister with books on this occasion.

We have seen that Stockdale had informed Jefferson in February 1788, that he was about to be prosecuted by the House of Commons, and that in June of that year the Virginian author had reached the end of his patience with his publisher: 'I am done with him irrevocably.' John Adams not only had the further contact with Stockdale just considered, but was also probably affected by his trial and the resultant Fox's Libel Act of 1792.

Like most writers, John Adams was in favour of freedom of the press on most occasions, but especially for himself. In the early days of the Revolution, like some others patriots, he was not averse to the freedom of speech of his opponents being curbed, as when John Mein, a loyalist publisher in Boston, was driven out of business for what he had written.[22] When in France, Adams lamented the government control of writers, which he contrasted with the position on the other side of the Channel where, 'The English papers are an engine by which every thing is scattered all over the world.'[23] Brown pointed out that Adams, as President, had signed the notorious Sedition Act of 1798, 'and then approved its use against his journalistic enemies', so that most scholars 'have agreed that Adams was much more an adversary than an advocate of free speech in the early republic'. If he had to model himself on Pitt the Younger,

---

[21] *American National Biography*. Monroe, the fifth President, is remembered for his Doctrine, which was largely the work of Adams.

[22] Hargreaves, Robert, *The First Freedom: A History of Free Speech*, Stroud: Sutton, 2002, 153.

[23] Brown, Richard D., 'The Disenchantment of a Radical Whig: John Adams Reckons with Free Speech', in Ryerson, Richard Alan (ed.), *John Adams and the Founding of the Republic*. Boston: Mass. Hist. Soc, 2001, 177.

it was a pity that he chose to copy that minister's repressive ways of dealing with his perceived enemies in the publishing world.

However, in mitigation of this rare black mark against Adams, Brown continued: 'Still, there were elements of the Sedition Act created under Adams's *aegis* that, as Professor [Leonard] Levy long ago pointed out, opened a path toward free speech as we have come to know it. In contrast to England's common law of seditious libel as articulated by Sir William Blackstone, the United States Sedition Act constituted an enlightened reform. The Federalist law empowered the jury, not the judge, to decide whether the words should be deemed libellous; and it also allowed the truth of the words to stand as a defense against the libel charge.' We have seen how Erskine's spirited speech in defence of Stockdale, and the English Libel Act of 1792, foreshadowed the American approach. The widely-read John Adams must have been aware of both Erskine's submissions and of the 1792 statute.

Paine's work, the Second Part of the *Rights of Man*, led to the prosecution of a number of booksellers, including Ridgway, for sedition, but it first led to Paine's prosecution. The trial was in his absence as he had fled from England to France to avoid it. John Quincy Adams's son, Charles Francis Adams, later referred to Paine's case. The Attorney-General of the day, who according to Stockdale had a high opinion of John Quincy's critical book, referred in his opening speech before Lord Kenyon, the Lord Chief Justice, to 'a publication by an American gentleman of the name of Adams', and read out several passages, claiming that they provided the complete answer to Paine. Charles Francis Adams added: 'It is told of Erskine, at that time engaged for the defence, that he at once retorted, "How much better would it have been for the government to follow Mr. Adams's example, and, instead of prosecuting Paine, to refute him!"'[24]

---

[24] Adams, Charles Francis (ed.), *Memoirs of John Quincy Adams*, Philadelphia: J. B. Lippincott & Co., 1874, 1: 26. The continuity provided by the

Erskine made a great speech, lasting over four hours, on the liberty of the press, developing matters touched on by him in his earlier defence of Stockdale in front of the same Chief Justice, but Paine's conviction was inevitable. He had not helped himself by writing a letter to the Attorney-General, that was read out to the jury, in which he said that he had been elected to the French National Convention. He had foolishly added: 'The duty I am now engaged in is of too much importance to trouble myself about your prosecution.' That prosecution certainly did not harm the sales of Paine's book: in Scotland, 'One bookseller increased his sale in three weeks from one copy to seven hundred and fifty.'[25]

John Adams and Thomas Jefferson eventually made up their quarrel and enjoyed exchanging letters for many years. By what must be one of the greatest coincidences of history – and by now, the best-known – the two men who had together drafted and signed the Declaration of Independence, died within a few hours of each other on the fiftieth anniversary of its approval by Congress. Both great men died on July 4, 1826, during the term of office of the sixth President of the United States, John Quincy Adams. John Adams had been unfairly accused of wanting his son to succeed him as monarch. Nobody could quarrel with John Quincy's election as President: he was one of the best qualified candidates ever. In any event, he had served his country for a quarter of a century after his father had been defeated by Jefferson and had retired from politics, so that nobody could fairly charge nepotism.

---

remarkable Adams family is noteworthy. Charles Francis Adams was appointed minister to London by President Lincoln in 1861. In the following year, while there, he presented a copy of his compilation, *The Works of John Adams*, published in Boston by Little, Brown in 1856, to the London Library – where the present writer has been able to consult it.

[25] Brown, Philip Anthony, *The French Revolution in English History*, London: Crosby Lockwood, 1918, 84.

Illus. 17. Jedidiah Morse by Samuel Morse

16

The Father of American Geography

Rev. Dr. Jedidiah Morse is now known principally for being the father of Samuel Morse, the painter who invented the famous signalling code. There was a time when he was better known as the Father of American Geography, as he was the first American to write a number of books of geographical interest, works on that topic having been sent over from England before the Revolution. Indeed, that was still the position after the Revolution as far as books generally were concerned. 'After independence no less than before, readers in the new republic continued to depend on books printed overseas for much of their reading matter.'[1]

Morse had discovered the need for a good geography book when teaching in 1783, in Connecticut, before he moved to Massachusetts and became the minister of a church near Boston. John Stockdale was introduced to him by David Ramsay, who shared Morse's patriotic view that it was outrageous that Americans should still be dependent on European writers for information about their own country.[2]

The Morse-Stockdale correspondence, now scattered around different libraries in the United States, gives a clear picture of the cut-throat competition that authors and booksellers had to face before adequate copyright laws existed. It is not clear which

---

[1] Amory, Hugh and Hall, David D., *The Colonial Book in the Atlantic World*, Cambridge U.P., 2000, 477.
[2] Shaffer, Arthur H., *To be an American*, Columbia: U. of South Carolina P., 1991, 94.

topic was the first to be discussed by author and bookseller, but Stockdale clearly upset Morse early on in their relationship, because on July 29, 1788, David Ramsay wrote to Morse, sympathising with him: 'Stockdale has used you cavalierly.' He went on to say that he personally had 'adopted another plan' to deal with booksellers: he had offered to barter his work for books from Charles Elliott in Edinburgh. He advised Morse, 'This proposition made to two or three booksellers would probably secure you a good library.'[3]

Morse nevertheless decided to stick with Stockdale and agreed to send him five hundred copies of his *American Geography*, which were privately printed for him at Elizabethtown, now Elizabeth, New Jersey, in 1789.[4] During their exchange of letters, Stockdale gave notice that he might produce his own edition of the work, writing to Morse on October 21, 1788, 'If it is necessary to reprint the book, I will not undertake it in London without having an equal profit with yourself.' Stockdale will have recalled that Ramsay's first book had been so badly printed in America, that he later felt obliged to reprint it, and probably guessed that Morse might have similar production problems. At that time, many American printers were still learning the finer points of their craft and were not only having to make do with second-hand machines and worn type imported from Europe, but also struggling with inferior paper. It is to be noted that Morse does not at this stage seem to have responded with an indignant protest at the very idea of reprinting by Stockdale. He may have assumed, not unreasonably, that he would be asked for his specific consent to any reprinting.[5]

---

[3] Brunhouse, Selections, 122.

[4] Sprague, W. B., *The Life of Jedidiah Morse*, New York: Anson Randolph, 1874, 201.

[5] Stockdale's letter has not been traced, but Morse reminded him of the above sentence in his letter to Stockdale, dated May 14, 1792. Morse Family Papers, Yale Univ. Library.

A letter from Morse in Boston to Stockdale on January 11, 1790, explained why the author felt he could not keep his promise to send five hundred copies – and included yet another complaint about an American printer. 'I forwarded forty copies of my *American Geography* last October to the care of Dr. Price, to be lodged with you for sale. I leave the price to be fixed by you. I could not spare more from the present edition, more than two-thirds of the work is already sold. Besides, the paper and printing are so inferior to what I expected, through the misconduct of my printer, that I did not wish to send more till another and better edition. I have completed and published *Geography Made Easy*. It is only an abridgment of my *American Geography*, and designed as a cheaper book for the use of schools. I send you fifty of them (the number you mentioned in your letter) on trial, and if you find they will sell, you will please to write for more. I leave the price with you. If you can produce maps of a more suitable size than those I send you, as you probably can, at a cheap rate, you will please me to do it, if you think it best.'[6]

It rather looks as though Morse had made enquiries about the choice of British booksellers from people other than the somewhat disgruntled Ramsay, and had received good reports of Stockdale and his geographical output, as he was prepared to give him other works as well. His letter continued: 'I have not yet completed my Gazetteer, but have it in such forwardness, that I hope to publish it next Summer. As "there is no copyright for any book printed out of England", what offers can you make me provided I send you the Gazetteer in manuscript before its publication? I trust your laws admit the privilege of copyright to books that are *written* (if they are not *printed*) out of England.' In a postscript, Morse asked the bookseller to send him certain books 'out of the avails of the books I send you.'

---

[6] Jedidiah Morse Papers, New-York Hist. Soc.

Morse, together with Ramsay and others, succeeded in persuading Congress – with 'a nudge from President Washington' – to pass the first United States Copyright Act in 1790, under the powers granted by the new Constitution. It drastically confined protection to citizens or residents of the United States, a matter not remedied until 1949, leading Steinberg to comment that it 'retained one of the worst features of the erstwhile English Licensing Act, namely the restriction of copyright to a privileged class of printers.' However, that new statute did not, and could not provide the world-wide protection Morse would have liked. The first British Act to provide for international copyright protection was not passed until 1838. Even then, it was only to be on a reciprocal basis: an Order in Council could be passed to protect the authors of any country granting British authors similar rights.[7]

Morse's books sold very slowly in the Piccadilly shop in the year 1790, and the first half of 1791, as Stockdale reported to the author on February 22, 1792, in a letter which contained information relating to a new edition of the *American Geography*, usually referred to as the second, dated 1792. Stockdale had published this without consulting Morse, writing: 'I will agree to take one hundred copies of your new edition in octavo and twenty-five of the *Abridgment*, though I have doubts whether it will answer my purpose or not, as yours will have so few maps and Guthrie has about twenty. Added to this there seems to be a general dislike in purchasing American printed books. I believe I was near a year and a half in selling your small number of copies, but in consequence of its having been well spoken of, it has been in much request lately, which has induced me to reprint it

---

[7] Gordan, John D., '*Morse v. Reid:* The First Reported Federal Copyright Case', *Law and History Review*, 1993, 11: 21; Steinberg, S. H., *Five Hundred Years of Printing*, new edition by Trevitt, John, London: British Library, 2001, 134; Holdsworth, W. S., *History of English Law*, London: Methuen, 1965, 15: 41.

in a handsome manner. It has cost me between two and three hundred pounds. I am advertising it in all the papers in this kingdom, which are above one hundred, and have printed and shall distribute above twenty thousand catalogues in different parts of the kingdom. How far it will answer in reimbursing me is uncertain.'[8]

The comments about the slow sale of American works generally – about which John Adams had complained – and about the extent of the advertising campaign, should be noted. Stockdale did not apologise to Morse for having printed a second edition without his authority, but he gave him an explanation of sorts. 'Two other booksellers had assured me that the book was reprinting, which was the reason that induced me to take the field before them. If this is the case they certainly cannot all succeed, and I must suffer considerably with the rest, but I have doubts whether what they asserted was the truth.' He added the revealing comment, 'If a book written in America is worth the risk of a bookseller in London – to venture the reprint – it will always be done by someone or other.'

On April 12, 1792, Stockdale sent gloomy tidings to Morse: 'The proprietors of Guthrie's *Geography* are very inveterate against me for publishing your *Geography*, and they assert it is all taken from their work. This you know is false, but they now inform me that they will copy the whole of it in their new edition which is coming out. This I cannot prevent. I am much afraid it will hurt the sale of mine, particularly so as theirs is near double the quantity, and a number of maps &c, being sold to the booksellers so very cheap as well as to the public.' Morse must have had mixed feelings on reading, 'Your book is well spoken of by all candid gentlemen that have seen my new edition.'[9]

Whether Morse was merely outraged by the proprietors of William Guthrie's work, or whether he was also spurred on by a

[8] Misc. Mss. Stockdale, John, New-York Hist. Soc.
[9] Misc. Mss. Stockdale, John, New-York Hist. Soc.

desire for increased earnings is not clear, but two years later, in response to a request from the Philadelphia bookseller Matthew Carey, he agreed to revise the United States section of Guthrie's *Geographical Grammar*, which had for some time been a standard work on both sides of the Atlantic. Morse imposed two conditions: the first, that his role should be kept secret, the second, that Carey should abstain for five years from publishing Guthrie's large geography, which was a rival to Morse's own book.[10]

Morse's work was indeed making a very good impression on many readers in England, partly because he made a point of including a great deal of information about life in America. In January 1792, William Wells, a dissenting minister, wrote to Morse shortly before emigrating from England: 'Stockdale has published an edition of your Geography, which I have – a valuable book and much read. A gentleman of distinction for abilities, character and fortune in this neighbourhood, tells his children, "Study the book, as North America is the place you will probably go to." Multitudes are on tiptoe to be gone, and were some to lead the way, and give a good account of things, multitudes would soon follow.'

Joseph Priestley, the distinguished dissenting minister and scientist, wrote to Morse on August 24, 1793, to compliment him on his book: 'We had but a very imperfect idea of America before, and it has contributed not a little to the spirit of emigration that now prevails in this country. One of my sons will deliver this, and it is my wish to settle them all with you, in order to follow them myself, some time hence. My friends, Mr. Wells and Mr. Toulmin, are already gone.' As is well known, Priestley followed his sons and friends across the Atlantic in 1794, some

---

[10] Moss, Richard J., *The Life of Jedidiah Morse*, Knoxville: U. of Tennessee P., 1995, 58. See also, Short, John Rennie, *Representing the Republic: Mapping the United States, 1600-1900*, London: Reaktion Books, 2001, chap.6 – which has the same title as the present one.

time after his Birmingham house had been burned down by a drunken mob, which objected to his approval of the French Revolution.[11]

In August 1792, Stockdale sent two further letters containing bad news. On August 3, he informed Morse: 'Your friend Mr Larkin has done me much harm, but very unintentionally, by reporting that a new edition of your book was coming out, which will, of course, make those I have lie heavy on hand. For this reason I must beg that you will not send any of your new edition. I have been at very uncommon expense in advertisements, catalogues &c. which, if the report of a new edition prevails, will be totally lost.'

Stockdale went on to offer £40 for two copies of each future edition of both the *Geography* and the *Gazetteer*, but he added the condition, 'that neither you, your printer or bookseller, shall send any copies of the above works to Great Britain, nor do I believe that it would answer your purpose. The *Abridgments* that I have paid for I am certain will not be sold in twelve months. Some of my books have been printed in America, of course without my leave, and I am certain there is not one of your booksellers would give me a shilling for such leave.'

On August 28, Stockdale wrote: 'I am sorry to inform you that a bookseller of Dublin has printed your *Geography*, which he sells to booksellers at about four shillings and sixpence a copy, and to the public at six shillings, and what makes it still more unfortunate for me, he supplies the booksellers in England with his trumpery edition, which in most instances is from my advertisements; so that it turns out as I apprehended, that it would be printed by some other bookseller. By this, my advertisements have served my opponent equally with myself. I am just informed that another bookseller in the country has, or is about to print a cheap edition; this will of course injure me, and

---

[11] Sprague, 219, 204. Priestley's house was destroyed on July 14, 1791, the second anniversary of the storming of the Bastille.

perhaps himself much more so, as I am very certain that it will not answer his purpose.'[12]

 Cheap Irish reprints of London books were certainly known to Stockdale, for they were commonplace. 'No less a bibliophile than Thomas Jefferson appreciated the cheapness of Irish reprints of English legal authorities.'[13] As related in chap.8, Jefferson's very first order to Stockdale included a request for the Irish edition of Blackstone's *Commentaries*. However, Morse may have been previously unaware of the problems that Irish reprints could create.

On September 1, Stockdale revealed his plan for dealing with John Jones, his Irish competitor (despite the Welsh name), whose edition was also dated 1792. 'In consequence of the Irish edition I have resolved to sell my edition at whatever they may fetch, should it be no more that two shillings and sixpence or three shillings a copy; this will, in a great measure, stop the Irish edition. Your proposition respecting a fictitious name &c. would not have the desired effect; as there is little doubt but different copies of your work will find their way to the booksellers. Notwithstanding the sale is now pretty well over, I should not be surprised to see different London booksellers bringing out new editions from your corrected copy. They may do it in a hurry, but they will certainly have sufficient time to repent of their rashness; but this of course is all surmise.'[14]

On November 12, 1792, Morse replied to all three letters. His plea for information will be read with sympathy by all authors. 'It would have been gratifying to me could I have known how large an edition of the *Geography* you printed, and what number remained on hand when you last wrote, but as you have not informed me of either, I conclude you wish not to communicate these particulars. If they are no secret, however, I

---

[12] Misc. Mss. Stockdale, John, New-York Hist. Soc.
[13] Amory, Hugh, 'Reinventing the Colonial Book', in Amory and Hall, 30.
[14] Misc. Mss. Stockdale, John, New-York Hist. Soc.

will thank you to inform me in your next. You know authors, though poor proverbially, have a little pride as well as other people and wish to know how their works sell. The circumstances of its being reprinted in Ireland, and by a bookseller in the country, are indications of its favourable reception and ready sale. I hope you will be no loser on the whole though these editions may possibly take off some of your expected profits.'

Morse continued: 'I should have made no objection to a proposal from you of printing an edition of the *Geography* in England at our joint expense, and of depositing a proportion of the expenses in your hands. And I would readily accede to a like proposal for an edition in London of the present edition, provided it could be printed so as considerably to precede any other edition. I do not think the terms of your offer are equal to what I ought to expect. If the privileges of sending you the sheets as they are struck off, and binding myself not to send any other copies into the kingdom, are worth anything, they are worth more.'[15]

Morse followed this argument with a detailed proposal for future editions, but on December 20, he sent a hasty withdrawal of his offer, as he had run into trouble with his Boston publishers. 'My printers and booksellers, Messrs Thomas & Andrews, will not bind themselves not to send any copies to England. They construe the contract between us as implying a right in them to sell the books in all parts of the world, and they will not relinquish that right, though I never meant to, and never supposed I had, conveyed it to them. As they are partners in the copyright, they insist on being concerned in the disposal of it in England – and I have accordingly relinquished it entirely to them, on condition they will make you the first offer.'[16]

It was now Stockdale's turn to take umbrage, as his letter of March 16, 1793, shows: 'I received your favour; immediately

[15] Yale Univ. Library.
[16] Yale Univ. Library.

after it one from your printers informing me that you had no right in disposing of the work, and that was I inclined to purchase it, it must be from them, which I declined. Whatever compliment I may be inclined to give, it certainly will be to you. I know nothing of them, nor am I under any obligations. I have unfortunately printed three thousand of your *Geography*, but have not yet sold one thousand, and have laid out more money in advertising than was probably ever done with any other book in the English language. Should another be printed here, or sent over from you, my loss must be very considerable, and I shall think myself very ill used, as it would of course make waste paper of all I have got.'[17]

Stockdale claimed he knew nothing of the printers mentioned, but they were the most successful ones in North America at the time: the partnership established by Isaiah Thomas and Ebenezer Andrews in 1788. By the 1790s they had as many as 150 men in one printing works, operating seven presses.[18]

In the next four months Stockdale sold more than six hundred copies. On July 29, 1793, he reported: 'I shall certainly never think of sending any to America; that would be acting very dishonourably indeed. I have still about 1400 copies on hand. I shall therefore not think of reprinting at present, unless it should be in my own defence.' The letter continued with a request which indicates how Stockdale was anxious to improve Morse's work, and also how he was interested in maps. 'One [John] Filson has printed an account of Kentucky, and [Gilbert] Imlay another account. You will oblige me very much by sending per first ship one perfect copy of each with the maps. Should I reprint your work, it may be proper to add Filson's account of Kentucky. I wish much at the same time to have your opinion of

---

[17] Jedidiah Morse Papers, New York Public Library.

[18] Chernofsky, Jacob L., 'Isaiah Thomas', in Franklin, Benjamin, V, *Boston Printers, Publishers, and Booksellers: 1640-1800*, Boston: G. K. Hall, 1980, 464, 467.

their authenticity, and, if not too much trouble, to mark what you think would be proper to bring into your work. They are both reprinted in London, but I do not think it safe to copy anything from a reprint. I mean to engrave the map or maps, should they be correct, at any rate. I must beg it as a particular favour that you will not fail to send me a correct copy of each, if it is possible to procure them.'[19]

Morse replied on December 26, referring to yet another Irish edition: 'A few days since, I sent you by the *Galen* a Dublin edition of Imlay's description of Kentucky, marked and accompanied with such remarks as occurred during my necessarily hasty perusal of it. I this day unexpectedly received Debrett's London edition of the work, printed in 1792, with Filson's account annexed, and illustrated with two maps. I think it needless to send it to you, as you can have it on the spot.' Morse had doubtless noticed that Debrett's address was almost the same as Stockdale's. He continued: 'Such marks and remarks as I have made on the Dublin edition may be easily transferred to the London edition. I think it would be advisable by all means to publish the map of Kentucky, and perhaps to correct my map of the Northern and Middle States, particularly the Territory northwest of Ohio, from the other large map. I think my account of Kentucky may be greatly improved from Imlay – and some useful remarks may be added to my account of the Territory northwest of Ohio.' Morse ended his letter in a friendly manner. 'Let me hear from you soon and frequently – depend on receiving from me every information in my power that may tend to perfect the *American Geography*, so that should you publish it, it

---

[19] Yale Univ. Library. Gilbert Imlay, who had served under Washington, nearly shortened the life of the author Mary Wollstonecraft, by playing Lieut. Pinkerton to her Butterfly. After she had borne his child, he left her for two other women. She threw herself into the Thames in 1795, but was rescued. She died two years later, giving birth to William Godwin's daughter, the future Mary Shelley. Todd, Janet, *Mary Wollstonecraft – A Revolutionary Life*, London: Weidenfeld & Nicolson, 2000.

may come out revised and corrected by the author.'[20] Stockdale's 1794 edition duly carried the reassurance: 'New edition. Revised, corrected and greatly enlarged by the Author.'

Before the end of 1793, Stockdale managed to publish John Filson's *The Discovery, Settlement and Present State of Kentucky*, but it is not clear where he got it from: possibly he cribbed it from Debrett's version.

On March 17, 1794, Stockdale wrote a letter in which he seemed to contradict himself: he referred to difficulties in selling Morse's work and yet announced another edition, albeit in quarto rather than octavo. 'The *Geography* goes off very slow: I have nearly 1000 on hand, notwithstanding I have risked to print it on quarto on a larger letter.' He recounted once again the great expense he had had, and how the Dublin edition had hurt him. He opposed Morse's claim for a monopoly in England and doubted the truth of a suggestion by Morse that an American author had been offered £700 for his book by an English bookseller. 'English booksellers are neither so rich, nor such fools,' Stockdale protested. 'If the fact is so, I will take care that the London bookseller shall pay for his folly.'

The letter also revealed another way in which a bookseller could defend himself. Stockdale added that he had frightened off some of the competition by pirated editions, which had threatened to cost him 'some few hundreds' of copies of Morse's book. He would have had a loss, 'had not the booksellers been sensible that I might have repaid them in their own coin, by reprinting some of their books, and which I am actually at the moment doing in retaliation for their attacking some of my property, namely, the *History of Sandford and Merton*. They will have time to repent of their folly, and I am certain it will be a lesson to others in this town.'[21]

---

[20] Samuel F. B. Morse Papers, Library of Congress, MS Division.
[21] Yale Univ. Library.

Reference has been made several times to the various advertisements placed by Stockdale in his own publications, as well as those in the newspapers. He managed to give the new quarto edition of Morse's book some additional publicity, when he published the second edition of John Adams's three-volume *Defence*, early in 1794. The first volume started with Stockdale's note; 'The publisher has prefixed the following short account of the author, which he hopes the reader will not be displeased with. It is extracted from the *American Geography* by the Rev. Jedidiah Morse, now printing in quarto.'

On October 3, Stockdale wrote to Morse again, first apologising for the delay in writing, which had been caused by his extended visit to the neighbourhood of Manchester, where he was engaged on his first topographical venture. He had more bad news for Morse. 'You will perceive by the first number that I have sent that three persons confined in Newgate are publishing in numbers the *Geography*.' He added that he hoped to have his quarto edition of Morse's book ready in a week or so, and that he still had hundreds of the octavo editions. He once more moaned about the cost he had incurred in advertising, and mentioned that he had embellished the work with twenty-five maps. After quoting Morse what he would charge him for copies of two of the maps, he added that he would need an advance of £400 before commencing work on them. Stockdale protested that he had the highest regard for Morse himself, but felt obliged to play safe, partly because the two countries seemed to be heading for war once again, 'as there seems to be a great inclination in your countrymen to quarrel with this, and I know by woeful experience the difficulty of getting payment from America'.[22]

---

[22] New York Public Library. It will be recalled that Stockdale had pointed out to Jefferson that payment was not easy to obtain from across the Atlantic.

Stockdale was slightly in error in referring to the Newgate publication as being a version of Morse's book; it merely plagiarised large sections of it. The story of that production in prison is quite extraordinary. We all know that some famous books have been written in prison, like John Bunyan's *Grace Abounding* and much of his *Pilgrim's Progress*, one of Benjamin Franklin's favourite books.[23] Newgate had its fair share of authors over the years. Anne Sutton has recounted how a recently discovered document proves that Sir Thomas Malory wrote his *Morte d'Arthur* while a prisoner in Newgate as early as 1469. She also had some interesting ideas about how he might have managed to write such a work, with the help of a small private library and the benefit of purchases from nearby Paternoster Row.[24] We have also seen how Walter Parker managed to edit his *General Advertiser* from his cell in Newgate until the Gordon rioters interrupted his work. The prisoners mentioned by Stockdale took the matter one step further: they jointly succeeded in producing a very large compilation while incarcerated.[25]

The year 1793 had seen the beginning of the war with France, which Stockdale, like many others on both sides of the Atlantic, feared might lead to the Americans siding with the French. The French Revolution, and works such as those of Tom Paine, had so alarmed Pitt and his government, that they overreacted and introduced a wave of repressive measures. Somewhat surprisingly, John Almon approved of those measures, having become a prosperous man and having hardened, or become more realistic, in his fifties. He wrote in 1793: 'We all remember the supineness of the magistrates at the time

---

[23] Stockdale, Eric, *A Study of Bedford Prison 1660-1877*, London: Phillimore, 1977, 9.

[24] Sutton, Anne F., 'Malory in Newgate: A New Document', *The Library*, 7th Series, 2000, 1: 243, 253.

[25] In 1810, William Cobbett continued to edit his *Political Register* in Newgate; one day, perhaps, someone will write a Ph.D. thesis and/or book about Newgate prison as a publishing house.

of the riots and conflagrations in the year 1780. The same scenes, or others more tremendous, might have been exhibited at the latter end of the year 1792 or beginning of 1793, had not the vigilance of ministers, armed with the authority of the laws, been ready to support, with energy and vigour, the duty and authority of the magistrates.'[26] One radical bookseller after another was prosecuted and imprisoned for publishing or selling works such as Paine's *Rights of Man Part II*. The visitor to Newgate prison might have been forgiven for thinking that he had strayed into the nearby Stationers' Hall by mistake.

A Baptist minister, William Winterbotham, was also confined there: a conviction for sedition, in respect of two sermons he had preached, had led to a sentence of imprisonment. His case illustrates the point that the Libel Act of 1792 was not enough, on its own, to protect the free expression of opinion. Winterbotham had been convicted by a jury, despite the judge's recommendation that they should acquit. As Leonard Levy has pointed out, 'The English seditious libel trials, like the American ones a few years later, proved conclusively that making juries judges of the criminality of allegedly seditious words did not have the effect of broadening the scope of free discussion, certainly not during times of stress – and there are rarely sedition trials at any other times.'[27]

While in Newgate, the convicted minister wrote *The Trial of William Winterbotham*, and dedicated it to the two juries who had convicted him. It appeared in 1794 with the dateline, 'State Side of Newgate, 23 January 1794', and bore the imprint: 'Printed by William Winterbotham. Sold by J. Ridgway, H. D. Symonds, D. I. Eaton, D. Holt, R. Phillips, J. Campbell and W. Page.' The first five-named were certainly confined in the prison with the

---

[26] [Almon, John], *The Causes of the Present Complaints*, London: J. Sewell, 1793, 11. See generally, Goodwin, Albert, *The Friends of Liberty*, London: Hutchinson, 1979.

[27] Levy, Leonard W., *Emergence of a Free Press*, Oxford U.P., 1985, 287.

author, and Ridgway and Symonds remained on friendly terms with Winterbotham after their release. A print, published by William Holland in 1795, shows the distinguished company of booksellers to be found in Newgate in that year: Ridgway, Symonds and Eaton appear in the picture.[28]

Winterbotham was apparently well pleased with his first venture in prison and so embarked on *An Historical, Geographical, Commercial and Philosophical View of the American United States.* It was this work, which first appeared in parts and then in four volumes, which Stockdale mentioned in his letter to Morse. The publishers this time were three of the above-named fellow prisoners: Stockdale's brother-in-law, James Ridgway, Henry Delahy Symonds and Daniel Holt. Winterbotham's preface indicated that he shared some of the views of Joseph Priestley and William Wells: 'One object has been constantly kept in view, namely, to afford the emigrator to America a summary of general information, that may in some measure serve as a directory to him in the choice of a residence, as well as in his after pursuits. This suggested the propriety of adopting the plan which Mr. Morse has laid down in his *American Geography.*' Morse must have choked when he reached this passage, but it got worse.

Winterbotham went on to explain the manner of his plagiarism: 'With respect to the printed authorities which the Editor has followed, he has not only borrowed their ideas, but, where he had not the vanity to conceive himself capable of correcting it, he has adopted their language, so that in a long narrative he has often no other claim to merit than what arises from selection and a few connecting sentences.' He did, however, have the grace to add that he had 'availed himself of the labour and abilities' of a number of named authors, including Franklin, Jefferson, Adams, Ramsay, Barlow and Morse. In a rare mention of

---

[28] Wardroper, John, *Kings, Lords and Wicked Libellers*, London: John Murray, 1973, pl.30.

the difficulties of publishing from inside a prison, Winterbotham apologised for typographical errors resulting 'from his situation, which rendered an easy communication with the printer not only difficult, but in many cases impracticable.'

Morse checked the contents of the compilation carefully, and found that no less than six hundred of the two thousand pages had been copied from his own work, while another large section had come from David Ramsay's *History of the American Revolution*. Winterbotham had also used large portions of Jefferson's *Notes on the State of Virginia* and of Franklin's two Tracts of 1784, all of which Stockdale had published.[29] Winterbotham was by no means the only author who had found Jefferson's book very useful. According to Merrill Peterson, 'When Jedidiah Morse, "the father of American geography", published his pioneer work in 1789, all he had to do with respect to Virginia and the vast western domain was to reprint the account from the *Notes on Virginia*,' adding, 'Some travelers offered Jefferson's depiction as their own!'[30]

Winterbotham provided further proof of his unscrupulous nature by stealing the poem, *Wat Tyler*, from Robert Southey. Southey had written it as a young man when under the spell of the French Revolution and had offered it to Ridgway when visiting him in Newgate in December 1794. Ridgway and Symonds, in the presence of Winterbotham, told Southey they would publish it, but later decided against publication – possibly because they did not want to risk another prosecution under Pitt's repressive laws. Southey forgot all about the manuscript he left in the hands of Ridgway, until Winterbotham, who had somehow acquired it, had it published twenty-three years later. He did so without permission, to embarrass the author, who by

---

[29] Syrett, Harold C., *The Papers of Alexander Hamilton*, New York: Columbia U.P., 1974, 20: 12.
[30] Peterson, Merrill D., *Thomas Jefferson and the New Nation*, Oxford U.P., 1975, 264.

then had left his Jacobin youth far behind and was not only a Tory but also Poet Laureate. On the death of Henry James Pye in 1813 ('No more – no more of that'), Sir Walter Scott had declined the post and it had passed to Southey. Scott may well have turned the offer down because, as the *Dictionary of National Biography* commented on the 1790 choice of Pye, 'No selection could have more effectively deprived the post of reputable literary associations.'[31]

When Stockdale wrote to Morse on August 5, 1795, he still claimed to be out of pocket as a result of their collaboration, partly because of 'that villainous Newgate compilation'. He advised Morse to protect himself in America against it. With the help of Alexander Hamilton – by then a lawyer as well as a politician – the author succeeded in obtaining both an injunction and a judgment for damages in the Federal court against the American publishers of Winterbotham's work, John Reid and his partners.[32]

On April 29, 1796, Stockdale expressed some surprise that Morse had difficulty in selling the quarto edition in America, 'as several American gentlemen on arriving here have preferred and purchased it'.[33] It is of interest to note that, despite political tension between the two countries, Americans were still visiting London and calling at the Piccadilly bookshop. In 1797, Morse discussed the possibility of Dilly publishing his *American Gazetteer*, 'but John Stockdale, protesting that Morse had a contract

---

[31] Manogue, Ralph Anthony, 'Southey and William Winterbotham: New Light on an Old Quarrel', in *The Charles Lamb Bulletin*, 1982, New Series, 38: 105. I am grateful the Prof. Manogue for drawing my attention to this incident. *Wat Tyler* was printed for Sherwood, Neely and Jones in 1817, and in the same year James Harper published an anonymous poem, *The Changeling*, which took Southey to task for moving from republicanism 'to the worthless and detested character of a Court Parasite.'

[32] Misc. Mss. Stockdale, John, New-York Hist. Soc.; Syrett, 1979, 26: 859; Gordan, 33.

[33] Yale Univ. Library.

with him for all his geographical works, demanded an equal share in this venture and threatened to bring out a competing edition if his demand was not met. Dilly yielded.'[34] Morse sought to explain his disloyalty to Stockdale with the excuse that he had not heard from him 'for years'. As one can see from the dates of the letters quoted above, despite the fact that Morse was a cleric, this was simply untrue.

The last letter that the writer has been able to trace between Morse and his English bookseller is one from Stockdale at the end of the century, dated September 7, 1799. It is full of misery once again and does not require separate consideration. However, it does leave one with the question of whether Stockdale made any money from the sale of the geography books in England. Since no accounts have been found, it is difficult to say. For what it is worth, Ramsay's nephew had bought a copy of one of Stockdale's Morse editions from his shop when visiting London. The uncle reported to Morse on March 13, 1794, 'My nephew informs me that he is very certain that Stockdale must have made money from it.'[35]

Perhaps the Morse books were selling like hot cakes during the visit. The visitor cannot have known of the costs of production and advertising, to which the bookseller was constantly adverting, but his guess may have been correct, for all that. Despite what he claimed in his letter of August 5, 1795, it is unlikely that Stockdale would have struggled on for years, trying to sell books which produced no profit, even though they had been written by a highly regarded author, one whose books helped him to make the point that his was the shop for readers to come to, if they wanted publications of a geographical, or of an American nature – or both. One thing is clear: Morse himself made a great deal of money from his various geographical

---

[34] Butterfield, Dilly, 300.

[35] Misc. Mss. Stockdale, John, New-York Hist. Soc.; Brunhouse, Selections, 137.

works. He was as successful financially as David Ramsay was unsuccessful. In 1794, he wrote to a German correspondent that he had sold over twenty thousand copies of his *American Geography* alone. Morse's latest biographer, Richard Moss, has pointed out that one of his Boston printers, Ebenezer Andrews, 'got so infuriated by Morse's greed that he coined the term "Morseish", which he defined as someone who "loves money and knows how to get it".'[36]

The story of Morse is one of an unusual cleric who earned a great deal from his books. He was entitled to his success because his books clearly filled a need. One of his good geography books could, and did provide more enlightenment than many another contemporary work. Print runs that were far too optimistic for Ramsay, proved to be attainable by Morse, time and again. Apart from anything else, this success showed the way ahead: there was no reason why, with properly equipped experienced printers and an expanding market, American authors should not outsell their English cousins before long. Perhaps more important is the fact that the success of Jedidiah Morse helped to prove that native-born American authors were capable of producing books that would sell well, both in the United States and in England, and that the historic dependence on English booksellers could be diminished and might, before long, be ended.

---

[36] Moss, 49, 59.

17

Stockdale's Topographical Works

John Stockdale's interest in geography was not confined to America, Australia and mainland Europe: he also published a number of books and maps on the British Isles. His first major undertaking of this kind was a very large work which appeared in 1795, *Description of the Country from 30 to 40 miles round Manchester*, 'the materials arranged, and the work composed by J. Aikin M.D.' The work had grown out of the mutual interest in the area of Stockdale and John Aikin, whose sister was the writer Anna Laetitia Barbauld. Stockdale had got to know some of the area in his youth, when he and his future wife were members of the Moravian congregation in Dukinfield, but he had also visited it later. Aikin had lived for some time in nearby Warrington, and while there had helped his friend, the philanthropist and penal reformer, John Howard, to prepare his great book, *The State of the Prisons*, for its publication in 1777.

Stockdale gave an account of the background of the Manchester book in the preface, referring to himself in the third person. 'His original idea was merely to give an account of the town of Mottram-in-Longdendale, and the singular country around it, with which he has much personal acquaintance, and where he enjoys a circle of valuable friends. At the urgent solicitation of some Lancashire gentlemen, he was induced to enlarge his plan, and to make Manchester the centre of a descriptive work, the circumference of which gradually extended itself further and further. With, perhaps, little reflection, he suffered himself to be engaged in a design of a magnitude and importance that involved him in toil and expense, the idea of which had he foreseen their extent, would probably have deterred him from the prosecution of it.'

Lucy Aikin later described her father's involvement. He earlier had the idea of a history of Lancashire, but dropped it for want of sufficient support. Then came the proposal for the new book. 'The materials for this book were to be collected by Mr. Stockdale, the preparation and arrangement of them, and the composition of the work, were alone undertaken by Dr. Aikin; but in fact it was from his exertions and the communications of his personal friends in that part of the country, that the most valuable portion of the matter proceeded; without which the performance would have been defective indeed.' If Aikin did indeed expect the London bookseller to collect all the material for him, he was certainly expecting rather too much of him.[1]

Both men clearly had a great deal of work to do in the preparation of the book, which turned out to be over 600 pages quarto, and contained 73 plates. While there is no correspondence to indicate the scale of the work involved for the publisher on this occasion, we can get some further idea of what was entailed from the letters Stockdale wrote in connection with his next mammoth undertaking, *The History of London and its Environs*. Stockdale's letters to one of the contributors to that work, the Rev. Mark Noble, are fortunately in the Bodleian Library.[2]

It was a pity that Stockdale always made a point of ignoring what the critics had to say, or he might have been put on his guard against Noble, whose reputation as a writer was a poor one. The reviewer in the *Gentleman's Magazine*, for example, had

---

[1] Aikin, Lucy, *Memoir of Dr. John Aikin*, London: Baldwin, Cradock and Joy, 1823, 170.
[2] Bodleian MS Eng. Misc. d.156.

said of the second edition of his *Memoirs of the Protectoral House of Cromwell*, that it was an 'ill-digested, over-loaded work'.[3]

In 1797, Noble offered to sell his *The Lives of the Regicides* to Stockdale, but he turned the offer down, writing on November 8, 'After the most mature consideration and consulting some of my great literary friends, on whose judgment I can rely, I find it prudent to decline purchasing.' As related earlier, Stockdale clearly relied on his friend Thomas Day for advice before his premature death; it would have been useful to know who his 'literary friends' were at the end of the century. Although he did not wish to buy Noble's new work, he did agree that he would publish it at his own expense, on the basis of shared profits. On December 26, 1797, he wrote another of his miserable letters: 'Before the War I could have sold an edition of such a work in a month. Whether it will sell or not I am utterly at a loss to say. I hope it will. But men's minds are so agitated and the taxes so heavy, that nothing sells. I shall, of course, give it every assistance in my power. It has exceeded the printer's calculation by at least six sheets. If all were sold at the price fixed, there would be nothing to divide. For this reason, when the work is finished I shall be obliged to fix it at 12 or 14 shillings.'

On January 12, 1798, Stockdale wrote to inform Noble that he had published his book that day, at 12 shillings a copy, adding: 'You may rest assured that it shall be well pressed. If it should not thrive, the fault will not be mine, though the loss will be. Yet as my friends are numerous, I shall endeavour to make the most of them. I have but little interest with reviewers, therefore I shall trust to my own strength and the merit of the work. I shall of course be glad to see you in Town. At my table you will receive my homely but hearty welcome.'

The speed of production should be noted. The printers had sent the first printed sheet with their letter of November 13, within a day or two of Noble's decision to accept Stockdale's

[3] *Gentleman's Magazine*, 1787, 57: 516.

offer. The Regicide book included an advertisement by Stock-dale relating to the topographical work in which Noble was to be involved. This announced the publication of Parts I, II and III of his *The History of London and its Environs*, and it mentioned that the next two parts were 'in great forwardness'. One of those parts was to include the county of Kent, where Noble lived. The whole work would in due course resemble the Manchester book.

On February 23, the unhappy author complained to his publisher that he had not pressed his book on the Regicides suf-ficiently: his friends had not known about his work. Stockdale replied on the same day, 'As to its not being sufficiently known, that cannot be.' He added a universal truth, too painful for most authors to accept: 'But those who do not purchase, of your acquaintance, must make some excuse.' He gave Noble an account of his advertising and added an extraordinary comment. 'The truth is that the public do not feel themselves interested in the reading such lives. I should never have advised you to have lost your time on such a work. Literary gentlemen are not such good judges of what will sell as booksellers.' His earlier letter suggested that his literary friends were not keen on Noble's manuscript, but in this letter Stockdale seems to blame them, or some of them, for his decision to publish it.

On April 10, Stockdale reported that the work was still selling slowly. Even the works of well-known authors, he com-plained, 'meet with very little encouragement, owing to the perpetual alarm for the safety of our islands &c.' The renewed threat of invasion by the French was causing that alarm, and members of the militia were even drilling across the road from his shop, which was immediately opposite the gateway of Bur-lington House. Leigh Hunt, one of the literary men responding to the call to arms – on a part-time basis – gave a delightful account of the warlike preparations in Piccadilly of the St. James's Volunteers.

'We had been a regiment for some time without a colonel. At length the moment arrived – the colonel was named; he was to be introduced to us; and that nothing might be wanting to our dignity, he was a lord, and a friend of the minister, and nephew to the victor [of Montreal]. Our parade was the court-yard of Burlington House. The whole regiment attended. We occupied three sides of the grounds. In front of us were the great gates, longing to be opened. Suddenly the word is given, 'My Lord is at hand!' Open burst the gates – up strikes the music. 'Present Arms!' vociferates the major. In dashes his lordship, and is pitched right over his horse's head to the ground.'[4]

One can tell how seriously the French threat was regarded, and how desperate the measures to meet it, from a story related about Henry James Pye – whose beautifully printed *Commentary Illustrating the Poetic of Aristotle* had been published by Stockdale in 1792. 'He translated the war verses of Tyrtaeus the Spartan, for the purpose of animating the British militia against the French; and a board of general officers, much impressed by their weight and importance, agreed to give all the effect in their power to his intentions. The verses were accordingly read aloud at Warley-common and Barham-downs by the adjutants, at the head of five different regiments, at each camp; and much was expected. But before they were half finished, all the front ranks, and as many as were within hearing or verse-shot, dropped their arms suddenly, and were all found fast asleep.'[5]

As we have digressed into the militia field, it is worth recalling that we earlier saw Erskine as one of the defenders of the Temple during the Gordon riots in 1780. Some twenty years

---

[4] Hunt, Leigh, *Autobiography*, Oxford U.P., 1928, 151. Somewhat surprisingly, Richard Brinsley Sheridan was the colonel for a while.

[5] Timperley, C. H., *Dictionary of Printers and Printing*, London: H. Johnson, 1839, 850. This reaction to Pye may be contrasted with that to Violet Hunt, who had three hundred soldiers within verse-shot during the Boer War. She so impressed them with her lecture on poetry, that they insisted on writing down, at her dictation, the lines of Browning she had declaimed. Altick, Richard D., *The English Common Reader*, 2nd ed., Columbus: Ohio U.P., 1998, 2.

later, he became Colonel of the Temple militia, ready to defend it against the French. It was said of the legal volunteers on manoeuvres, that when they received the order 'Prepare to charge!', they pulled out pen, ink and paper, ready to draw up their customary demand for payment.[6]

After this frivolity, it is necessary to make the serious point that Stockdale, like other booksellers, will have been justified in claiming that his business was badly affected by the war and the continued alarms and excursions. The highly successful bookseller, James Lackington, pointed out that people visited bookshops much less in times of turmoil. The increase in the cost of books, caused by the Napoleonic wars, did not help either: a printer told a House of Commons committee in 1818, 'Books are a luxury, and the purchase of them has been confined to fewer people.'[7]

On June 8, 1798, Stockdale wrote a letter to Noble which indicated that the part including Kent was not quite so forward as the January advertisement had suggested. One of the contributors to the Kent section had given up on the grounds of ill-health, so he had a proposal for Noble. 'It is not improbable but that it would be much more to your advantage to be employed by me than being author, one being certain, the other uncertain. You mentioned that you could not bear being unemployed. Should you approve of my proposition, I will instantly send you town books and instructions.' The reference to unemployment has to be read in the light of the fact that Noble was Rector of Barming at the time, but he jumped at the novel offer of paid work as an author. The pay was to be thirty shillings per printed sheet, payable on publication or earlier if Noble wished.

---

[6] Hostettler, John, *Thomas Erskine and Trial by Jury*, Chichester: Barry Rose, 1996, 172.

[7] Barnes, James J., 'Depression and Innovation in the British and American Book Trade, 1819-1939', in Carpenter, Kenneth E. (ed.), *Books and Society in History*, New York: R. R. Bowker, 1983, 232, 233.

The historian in Noble made him repeatedly enter into detail when mentioning people's names, so Stockdale kept urging him, 'Do not go into pedigree more than necessary.' He also informed him that he should be more careful with his manuscript as 'the corrections, though absolutely necessary, come expensive and ought not to fall on me.' He suggested that Noble might get his wife to check both his manuscript and the proofs, making the valid point, 'You will find her a great assistant, as few authors will detect their own errors as soon as another.' Noble took umbrage when reproved and Stockdale tried to mollify him. 'I am confident your good understanding will not be offended at my alterations and suggestions, as they will most probably be fair.' He added the fair point, 'My reputation is greatly at stake in this work, as it is on my character the public trusts, no ostensible author standing forward.'

Stockdale knew what a nuisance typographical errors could be; he had probably been warned against them in his early days with John Almon and had never forgotten his advice. Stockdale had probably started with him in 1774 and in that year his master published one of his humorous collections called the *Fugitive Miscellany*. He included in it a long letter to the editor about misprints, signed *Emendator*. Sadly, a short extract must suffice: 'I have known you throw an injurious reflection on all the crowned heads in Europe at one stroke, for instead of *potentates* you have called them *potatoes*, as if they had been mere vegetables. As to the King of Prussia, you talk of him in a different style, for instead of the *Hero*, you have made him the *Nero*. Next day comes your apology, or your erratum, which sometimes, instead of mending matters, makes things worse, and, like an arch tinker, in stopping one hole makes two, as I remember my old friend Alderman Faulkner, of Dublin, corrected an error in his *Journal*, "Erratum in our last; for *his* Grace the Duchess of Dorset, read *her* Grace the Duke of Dorset".'

In September, despite ill-health, Stockdale travelled to Liverpool in connection with another major projected topographical work, *The History of Liverpool.* During his absence, his eldest son, John Joseph dealt with Noble. A note dated October 18, written by him, gives an indication of the scope of the London work and mentions the beginnings of London's famous tunnels. 'Mr. Noble will be so good as to finish the sheet in a dozen or fourteen lines on the three subjects hinted at on the bottom of that sheet. It is not probable that there can be any other difficulty in driving a tunnel under the Thames except its expense, as it is known to be of chalk rock bottom, and the intention is to make the tunnel 30 feet under the bed of the river. To be arched with brick or what is much more durable, stone masonry. S. has no knowledge of the docks. Probably Mr. N. may be shown them. If not, make the best of the hint.'

On November 5, John Stockdale apologised for not answering a letter of Noble's earlier, 'partly from hurry of business but still more from indisposition. I cannot yet bear the anxiety attendant on the different works in which I am engaged.' This comment is rather strange, in view of the fact that he had been a publisher in his own right for eighteen years. The war seems to have been affecting the business less than earlier, for on May 2, 1799, the bookseller complained to Noble, 'My shop is so surprisingly thronged, that it is with difficulty I can get a minute to myself.'

It looks very much as though Stockdale was working too hard while in poor health. He had been seriously ill in 1797. His daughter Mary had then been inspired by the sight of her sleeping five-year-old brother, George, to write:

> Spare, spare a parent, raise his dying head;
> Let not the iron-sceptred monarch sway;
> Station a guard of angels round his bed.

Later, she referred to her long period of angelic 'night-watchings' at her parent's bedside, adding, 'My father, who had for some time seen me only through the gloom of his sick room, could not, the moment he beheld my features in the clear light of day, forbear expressing how much he was shocked at the alteration he discovered in my countenance. I replied with a resigned smile, "Yes, I feel it is my turn next".' The fond daughter kindly left unsaid, 'After you have died in the near future.'[8]

John Joseph later summed his sister up neatly. When in the Fleet prison as a debtor, he commented on her lack of concern in a letter to his wife, adding: 'How anxiously she would have attended my prison-couch if she could have ensured herself an opportunity to write an elegy on my death by starvation!'[9]

The travelling in connection with the large topographical works kept Stockdale away from the shop for significant periods, but much of the work was waiting for him when he returned. It is not clear how much Mrs. Stockdale helped with the business. Thomas Day wrote shortly before his death, as mentioned earlier, that he would only accept an account signed by her, but that was in a jocular vein. She may well have helped in the shop, and possibly with the account books, but Stockdale may have made a point of 'keeping his own accounts, which, however multifarious, he has ever since [learning to read], done without a clerk.'[10]

Stockdale referred at different times to the assistance of his eldest son, but he never mentioned anyone like a manager, only clerks. Once John Joseph left him, to set up on his own in 1806, in nearby Pall Mall, he had even less help. After Stockdale's death in 1814, his daughter Mary and son William (who married his cousin Caroline, Ridgway's daughter) tried to keep the business going but failed to do so for long. At first they continued to use their father's name, but then used their own. If they gave help to their father in his lifetime, then it probably did not

---

[8] Stockdale, Mary Ridgway, *The Mirror of the Mind*, London: John Stockdale, 1810, 1: xl.

[9] *The Memoirs of Harriette Wilson*, London: John Joseph Stockdale, 1831 ed., 6: 641.

[10] Granger, William, *The New, Original and Complete Wonderful Museum and Magazine Extraordinary*, London: Alex. Hogg, 1807, 5: 2469.

amount to much. Almon had entrusted Stockdale and others
with his shop when busy being a journalist or pamphlet writer,
but we have seen that he felt betrayed by his staff. Stockdale
seems not to have employed outsiders in any post of respon-
sibility; possibly a guilty conscience reminded him of the risks
entailed in letting subordinates learn too much about a business.
In any event, he was clearly overworked in the late 1790's and
after the departure of his first-born, that situation must have got
markedly worse.

Stockdale was not wholly satisfied with Noble but, doubtless
because the clock was ticking, asked him to work on the Essex
part as soon as he had finished his Kent section. On June 9, he
referred to his ill-health once more, writing to Noble: 'I long to
get into the country, but business that cannot be neglected will
not permit it. I must however soon give way, or I fear a relapse.'
As will become apparent later, 1798 was a very bad year for
Stockdale; a number of matters may well have conspired to delay
the recovery of his health. Constant worries about Noble's contributions cannot have helped. Stockdale was not the only one
to have adverse comments to make: the *Dictionary of National
Biography* was scathing about him. 'Noble's writings are those of
an imperfectly educated vulgar-minded man. His ignorance of
English grammar and composition renders his books unintelligible, while the moral reflections with which they abound are
puerile.'

Stockdale had earlier, as we have seen, published maps of
European countries by Chaucard, which were used by Wellington (or Wellesley as he then was) in his campaigns. They had
been massive undertakings, for they had been printed by Gillet
so that they could be mounted as fourteen large sheets, each
nine feet by seven, roughly three metres by two. Early in 1801,
Stockdale advertised a similarly ambitious project for maps of
the British Isles: 'Two grand imperial topographical maps of the
United Kingdom of Great Britain and Ireland. On 48 large
sheets of Atlas paper, each sheet measuring two feet ten inches.

To be published by subscription. Mr. Stockdale takes the liberty respectfully to inform the public that he has for a considerable time past been preparing, under the sanction of His Majesty, a grand map of Ireland, on the most extensive scale hitherto attempted; also a map of Great Britain, of even still greater magnitude. The expense of the two will not, it is conceived, amount to less that £20,000. Notwithstanding the subscription is only just opened it is daily filling with rapidity, and will certainly soon exceed the numerous list for the maps of Chaucard, which was, by much, the largest ever known in England.' At the date of the advertisement there were already several members of the Royal Family recorded as subscribers.

Stockdale did not use subscription lists very often. As W. A. Speck pointed out, 'Only a tiny percentage of books published in the eighteenth century were brought out by subscription, and these tended to be fairly expensive productions, confined to the more affluent members of society.' He added that all sorts of pressures could explain some of the signatures on subscription lists: ties with the author of party, college or profession, 'or even of simple friendship, might well overcome a complete lack of interest in the subject matter of a book acquired in this way.' He ended by quoting Colonel James in Henry Fielding's *Amelia*: 'Heaven forbid I should be obliged to read half the nonsense I have subscribed to!'[11]

Back in 1772, John Almon had been one of the many publishers who had jointly put out a new edition of Camden's *Britannia*, with maps by Robert Morden. Stockdale joined his shop soon afterwards, and must have sold quite a few copies of the work for his master. In 1789, Richard Gough published another edition of Camden. Stockdale's four-volume edition of

---

[11] Speck, W. A., 'Politicians, peers, and publication by subscription 1700-50', in Rivers, Isabel (ed.), *Books and their Readers in Eighteenth-Century England*, Leicester U.P., 1982, 50.

Britannia, with maps by John Cary, appeared in 1805. The Cary maps were up to that cartographer's usual high standard.[12]

Stockdale does not rate very highly as a producer of maps, whether British or overseas. However, when one looks at the whole of his output of geographical works, from Jefferson's *Notes on the State of Virginia* and the early books on Australia, via his sales of the books of Jedidiah Morse, down to the Chaucard and Cary maps and the topographical works of men like Aikin and even Noble, one has to acknowledge that his contribution in this field was not insignificant. He was fortunate enough to publish these various works at a time when the reading public was anxious to be further enlightened, hungry for news of the world outside, and when information about Virginia, Australia and even Manchester, was eagerly awaited and devoured. The fact that he was aware of what the public wanted – with some advice from others – and was able to respond speedily to market forces, helped to make him the success he undoubtedly was, until he overreached himself early in the nineteenth century.

---

[12] The map of Hertfordshire (spelled with an 'a') by Cary, published by Stockdale in 1805, hangs above the present writer as he processes his words. It is so carefully executed that the writer can easily spot the road where he lives.

18

Stockdale Lampooned by Gillray

During the course of his long career John Stockdale inevitably
made a number of enemies. Some, obviously, were more dangerous than others. One of the main causes of strife with competi-
tors, as we have seen, was the ever-present problem of piracy.
One day Stockdale was complaining bitterly about the effrontery
of a rival who had dared to breach his copyright; on the next he
was defending himself against another bookseller making a
similar complaint against him. One of the basic causes of the
problem was that the Copyright Act of 1709, even after minor
amendments, was very much a first effort at detailed legislation
on this important and complicated subject, with many questions
of law remaining open to doubt. Having said that, one is bound
to have the sneaking feeling that a publisher who had been sued
several times for breach of copyright, and may have been a
plaintiff as well on occasion, will have had some grasp of the
essentials of the law.

As related earlier, when George Nicol sued Stockdale in connection with Captain Cook's *Voyage* in 1784 and 1785, John
Scott argued that Stockdale had not been guilty of any breach of
copyright as he had merely abridged Nicol's book. Scott, a distinguished lawyer, who was to become Lord Chancellor, argued
that the abridgment amounted to a new work. That was not
such a ridiculous argument as might now be thought. Until the
Copyright Act of 1911, the point was certainly one which could
be argued with some prospect of success. That is not to say that

Stockdale's abridgments were ever regarded as innocuous by the original publishers.

In 1797, Nicol and Stockdale clashed again. In that year Nicol, by then bookseller to the King, published *An Authentic Account of an Embassy from the King of Great Britain to the Emperor of China*, by Sir George Staunton, in two quarto volumes, together with a folio volume of plates. Later in the same year Stockdale produced *An Abridged Account of the Embassy* by Staunton, in one octavo volume, at the low price of 3s. 6d., in boards. He had first issued the work in ten parts. In his own introduction to the tenth part, which was repeated in the bound volume, Stockdale not only pulled Nicol's leg about his charging four guineas for the full work after advertising it for three guineas, but showed that he was ready to do battle with him once more. (For the younger reader, who does not recall it and has so far not been able to work it out, it should be pointed out that the guinea, much loved by the professions in England, as it wrested an extra five per cent out of the clients' hands, was twenty-one shillings, that is, £1.1.0d., as there were formerly twenty shillings to the pound sterling.)

'But as he has unprovokingly been dared to combat', wrote Stockdale of himself – although the florid style is that of his eldest son, John Joseph, 'like a prudent general, he has reserved the fire of his artillery till the day of battle in Westminster Hall [where the courts sat], when he will be able to shower upon his antagonists such volleys of secret information, and irresistible arguments, relative to the folio volume of plates, as well as the quarto volumes &c., as may bring suffusion on the cheeks of some, and make them lament they had ever excited such disclosures.' Whether Nicol dreaded his cheeks becoming suffused, or whether he shunned battle for more important reasons, the writer has been unable to discover. Although Nicol did not rise to the challenge, Stockdale was to have cause to regret his abridgment, which did not go unnoticed by others.

Another bookseller Stockdale succeeded in crossing was John Wright, who moved into 169 Piccadilly in 1797, and who did so well, for a short while at any rate, that in 1799, he also took on the shop next door at No. 168, where John Owen had published Burke's pamphlets.[1] Unfortunately for Stockdale, Wright became a direct rival as he also tried, with some success, to attract the Pittites into his shop. In 1797 and 1798, he published the *Anti-Jacobin* magazine, which was edited by William Gifford and supported by George Canning. The two booksellers seem initially to have tried to co-operate. In 1798, Wright published William Playfair's *History of Jacobinism*, in two volumes, and Stockdale also sold it. The British Library copy has two pages of Stockdale's own advertisements in the back of the second volume and they, unusually, were numbered 815 and 816, to follow on the final page number in Wright's book. That may have irritated Wright.

At some stage the men's rivalry led to an allegation of violence. As a result, Stockdale found himself in the dock at Bow Street magistrates' court, charged with assaulting Wright. He was committed for trial at Middlesex quarter sessions. He was granted bail pending his trial, and his sureties were the two printers, Thomas Gillet and Samuel Gosnell. The outcome of the dispute at the sessions was satisfactory for the defendant, because Wright, the prosecutor, dropped the case and ended up paying something towards Stockdale's costs. John Tarrant was Stockdale's attorney, and his brief to counsel, dated June 1798, included the information, 'All matters in difference between the parties was last Term by order of the Court of King's Bench referred to the arbitration of Henry Dampier of the Inner Temple, Esq., who has since made his award, and among other things awarded that the prosecutor pay the defendant £3.3.4 towards his costs of this indictment.'[2]

---

[1] *Survey of London*, London: Athlone Press, 1960, 29: 252.
[2] London Metropolitan Archives, MJ/SP/1798/07/25.

On March 12, 1798, Wright published a second edition of the *Speech of the Rt. Hon. John, Earl of Clare,* Clare being Pitt's Lord Chancellor of Ireland. The first edition produced by him had apparently been a reprint of a Dublin version, and the subject of rude comments by Stockdale, for Wright included a note about them in the second edition. 'It was a faithful copy of this publication which Mr. Stockdale was wantonly pleased to call spurious; though no first transcript, perhaps, ever bore greater marks of authenticity.'

Wright added that the Dublin printer, John Milliken, was preparing an improved version of the speech, and continued, 'If this be the pamphlet Mr. Stockdale is about to reprint, it is well. The field is open to all; and his zeal in the cause which I conscientiously espouse would have had my praise, had he not made it a stalking-horse to level his abuse at me – abuse which I know not how I have provoked, unless by peacably and honestly following the fair line of my profession.'

Wright followed the 'fair line' of his profession by arranging for a simultaneous attack on Stockdale by one of the deadliest weapons known to the trade: a cartoon by James Gillray. Stockdale should have chosen his enemies more carefully. He must have known that Wright was the publisher of the *Anti-Jacobin,* and that Gillray was its cartoonist. As Canning's biographer pointed out, 'In Gillray, the paper possessed the greatest cartoonist of the day. It is not difficult to realize the effect which his pencil produced upon his contemporaries.'[3]

Immediately after Stockdale's appearance at the Bow Street court, the cartoon by Gillray appeared, dated March 13, 1798.[4] Gillray lived near Stockdale, in St. James's Street, over the shop of Hannah Humphrey, who published most of his work. One of

---

[3] Petrie, Charles, *George Canning,* London: Eyre and Spottiswoode, 1930, 23.
[4] British Museum, Political Satires 1798, No.9186. The text it contains has been lightly edited.

the greatest fears of public characters in the latter part of the eighteenth century must have been to be the target of one of the many cartoonists, but particularly of Gillray, who could be really vicious and very weird, and who eventually had a complete mental breakdown. Stockdale learned what it was like to be at the receiving end of one of Gillray's devastating attacks. With a disregard of the *sub judice* rule, Gillray portrayed Stockdale in the dock in Bow Street court, although his trial at the higher court had not yet taken place – and was never to take place. The cartoon was entitled, 'Effusions of the Heart' or 'Lying-Jack the Blacksmith at Confession'. The first part of the caption was a cheap crack, based on the fact that Stockdale had just published his daughter's book of poems with that title. The second part referred to the fact, previously noted by Thomas Rowlandson in his cartoon, that Stockdale had worked as a blacksmith. Underneath the title Gillray wrote: 'Scene. Bow Street – with Lying Jack answering a charge of abuse and blackguardism.'

The drawing itself showed Stockdale pleading with the bench, with tears in his eyes, saying: 'Oh! God dang it, your Worship, do take bail, your Honor tw'ant my fault your Majesty, that I com'd the black-guard over him; God dang it, didn't he say that his thing was printed before mine? & that all my things were only copies and piracies? God dang it, your Worship, ax Almon the bookseller if I was a blackguard all the while I was a porter! or ax the people where I & wife kept a small-coal cellar in Leather Lane if I'm a blackguard! God dang it, was I act like a blackguard when I let that Cooper the printer pull my by the nose, only for saying he was a liar? God dang it, your honor, was it like a blackguard when I Offer'd to beg Ridgeway's pardon, after he had kicked my own arse in my own shop? but I sees how the booksellers all hates me! and wants to ruin me! & says I livs by only copying other peoples works, your Worship! tho' I only 'bridges 'em! yes your Worship, they all hates me; & respires against me: and calls me Lying-Jack, your honor, &

Filching Jack the plagurist! & Stock'ee Jack the Informer! your honor – ah God dang it, they'll be my ruin your Honor!'

It is possible that James Ridgway had contributed some of the background material for Gillray. As was common with his cartoons, there were a number of other barbs to be found in his drawing. He had Stockdale referring to only abridging other people's work, and one of the books shown in the cartoon was *The Abridged Embassy to China*. On the wall he showed an injunction restraining Lying-Jack's copy, and on the floor, a porter's knot (essentially a shoulder sling) to make the point that Stockdale had started out as Almon's porter.

The cartoon obviously amused Stockdale's enemies and rivals. One of the great gossip shops of the trade was that of Tom Lewis in Russell Street, Covent Garden. The author of the article on Stockdale in William Granger's *New, Original and Complete Wonderful Museum*, 1807, stated that the Gillray cartoon 'was a long while exhibited' by Lewis. He added, 'We have heard it said for truth, that a copy of this print coloured was sent to all the shops in the trade in town and country to be publicly hung up.' The effect of this cartoon on Stockdale can readily be imagined. During 1798, he suffered from a great deal of ill-health; how much the cartoon was responsible cannot now be gauged, but it cannot have helped.

Wright and Stockdale were also in conflict over a pamphlet written by the Congressmen for South Carolina, Robert Goodloe Harper, who had wanted David Ramsay to be a United States Senator for the State, and who was to sponsor the United States Sedition Act for President Adams. Stockdale had a particular interest in South Carolina, of course, because of his links with Laurens and Ramsay. Harper's topic, *Observations on the Dispute between the United States and France*, would have been of additional interest to Stockdale in view of his involvement in the Paine-Jefferson-Adams controversy over France. Harper, like many others, at first welcomed the French Revolution, but changed his mind completely when the truthful reports of atrocities came out. He then became very pro-British and anti-French, and strongly supported President Adams and his re-armament programme. However, when the British invaded Maryland during the 1812 War, near his then home, he was, not unreasonably, less of an Anglophile and sprang to arms to repel the invaders. He probably felt, like many another American who remembered the earlier war: Not again![5]

The third edition of Harper's pamphlet appeared in 1798, with the most unusual imprint: 'Philadelphia printed. London: Reprinted, by direction of the Editor, at the Philanthropic Society, London Road, St. George's Fields; and sold by Debrett and Wright, Piccadilly; Hookham and Carpenter, Bond Street; Egerton, Whitehall; Kearsley, Fleet Street; Vernor and Hood, Poultry; Richardson, Royal Exchange and by all other book-sellers except John Stockdale, Piccadilly.'

The pamphlet bore the stern warning: 'The Public are requested, by the Committee of the Philanthropic Society, to beware of a spurious 3rd. edition, advertised to be published by John Stockdale, Piccadilly, but which is, in fact, only his first edition. It is hoped that as the original editor of the pamphlet devoted the profits of the sale to the exclusive benefit of this benevolent institution, that the public, nor any of the book-sellers, will give countenance to the sale of such spurious edition; such conduct being so very illiberal in itself, and injurious to the Charity.'

In view of Stockdale's interest in the subject-matter, one can understand his wishing to be involved. However, the warning in the pamphlet claimed that he had turned down the opportunity to publish it. 'And it ought to be known, that the editor had, in the first instance, actually offered the American copy to Mr. Stockdale, to publish for his own benefit, but apprehensive *then* of the risk, he rejected it, − *now* finding it to have such an

---

[5] Cox, Joseph W., *Champion of Southern Federalism: Robert Goodloe Harper of South Carolina*, Port Washington, N.Y.: Kennikat Press, 1972.

extensive sale and call, he is, for the sake of a little paltry profit to himself, violating the confidence reposed in him by the Editor.'

Assuming the charges to be correct, Stockdale had behaved badly, but the response was perhaps a trifle over the top. We have read in his correspondence with Morse, how Stockdale and his colleagues used retaliation publishing as a weapon, but personal attacks were rare. It is highly likely that the explanation for the intensity of the attack is that Wright, stung by Stockdale's insults, was behind it. It is to be noted that Gillray's cartoon also depicted the Harper pamphlet, with a note, 'Price 6d. for the benefit of the Philanthropic Society'.

Wright did not remain a rival for long. He acted as the English agent for William Cobbett while he was in America, where he had set up a newspaper in Philadelphia, *Porcupine's Gazette*. When Cobbett returned to London in 1802, having lost an expensive libel suit brought against him by Dr. Benjamin Rush, he lived with Wright for a while, but he was soon afterwards one of the creditors responsible for his committal to the Fleet prison. Wright's departure is evidenced by the imprint and text of *The Picture of London for 1802*, which was published by Richard Phillips and 'sold also by J. Ginger, 169 Piccadilly [Wright's former address], and by all booksellers and at the bars of the principal inns and coffee-houses'.[6]

That 1802 publication included a passage of general, as well as of specific interest. 'At the west end of the town are booksellers shops, particularly Debrett's, Stockdale's, Ginger's (late Wright's) in Piccadilly; Ridgway's, York Street, St. James's Square; the Hookhams in Old and New Bond Street, Earle's,

---

[6] In 1810, Cobbett also went to prison. He was sent to Newgate for his criticisms of the sentences of five hundred lashes for certain soldiers, but in the best traditions of that prison, continued to edit his *Political Register* while in custody. Hargreaves, Robert, *The First Freedom*, Stroud: Sutton, 2002, 198, 202.

Albemarle Street and Lloyd's, Harley Street, furnished with all the daily newspapers, which are much frequented about the middle of the day by fashionable people, and are used as lounging-places for political and literary conversation.'

Illus. 18. Hester Lynch Piozzi by Marino Bovi

19

'Loyal' Stockdale and Hester Piozzi

We have already seen that Stockdale, like some other book-sellers, received government money for publishing various items at different times. There was little secret about the payments, and even Abigail Adams was able to mention the matter to John Quincy Adams. In 1784, Stockdale received £228 from Pitt's secret service funds, and in 1793, £51 in respect of various pub-lications.[1] John Wardroper has pointed out that James Gillray, the deadly cartoonist, in 1788, 'sold his services to Pitt's side during a hotly contested election in the Westminster constitu-ency'. Despite taking this money, within two weeks he produced a cartoon, showing 'Election Troops bringing in their accounts to the Pay Table'. This showed newspaper editors and other hired supporters – less Gillray – asking Pitt for payment at the entrance to the Treasury. Gillray was possibly manifesting early signs of a split personality. As a critic, he was able to pour scorn on those who took money from the government; as a recipient himself of such filthy lucre, he kept out of the picture: his own picture. Gillray showed Pitt telling the applicants to 'go to the back door in Great George Street under the Rose'. This was a reference to George Rose, the Secretary of the Treasury, who dispensed the funds to booksellers and others, *sub rosa*.[2]

---

[1] Butterfield, *Adams Family Correspondence*, 6: 360; Aspinall, Arthur, *Politics and the Press 1780-1850*, London: Home and Van Thal, 1949, 153, 166.

[2] Wardroper, John, *Kings, Lords and Wicked Libellers*, London: Murray, 1973, 10 and pl.22.

In 1795, James Ridgway, Mrs. Stockdale's brother, published *The Rolliad*, a collection of verses by literary members of the opposition. One verse was entitled 'Rose; or the Complaint'. The complaint was that of George Rose, who was vexed at being left to hold the fort at the Treasury while his colleague, Thomas Steele, was enjoying himself with Pitt at the seaside at Brighthelmstone (now Brighton). The snobbish versifier included the following lines:

> In one sad joy all Rose's comfort lay;
> Pensive he sought the Treasury, day by day;
> There, in his inmost chamber, lock'd alone,
> To boxes red and green he pour'd his moan
> In rhymes uncouth; for Rose, to business bred
> A purser's clerk, in rhyme was little read;
> Nor, since his learning with his fortune grew,
> Had such vain arts engag'd his sober view,
> For Stockdale's shelves contented to compose
> The humbler poetry of lying prose.

Towards the end of 1795, there was a considerable amount of unrest in London, owing to the hardship caused by the war with France, and in particular by the price of bread. On October 29, the King went to the Opening of Parliament from Buckingham House. Much to his consternation, he was 'violently hissed and hooted, and groaned at the whole way; but no violence was offered till he arrived opposite the Ordnance Office, when a small pebble, or marble, or bullet, broke one of the windows'.[3]

On the return journey through the park, 'the mob surrounded the carriage, and prevented it from proceeding, crying out, "Bread! Bread! Peace! Peace!" Three or four persons were apprehended on suspicion of having thrown stones &c. at the King, and one of them was charged with having called out "No King", and other such expressions.' The call for peace – like that for bread – can be readily understood. The country had been at

---

[3] *Annual Register*, 1795, vol.37, Chronicle 37; 1796, vol.38, Chronicle 6, 17.

war for nearly half of the forty years since the start of the Seven Years' War in 1756.

The man charged was Kyd Wake, a Gosport bookbinder; one of the two special constables who arrested him was – perhaps appropriately – a bookseller from Piccadilly. The *Annual Register* report makes it clear that the 'special' and defending counsel had met in court before. 'Mr. Stockdale, the bookseller, and Mr. Walford, the linen draper, who acted as constables on the day, were examined, and fully proved the facts charged in the indictment; upon which the jury without hesitation found a verdict, guilty.' A large number of character witnesses had attended to support Wake, but 'Mr. Erskine, the prisoner's counsel, declined calling upon them, reserving their testimony to be offered in mitigation of punishment, on the first day of next term'.

On May 9, 1796, neither the character witnesses nor even Erskine's oratory were of much effect. Wake was sentenced to imprisonment with hard labour for five years, and to be pilloried. He was also ordered to find, on his eventual release, sureties for £1000 for his good behaviour for ten years. E. P. Thompson stated that Wake died in prison, but this was not the case: he was released from Gloucester prison on May 7, 1801.[4]

One unfortunate consequence of the Kyd Wake incident was that the ministry became even more apprehensive about a revolution and pushed through the 'Two Acts' to increase their powers, during the session of Parliament that the King had opened.[5]

---

[4] Thompson, E. P., *The Making of the English Working Class*, Harmondsworth: Penguin, 1968, 193; Whiting, John R. S., *Prison Reform in Gloucestershire 1776-1820*, London: Phillimore, 1975, 70. Whiting's book features a plate, showing Wake at his hard labour in his cell, which was also used on the dust jacket.

[5] 36 Geo. III, cc. 7 and 8; Brown, Philip Anthony, *The French Revolution in English History*, London: Crosby Lockwood, 1918, 152.

Dr. Samuel Johnson, another King's man, had died at the end of 1784. Since he had been a legend in his own lifetime, it came as no surprise to the publishing world when a number of works relating to the great man appeared. James Boswell is the name that is most immediately linked with that of Johnson, but the Doctor's friend, Hester Lynch Thrale, has also left us memorials of him. In 1789, Peter Pindar (John Wolcot) commented on the rivalry of Boswell and Mrs. Piozzi (as Mrs. Thrale had become) in a poem entitled 'Bozzy and Piozzi; or, The British Biographers'. The poem included the lines:

> At length, rush'd forth two candidates for fame
> A Scotchman, one; and one a London Dame:
> That, by th'emphatic Johnson, christen'd Bozzy;
> This, by the Bishop's Licence, Dame Piozzi;
> Whose widow'd name, by topers lov'd, was Thrale,
> Bright in the annals of election ale.

Johnson was rather fond of the lady, who had taken him into her matrimonial home and looked after him when he had a breakdown in 1766. Her husband, the well-known brewer Thrale, died in 1781, and three years later she married her daughter's music teacher, Gabriel Mario Piozzi, shortly before Johnson's death, but not before the good Doctor had opined, 'Sir, she has done everything wrong, since Thrale's bridle was off her neck.' One thing that Mrs. Piozzi did that was right, was to take her new husband on a Grand Tour, and to get Thomas Cadell to publish her *Observations and Reflections in course of a Journey Through France, Italy and Germany* in 1789. Stockdale, with his great interest in geographical books, will have been aware of this work. Although Stockdale may never have met Dr. Johnson, he later published Hester Piozzi, and got to know her quite well.

The *Works of Johnson*, edited by Sir John Hawkins, were published in 1787, in eleven volumes by a number of booksellers, of whom Stockdale was not one. For a number of publishers to get together in a loose partnership or 'conger', was not unusual in the eighteenth century: the arrangement enabled the risks to be spread, as in ship insurance. In the latter business the risks were traditionally taken on in sixty-fourths: in the congers the usual division was into shares of twenty-fourths. S. H. Steinberg pointed out that Johnson's *Lives of the Poets* had initially been shared between as many as thirty-six booksellers. He added: 'The congers eventually disappeared because the increasing wealth of the individual publishers made them face the inevitable risks of their trade with less apprehension, and chiefly because by the end of the century the spirit of co-operation had given way to the fierce tenets of unrestricted competition.' Stockdale, as will have been noted, nearly always published on his own and was possibly a prime example of the change referred to by Steinberg. However, he occasionally joined in the form of looser and smaller association that began to replace the conger at about the time he started his own business, as with the first of his Berquin books of children's stories.[6]

Before the congers disappeared, Stockdale participated in several of them – comprising less than thirty-six booksellers – which produced not only Johnson's *Lives of the Poets*, but also various editions of his dictionary.[7] Stockdale clearly had advance knowledge of Hawkins's eleven-volume Johnson collection and published what he opportunistically called volumes 12 and 13 of Johnson's *Works* in the same year, making them look similar to the original eleven. These contained Johnson's early parliamentary reports and were edited by George Chalmers, who had written a number of books for Stockdale, including the

---

[6] Steinberg, S. H., *Five Hundred Years of Printing*, new edition by Trevitt, John, London: British Library, 2001, 112, 113. For a valuable account of the congers and the linked topic of the sale of copyright, see, Belanger, Terry, 'Publishers and writers in eighteenth-century England', in Rivers, Isabel (ed.), *Books and their Readers in Eighteenth-Century England*, Leicester U.P., 1982, 5.

[7] See the references to Stockdale in the comprehensive two-volume work of Fleeman, J. D., *A Bibliography of the Works of Samuel Johnson*, Oxford U.P., 2000.

government's attack on Tom Paine, using the pseudonym Francis Oldys. There is some doubt about the usefulness of Johnson's reports because, as Michael Harris politely pointed out, 'his literary contribution in making up the majority of the debates puts him in rather a special category.'[8] In the following year Stockdale, together with Robinson, published a matching volume 14, containing miscellaneous pieces of the Doctor's.

At the close of the century Mrs. Piozzi was looking for a publisher for her new book, *Retrospection*, a history of the preceding eighteen centuries – in a few choice pages. She tried George Robinson, who had not only joined with Stockdale in putting out volume 14 of her late friend's work, but had also published her *British Synonymy* in 1794. The proud author thought that her new masterpiece was worth £1000, but Robinson declined her kind offer of the manuscript. On June 10, 1800, Mrs. Piozzi wrote to her friend and agent, Rev. Leonard Chappelow, 'Here is a letter from Robinson to say he is grown sick and old, and going to leave off, and will take no engagement, but wishes me success, and doubts not but many in the trade (those are his words) will give the money I have asked from him. It is vexatious enough, but when the world is full, as Dr. Johnson said, of sin and sorrow, I must not be talking of *paper and packthread*.'[9] The situation was even more vexatious for George Robinson: he died in the following year.

Chappelow suggested Stockdale to Mrs. Piozzi, who replied on November 1, 'Robinson and I are number *two* now and everything is over between *us*; and your friend Stockdale as next oars commands my attendance with the manuscript. I threw myself on his daughter's mercy and his own by the same post

---

[8] Harris, Michael, 'Journalism as a Profession or Trade in the Eighteenth Century', in Myers, Robin and Harris, Michael (eds.), *Author/Publisher Relations during the Eighteen and Nineteenth Centuries*, Oxford Polytechnic Press, 1983, 43.

[9] John Rylands University Library of Manchester, Rylands English MS collection, 560/96.

which carried this and desire a speedy answer.' She got her speedy answer: 'Memorandum of agreement between Mrs. Hester Lynch Piozzi and John Stockdale, bookseller of Piccadilly, Westminster, 3rd. November 1800. The undersigned mutually agree that the work intituled "Retrospection or a glance backward upon the most striking and important events, characters, situations and their consequences, which the last 1800 years have presented to the observation of mankind" be published at the sole risk of the said John Stockdale, who shall not have it in his power to make any demand therefor on Mrs. H.L. Piozzi, for any expense so incurred. And it is further agreed that after the expense so incurred shall be reimbursed to the said John Stockdale, the whole profit shall be divided equally between the two undersigned, and that the property of the copyright in the aforesaid work be the equally divided property of the two undersigned.' The contract was written out by Stockdale's eldest son, John Joseph, who also signed as a witness. 'So Stockdale bears me harmless of expense, and we share the profits,' the author wrote in her diary, adding gloomily, 'which will be *none*.'[10]

On November 5, Mrs. Piozzi wrote to her friend, Penelope Pennington: '*Retrospection* is already disposed of, and you will be pleased that 'tis launched from a good aristocratic house. We have been but once in Town yet, and that for two hours only, one spent with Stockdale, and one with [the actress Sarah] Siddons, who is lean and nerve-shaken, but lovely as ever.' She later wrote to Dr. Robert Grey in a similar vein: 'Stockdale is a good *hoper*, and seems to think well of it upon the *launch*. He is a good aristocrat, too. I am pleased that it comes out from his loyal shop.'[11]

---

[10] Ryl. Eng. MS 560/140, 557/201; Balderston, Katharine C., *Thraliana*, Oxford U.P., 1951, 2: 1015.

[11] Knapp, Oswald G., *The Intimate Letters of Hester Piozzi and Penelope Pennington*, London: John Lane, 1914, 202; Hayward, A., new ed. by Lobban, J. H., *Dr. Johnson's Mrs. Thrale*, Edinburgh: Foulis, 1910, 283.

The label 'loyal' can easily be understood in view of Stockdale's pro-government stance, coupled with the arrest of Kyd
Wake during the 1795 riot, but the use of the words 'aristocratic'
and 'aristocrat' must be put down to Mrs. Piozzi's fulsomeness.
Incidentally, the reputation for loyalty lasted a long time.
Although John Stockdale died in 1814, as late as September 23,
1839, the printer, Luke Graves Hansard, whose family had
massive litigation problems with young Stockdale, noted in his
diary: 'And even old Stockdale was patronised for collaring a
poor devil who was charged with throwing stones at Royalty.'[12]

Stockdale set his printer, Thomas Gillet, to work at once, so
that the author was able to write to Chappelow as early as
November 14, 'Stockdale plies me pretty hard with proofs, and
promises the present *Retrospection* as a New Year's gift to the
Town very early in January.' She also wrote to her friend
Penelope, urging her to get her friends to place orders in
advance of publication, adding, 'Stockdale shows his numerous
orders as nest-eggs or decoys.' On December 15, Mrs. Piozzi
informed Chappelow that her friend Mrs. Clay had been to the
Piccadilly shop to order three copies. She added: 'What a pretty
woman she is, says Stockdale. Ay, I replied, so she is, a *very*
pretty woman sure enough; but such an errand would have
made almost any woman pretty: and he has a particular pane of
glass to look at subscribers through, I suppose.'[13]

Mrs. Piozzi was extremely upset by Gillet's many typographical errors when she read the proofs. She nevertheless
missed, or failed to correct many of them, so they appeared in
the book in due course. She was particularly unlucky with the
timing of the printing, as she ran into an industrial dispute that
affected all the printers in London and Westminster, including

---

[12] Ford, P. and G., *Luke Graves Hansard, His Diary*, Oxford: Blackwell,
1962, 202. For the saga of *Stockdale v. Hansard*, see the Appendix to the
present work.
[13] Ryl. Eng. MS. 560/105; Knapp, 206; 560/106.

Gillet. On November 29, the Master Printers agreed to pay an increased rate for some of the compositors' work, but the employees were not satisfied. At a meeting of the Masters on Christmas Eve, 'It was stated that a general dissatisfaction still remained among the compositors, concerning the advances granted them at a former meeting; they expected to have an additional allowance of one half-penny per thousand on works printed from MS copy'. The complaint about authors' bad hand-writing was conceded by the employers and the additional allowance was agreed, to start on January 1, 1801. It is not beyond the bounds of possibility that Mrs. Piozzi's manuscript pages, and perhaps those of other authors at about the same time, were deliberately found to be exceptionally difficult to read, by compositors making their point.[14]

'On 1 January 1801 we dined in company of kind Mr. Gillon at Stockdale's house, Piccadilly,' Mrs. Piozzi wrote a little later. 'The man's ineffable delight when that diligent friend produced his list of demands for 92 copies, was even comically pleasant; and he said it took away his breath and appetite.'[15] Mrs. Piozzi probably lost her appetite when the reviews began to appear. The many misprints were bound to draw unfavourable com-ment, as she had realised would happen, but she cannot have anticipated how biting some of the reviews would be. Towards the end of her preface, the author had stated, 'But I will run

---

[14] Howe, Ellic, *The London Compositor 1785-1900*, London: Bibliographical Society, 1947, 79.

[15] Balderston, 2: 1031. This is a rare reference to Stockdale socialising with an author, other than Thomas Day. He seems not to have followed the custom of Joseph Johnson and some other publishers of having regular literary dinner parties. Tyson, Gerald P., *Joseph Johnson: A Liberal Publisher*, Iowa City: U. Iowa P., 1979, 91. The Dilly brothers 'had the agreeable habit of stuffing rather than starving authors.' Butterfield, L. H., 'The American Interests of the Firm of E. and C. Dilly', *Papers Bib. Soc. of America*, 1951, 45: 285.

down my own book no more.' The critics took up where she had left off.

The *Anti-Jacobin* described the work as 'history cooked up in a novel form, reduced to light reading for boarding school misses, and loungers at watering places,' while the *Critical Review* claimed that it was unsuitable for any class of reader. Mrs. Piozzi's biographer and Samuel Johnson scholar, James Clifford, commented: 'On the whole it is Mrs. Piozzi's most uninteresting book. She seemed unable, in the dreary and tedious summaries of Roman and medieval history, to combine her talent for telling a good story with the miscellaneous information she had culled from her wide reading.'[16]

On February 2, Mrs. Piozzi had written to her agent, over-looking the fact that she had herself read the proofs, 'Pray reproach Stockdale slily with the typographical errors, which are innumerable – and especially in the quotations. The rebellion among our printers was a terrible blow upon us, and now people wait for the second edition, and resolve to stay till they can get a correct copy.'[17] The critics made it clear to the public that they felt the book had some rather more fundamental shortcomings than those caused by the industrial dispute, so the first edition was not sold out and no second edition ever appeared.

In attempting a history of eighteen centuries the author had inevitably run into all sorts of difficulties, one of which she had indicated in a letter to her daughter as early as April 27, 1796. 'The eternal difficulty is to judge where to contract most and where to amplify, lest one should at last resemble Johnson's Macbean, whom he set a long time ago to compile a Geographical Dictionary, and looking it over said he had dwelt too little on the article 'Athens'. "Ah Doctor", says the man, "but if I make so much writing about *Athens*, what room will be left for me to

---

[16] Clifford, James L., *Hester Lynch Piozzi*, Oxford U.P., 1952, 402.
[17] Ryl. Eng. MS. 560/108.

talk of *Abingdon*?" "After this conversation," cries Johnson, "you may be sure we talked no more of work." ' [18]

In the preface to *Retrospection* Mrs. Piozzi changed that charming story somewhat, proving once again that anecdotes about the great must always be regarded with some scepticism. In less than five years, her own account of Dr. Johnson's exchange was altered by her to the following: ' " Ah, but dear Sir", exclaimed the admiring parasite, "if I am to make all this eloquent ado about Athens and Rome, where shall we find place, do you think, for Richmond or Aix la Chapelle?" '

Despite the misprints and the cool reception given to the book by the critics, Stockdale's final account shows that both he and the author managed to make a small profit. His account records that 516 copies were sold at £1.12.0 each, producing £825.12.0. Only 750 had been printed, so a sale of the whole edition would not have made much more of a profit. Stockdale showed the costs of production and advertising in 95 newspapers as £577.4.6 in all, so that there was only £248.7.6 left for the partners in the venture to share equally. One of the items he had wrongly shown as a disbursement was the full sale price of the nine public deposit copies of the book supplied by him without charge, as required by law. He had, of course, not paid for those books.[19]

Although the parties never collaborated again on any other publishing venture, Mrs. Piozzi continued to patronise the bookshop. Unfortunately, that patronage was not of much value to Stockdale, who had to write to his customer in August 1807, requesting her to settle a bill of some £5, the major part of

---

[18] Lansdowne, Marquess of, *The Queeney Letters*, London: Cassell, 1934, 256.
[19] Ryl. Eng. MS 557/203 is the account, 557/202 is the complete list of periodicals carrying the advertisements.

which had been incurred in 1802. The request referred to 'Mr. Stockdale being greatly distressed for money'.[20]

Stockdale's reputation for loyalty persisted, as we have seen from Hansard's comment, but there must have been occasions when he wished that he were less well known for that characteristic, and that he had not been known as the man who collared that 'poor devil' Wake.

A near neighbour of his in Piccadilly was the radical Sir Francis Burdett, who had followers quite as turbulent, at times, as those of Wilkes. On August 10, 1804, *The Times* reported: 'We congratulate the County of Middlesex on the close of its election for a representative in Parliament. Yesterday the Sheriffs, who throughout this long and tumultuous contest have acted with a degree of firmness, spirit, vigilance and impartiality made the following declaration of the numbers at the close of the poll: For Mr Mainwaring 2828; Sir Francis Burdett 2823; Majority for Mr. Mainwaring 5. In consequence of which that gentleman was declared duly elected. Around Sir Francis Burdett's house a still greater crowd was assembled who seemed exceedingly ripe for mischief. About 9 o'clock six ruffian-looking figures went along Piccadilly, and with large bludgeons. This sight seemed to enliven the mob, who cheered them with clamorous outcries of "Burdett for ever".'

Stockdale had experienced very similar incidents two years earlier, and grew extremely alarmed. At 4 p.m. on August 8, Stockdale had written an urgent plea for help to Lord Hawkesbury, at the Home Office, which stated that the mob had threatened him personally. 'My Lord, Having reason to believe from the numerous threats of the mob, for some time past, but more particularly within the last two hours, that my house will very shortly be attacked, I have taken the liberty to inform your

---

[20] Ryl. Eng. MS 557/205.

Lordship thereof and have no doubt that measures will be taken for the protection of my family and property.'[21]

The Times report, which deals with a slightly later time, suggests that the matter never became as serious as a riot, thanks to 'the constables and police officers showing themselves', with the 3rd Regiment of the Loyal London Volunteers in the background. With problems of health, finance and criticism on both professional and political grounds, and with direct threats of violence to his shop, home and family, Stockdale must have wondered how much longer he could, or should shoulder the burdens of a bookseller.

[21] British Library Add. MSS 38,571, f.84; the earlier incidents are described by Ignatieff, Michael, *A Just Measure of Pain*, London: Macmillan, 1978, 138.

20

Stockdale's Final Years

We have now seen how Stockdale, during his first twenty years from 1780 to 1800, built up his areas of special interest: America, political works, geography/topography and children's books. He was probably required to keep some novels for sale, but he showed no interest in publishing them. It might be thought by some readers that there were not many novels published in the eighteenth century, in any event, but that was not the case. Before he left his Boston bookshop to become Washington's senior artillery officer, Henry Knox, over a period of four years, imported no less than five hundred copies of novels from London. The most popular one was not, as one might have expected, one of Samuel Richardson's novels but Henry Mackenzie's *The Man of Feeling*.[1] Stockdale appears to have had no feeling for the novel but there was one line that he was keen on that we have not yet considered: Shakespeare. Stockdale first published his complete works in 1784, in one octavo volume. In his classic *Introduction to Bibliography for Literary Students*, Ronald McKerrow pointed out that, 'Stockdale was able to offer his book in the following versions: "boards, 15s.; calf, 17s.6d.; calf gilt, 18s.; russia, 19s.; vellum, 21s. [one guinea]; morocco extra, 25s.; tortoiseshell 63s. [three guineas]".'[2]

---

[1] Reilly, Elizabeth Carroll and Hall, David D., 'Customers and the Market for Books', in Amory, Hugh and Hall, David D. (eds.), *The Colonial Book in the Atlantic World*, Cambridge U.P., 2000, 1: 389.
[2] McKerrow, Ronald B., *An Introduction to Bibliography for Literary Students*, Oxford U.P., 1927, 125n.

In one of his many advertisements, after stating that he was providing the work for 'the middling and lower ranks', Stockdale aimed at that difficult customer, the man who has everything. 'Nor is the utility of the present publication confined to persons of the rank already described; it will be found serviceable even to those whose situation in life hath enabled them to purchase all the expensive editions of our great dramatist. The book now offered to the public may commodiously be taken into a coach or a post-chaise, for amusement on a journey.'

The publication was a success and on April 5, 1788, Stockdale entered into a contract that was to build on that success. 'Memorandum of an agreement between John Stockdale of Piccadilly, bookseller, and the Rev. Samuel Ayscough, of the British Museum, that Mr. Ayscough shall make an Index to the Plays of Shakespeare, with reference to the play, act and scene, and also to the page and line of Mr. Stockdale's edition. That Mr. Stockdale will print it with type and sized pages as the volume itself is printed, and will pay Mr. Ayscough five guineas for every sheet or sixteen pages so printed, and in proportion for any part of the sheet. Twenty guineas to be paid to Mr. Ayscough when the Index goes to the press, and the remainder three months after publication. The Index shall remain the sole property of Mr. Stockdale or his assigns.'[3]

Ayscough, who was a curate, had already prepared an index for the *Monthly Review* and, as the contract indicated, worked at the British Museum on the index of books there. He also compiled one for the *Gentleman's Magazine* and another for the *British Critic*. He completed his massive task for Stockdale in time for his second Shakespeare edition in 1790. From then on customers had the choice of buying the work with or without index, as well as with the various binding options. In his advertisement inviting subscriptions for the new edition, Stockdale, as usual, referred to his heavy expenditure. This time it was said to be

---

[3] Folger Library, Washington, Y.c. 59 (2).

'near £2000', but he probably recouped his outlay, and more, over the next few years.

John Stockdale and his wife had met through a Moravian chapel, and she was a member of the congregation of the Fetter Lane Chapel for some years. Stockdale as an adult never indicated any religious preference in any of the existing documents – unlike his son, John Joseph, who later displayed classic signs of religious bigotry, in his case, of the militant Protestant variety. Stockdale's daughter Mary wrote later that she herself, as an adult, had worshipped at Christopher Wren's beautiful St. James's parish church, only a few doors along in Piccadilly. However, the publication of the Shakespeare gave rise to a rare mention of the Moravian connection. 'I recollect, when a boy, on my father publishing Shakespeare in one volume,' John Joseph wrote to his wife, 'that old Benjamin La Trobe, the celebrated Moravian minister, called in, and my father, anticipating a lecture from his venerated friend for having published plays, made some apologetical remark, to which the worthy pastor replied, "Everybody reads Shakespeare, Mr. Stockdale. Even I have Shakespeare in my little library".'[4]

It is clear that Stockdale, despite his various protestations that enormous costs made a profit on books almost unattainable, was successful financially in the 1790s, if not earlier. He managed to send all four sons to boarding school at Apsley in Bedfordshire and, according to his obituary in the *Gentleman's Magazine* in 1815, the year after his death, 'by several speculations he acquired considerable property.' The obituary added the telling comment, 'but, being rendered too confident by success, he latterly overstepped his powers.' It may well have been the death of his fellow-publisher, George Robinson, that first led to his overstepping his powers in a significant manner.

---

[4] *Harriette Wilson's Memoirs*, London: John Joseph Stockdale, 1831 ed., 6: 483.

In June 1800, Mrs. Piozzi wrote that Robinson had declined her *Retrospection*, as 'he is grown sick, and old, and going to leave off.' Because of that, as related earlier, she had let Stockdale (then only 50) have her new book. Robinson had taken his only son, also George, and his brother John into partnership in 1786, and in 1793, was one of those prosecuted for publishing Paine. After his death on June 6, 1801, his stock was sold, the sale being conducted by his brother-in-law, John Walker, of whom William Granger wrote, 'He is also (and has a long time been) an eminent auctioneer for the booksellers.' Granger continued: 'When disposing of the immense stock of his deceased brother-in-law, Mr. George Robinson, he sold in three days' time, to the amount of £54,000, of which Mr. Stockdale bought nearly one-half of that amount, a circumstance unknown in the annals of bookselling.'[5]

Presumably Stockdale had to borrow a substantial sum in order to pay some £25,000 for his share of Robinson's stock. Even with a low interest rate, such an additional burden, at the height of the war with France, was probably too much for him. He gained a number of titles from Robinson which fitted in with his own lists, such as George Vancouver's *Voyage Round the World*. The *New Annual Register*, which had been started in 1781, and which was originally edited by Andrew Kippis and then by Thomas Morgan, also came into Stockdale's hands in this way. As related before, in 1807, he published *The Works of Sir William Jones*, which the Robinsons had earlier put out in fewer volumes, but it is unlikely that this, or any other single Robinson work, made much money. Stockdale probably succeeded in doubling the number of the problems he had to cope with in his business, rather than its net profit.

For example, one of Robinson's titles that may have attracted Stockdale, was Camden's *Britannia*. Richard Gough had been

---

[5] Granger, William, *The New, Original and Complete Wonderful Museum and Magazine*, London: Alex. Hogg, 1808, 6: 3153, 3157.

preparing a new edition and the first volume 'was far advanced in the press'. Unfortunately, Gough suffered a number of epileptic fits and let it be known that he, 'finding it of importance to his health that he should suspend such pursuits, considered himself at full liberty to decline proceeding any further than to complete the volume which Messrs. Robinson had begun to print.'[6]

At the end of 1806, John Joseph decided to set up on his own nearby, at 41 Pall Mall. Perhaps he saw that his father's ship, if not sinking, had sprung a few leaks, and decided to leave it for that reason. Young Stockdale, who turned out to be a rogue of the first order, undoubtedly exaggerated his previous role at his father's shop when he advertised: 'He hopes that his immediate attention to whatever orders he may be honoured with, will ensure him a continuance of that favour which he has uniformly experience during nearly fourteen years that he conducted his Father's business in Piccadilly.' It is impossible to say whether his father told him to go, for financial or other reasons, and also whether he regretted his departure or welcomed it. It is clear that they were not on the best of terms two years later.

John Joseph was then about to publish, as one of his earliest productions, the documents relating to the Cintra Convention. General Sir Arthur Wellesley had been criticised – shades of the Saratoga Convention – for being too generous with the surrender terms offered to the enemy during the Peninsular campaign. The General, who as the Duke of Wellington was to tell John Joseph Stockdale to PUBLISH AND BE DAMNED!, had promised to provide him with some relevant documents, which would vindicate his decision. The name Stockdale, bookseller, clearly still indicated a Piccadilly address only to some people. On December 16, 1808, John Joseph wrote to Wellesley: 'Owing to the accidental direction of your packet to my father, it has not

---

[6] Nichols, John, *Literary Anecdotes of the Eighteenth Century*, London: Nichols, Son & Bentley, 1832, 2: 273, 283.

yet reached me, and even scruples are made to let me have it – very unhandsomely, I must say. Lest a difficulty should be made, do me the favour to let me have an order for the delivery of it.'[7]

The fifth volume of Granger's *Museum*, which came out in 1807, contained a long anonymous article, entitled 'Biographical Memoirs of John Stockdale, Esq., a Remarkable and Eminent Bookseller and Publisher in Piccadilly'. Granger was assisted with his book by James Caulfield, also a bookseller, so he may well have been the author of the article. It is not reliable as far as Stockdale's early history is concerned, but is probably fairly accurate when dealing with the early years of the nineteenth century.[8]

The author commented on the fact that Stockdale had published many political pamphlets, adding that he had persuaded the ministerial party 'to make his shop the market for their political effusions. Thus his warehouse became filled, for every gentleman published at his own expense, and when a number of copies had been sold, or sent according to the author's direction to friends, the remainder was piled up for another use, as it seldom happens that evanescent leaves are ever after called for, hence the lining of trunks, fruit stalls and fishmongers are supplied with that useful article, waste paper.'

Although the writer disapproved of the ministerial party and appears not to have liked Stockdale, he was objective enough to give him his due. 'It must be observed he had always at his elbows the demagogues of the richest and strongest party, who were loud in their approbation of all his works. Thus we see a country blacksmith raised to a connection with the rulers of a great nation, and imparting advice to the Solomons of the age.

---

[7] Letter in the possession of Robin Myers. For the latest account of John Joseph Stockdale, Harriette Wilson and the attempted blackmail of the Duke, see, Wilson, Frances, *The Courtesan's Revenge*, London: Faber and Faber, 2003.

[8] Granger, 5: 2469.

Assurance, confidence, resolution and a strong tincture of common sense, accomplished this most valuable purpose. Booksellers read this, and do so likewise.' We now know enough about Stockdale's American contacts to add that perhaps the reference to the rulers of a great nation, should have been to the rulers of two great nations.

The Granger article reveals a little of the bad feelings between Stockdale and Debrett. At what was probably in the early years of the two men's relationship, when Stockdale was once 'dissatisfied with Debrett's conduct in not forwarding the sale of some of his pamphlets, a very warm debate took place in the latter's shop [where Stockdale had worked for Almon], when in the most exalted attitude of pomposity, he demanded an immediate return of every *thing* that belonged to him; on which Mr. Debrett immediately went backwards and brought him his knot, which he laid before him in the public shop, observing at the same time that it was originally his own, and he hoped he would take it away directly. This occasioned much laughter.'

Stockdale had the last laugh, for when Debrett went out of business in 1803, Stockdale was the beneficiary. 'He is the greatest publisher of Piccadilly, and since the commercial demise of Debrett does double the business he did before.' It doubtless gave the surviving bookseller great satisfaction to be able to advertise: 'Mr. Stockdale respectfully informs the Public that he has purchased from the assignees of John Debrett, bankrupt, all the remaining copies of the Parliamentary Register; and that he has now reprinted the seventeen volumes so long out of print, and many scarce numbers, whereby he is enabled to complete 100 sets, containing the proceedings of both Houses of Parliament from 1743 to 1802, in 87 volumes, price half-bound £58.2.0.' Debrett had taken over the parliamentary series published by Almon, who had, with Wilkes, opened the door to such reporting. Almon, who was nearing his end, was probably happy to see his reports continued, but not best pleased that his former assistant had acquired them.

Debrett obtained one final moral victory over his rival. Two clerks at the India Office had agreed to compile an East India calendar or directory for Stockdale, but had fallen out with him when he declined to increase their agreed annual fee. They had got Debrett to publish it for them instead. Stockdale republished it, and was successfully sued for an injunction by the authors. The Whigs were at last in office, and the plaintiffs were represented by the new Solicitor-General, Sir Samuel Romilly. An application was heard on February 27, 1806, by the new Lord Chancellor, who had also just been appointed as a member of the ministry of 'All the Talents'. He was none other than the highly successful defender of Stockdale and others, the newly ennobled Lord Erskine.

Counsel argued on Stockdale's behalf that a publisher could not alter basic facts, just to avoid publishing the same information as his rival. The names of civil servants, or the true locations of places on maps, could not be changed merely to avoid identical true facts being used by both. Romilly pointed out that Stockdale had done rather more than use the same basic information: he had slavishly copied Debrett's work, even including his odd un-alphabetical listing and his misprints. To make it worse, he had undercut Debrett, by charging 2/6d. to his 5/6d. Lord Erskine had little difficulty in finding against his former client and continued the injunction until trial.[9]

To complete the story, one should add that Debrett's name is today remembered, while Stockdale's is known only to collectors and librarians, by pure chance. Almon had first published *The New Peerage* in 1769, and Debrett in due course published it as his successor. When he brought out the fifth edition in 1802, shortly before his 'commercial demise', he changed the title to *Debrett's Peerage*, under which name it still makes a regular

---

[9] *Matthewson v. Stockdale, English Reports*, 33: 103.

appearance in bookshops. Debrett had changed the name just in time to secure his immortality.[10]

Stockdale may have been named 'the greatest publisher of Piccadilly' because of the limited competition. We have seen that Wright went to the Fleet prison in 1803, the year in which Debrett lost his double shop. John Hatchard, whose bookshop is now the sole surviving eighteenth-century one in Piccadilly, only arrived in 1797, the same year as Wright. According to William Beloe, Hatchard was 'a Godly bookseller, a worthy and conscientious man, whose principal dealings were in religious books and tracts'. Hatchard made an appropriate entry in his diary for June 30: 'This day by the grace of God, the good will of my friends and £5 in my pocket, I have opened my bookshop in Piccadilly [at no. 173].' Hatchard in fact very successfully sold more than religious works and also supported the Tories, but he did not publish much. Despite that important distinction between the two booksellers, his success may well have been partly at Stockdale's expense.[11]

When David Ramsay, the South Carolina historian, lost his wife, the daughter of Henry Laurens, he wrote a memorial of her which included various letters to demonstrate what a pious lady she had been. The English edition of his *Memoir of the Life of Martha Laurens Ramsay* was published in 1815, the year after Stockdale's death, by Hatchard, as one might have expected. Without her husband's book, Martha Laurens Ramsay might well have been forgotten; with it, she is sufficiently well

---

[10] I am obliged to Patrick Montague-Smith, former editor of *Debrett*, for this information.

[11] Beloe, William, *The Sexagenarian, or Recollections of a Literary Life*, London: F. C. & J. Rivington, 1817, 2: 281, 243; Laver, James, *Hatchards of Piccadilly 1797-1947*, London: Hatchards, 1947, 11. Hatchard was at no.173 from 1797 to 1801 only, and then leapfrogged over Stockdale and Duke Street to no.190, near St. James's Church, where he had to pay a thousand guineas to acquire a lease for twenty-four years. Most of the old house numbers in Piccadilly have since been reduced by two.

remembered to have her own entry in the new *American National Biography*, like her husband, father and brother John, all of whom certainly merited such recognition.

It is possible that Beloe was referring to Stockdale when he wrote: 'There was also a bookseller to whom the epithet B-----d is attached, but anecdotes of vulgar rudeness, over-reaching cunning, and total disregard of the civilities of life, would only deform these pages.' As Beloe, apart from being an assistant librarian at the British Museum was, like his colleague, Samuel Ayscough, a cleric, it is probable that the epithet he found too shocking to spell out was 'blackguard', rather than the more customary term of abuse with the same two letters. The word 'blackguard' had figured in Gillray's cartoon.

Beloe painted a delightful picture of some visitors to book-shops in general, but which doubtless also resembled the scene at Stockdale's shop: 'The first resort of young men who possess any literary curiosity is usually a bookseller's shop, and if the proprietor be a man of experience in his business, and of a courteous communicative disposition, an acquaintance with him may prove of considerable benefit to the student. He learns from him the value, not in a professed collector's sense of that word, but the relative excellence of different editions. He hears also of new works in contemplation; he meets individuals of similar propensities with himself, and an agreeable interchange of knowledge and information is thereby promoted. Above all, he obtains the enviable privilege of seeing publications which his finances will not suffer him to purchase, and enjoys the no small indulgence of an early sight of the periodical publication.'

Granger's 1807 article revealed that Stockdale's purchase of much of the Robinson stock had not been his only investment. 'He has himself declared that, including the above, he purchased in the course of one year nearly to the amount of £50,000. To do this in time of war like the present requires a mind a little more enlarged than a vinegar cruet, which is mostly the case with his companions in business, who on seeing him buy thus largely, prophesied his quick downfall; but, like the knotted oak, he gives way to nothing, and has lately opened a house of public auction in Piccadilly.' The article added that John Joseph, who had recently opened his own shop in Pall Mall, possessed 'a great share of his father's perseverance and industry'.

The writer next referred to another of Stockdale's problems, namely 'milestones', and revealed an interesting new social phenomenon: 'Editions are more numerous as well as readers, and books are now held necessary as well as ornamental, to complete the furniture of a genteel house.' Granger continued, 'Mr. Stockdale is now become remarkable for producing new and expensive works, all of which do him more credit than the politics he prints, however he may serve the party that has hitherto supported him. If we might venture to advise him, and he seems to want such sort of assistance since he has stumbled on some milestones, for so booksellers call heavy works that stick on hand, he would do well to print a topographical dictionary.'[12]

It is not clear why Stockdale started book auctions, unless it was because he had so much unsold stock on his hands after making his major – and probably foolhardy – purchases. He presumably thought that auctions could help ease his financial pressures. He seems to have failed in that endeavour, but he succeeded in antagonising some more of his colleagues. His obituary in the *Gentleman's Magazine* made the point, 'He had lately dealt in the over-printed stock of other publishers and, to dispose of his purchases, had established a series of sales by auction in London and the various great towns of the United Kingdom, a system of business which had justly excited the jealousy of the regular traders, and which, judging by the consequences, had not met the expectations of the proprietor.' The sales included more than over-printed stock. John Symmons, a bidder at an auction managed to buy a 'valuable' Bible at below

---

[12] Granger, 5: 2486.

the reserve price. When Stockdale wrote to him to draw attention to the error, the customer returned the book adding,
reasonably, on January 28, 1808, that he had thought that 'you
had taken proper precautions for the security of your more
valuable lots, so that none of them should be sold below the
prices you had affixed.'[13]

The Granger article concluded with a passage which shows
how prominent John Stockdale was in 1807, immediately before
his decline began. It also shows that he was not universally
admired. 'It has been observed that since the day of the pro-
jecting Dunton, a bookseller remarkable for his schemes, but
none of which did him any service, no bibliopole has occupied
so much of the public's attention as Mr. Stockdale, and perhaps
the cause has been owing to his large purchases and long puffs
in the papers: a proof that he possess considerable advantages
with the public, that he is not without some merit, as well as a
considerable share of spirit; yet his contemporaries say he's a
proud upstart, high today, and low tomorrow; but we must in
truth say,

> He's a bookseller meritoriously by fortune raised,
> By Whigs admired, and by Tories praised.'

On March 11, 1809, Stockdale found himself appearing
before the Lord Chief Justice as a defendant once again, but on
this occasion the Attorney-General appeared for the defence.
The Chief Justice was Lord Ellenborough (who, as Edward Law,
had defended Warren Hastings), and the Attorney was Sir Vicary
Gibbs, but the trial was on this occasion that of an ordinary civil
action. Once again Stockdale had been at the receiving end of a
writ, as he had published the offending item in his *New Annual
Register* for 1807. The plaintiff was Joseph Nightingale, a former
Methodist minister, who had written a book critical of Method-
ism. The anonymous reviewer in the periodical had written of

---

[13] Henry E. Huntingdon Library, San Marino, Cadell and Davies Collection.

the author: 'There is a depravity indeed, in this man's heart, if we may reason from his publication before us, that unqualifies him for giving evidence in any court. The Methodists may be fools, but their present historian is obviously a knave.'

Counsel for the plaintiff, Mr. Pollock, addressed the jury in the stirring language of Charles Dickens's Serjeant Buzfuz in the case of *Bardell v. Pickwick*: 'Gentlemen, I will put the question to you calmly and deliberately. Can the language of libel be more malignant than this? Is it possible to crowd more defamation into the same space? For this, you will observe, is not one of those protracted, tedious, long-winded libels that is half neutralised by its prolixity. It is not a libel which compels you to dig for its meaning amongst the dust and rubbish of inference and innuendo. It is not a libel of that kind which is rendered comparatively harmless by spinning out its insinuations into a detail too long to be remembered, or too obscure to be understood.' In short, it was short.

The first witness told the court that he had bought the offending volume in Stockdale's shop in Piccadilly. 'I purchased it of a young man who I afterwards understood was young Mr. Stockdale.' Stockdale junior was called next. This was clearly William, the second son, who according to his sister Mary, was 'a gentle pious soul'. It may have been his piety that made him very careful with the evidence he gave on oath, or the black looks of Serjeant Buzfuz, but whatever the reason, his testimony reads rather like that of Sam Weller.

'Does your father keep the shop opposite Albany Buildings – the bookseller's shop?'

'No, sir.'

'Where then, pray?'

'It is opposite the Duke of Portland's.'

'He keeps a shop in Piccadilly?'

'Yes, sir.'

'Is there any other bookseller of the same name who keeps a shop in Piccadilly?'

William clearly thought carefully about his elder brother John Joseph's bookshop in Pall Mall, and possibly about his uncle Joseph's business in Bermuda, before replying, 'Not in Piccadilly.'

His father lost the action and was ordered to pay £200 damages. In his preface to the published account of the trial, the successful plaintiff, Nightingale, was good enough to say that although the libel had been dictated by malevolence and a wish to defame, 'I do not, however, impute this spirit to Mr. Stockdale, with whom I could not have had any personal quarrel, and I should much have preferred prosecuting the real author, could I have been furnished with legal evidence to support an action.' Possibly Stockdale had refused to provide the name of the author because of the established rule, that sources were protected by booksellers and printers.

The writer has been unable to find any letter from Stockdale referring to his move in 1809 or 1810, from no.181 to 180 Piccadilly – and his imprint never gave any house number. However, the *Survey of London* and supporting rate books show that he did so. In view of what is now known about his straitened financial circumstances at the time, one might think that his move, after some thirty years at no. 181, was attributable to a desire to save on rent. This was clearly not the reason, for his rent at no. 181 had been £75 a year, while after his move to 180 it was up to £95, so the reason for the move remains a mystery.[14]

If the *New Annual Register* for 1807 cost Stockdale £200 in damages for the libel on Nightingale, at least the issue for 1810, which he published in the following year, secured him a place in the history of printing. In 1807, Friedrich Koenig, the German inventor of the very first printing press operated by steam, entered into a partnership with Thomas Bensley, the printer who

---

[14] *Survey of London*, London: Athlone Press, 1960, 29, 253; rate books in the Westminster City Archives Centre, especially D134.

produced a number of Stockdale's books. 'All the machine had to perform was reduced to a rotary motion, so that it could be moved by the power of steam, and the workman had not to do anything but to put the sheets upon the tympan and to take them off again.'[15]

As the expense of development was considerable, two more printers joined the partnership, George Woodfall and Richard Taylor. Koenig described the success of their efforts: 'After many obstructions and delays, the first printing-machine was completed exactly upon the plan which I have described in the specification of my first patent, which is dated 29 March 1810. It was set to work in April 1811. The sheet (H) of the *New Annual Register* for 1810, "Principal Occurrences", 3000 copies were printed, the first part of a book ever printed with a machine.'[16]

The new technology transformed the printer's art, especially once John Walter had installed Koenig's machines to print his newspaper, *The Times*. A good printer could print about 250 sheets an hour on the traditional hand-press. Koenig's steam machines raised the rate to 800, and by the time Walter started using them, to 1,100 sheets per hour. Printing costs were at once reduced by 25 per cent. In the first issue of *The Times* printed on the new machines, that of November 29, 1814, Walter proudly and accurately stated, 'Our journal of this day presents to the public the practical results of the greatest improvement connected with printing, since the discovery of the art itself.' He was not exaggerating. Stanley Morison, in his classic lecture on 'The Typographic Arts', stated, 'This was the greatest revolution since Gutenberg.'[17] Possibly without appreciating the full significance of what was happening to his *New Annual Register*, for he was not

---

[15] *A. F. Bauer, 1783 bis 1860*, Würzburg: Koenig & Bauer A.G., 1860.

[16] *The Times*, December 8, 1814.

[17] See also, Bowman, W. D., *The Story of The Times*, London: Routledge, 1931, 94; Morison, Stanley, *The Typographic Arts* – Two Lectures, London: Theodore Brun, 1949, 39.

a printer himself, Stockdale had played his small part in 'the greatest improvement' – greatest, that is, until the arrival of the computer.

The account books of Richard Taylor, now in St. Bride Printing Library, show how the sales of the *New Annual Register* dropped off towards the end of Stockdale's life. From the edition for 1804 until the historic issue for 1810, Taylor printed three thousand copies annually for Stockdale. The issue for the year 1811 was limited to two thousand, and those for the next three years were down to 1500 only. Taylor also recorded that Part 3 of the book was on occasion printed by Gillet or Bensley: it was Bensley who shared the printing of the 1810 edition with Taylor.

Taylor's account books contain a number of other indications of Stockdale's financial decline. The first clue is not significant on its own, but fits in with the others. In the years 1806 to 1809, Stockdale was paying his printer thirty guineas a year rent for the storage of the books he had printed and looked after, but from 1810 on the rent was down to twenty guineas annually.

The advantage for a bookseller in paying his printer to store his printed stock for him is obvious: he did not have to fill his shop with books or sheets not immediately required, nor did he need to rent a warehouse for such items. The disadvantages were that printers charged rent and that their warehouses were regularly victims of one of the classic 'enemies of books', fire, with serious consequences not only for them but also for their bookseller clients. Clearly, the more printers a bookseller used, the better the spread of risk, but a bookseller could scarcely expect most-favoured client status from a printer if he used him, say, as one of a dozen only. Granger in 1807 referred to Stockdale having his own warehouse, but even if his Robinson purchase had forced such an expedient on him, he still had some stock at printers' premises.

Both Almon and Stockdale seem to have escaped major disaster as the result of fire, but Stockdale was affected by the fire at the Salisbury Square address of Thomas Gillet, the printer, on July 28, 1810. The premises were destroyed with all the contents, including 'a great amount belonging to Sir Richard Phillips, Mr Stockdale and other booksellers.' The reference was almost certainly to John Stockdale, rather than to his son, who also used Gillet. Stockdale possibly did not lose much, but times were hard enough for him already, without this additional blow. His son, John Joseph, who had only been in business on his own under four years, was more seriously affected, and put out an advertisement soliciting orders because of 'the entire destruction of a great part of his property, almost wholly uninsured, by the late fire in Salisbury Square.'[18]

The fire was also extremely hard on Gillet, as his premises had been destroyed by fire only five years earlier. After that earlier incident, when Gillet had sued Mawman, the successor to Charles Dilly, for the price of printing work done, but later consumed by the fire, he had been met by the defence that a custom of the trade put the loss by fire on the printer. Gillet, who had not only done a great deal of work for John Stockdale by then, but had also stood bail for him when he was charged with assaulting Wright back in 1798, subpoenad Stockdale as one of his witnesses, to disprove the existence of any such custom.[19]

In November 1811, Taylor printed two thousand copies of Volume 2 of Williams's *Justice of the Peace* for 'John Stockdale and other proprietors', and some time later lent the bookseller £300 against the security of this work. It did not sell well and only

---

[18] *Gentleman's Magazine*, 80: 85; John Johnson Collection of Printed Ephemera, Bodleian Library.

[19] *Annual Register*, 49: 455; the subpoena is in the St. Bride Printing Library, Richard Taylor Papers. One of the most serious fires was that of January 1782, which burned down the Leadenhall Street warehouse and home of James Woodmason, the stationer used by Jefferson. All seven of his children died in the blaze. *Laurens Papers*, 16: 340n.

£200 was repaid. More significant is the fact that Taylor entered both the issues for 1813 and 1814 as being for the Trustees of Stockdale. The sad truth was that Stockdale had been obliged to enter into an arrangement with his creditors.

Stockdale owed Taylor a further £695, and only a part of this debt was cleared off after his death on June 21, 1814 at the age of 64. His third son Thomas had died on May 3, but Stockdale will have been spared that sad news, as his son's death was in India. In 1817, his estate managed to pay his outstanding creditors six shillings in the pound, and as late as May 1822, another shilling, making a total of 35 per cent.[20]

It was a sad ending for a man who had pulled himself up by his own bootstraps, had impressed several leading American statesmen, as well as many English authors, and had built up a very good business over his first twenty-five years in Piccadilly. His shop had been one of the hubs of bookselling and publishing in the West End of London. It had also been a port of call for information. Had he not overreached himself, Stockdale might well have ended his days like Almon, a financially successful man. Whatever else may be said about him, John Stockdale is still entitled to be considered as 'the greatest publisher in Piccadilly'. It is highly unlikely, given the current rentals, that any publisher, as opposed to bookseller, will ever attempt to deprive him of that hard-won title.

When one looks back over the highlights of Stockdale's career, it is striking how often he happened to be at the right place at the right time. When Almon gave up his shop with its American links, Stockdale was ready to open his own and to fill the need for a West End bookshop with an interest in American matters. After Henry Laurens emerged from the Tower, Stockdale was there to accommodate him whenever needed. When John Adams needed rooms in London for two months for himself and his son, John Quincy, Stockdale's home was made

---

[20] *Gentleman's Magazine*, 84: 701; 85: 179, 649.

available. *The Times* was launched, then named the *Daily Universal Register*, on January 1, 1785: Stockdale figured in the first day's issue. When Jefferson was worried about an unauthorised English edition of his only book appearing, Stockdale came to his aid, with an offer to publish it for him, at precisely the right moment. At a time when the rights of juries to make the crucial decision in libel cases was in doubt, Stockdale appeared as a defendant in a historic state trial and sensibly instructed Thomas Erskine to defend him. On the famous occasion when the King was insulted and had stones thrown at him, Stockdale was there to arrest the offender – ironically a bookbinder – this time acting as a special constable. When Hester Piozzi needed a new publisher for the new century, 'loyal' Stockdale was ready to help her. During the crucial minutes when Koenig and Bauer's steam printing machine was first tried out on a book, Stockdale was the supplier of the first sheet, for one of his annuals.

John Stockdale clearly made a number of enemies during the course of his career. However, he also demonstrated what hard work and determination could achieve in an occupation that was open to all comers. He is not known today as a publisher of a large number of classic books but he did his share of producing what the public wanted. In all, he contributed some 1500 book and pamphlet titles for the English-speaking world, at a time when men hungered for enlightenment by the printed word, on both sides of the Atlantic. For a man from a humble background, with no formal training for the book trade, this was no mean achievement.

THE UNNECESSARY CRISIS: THE BACKGROUND TO THE PARLIAMENTARY PAPERS ACT 1840

ERIC STOCKDALE*

LORD Campbell stated that *Stockdale* v. *Hansard* would be spoken of in 300 years' time.[1] The writer is unable to wait that long but the 150th anniversary of the Parliamentary Papers Act of 1840 may perhaps justify another look at the background of the litigation that led to the passing of the Act. Constitutional cases often owe their very existence to the character of one or more of the principal protagonists. The stubborn Englishman who knows his rights and is determined to fight for them, no matter how inconvenient for the police, the Home Secretary, the government or Parliament, is the man who is largely responsible for our rich constitutional case-law, as Sir Alan Herbert M.P. amongst others realised.[2] The litigant in question, be he a plaintiff in a civil action or an accused in a criminal case, may be thoroughly rational, bordering on the insane, or somewhere in between. Nearly always he will have a determination that can be understood the better if one knows something of his background. There were three principal actors involved in the saga of *Stockdale* v. *Hansard*, but the defendant, though important, was not one of them.

We shall meet in this article principally the plaintiff, John Joseph Stockdale; next, Lord Denman C.J., whose rulings greatly annoyed many members of Parliament; and finally Sir John Campbell, the Attorney-General, who was for all practical purposes Stockdale's opponent.

JOHN JOSEPH STOCKDALE'S PUBLISHING BACKGROUND

John Joseph Stockdale was born in 1776 at about the time his father, John, started working for the well-known Whig pamphleteer and bookseller, John Almon, at his London bookshop in Piccadilly. His mother was the sister of James Ridgway, who also became a substantial publisher—and a stern critic of his brother-in-law, John Stockdale. Almon was John Wilkes's publisher and biographer and was involved in a number of public law cases, including one of the first reported cases on contempt of court.[3] One of the many powerful people he managed to annoy was Lord Mansfield C.J. John Stockdale

---

* Circuit Judge; Visiting Professor, Queen Mary and Westfield College, University of London.
[1] The Hon. Mrs. Hardcastle (ed.), *Life of John, Lord Campbell* (1881), Vol. 2, p. 114.
[2] See A. P. Herbert's autobiography, *Independent Member* (1970), *Uncommon Law* (1969), and *R.* v. *Graham-Campbell, ex parte Herbert* [1935] 1 K.B. 594.
[3] *R.* v. *Almon* (1765) 97 E.R. 94; and see *R.* v. *Almon* (1770) 98 E.R. 411.

was employed as Almon's shopman or porter, but he was bright enough to learn the trade from his master speedily. There is some evidence to suggest that he managed to divert sufficient of his master's funds to set up on his own, as he did in 1781, when Almon handed over his business to John Debrett. Unlike Almon, John Stockdale was not a writer himself, and unlike Almon he seems to have preferred the Tories, who increasingly used his shop. A number of Almon's customers followed Stockdale to the shop which he set up so close to his former master's that the imprint at both addresses was "Opposite Burlington House, Piccadilly." The booksellers of the day were the publishers, so that a customer could buy his books and pamphlets in the shop and at the same time commission the owner to publish his latest thoughts, whether originally expressed in the House of Commons, at a political meeting or simply to friends or family who would not listen.

Whilst still working for Almon, John Stockdale must have realised how close his master's links were with the American colonists. Benjamin Franklin had made use of Almon's shop and it became the principal source for statements of the case for the colonists. Stockdale was extremely lucky that in his first year on his own, John Adams got in touch with him: as a result of that Stockdale in due course published works by the second, third and sixth presidents of the United States of America. During his two-month visit to England after signing the Peace Treaty in Paris in 1783, John Adams and his son, John Quincy Adams, stayed with the Stockdale family over the bookshop. On Adams's recommendation, Thomas Jefferson also patronised the shop and in 1787 Stockdale published Jefferson's only book, *Notes on the State of Virginia*.[4] Stockdale published a mixed list of works, but political and geographical works were always available at his shop.

Almon had been one of the booksellers who had successfully challenged the claim of Parliament that its privileges included the right to ban the publication of any report of its proceedings.[5] Almon had thereafter published the proceedings of both Houses, under the name of *The Parliamentary Register*. His successor, John Debrett, continued the series until he went bankrupt in 1803, when Stockdale took it over. William Cobbett also published his own reports, *Parliamentary Debates*, and this series was acquired by the Hansard family, who had the advantage over all the other publishers that they were themselves printers, and so did not need to rely on outside printers. The Hansards increasingly obtained printing work direct from Parliament

---

[4] E. Stockdale, "John Stockdale of Piccadilly: Publisher to John Adams and Thomas Jefferson" in R. Myers and M. Harris (eds.), *Author/Publisher Relations During the Eighteenth and Nineteenth Centuries* (1983), p. 63.

[5] J. Almon, *Memoirs of an Eminent Bookseller* (1790), p. 118; P. D. G. Thomas called Almon "the bold pioneer of newspaper reporting" in "Sources for Debates of the House of Commons 1768–1774" (1959) *Bull. of the Inst. of Hist. Research*, Special Supp. No. 4.

and ultimately gave their name to the official reports which continue to this day.

Stockdale was involved in litigation a great deal, often over alleged piracy. The very first issue of the *Daily Universal Register* (now *The Times*) on January 1, 1785, contained an announcement by Stockdale and others, complaining about the fact that a rival had obtained an *ex parte* injunction against them in connection with their edition of Captain Cook's *Voyage*.

Stockdale prospered sufficiently to send his four sons to boarding school in Bedfordshire, so John Joseph was perhaps better equipped for the trade than his father on entry into it, for John had had very little education. In 1789 John Stockdale was prosecuted by the Attorney-General, acting on the instructions of the House of Commons, for having published a pamphlet that was critical of the House for its handling of the Warren Hastings impeachment.[6] Stockdale had the good fortune to secure the services of Thomas Erskine, the future Lord Chancellor, whose closing speech was later described by Lord Brougham as being the finest ever made by an advocate. Erskine complained that the Attorney-General had taken selected passages of the pamphlet out of context, and made the point that anything, including passages from the Bible, could be distorted in that manner. He asked that the whole of the work be considered by the jury. Lord Kenyon C.J. in his summing-up, unlike some earlier judges, acceded to this suggestion, saying: "You have a right to look at the whole book; and if you find it has been garbled, and that the passages selected by the Attorney-General do not bear the sense imputed to them, the man has a right to be acquitted; and God forbid he should be convicted." The jury duly acquitted.

There were a number of repercussions from the case. Edmund Burke, for one, certainly had his enthusiasm for the Warren Hastings impeachment dampened, writing to Philip Francis, "Now for one word on our own affairs. The acquittal of Stockdale is likely to make a bad impression on them. . . . I confess that at last I totally despair, and think of nothing but an honourable retreat from this business."[7] More important was the fact that the outcome of the case contributed to the passing of Fox's Libel Act in 1792. For John Stockdale, the most important task was to raise sufficient money to pay for his defence. One of the steps he took was the publication in 1790 of a full account of the trial, based on Joseph Gurney's shorthand note. Young Stockdale was now 14, and the experience of his father's prosecution by the House of Commons and the Attorney-General, capped by the triumphant acquittal and amending legislation, must

---

[6] *The Whole Proceedings . . . against John Stockdale* (1790).
[7] A. Cobban and R. A. Smith, *The Correspondence of Edmund Burke* (1967), Vol. 6, p. 54.

have made a considerable impression on him—though it was to be
nearly half a century before he attempted to emulate his father's role.
   In 1793 John Joseph, then aged 17, started to work for his father in
the Piccadilly bookshop; he was to remain there for nearly 14 years.
In that year, Lord Loughborough was the new Lord Chancellor and
John Stockdale published his *Observations on the State of the English
Prisons*. Loughborough, who had been Solicitor-General, Attorney-
General and Chief Justice of the Common Pleas, made a number of
suggestions about prisons, including the following:

> "A jail requires as constant inspection as a house of correction, for
> although the judges of jail delivery have an inspection over it, yet they
> have little means of applying any specific redress. The justices must
> therefore undertake this charge by appointing inspectors, who should be
> different from the directors of the house of correction."

More than 40 years were to pass before Parliament provided for the
appointment of inspectors.[8] Two years later, John Stockdale was able
to demonstrate in a sensational manner what a good King's man he
was. As George III was being driven from Buckingham House to the
opening of Parliament, a mob surrounded his carriage, crying out for
bread and peace. A bullet or stone broke a window of the King's carriage. One of the crowd, a bookbinder named Kyd Wake, went
further and called out "No King!" He was promptly arrested by two
special constables, one of whom was Stockdale, who later gave evidence at Wake's trial. Erskine appeared for the defence once more,
but was not so successful as he had been when Stockdale and he had
met in court before: Wake was sentenced to five years' hard labour
and to be pilloried.[9] At the turn of the century, Stockdale published
Retrospection by Hester Piozzi (Dr. Johnson's friend, Mrs. Thrale),
who wrote, "I am pleased that it comes out from his loyal shop."[10]
His reputation for loyalty was noticed by the opposition also, a
matter the bookseller had occasion to regret when Sir Francis Burdett, a near neighbour, lost the Middlesex election in August 1804 by
five votes. Burdett's supporters were not best pleased and alarmed
Stockdale, who wrote an urgent plea for help to Lord Hawkesbury,
the Home Secretary:

> "My Lord, Having reason to believe from the numerous threats of the
> mob, for some time past, but more particularly within the last two hours,
> that my house will very shortly be attacked, I have taken the liberty to
> inform your Lordship thereof and have no doubt that measures will be
> taken for the protection of my family and property."[11]

---

[8] Prisons Act 1835, and see n. 22, *infra*.
[9] *Annual Register*, 1795, Vol. 37, Chronicle p. 37, and 1796, Vol. 38, pp. 6, 17.
[10] A. Hayward (ed. J. H. Lobban), *Dr. Johnson's Mrs. Thrale* (1910), p. 283.
[11] British Library Add. MSS 38, 571, f. 84. Stockdale doubtless recalled with alarm the very similar incidents two years earlier, described by M. Ignatieff, *A Just Measure of Pain* (1978), p. 138.

John Stockdale's business got into grave financial difficulties after this and he was insolvent at the time of his death in 1814. His son William and daughter Mary tried to keep the business going, but John Joseph had left it some years before his father's death. In 1806 John Joseph had set up on his own in Pall Mall. He had had the prudence in 1805 to marry a niece of Philip Box, the Grenville family banker, and he was granted some financial assistance by that influential family. He seems to have fallen out with his father at some stage, judging from a letter he wrote to the future Duke of Wellington in 1808. Young Stockdale had persuaded Sir Arthur Wellesley to let him have some of his papers relating to the Convention of Cintra, for which the General was being criticised. In due course John Joseph produced a pamphlet about the Convention, but while preparing it he had written to the General: "Owing to the accidental direction of your packet to my father, it has not yet reached me, and even scruples are made to let me have it—very unhandsomely, I must say. Lest a difficulty should be made, do me the favour to let me have an order for the delivery of it."[12]

At about the time that John Joseph and the General were communicating with each other, the General also made contact with an ambitious courtesan, Harriette Wilson. Wellesley was not the only military man to get involved with a potentially troublesome bedfellow: the Duke of York, the Commander-in-Chief, was much in the public gaze. Gwyllym Lloyd Wardle, a Whig M.P., had revealed that the Duke's mistress, Mary Ann Clarke, had been taking money from Army officers with a promise that she would intercede on their behalf at an appropriate moment. The grand old Duke of York acted decisively: he changed mistresses. Mary Ann Clarke quickly arranged for 18,000 copies of her memoirs to be printed. The government bought them all up for £10,000 plus an annuity for the author and her daughter.[13] John Joseph published a criticism of Major Wardle for his betrayal of the Duke, and much later claimed that he had advised the Duke about the memoirs of Mary Ann Clarke. That claim may not have been true, but the incident undoubtedly left an indelible impression on the bookseller.

John Stockdale had been a member of the Moravian church, but John Joseph demonstrated very clearly that he was a militant Protestant with a loathing of Roman Catholicism. It doubtless gave him great pleasure to publish tracts "exposing" various Catholic plots. Some of his early publications were printed for him by the Hansards. His intense bigotry led to numerous conflicts. In 1810 John Joseph published young Percy Bysshe Shelley's second novel, *St. Irvyne or*

---

[12] Letter in the possession of Robin Myers.
[13] P. Berry, *By Royal Appointment* (1970).

the Rosecrucian, but he soon decided that the young poet was in danger of going to the devil, passed that opinion on to Shelley's father when he called at the shop, and made it impossible for the author-publisher relationship to continue. John Joseph did, however, have one outstanding success at this time. He published a weekly, *Covent Garden Journal*, in which he described the rioting at the Opera House, caused by the increase in prices. He later published the parts in two volumes that were favourably reviewed in the *Gentleman's Magazine* for 1810. The review contained the comment, "He is a young bookseller of great promise, and has hopes of being Lord Mayor." This praise came in May and perhaps marked the high point of his career. On July 28, almost all his stock was destroyed in a fire at his printer's. Thereafter John Joseph was never a proper publisher: his fortunes went steadily downhill, with minor rests on the way. Before his battle with the House of Commons led to his final incarceration in Newgate, he managed to land in the Clare Street "sponging house" for debtors in 1819, in the Fleet in 1826 (a bad year for many booksellers), in the Whitecross Street prison in 1830 and in the King's Bench prison—where Almon had regularly visited Wilkes—in 1834.

In 1819, John Joseph (who will from now on be called Stockdale) demonstrated in a graphic way that he had a very thick skin. In the previous year he had published a poll book showing how everyone had voted in the Westminster election, and in 1819 he published a second edition which differed only because of a bizarre addition. Stockdale added a selection of the abusive and threatening letters that he had been sent as a result of his original announcement that he intended to reveal how everyone had cast his vote. One such letter came from a knacker, who wrote: "Hiff yoo poublishis hour names has woted for Burditt, dam my blud hiff i wont nok yoor branes hout the fust time i ketchis yoo." Another letter accused Stockdale of robbery and plunder, adding, "Why, a few days ago, at a meeting in the vestry-room of Paddington Church were you induced so furiously to resist a monthly inspection of the parish overseers' accounts?" Stockdale was indeed interesting himself in parish matters in Paddington, where he then lived. On April 13, 1819, a man called Thatcher asked him at a parish meeting whether he intended to stand for the office of churchwarden. "Certainly," replied the bookseller. "Then it is my painful duty to tell this vestry," said Thatcher, "that the money is not safe in your hands. The parish has been robbed of £2500 already, and as you now have two sets of creditors to whom you have to pay a dividend shortly, it will not be advisable for the parish to trust so much money in your hands." John Hunt was present and reported those remarks in his famous periodical, *Examiner*, on April 19.

Stockdale responded with an action for libel, which Hunt obligingly reported on December 13. The defence was one of justification and the evidence called in support of that plea dealt in great detail with the plaintiff's financial difficulties. Among other witnesses was a sheriff's officer who told the court that he had arrested Stockdale for debt as recently as February 23 and had lodged him in the lock-up house in Clare Street. He was followed by the overseer of the Paddington parish, who recounted that in 1817 he had had to distrain on the plaintiff's goods for the poor rate of £1. 14s., after repeated and ineffectual applications for payment. At this point the Chief Justice of the Common Pleas asked Serjeant Lens whether the plaintiff intended to persist with his claim. After a brief consultation, Stockdale abandoned it. Unfortunately, the danger of a defence of justification succeeding was not something that registered adequately with Stockdale.

By 1825 Stockdale's business affairs were in no healthier state, but in that year came what he clearly hoped would be the answer to his prayers. He published *Harriette Wilson's Memoirs*, and these sold like hot cakes. Harriette had certainly had some distinguished clients, including the future Duke and Prime Minister, Wellesley, and the future Lord Chancellor, Henry Brougham.[14] Shortly before publication, Stockdale wrote to the Duke of Wellington, drawing attention to the fact that the impending work would contain "various anecdotes of your Grace which it would be more desirable to withhold, at least such is my opinion. I have stopped the press for the moment." Harriette wrote in her memoirs that the Iron Duke had replied to her publisher "to menace a prosecution if such trash be published," but she went on to ask, "What trash, my dear Wellington?" Stockdale wrote once more to the Duke with the modest suggestion that omitting all references to his Grace "would diminish the interest in the work, and its consequent produce, perhaps not less than £5000." He added that the details of the manuscript could not "fail to give it an interest and circulation exceeding all which was anticipated of the suppressed Memoirs of Mary Ann Clarke." The Duke's reply is immortal: *Publish and be damned!* Unfortunately there is no written evidence that those were the precise words of the curse, but Stockdale did publish with details of the Duke's indiscretions, and he certainly was damned. Unlike the Duke's indiscretions, those of Henry Brougham were omitted from the publication. The explanation for the omission has been produced by Kenneth Bourne: the future Lord Chancellor paid the blackmail price demanded by the author, as his correspondence still shows.[15]

The first person to sue Stockdale successfully in respect of the

---

[14] E. Longford, *Wellington: The Years of the Sword* (1971), p. 209; K. Bourne, *The Blackmailing of the Chancellor* (1976). J. J. Stockdale's 1831 edition of the memoirs contains his own account of the publication.
[15] See Bourne, *supra* n. 14; University College, London, Brougham MSS.

memoirs was one Blore, whose case came on very speedily in the King's Bench before Abbott C.J. on July 1, 1825. The jury awarded £300 damages. On November 12, Henry Brougham, no less, appeared for Stockdale to ask the Chief Justice and a colleague to set the award aside.[16] The Chief Justice asked, "Pray, Mr. Brougham, what was it that I ought to have done at the trial which I did not do?" The great advocate found himself in great difficulties in answering, so Blore kept his judgment. The next plaintiff, Fisher, was awarded £700, prompting *Bell's Life in London* to publish a poem on May 8, 1826, that had Stockdale lamenting:

"I like it not: some speedy plan
Must be adopted, or, by Heaven!
Three hundred first, and after, seven,
Will take away all sort of profit.
You laugh! but I am certain of it,
'Twill take the gold, as has been said,
Entirely off the gingerbread."

This was fair comment: in September and October Stockdale spent seven weeks in the Fleet for non-payment of Fisher's damages. He was not too uncomfortable in prison. One of his letters to his wife contained a passage not often seen in prison correspondence: "At seven o'clock, when I went to open my door, I found that some trick had been played with the lock, so that I could not undo it, and was obliged to send for a smith."

Another matter which helped to de-gild the gingerbread was the piracy of Harriette Wilson's book by other booksellers, including one Onwhyn. Stockdale sued Onwhyn and once again secured Brougham's services.[17] Again the case came on before Abbott C.J., who knew the work as he had tried Blore's action. He upheld the defence submission that the book was so immoral that the courts would not afford it any protection, stating firmly: "I want no authority for pronouncing such a judicial opinion." Brougham called the defence the most immoral that he had ever heard, but his opponent, James Scarlett (soon to be Attorney-General), neatly demonstrated that a similar plea had been raised in the courts a short while before. Stockdale's 18-year-old son was cross-examined about the action that Poplett, the printer of the book, had brought against his father for the cost of printing. The young man could not recall what his father's defence had been, although the case had been heard only six weeks earlier. "Well, perhaps I can assist you," said Scarlett, misusing the word "assist" in the traditional manner of the cross-examiner. "Was it not that the work was so immoral and licentious that labour bestowed upon it could not be recovered at law?" The witness conceded

---

[16] *Annual Register*, 1825, p. 13; *The Times*, November 14, 1825.
[17] *Stockdale* v. *Onwhyn* (1826) 108 E.R. 65.

that something like that had been pleaded and that the plea had led to his father's succeeding in defeating his printer's claim. Stockdale was livid when he lost, protesting that the defence against Poplett had been raised without his instructions by his counsel, Serjeant Wilde. He had wanted to win on the merits, he claimed.

It is perhaps a little surprising that Brougham should have appeared twice for Stockdale, and that he should always have treated both the bookseller and Harriette Wilson with great courtesy and patience. The Bar's cab-rank rule does not afford a sufficient explanation. The truth is probably to be found in the combination of Brougham's ambition and his nervousness about the fact that the revelation of his indiscretions with Harriette would rule out high office. The truth might well have made it difficult for him to become Lord High Chancellor and Keeper of the King's Conscience—although if the King in question were to be one of the reprobate sons of George III, the conscience might then have been in appropriate hands.

In 1830 Stockdale applied to the trustees of the Royal Literary Fund for assistance, stating that he was in prison for debt once more, this time in the Whitecross Street prison in the City. His request was ignored but he tried again in 1833 enclosing a copy of his new penny publication. This appeal was also ignored. Stockdale also sent a copy of an advertisement for his new publication, *The Probe*, to Brougham, by then Lord Chancellor and, yes, Keeper of the King's Conscience.[18] He sent him a number of other documents, including a petition to the "Lords of Parliament for impartial Justice"; a petition to Brougham as Lord Chancellor, seeking to reopen his old case against Onwhyn, in which Brougham had acted for him; and, rather more sensibly, proposals for reform of the law relating to imprisonment for debt.

LORD DENMAN'S FIRST ENCOUNTERS WITH STOCKDALE

On February 10, 1834, Stockdale made his first appearance in the court of Denman C.J. Denman was perhaps best known for having, with Wilde and others, assisted Brougham in the defence of Queen Caroline in 1820. It was his unfortunate reference at the end of his speech to the woman taken in adultery, that had led to the immortal rhyme:

> "Most gracious queen we thee implore
> To go away and sin no more;
> Or if that effort be too great,
> To go away at any rate."

The Chief Justice was to get to know Stockdale rather better in the

---

[18] Archives of the Royal Literary Fund; University College, London, Brougham MSS 46, 105.

years 1837–39 when dealing with his litigation with Hansard. He
referred to Stockdale's later case as "the most important event of my
life, and that on which my future reputation must mainly depend."[19]
In 1834 Stockdale stood before Denman charged with extortion of a
kind closely resembling that connected with the Wilson disclosures.
Sir James Scarlett appeared for the prosecution on this occasion. In
the dock with Stockdale was a man called Mountprivat, who was married to the sister of the Countess Cornwallis. Stockdale wrote to Earl
Cornwallis saying that he had interesting documents relating to his
Countess that he intended publishing, unless he received an intim-
ation that would render such a step unnecessary. Stockdale tried his
hand at advocacy at the conclusion of the evidence. The *Morning
Post* reported next day: "The defendant Stockdale addressed the jury
during four hours, and introduced a variety of topics, attacking private characters and persons not before the court. His defence was
that he had taken up the case of his co-defendant from motives of
charity." The jury was uncharitable enough to doubt the latter point
and duly convicted. The defendant was sentenced by Denman to a
year's imprisonment, which he served in the King's Bench prison in
Southwark. Stockdale's four-hour harangue of the jury was one of
the matters justifying the comment: "Stockdale's fluency, with the
tongue or the pen, can only be described as appalling. On the faintest
pretext, or no pretext at all, he ran into thousands of words; closely
printed pages, or unquenchable oratory."[20]

Stockdale's departure from prison at the end of the year was also
attended by elements of farce. The story came to light when he
appeared in front of Denman once again on December 3, 1835, this
time as a plaintiff.[21] Stockdale was suing the prison authorities for
wrongful imprisonment, claiming that he had been detained after the
expiry of his sentence. The clerk to the Marshal said in evidence that
he had told Stockdale he could apply for remission of prison fees, that
is, fees for commitment and discharge, and also for chamber-rent.
The prisoner had declined to make any such application and would
not leave the prison after the expiry of his sentence. The witness said
that he had told Stockdale that it was a pity he would not leave, and
continued: "The plaintiff said: 'I shall not leave; I have written to the
Chief Justice and shall not leave until I get his answer.' " Two days
later Stockdale had said that he had not heard from Denman and so
would take his leave. The witness had indignantly pointed out to him,
"Why, the doors of the prison have been open to you ever since the
10th."

The Chief Justice ruled that whilst the prisoner could have been

[19] J. Arnould, *Memoirs of Thomas, First Lord Denman* (1873), Vol. 2, p. 45.
[20] A. Thirkell, *The Fortunes of Harriette* (1936), p. 223.
[21] *Stockdale v. Chapman* (1835) 173 E.R. 162; (1836) 111 E.R. 845.

40 *Public Law*

legally detained for rent, there was no justification for detaining him for his fees. Accordingly he found that Stockdale had been wrongly imprisoned for a while after the unjustified demand. The jury awarded £70 damages. Stockdale must have been delighted to win for a change. It may have been this victory which encouraged him to embark on his historic litigation before the same judge in the following year. Despite the various court findings against him, Stockdale was clearly still convinced of his innocence of any evil motive or action. When he wrote to Brougham a few days after his release from prison, he signed himself, "J. J. Stockdale, late of the King's Bench prison, but neither conspirator nor extortioner."

THE INSPECTORS OF PRISONS' REPORT

In 1835 Parliament made two important decisions. If either one had not been made, the case of *Stockdale* v. *Hansard* could not have come about. The first decision was the acceptance of the major recommendations of the House of Lords select committee on gaols and houses of correction, chaired by the Duke of Richmond. As a result, the Prisons Act 1835 provided for the beginnings of a national prison system, including a power for the Home Secretary to appoint inspectors of prisons for the first time.[22] The inspectors appointed would be required to report annually to the Home Secretary, and he in turn would inform Parliament in the usual way. The second decision was that made relating to the publication of parliamentary papers. Joseph Hume and other M.P.s had been concerned for some time to reduce the cost of supplying printed papers that were not made available to the public, and also anxious to ensure that the public should know what was happening in and around Westminster (within limits, of course). In 1835 Parliament finally decided that its printed papers should be put on sale to the general public.

Newgate prison was inspected immediately by one of the two newly-appointed Inspectors of Prisons for the Home District, Whitworth Russell, who as chaplain of the Millbank penitentiary had given evidence to the House of Lords select committee. A later inspector commented on Russell's intensive pastoral care in Millbank, "The prayers, expositions, and genuflexions were more in keeping with a monastery than a gaol full of criminals." Russell was a complex cleric, who later lost heavily on investments and then committed suicide.[23] During his inspection of Newgate, Russell was appalled to find what he regarded as an obscene work, and his comments duly went into the report presented by him and his colleague, William Crawford. The Home Secretary placed the report before

---

[22] E. Stockdale, "A Short History of Prison Inspection in England" (1983) 23 J.J.Crim. 209.
[23] E. Stockdale, "The Rise of Joshua Jebb, 1837–1850" (1976) 16 B.J.Crim. 164.

The Unnecessary Crisis   41

Parliament and it was published with the following historic passage in it:

> "We also found several books: amongst them Guthrie's Grammar, a song book, the Keepsake Annual for 1836, and the —— by ——, 18 plates, published by Stockdale, 1827. This last is a book of a most disgusting nature, and the plates are obscene and indecent in the extreme. It was claimed as his property by a prisoner named ——, and was kept in the cupboard without any attempt at concealment."[24]

It will have been noted that the report carefully omitted the title of the work and the names of author and owner: the only name mentioned was that of the publisher. Any inspector other than Russell might have made a few inquiries before reporting as he did. The City aldermen who were responsible for Newgate were indignant about Russell's comment and stated:

> "Upon reading the Report of the Inspectors . . . we were prepared to have met with a publication very different from that which was handed to us, as being the identical book referred to by the Inspectors. We found that it bore the title of 'The Generative System of John Roberton,' and that it was dedicated by permission to the late Dr. Baillie. It appeared, on a careful examination, to be a scientific book; the plates to be purely anatomical, calculated only to attract the attention of persons connected with surgical science, and we learnt from Mr.Cope [W. W. Cope, Keeper of the Prison] that it belonged to the before-named prisoner, Foulger, who had been a captain of a whaler, and had devoted himself to such studies."[25]

The inspectors were asked to comment on the views of the aldermen. They informed the Secretary of State that they adhered to their original description of the book, adding: "We also applied to several medical booksellers, who all gave it the same character. They described it as 'one of Stockdale's obscene books.' " This comment was also published by the Hansards on the orders of the Commons.

Was the book obscene? The answer is as unimportant as that to the classic question, "Was there a snail in the ginger-beer bottle?" but perhaps a short discussion is justified. We have seen what the aldermen thought. The Treasury Solicitor's views are clear from his brief to counsel, which also indicates the possibility that not everyone was looking at the same edition of the book. After referring to the aldermanic view, he wrote:

> "The absurdity of this commentary will be best proved to the jury by reference to the several editions of the work itself. The identical copy found in the hands of Foulger, the edition of 1827, is not forthcoming, nor can any copy with the same year's title page be found in London after diligent search. Several copies however from the same type sheets with different title pages and different plates will be produced and iden-

[24] Parliamentary Papers, 1836, Vol. 35, p. 7.
[25] Parliamentary Papers, 1836, Vol. 42, p. 235. The inspectors' comments are at p. 284.

42   *Public Law*

tified by Mr. Cox, the printer, as sheets, all but the title pages and plates, printed by him for the plaintiff Stockdale."[26]

The British Library has a copy of the 1824 edition in which Stockdale, using his pseudonym Thomas Little, wrote that his own additions had been "confined to some new plates." The book does indeed look like a bona fide medical book, but the half dozen additional plates, whilst not obscene by modern standards, look as though they were added to appeal to the non-scientific reader. There appears to be no valid reason for the additions. In due course a special jury was to uphold the Attorney-General's plea of justification, so that jury seems to have been satisfied that the work was obscene by the standards of the day.

Stockdale sued the Hansard family who had published the inspectors' report, claiming £500 damages for libel, and in October 1836 Park J. assigned John Curwood and Thomas Burton Howard as counsel and attorney for the plaintiff, who was suing as a poor person. The defendants had notified the Speaker of the House of Commons when sued, as they regularly printed for the House, and the Attorney-General thereafter appeared for the defendants. That post was then held by Sir John Campbell, later to be Chief Justice and Lord Chancellor—and a considerable author. At this stage of his career, Campbell was just about to have his pamphlet, *Letter to the Right Hon. Lord Stanley on the Law of Church Rates*, published by the firm founded by Stockdale's uncle, James Ridgway. Campbell threw himself into the fray with the utmost zeal in due course, but at first he was not unduly concerned, for he was confident that the court would uphold the defendants' pleas that the orders of the Commons constituted a sufficient answer, and that the words complained of were justified in any event. He probably felt that Lord Denman, the Chief Justice of the King's Bench, as a former House of Commons man and former Attorney-General, would share his views on the "undoubted" privileges of Parliament.

Lord Denman Shocks the Attorney-General

Much to Campbell's surprise, Denman summed up to the jury in Stockdale's favour on the constitutional point at the first trial in February 1837, saying:

> "I entirely disagree from the law laid down by the learned counsel for the defendant. I am not aware of the existence in this country of any body whatever that can privilege any servant of theirs to publish libels of any individual. Whether arrangements may be made between the House of Commons and any publisher in their employ, I am of opinion, that the publisher who publishes that in his public shop, and especially for

[26] P.R.O. TS 11/158.

The Unnecessary Crisis   43

> money, which may be injurious, and possibly ruinous to any one of the
> King's subjects, must answer in a court of justice to that subject if he
> challenge him for a libel, and I wish to say so emphatically and distinctly,
> because I think that if, upon the first opportunity that arose in a court of
> justice for questioning that point, it were left unsatisfactorily explained,
> the judge who sat there might become an accomplice in the destruction
> of the liberties of the country, and expose every individual who lives in it
> to a tyranny that no man ought to submit to."

The jury followed the clear direction of the Chief Justice and found
for the plaintiff on that point. Hansard's diary reveals that there was a
certain amount of confusion on the part of the jury about the second
defence. The jury first of all awarded the plaintiff a farthing damages,
stating that they were not unanimous about the book being disgusting, although they were all agreed that it was both indecent and
obscene. The Chief Justice not unreasonably said that he could not
understand that reasoning. The jury conferred a short while and then
found for the defendants on justification, so Stockdale did not even
get his farthing.[27]

Campbell later complained:

> "I relied upon a plea of justification that the book was obscene, contend-
> ing at the same time that the authority of the House of Commons was, at
> all events, a defence. The jury found the special plea in my favour, and
> the judge might easily have avoided giving any opinion upon the ques-
> tion of privilege, in which case it would have quietly gone off to rest. But
> he chose to deliver a strong tirade against the House of Commons for
> ordering to be published what might be injurious to the character of
> others, and a peremptory opinion that their authority did not amount to
> any defence."[28]

Campbell and some of his parliamentary colleagues, notably Serjeant Wilde, soon to be Solicitor-General and eventually Lord Chancellor (as Lord Truro), were gravely disturbed by Denman's ruling,
and so nine days after the trial another select committee was set up,
this time on the publication of printed papers.[29] The very good point
was made by a committee member that it might be as well to let sleeping dogs lie, as Stockdale had not succeeded. As it happened, Stockdale was not prepared to adopt such a course, bought a copy of the
inspectors' comments on the aldermen's views, and started his second
action for libel against the Hansards. Also, Campbell and his colleagues on the committee felt strongly enough about Denman's ruling
to publish a report asserting the privilege of the Commons to publish
what they thought fit, and insisting on the immunity of any servant of
the House. The full House adopted the report on May 30, 1837.

---

[27] 3 St.Tr. (N.S.) 723; P. and G. Ford, *Luke Greaves Hansard: His Diary, 1814–1841* (1962),
p. 168.
[28] Hardcastle, *supra*, n. 1, p. 97.
[29] Parliamentary Papers, 1837, Vol. 13, p. 97: this volume includes some documents relating to
the first trial in February 1837: p. 167.

44 *Public Law*

The second action eventually came on in April 1839 before Denman, sitting with Littledale, Patteson and Coleridge JJ., but without a jury. This time Campbell was determined to win on the constitutional point. In August 1837, as the Treasury Solicitor's papers show, he had written, "I begin to feel some anxiety about the argument in Stockdale v. Hansard. Of course I must argue the case myself. But I should wish to have some effective assistance. This I can hardly expect from any silk-gowned colleagues or even from Wightman [Treasury counsel]." A week later he added, "We must find some person such as I described to you either in or out of London." As his autobiographical notes show, Campbell did a tremendous amount of preparation for the case, and without much assistance. Curwood in opening the case for the plaintiff stated, "The question is, whether the imperial majesty of the law should bow to the decision of the House of Commons." He was in the happy position of being able to rely on Denman's earlier ruling.

Campbell addressed the court for 16 hours over a period of three days. He dealt with every case which might support the Commons and their privileges, but first he dealt with the importance of the case and Stockdale's lack of merits.

> "My Lords, my learned friend, Mr. Curwood, has addressed to your feelings a very eloquent and a very affecting appeal. My Lords, he has expressed his great anxiety in approaching such a subject; what, then, must be my anxiety? He represents Mr. Stockdale, who, I must say, without at all travelling out of this record, can hardly have any object, except to gratify a morbid love of notoriety. The result to Mr. Stockdale is of no importance; he could not expect, I apprehend, if he were to succeed, more than a farthing damages; and costs, from the manner in which he sues, must be of small importance to him either in the event of success or failure. My Lords, I represent here the House of Commons of the United Kingdom, who are called before an inferior tribunal for making public that which they thought essential for the discharge of their legislative functions—for exercising a privilege which they have enjoyed from ancient times—long before the Revolution—a privilege which is recognized by the Bill of Rights, and which since the Revolution has never been questioned by any one but Mr. Stockdale."

One of the odd features of the case was that Brougham, by then ex-Chancellor, sat in court and chipped in occasionally to make a point during Campbell's submissions. He was neither expelled nor told to keep quiet.[30] The court reserved judgment until the end of May, but then unanimously declared the law to be as stated by the Chief Justice in the first trial. As Campbell had decided that the alternative plea of justification should not be argued, judgment was entered for the plaintiff for damages to be assessed—and a jury in the following month fixed them at £100 with £1 costs.

---

[30] Parliamentary Papers, 1839, Vol. 43, p. 435.

Campbell went straight from court to the House of Commons, where he indignantly reported the Chief Justice's ruling that "the courts of law have supreme jurisdiction respecting all parliamentary privilege." He later wrote: "There was no resolution I could have proposed—if it had been at once to commit Lord Denman and the other judges of the Queen's Bench to the Tower—which would not have been carried by acclamation. But I advised them to set an example of forbearance and moderation." He also advised that yet another select committee should be appointed, and that was done. In a letter to his brother written before the judgment was delivered, Campbell made an extraordinary comment about the judges: "Then I had the misfortune of addressing Denman, he being vehemently against me. Out of hatred to the reformed House, the other judges, as Tories, were all strongly inclined to agree with him. Brougham and Lyndhurst, ex-Chancellors, coalescing, came in to back Denman." He added, "It was a most memorable case, and will be quoted three hundred years hence, if the British Constitution last so long."[31] The judges were certainly aware of the hostility of the majority in the Commons. One of the judges involved, Coleridge, who was also to become Chief Justice, later wrote: "I would not retire a step I have taken. One thing, however, does mortify me, and that is the public apathy in a cause which touches English Freedom so nearly. I fancy the Commons might have sent us to Newgate, and the world would have risen, dined, and gone to bed with much the same complacence."[32] Coleridge may have been overstating the degree of public apathy. There was probably considerable support for the judgments and opposition to the claims of the Commons majority. Peel's biographer, Norman Gash, has pointed out: "Outside the House it was clear that the legal profession in general and a majority of the peers, including Wellington, were equally ranged against them."[33]

Campbell and the House of Commons decided to accept defeat on this occasion and to pay any damages and costs "under the special circumstances of the case." The decision was taken that future actions would not be defended but that anyone offending against the resolution of the House on its privileges should be dealt with by way of contempt sanctions. Stockdale's response to these decisions may be guessed by the attentive reader: he sued Hansard for a third time in respect of another copy of the inspectors' report. Judgment was entered in default and a sheriff's jury was summoned to assess the damages. These were assessed at £600 and a writ of execution was issued to the Sheriff of Middlesex (two men shared the office).

---

[31] Hardcastle, *supra*, n. 1, pp. 113–114.
[32] E. H. Coleridge, *Life and Correspondence of John Duke, Lord Coleridge* (1904), Vol. 1, p. 74.
[33] N. Gash, *Sir Robert Peel* (1972), p. 244. Gash also makes the point that it was probably Peel's example that helped to keep the debates on a non-party basis.

46   *Public Law*

THE AFTERMATH OF THE LITIGATION

The Sheriffs duly seized Hansard's presses and raised £695 on a sale
to a builder called Winsland. Hansards later petitioned the House of
Commons for relief and stated that they had informed the Sheriffs'
bailiff that they had not been able to find a better purchaser. This was
true in one sense: the helpful builder was secretly buying the presses
back for the Hansards, who presumably felt by now that all was fair in
war with Stockdale, even if it meant deceiving their best customer,
Parliament. The Sheriffs were reluctant to pass the proceeds over to
Stockdale, who called on them to show cause. On January 11, 1840,
Denman once again asserted the supremacy of the courts.[34] The
Chief Justice said:

> "What is to prevent him from obtaining the fruits of that execution?
> Nothing that I am able to perceive. I infer, from the resolutions brought
> before us, that the House of Commons disapproves of our judgment in
> the former case between these parties, and I deeply lament it; but the
> opinion of the House on a legal point, in whatever manner communi-
> cated, is no ground for arresting the law, or preventing the operation of
> the Queen's writs in behalf of every one of her subjects who sues in her
> courts."

Campbell later wrote:

> "If the damages had been levied and paid over to the party before the
> meeting of Parliament, the privileges of the House would have been
> gone by such a precedent. This would have been the result had Parlia-
> ment not met till the usual time in the beginning of February. I made
> representation on the subject, and a Cabinet was called, which I
> attended. Some were swayed by the inconvenience of facing a trouble-
> some assembly prematurely, but Lord John Russell, ever eager for the
> dignity of the House of Commons, and regardless of personal labour,
> took my side, and the meeting of the two Houses was fixed for the 16th
> of January."[35]

On that day, Russell asked the House to deal with Hansard's petition
and the Stockdale problem as a matter of urgency before the Queen's
Speech was read. The House agreed and ordered the successful plaintiff to attend next day.

On January 17, 1840, Stockdale appeared at the bar of the House
and was examined by Campbell, who asked him whether the jury at
the first trial had been a special one. Stockdale replied: "That I really
don't know, but I do know that the Lord Mayor and Court of Aldermen have stated that the book was strictly a professional book, and
that neither the book itself nor the plates were obscene." In answer
to further questioning he admitted that he had been aware of the
resolutions of the House about its privileges when starting his third

---

[34] *Stockdale* v. *Hansard* (1840) 113 E.R. 411.
[35] Hardcastle, *supra*, n. 1, p. 127.

action. "And that it would be a breach of the privileges of the House to question its power to order such a publication?" the Attorney-General asked. The answer sealed Stockdale's fate: "Yes; but from my own reading and my acquaintance with the great statesmen of other times, I knew that the House did not possess that power." Shortly afterwards he was asked to withdraw and Sir Robert Peel drew attention to the letter Stockdale had written to Hansard on August 27, 1839, which began: "The Commons, in Parliament, has usurped a tyrannic despotism, and having, with the reckless audacity characteristic of all vulgar assemblies or mobs . . . . . . " Stockdale was recalled and did not deny being the author of that letter. Lord John Russell moved that his bringing the third action was contempt and breach of privilege, and the House voted 249 to 100 in favour of the motion. Russell then moved for the contemnor's committal and that motion was carried by 239 votes to 135. By what may be called an act of poetic justice, Stockdale was duly taken to Newgate, the source of all the bother!

The Sheriffs were ordered by the House to restore the money in their possession to the printers of the House, but they refused to do so in view of the ruling of the Chief Justice, so they were also committed to custody by the House. It was one thing for a disreputable publisher to be locked up, but a committal of the Sheriffs for obeying an order of the Chief Justice was another matter. A crisis of major proportions was looming up. Campbell was acutely aware of the dilemma facing the House, and later recalled:

> "Next came a proceeding which placed me in a most difficult position, and the public never knew the danger which existed of a convulsion unexampled in our history. The sheriffs sued out a writ of Habeas Corpus directed to the Serjeant-at-Arms, commanding him to produce before the Court of Queen's Bench the Sheriffs of Middlesex, alleged to be illegally in custody, with the cause of their detention. Wilde, the Solicitor-General, was strong for refusing to make any return to the writ, and for setting the Court of Queen's Bench at defiance. Had I concurred in this opinion, it certainly would have been acted upon. The consequences would have been that the Serjeant-at-Arms, even with the mace in his hand, would have been sent to Newgate by the Court of Queen's Bench. The House must have retaliated by committing the judges. The Crown would then have had to determine on which side the army should be employed, and for a time we must have lived under a military government."[36]

Fortunately both Campbell and Denman realised that each side had to pull back from the brink. Campbell produced the prisoners and Denman returned them to the custody of the House, saying that he could not go behind the affidavit which proved they were imprisoned under parliamentary privilege. Campbell later wrote of:

36 *Ibid.* p. 129.

"the practice which I had the honour to introduce in the case of the Sheriffs of Middlesex, arising out of the famous case of *Stockdale* v. *Hansard*, of returning to the *habeas corpus* in general words a commitment for *breach of privilege*—which is allowed, on all hands, entirely to oust the jurisdiction of the Common Law Courts."[37]

The Sheriffs remained in custody for a short time, and for good measure—exasperated by the commencement of a fourth and a fifth action—the House also committed Stockdale's attorney and two of his clerks. Stockdale managed to irritate the House one last time by petitioning for the release of the latter in terms found, by the majority of the Commons, to be insolent.[38]

The Duke of Wellington now makes his final appearance in our story. According to Campbell, the Duke proved to be "the great obstacle to a settlement" of the problems caused by Stockdale. He was sure that the sale of libels must be unlawful, doubtless taking the view that anyone who published them deserved to be damned: no injury without damnation. Eventually the Duke gave way and so the road was clear for the passing of the Parliamentary Papers Act 1840 which, as Campbell wrote with considerable relief, "secured to the two Houses of Parliament the right to publish what they please without the control of any court of law." Parliament had finally managed to put an end to John Joseph Stockdale's actions.

The crisis could have been averted on a number of occasions. Had Whitworth Russell been a little more tolerant, the report on Newgate might never have contained a mention of the book in question. Had Stockdale's name been omitted from the printed version of that report, he could not have sued. Had the Attorney-General been content to rely on justification, Stockdale would have been stopped in his tracks. Perhaps if Lord Denman had toned down his comments on parliamentary claims of privilege, Campbell and his colleagues in the House of Commons would have been less militant. Stockdale was not heard of again: he did not manage to stage any comeback and died in 1847, the year in which the two prison inspectors for the Home District died. Crawford died while on an official visit to Pentonville and Russell shot himself on a visit to Millbank penitentiary. At least Stockdale had the benefit of dying outside prison at Bushey in Hertfordshire.

Stockdale was clearly a rogue, but without rogues like him our rich constitutional law would be the poorer. In fairness to Stockdale, one should perhaps consider whether the crisis he provoked was an unnecessary one. At some stage, it might well be argued, someone had to challenge the claim of the Commons to be able, in effect, to

---

[37] John, Lord Campbell, *Lives of the Chief Justices of England* (1874), Vol. 3, p. 48.
[38] *Hansard's Parliamentary Debates*, 3rd series. Vol. 52 (1840), 1257. This volume contains numerous references to the Stockdale problem.

legislate on its own. Keir and Lawson have pointed out: "Never in fact since *Stockdale* v. *Hansard* has the House of Commons refused to admit the jurisdiction of the courts when matters of Privilege arose. It has thus by implication recognized that the nature and extent of parliamentary Privilege are only such as the law allows."[39] In view of all that we now know about John Joseph Stockdale's character, it is difficult to feel at all sympathetic to him, but we should perhaps accord a measure of gratitude to the man who made it possible for the courts to test the extent of that right claimed by the Commons.[40] *

---

[39] D. L. Keir and F. H. Lawson, *Cases in Constitutional Law* (6th ed., 1979), p. 256.

[40] The State Trials Volume cited in n. 27 contains the fullest account of the various rounds of the contest discussed above. See also the discussion in, *e.g.* E. C. S. Wade and A. W. Bradley, *Constitutional and Administrative Law* (10th ed., 1985), pp. 216, 221; G. Wilson, *Cases and Materials in Constitutional and Administrative Law* (2nd ed., 1976), p. 238; O. Hood Phillips and P. Jackson, *Leading Cases in Constitutional and Administrative Law* (6th ed., 1988), p. 65; Erskine May, *Treatise on the Law . . . of Parliament* (21st ed., 1989), pp. 150–154.

* A further article marking the 150th anniversary of the Parliamentary Papers Act 1840 will appear in the Summer issue. By Patricia M. Leopold of the University of Reading, it will examine the present application of the 1840 Act and will consider the need for legislative reform. [Ed.]

Index